Collection Management Basics

Collection Management Basics

Seventh Edition

Margaret Zarnosky Saponaro and G. Edward Evans

Library and Information Science Text Series

 LIBRARIES UNLIMITED

AN IMPRINT OF ABC-CLIO, LLC
Santa Barbara, California • Denver, Colorado • Oxford, England

Library of Congress Cataloging-in-Publication Data

Names: Evans, G. Edward, 1937– author. | Saponaro, Margaret Zarnosky, author.
Title: Collection management basics / Margaret Zarnosky Saponaro
    and G. Edward Evans.
Other titles: Developing library and information center collections
Description: Seventh edition. | Santa Barbara, California : Libraries Unlimited,
    an Imprint of ABC-CLIO, LLC, [2019] | Series: Library and information science
    text series | Includes bibliographical references and index.
Identifiers: LCCN 2019000144 (print) | LCCN 2019002709 (ebook) |
    ISBN 9781440859656 (ebook) | ISBN 9781440859649 (pbk. : alk. paper)
Subjects: LCSH: Collection management (Libraries) | Libraries—Special
    collections—Electronic information resources.
Classification: LCC Z687 (ebook) | LCC Z687 .E918 2019 (print) |
    DDC 025.2/1—dc23
LC record available at https://lccn.loc.gov/2019000144

ISBN: 978-1-4408-5964-9 (paperback)
      978-1-4408-5965-6 (ebook)

23 22 21 20 19   1 2 3 4 5

This book is also available as an eBook.

Libraries Unlimited
An Imprint of ABC-CLIO, LLC

ABC-CLIO, LLC
147 Castilian Drive
Santa Barbara, California 93117
www.abc-clio.com

This book is printed on acid-free paper ⊗
Manufactured in the United States of America

We wish to dedicate this edition
to all the students,
who will begin developing the collections of the future,
and their instructors who will assist them in their learning.

As a personal dedication:
to the young readers Katie Saponaro and Ezra Harrington

Contents

Illustrations

Figures

Tables

Preface

The first edition of this title (originally called *Developing Library and Information Center Collections*) was published in 1979. Since that time, the manner and method of collection management has radically changed in libraries of all types with some of that change occurring as we prepared this text. Despite this radical change, collections remain an essential component of library operations. In this current age of diverse and clashing opinions, library collections continue to facilitate the unbiased, open exchange of ideas and information. A balanced collection means a person can access varying points of view either alone or with others without a real concern that hostility may arise. For example, as suggested by one of our Advisory Board members, Wendy Bartlett, in a public library setting, newspapers are a very important source as readers have been known to engage in lively discussions about sports or local politics after reading the copy available at the library— showing the community-building effect these resources can cultivate.

With this framework in mind, the chapters in this text are grouped to cover the background and process of collection management from start to finish, as well as addressing special issues in collection management. The first three chapters provide the reader with the foundations of collection management, its history and philosophy, as well as intellectual freedom and personal bias in selection. Beyond these introductory chapters, we next focus on policies, user needs assessment, and selection activities. Recognizing the important role technical services plays in the collection management process, we have added a new chapter exploring core technical services functions and workflows. After addressing methods to assess the collection, the remainder of the text focuses on special issues of concern for collection management practitioners, including collaborative collection development, material types, preservation, and legal issues. Each chapter includes sidebars with suggested resources, issues to watch, "points to ponder," and the like.

This work would not have been possible without the contributions of a great number of individuals. We are especially grateful for the comments, suggestions, and insight of our three Advisory Board members, who all brought a unique perspective and insight to the work: Wendy K. Bartlett, Collection Development and Acquisitions Manager, Cuyahoga County Public Library,

Parma, OH; Holland Christie, Branch Manager, Battle Ground Community Library, Vancouver, WA; and Susan Koutsky, Media Specialist, Westover Elementary School, Montgomery County Public Schools, Silver Spring, MD. You will see some of their many contributions to this work appearing throughout the text as "From the Advisory Board" sidebars.

We would also like to extend a very special thanks to Leigh Ann DePope, Head, Acquisitions & Data Services; Daniel Mack, Associate Dean, Collection Strategies and Services; Carla Q. Montori, Head, Preservation; and Celina Nichols McDonald, Government Documents & Criminology Librarian at the University of Maryland Libraries for their assistance. The input of each of these individuals greatly improved the manuscript. However, they are not responsible for errors in content.

Margaret Zarnosky Saponaro
Rockville, MD

G. Edward Evans
Flagstaff, AZ

1
Introduction

The goal of any collection development organization must be to provide the library with a collection that meets the appropriate needs of its client population, within the limitations of its fiscal and personnel resources.

—Bonita Bryant, 1987

Much of the literature on library collections and access to information focuses on academic libraries. . . . There are some similarities between the challenges faced by academic libraries and public libraries. . . . The issues of concern are far-reaching and transcend traditional topics that collection development and management has included.

—John Budd, 2014

In a rapidly evolving information environment, libraries need to "do more than just prevail." Instead they need to reimagine and reinvent themselves taking advantage of the new opportunities that this environment has created.

—International Federation of Library
Associations and Institutions, 2016

Bonita Bryant's opening quotation is as valid today as when she first "penned" it. We believe it will remain valid well into the future, even as the content of library collections changes. The overarching purpose of collection development and management will not change—money and people in a library are finite and will always be. Even so, collection development and collection management are relatively new concepts for libraries, in light of library history.

As a societal institution, the notion of a library is old—more than 4,000 years, in fact. Clearly that type of longevity suggests that libraries have changed with the times. Both the medium for conveying information (technology of a sort) and access to the library's resources shifted with the times. The earliest known libraries housed clay tablets and only a few select individuals could access the collections. Papyrus and vellum scrolls came along next and a growing number of people were capable of accessing and using the information. With the advent of the printing press and paper the boom truly began for libraries and society's members having significant access to information. Until recently, in terms of library history, gaining access to a library's resources required an in-person visit to the library (library as place). In today's digital world, much of a library's resources are remotely accessible 24/7 online. Even with this shift the "place" aspect of libraries has not disappeared and is unlikely to do so in the foreseeable future.

There is every reason to think that libraries will be able to "reinvent and reimagine" themselves, as the International Federation of Library Associations and Institutions' (IFLA) opening quotation suggests. It is essential for long-term survivability. There is little doubt that such creative efforts are necessary, and there is significant evidence those efforts are well underway. We address such evidence, in terms of collection development and collection management, in later chapters.

There is no doubt there are threats to libraries in today's digital environment, but the reality is there has always been the potential for some societal institution to, in time, replace the concept and the value of libraries. Elisabeth Jones (2013), when writing about her view of where libraries would be in 2020, noted that "opportunities and threats will, I suggest, fall roughly into six axes: (1) changing the calculus of preservation vs. access, (2) increasing impetus for collaboration, (3) reimaging library spaces, (4) disintermediation between reader and resource, (5) continuing—or even magnifying—the need for guidance and instruction, and (6) increasing expectations of digital universality" (p. 17). All of those topics come into play either directly or indirectly in collection management activities.

Throughout time, complex societies around the world have had several basic beliefs about the library:

- It is a physical place,
- It is a collection of what is deemed societally important information,
- It will allow for appropriate access to its resources (the definition of what is appropriate has changed over time),
- It organizes those resources to enhance access and provides assistance in their use, and
- It preserves the information for future users.

The last point is important in today's digital environment. Libraries are the only institution that society expects to provide long-term preservation of important information. (We explore preservation in some detail in chapter 14.) Why is long-term preservation a concern? Libraries connect people to the world of information and knowledge. People use that information/knowledge to improve their lives and society and, in the process, they create new knowledge that requires preservation. Whether that information was contained on a clay tablet or in a digital file, libraries perform a vital preservation function that helps improve society. Verlon Jose (2017) stated the case for library preservation effectively when he wrote on Martin Luther King Day, "Today recognizes a great man who told great truths about humanity.

Check These Out

Perhaps one of the most comprehensive recent histories of libraries is the three-volume set entitled *The Cambridge History of Libraries in Britain and Ireland*, edited by Peter Hoare (Cambridge: Cambridge University Press, 2008). Volume 1 covers up until 1640, volume 2 covers 1640 to 1850, and volume 3 covers 1850 to 2000.

Michael Harris' *History of Libraries in the Western World,* 4th ed. (Lanham, MD: Scarecrow Press, 1999) is an excellent summary of library history.

An easy to read title about publishing, the book, and society is Ted Striphas' *The Late Age of Print: Everyday Book Culture from Consumerism to Control* (New York: Columbia University Press, 2009).

The Library History Round Table of the American Library Association also publishes a semi-annual bibliography of library history: http://www.ala.org/rt/lhrt/popularresources/libhistorybib/libraryhistory.

His words are written down for all to read, recorded for all to hear. They are in every library in the nation" (p. 10A). We also believe that libraries will continue to do so well into the future.

Rivkah Sass (2017) shared an interesting thought about today's library environment, noting: "Sometimes I worry that in our quest to find the next new library thing, we are so busy debating whatever our current library buzzwords are—future, relevancy, outcomes, library service—and so busy competing with one another to be the first to offer the latest new 'thing' in library service, whatever that may be, that we forget the fundamentals of why we exist" (p. xi). Although not explicitly stated by Sass, clearly one of those "fundamentals" is the library's role in providing access to information in all its forms. This book addresses how a library goes about creating and maintaining appropriate collections of information resources for its users.

What Is Collection Management?

Today, the short answer to that question is the process by which library staff members determine what resources will be available to users—the "collection." Needless to say, what constitutes the collection is very different from its makeup not all that long ago. As the components of the collection have expanded, so have the challenges in creating the most appropriate content while balancing those money and staffing constraints Bryant identified. Another term in use for the process is *collection development* (CD). That term relates to an aspect of collection management. CD focuses on the identification and acquisition of information materials that address user interests/needs while staying within established policy guidelines and financial constraints. CD also has some role in collection policy and budget development. (CD policies are covered in chapter 4, while budgeting is covered in chapter 8.)

Collection management (CM), however, involves those activities and more. One important aspect is proposing a budget for acquiring resources and managing the funds that become available. Another difference is CM involves the ongoing assessment of the collection—what is still of interest to users, what is not, and how to handle the less important materials as well as taking into consideration preservation responsibilities.

Other types of organizations also have information management/transfer issues; some of the terms used in these environments are information resource management, knowledge management, content management, and records management. The terms cover similar activities and differ primarily in organizational context. *Information resource management*, as used today, relates to any organizational context, often without any centralized collection of materials, in which the information resource manager is responsible for identifying and making available to appropriate staff members both internal and external sources of information. Practitioners in computer science and information systems often define *knowledge management* as the "management of objects that can be identified and handled in information systems" (Brogan, Hingston, and Wilson, 2002, p. 2). Martin White (2002) defined *content management* as software that "provides a platform for managing the creation, review, filing, updating, distribution, and storage of structured and unstructured content" (p. 20). *Records management* is the process of handling the working records of an organization with an emphasis on retention, retrieval, and access issues. No matter which term is most familiar to you, the resulting goal of each is to provide accurate information in a timely and cost-effective manner to all members of the service community.

With the addition of e-resources another activity became part of CM—handling vendor agreements. Such resources are almost always more complex in terms of what and how a library may make the material accessible to its service community. (We look at e-resources in some detail in chapters 12 and 13, a reflection of this category of library collections.)

In essence, CM is a major library activity that is fundamental to people having access to information. It is important as its activities determine what will and will not be easily accessible from the universe of information materials for the library's service population. That universe is far too large for there not to be a necessity to make choices, often between many potentially appropriate items and the reality of limited funds.

Access to Information

An obvious proposition is, why preserve information if there is to be no access? As we noted above, access to information in library collections has changed through time. Today, anyone in the U.S. with an Internet connection can access at least some information from some library at any time, if nothing more than the Library of Congress catalog; the reality is there are a great many other library options that are also available 24/7.

Expansion of access has been a slow process until relatively recently. Even today not everyone has the same access options. One limiting factor is that not everyone agrees universal accessibility is desirable. In the U.S., during the first two hundred years of academic library development, students either had no access or access only under the direct supervision of a faculty member. U.S. public libraries began as subscription libraries—you needed money to have access. One of the country's largest public libraries reflects that fact in its name—The Free Library of Philadelphia (established 1891). The concept of school libraries is very recent, in comparison to the overall history of libraries, and school libraries do have restrictions on students' access to information (chapter 15 covers this topic in more depth).

In the next chapter, we explore the concept of intellectual freedom (IF) more fully; here we look at the more general issues of library access. Library access goes well beyond collections. The notion of access applies to all library programs and services, all of which are interconnected. Collections underlie most services and programs to a greater or lesser extent.

From the Advisory Board

With regard to Internet access, Advisory Board member Susan Koutsky notes the following:

> Yes, anyone with a connection can access information, but for students, the key is the Internet and computer access. In my experience as a media specialist in a Title 1 school in Maryland, approximately 40 percent of my students did not have access to digital information at home either because there was no internet access at home, there was no computer at home, or parents would not let students use the computer at home. After school hours, students could potentially use the public library, but most of my students went to an aftercare program and did not even get home until dinner or bedtime.

I want to point out some findings from papers shared by my husband, Tom Koutsky, who worked on Internet access issues at Connected Nation and now is a Senior Connectivity Advisor at the USAID Global Development Lab:

Horrigan, John B. 2015. "The Numbers Behind the Broadband 'Homework Gap.'" *Pew Research Center.* http://www.pewresearch.org/fact-tank/2015/04/20/the-numbers -behind-the-broadband-homework-gap/.

> This article finds that some 5 million school-age children do not have high-speed Internet access at home, with low income and black or Hispanic families making up a disproportionate share. This creates a "homework gap."

McHenry, Giulia, Edward Carlson, Maureen Lewis, Rafi M. Goldberg, Justin Goss, and Celeste Chen. 2016. "The Digital Divide Is Closing Even as New Fissures Surface." *TPRC 44: The 44th Research Conference on Communication, Information and Internet Policy 2016.* https://papers.ssrn.com/sol3/papers.cfm?abstract_id =2757328.

> One of the findings in this paper is that rural communities are low adopters of Internet use, due to a number of reasons.

Purcell, Kristen, Alan Heaps, Judy Buchanan, and Linda Friedrich. 2013. "How Teachers Are Using Technology at Home and in Their Classrooms." *Pew Research Center.* http://www.pewinternet.org/2013/02/28/how-teachers-are-using-technology-at -home-and-in-their-classrooms/.

> This article finds that of the teachers surveyed, more than half say their students have the digital tools they need at school, but only a fifth say they their students have access to the digital tools they need at home. Again, low income and rural communities are greatly impacted.

Fox, Christine, and Rachel Jones. 2016. "The Broadband Imperative II: Equitable Access for Learning." Washington, DC: State Educational Technology Directors Association (SETDA). http://www.setda.org/wp-content/uploads/2016/09/SETDA -Broadband-ImperativeII-Full-Document-Sept-8-2016.pdf.

> This report from SETDA gives recommendations to address the digital divide.

Although for many people the notion of 24/7 access to information is a reality, the amount that is available is a small percentage of the information universe. Further, who has access to what varies; thus the notion of universal access has limits and likely will never be achieved. In the U.S. there is, broadly thinking, universal physical access to some library somewhere, but even that access does have some constraints in terms of time. For example, K–12 students have access to their primary library (the school library) only when the school is open (it is rare for the students to have access on the weekends). Some academic libraries restrict physical access, usually in the form of limiting noncampus individuals' entrance. (Often such limitations are removed if the "outsider" pays a fee.) There are instances of public libraries placing limits on behaviors and even hygiene, and allowing the removal of a person failing to meet the requirements. Beyond physical access, there are a variety of restrictions on who has access to what services and programs. Both academic and public libraries control who may use their document delivery services. School libraries rarely offer access to materials not in their collection (analog or digital).

Such constraints on access are a realistic reflection of Bonita Bryant's comment in the opening quotation: "within the limits of its fiscal and personnel resources." No library, no matter how big, has the resources to meet all information needs of all individuals. Libraries must prioritize their efforts and define their "primary service population." Most libraries would like to do more; however, reality checks this desire.

Accessibility is also a factor in how supporters/funders of a library view the library. Who gets service and how cost effective those services are play a major role in both the level of fiscal support as well as staffing. Staffing comes after funding, so how society perceives the library is important in what funds the library has for staff and for providing access to its services and programs.

Access and Value

Historically libraries have been viewed as a public good (rather like motherhood and apple pie). Most people probably still hold that view (at least in the abstract). However, when the financial reality hits and monies are scarce, practicality displaces most theoretical values. Difficult economic times almost always lead to leaner library budgets and, as Jill Grogg (2009) noted, "Budgets are shrinking and, often, one of the first cuts libraries make is to their collections budgets" (p. 127). Collection management personnel should always be concerned with stretching collection funds as far as possible, but in bad times, it becomes imperative to do so. (We look at why collections are among the first cuts in chapter 8.)

Libraries receive the vast majority of their funding indirectly from taxpayers and student fees. Further, the taxes and fees apply to everyone, not just those who make use of the library. Carol Tenopir (2009) made the point that: "When perceptions of the importance of a product or service decrease, but the price of that product or service increases, a gap is formed. . . . That gap puts pressure on libraries to justify their budgets in the future or to decrease their expenditures" (p. 20). For those who make little or no use of libraries, the gap that had existed in the best of times grows wider when the economy goes bad.

In the past, and to a much greater extent today, libraries have used output measures to demonstrate they were making effective use of the funds provided. Some examples of such measures were and are gate counts (people

---

Check These Out

A good website that lists a growing number of state and community public library ROI surveys/reports is the "Economic Impact of Public Libraries" site from the Wisconsin Department of Public Instruction: http://dpi.wi.gov/pld/data-reports/economic -impact. Another site worth investigating is the "Return on Investment for Public Libraries" site: https://www.lrs.org/data-tools/public-libraries/return-on-investment/, maintained by Library Resource Services (LRS). The site includes both personal and library ROI calculators, as well as ROI reports from several public library districts.

---

entering the facility), total circulation, cost per item circulated, titles purchased, cost per title purchased, reference questions answered, and user surveys. While useful and perhaps interesting to some people, such measures do not truly address the value to users or the people providing the funding. Did I/we get more back in value than we put into the service? That is the question libraries must answer today. It is the ultimate assessment/accountability question. (We explore collection assessment issues in chapter 9.)

One of the most frequently employed and more sophisticated methods of demonstrating organizational value with hard data is to perform a Return on Investment (ROI) study. ROI is a methodology for assessing whether or not an organization/department/activity produces more value/income/profit than it expends on the outcome/product/service. Libraries have taken to using this approach to help bolster their contention they provide a tangible value for their parent organization. Public libraries have been engaged in ROI efforts for some time now. Reported ROI data shows that the average return from a public library to a community is $4 or more for every dollar the community expends on the library. Stephanie Zurinski's (2007) article about public libraries' impact on small communities (populations of fewer than 10,000 people) provides some surprising ROI results. She noted, "Small libraries operate with minimum staff and small budgets. Yet, the average ROI for the small libraries in west Texas is $12. The communities served by these small libraries receive an average value of $407,322 in return for the dollars they can afford to invest" (p. 127).

Access Philosophy and Staff

Once there is funding and staffing the process of providing access starts. U.S. librarianship rests on several deeply held beliefs about the basic functions of a library—provide access to as much of the world's information as possible and to as many people as possible. Those values/beliefs are reflected in a number of position statements from the American Library Association (ALA). Two of the most important statements are:

Library Bill of Rights—1939; revised 1944, 1948, 1961, 1967, 1980, 1996; (http://www.ala.org/advocacy/intfreedom/librarybill)

Freedom to Read Statement—1953; revised 1972, 1991, 2000, 2004; (http://www.ala.org/advocacy/intfreedom/freedomreadstatement)

The *Library Bill of Rights* (LBR) states, among other topics, that library resources should provide for the interests of the entire service community and that the materials should reflect all points of view on controversial topics.

Further, libraries must not restrict anyone's access to these resources on the basis of national origin, age, background, etc. A more detailed statement regarding this issue is ALA's *Diversity in Collection Development* (http://www.ala.org/advocacy/intfreedom/librarybill/interpretations/diversitycollection), which goes into more detail on the subject of allowing all people full access. Several of the other documents listed above also relate to access issues, especially for children and young adults. The LBR also states libraries should resist efforts to censor materials or restrict access to resources. (We look at such concerns in greater depth in in the next chapter and chapter 15.)

The *Freedom to Read Statement* (FR) links the concept of unfettered reading to the U.S. Constitution, particularly the First Amendment. As a result, you will see IF and FR linked to the First Amendment without any additional reference to the U.S. Constitution. FR contains seven "propositions" calling for libraries, publishers, and booksellers to collaborate in assuring that both the freedom of expression and the freedom to access those expressions are protected. Most, if not all, censorship challenges are related to FR and its links to the First Amendment.

Yet another collection management–related document is the *Code of Ethics of the American Library Association* (http://www.ala.org/advocacy/proethics/codeofethics/codeethics). It contains an acknowledgment that "ethical dilemmas occur when values conflict." Nevertheless, it delineates eight guiding principles for the ethical behavior of librarians. The first three on the list and the seventh are all related to CM activities to a greater or lesser degree. Many of the documents listed above have ethical issues built into them, although they do not always employ the words ethics or ethical. Again, we explore ethics in the next chapter.

Access and Literacy

A basic requirement for gaining access to information is to have some degree of literacy in the various formats if there is to be any comprehension and value. Libraries of all types engage in efforts to expand individuals' skills in understanding and evaluating both print and digital information resources. School libraries are increasingly putting emphasis on identifying resources and evaluating information and inquiry, while reading and comprehension are addressed more by the classroom teacher. Public libraries tend to place their emphasis on the reading and comprehension aspect of literacy, while academic libraries put their emphasis on identifying appropriate resources and evaluating sources (both print and digital).

More than a few pundits have been vocal about the imminent demise of print and reading. So far, their predications have failed to materialize and are unlikely to do so during this edition's lifetime. In fact, a 2017 Gallup Poll survey reported that 53 percent of young people read 1 to 10 books in the past year. (Of that number, 35 percent read more than 10 books.) One fact that probably surprised the pundits who expect the rapidly approaching death of print books was that 73 percent of all respondents preferred the printed book rather than the electronic version. The reported stated, "Additionally, while some have alleged that technology would displace printed books, this shift has not been as swift as expected. In fact, recent industry data shows that sales of printed books have been increasing" (Swift and Ander, 2017).

It seems likely that library literacy efforts must continue to have a dual focus. Bill Ptacek (2013) made the following observation, "Two other crucial areas that will define the public library of the next decade are its role in

---

From the Advisory Board

Advisory Board member Susan Koutsky suggests the following resources from the State of Maryland regarding school library media programs:

Maryland's *School Library Media State Curriculum PreK-8* (2010): http://mdk12.msde.maryland.gov/share/vsc/vsc_librarymedia_grpk8.pdf.

Also check out Maryland's annual report, *Facts about Maryland's School Library Media Programs 2015–2016*, especially chart 2 on page 7: http://marylandpublicschools.org/programs/Documents/ITSLM/slm/SLMReport20152016.pdf. The chart shows how school librarians spent percentages of their time. School libraries are engaged in efforts to teach students research skills using both print and digital information.

---

supporting the information needs of K–12 students and its position to lead community efforts for early-childhood literacy" (p. 119). Assuming those two "predictions" are close to accurate, it will mean a shift in thinking about public library collection content, close collaboration with school libraries, and rethinking funding priorities.

Blended Collections

The above is not to suggest that e-resources are not increasing in importance for libraries; they are. One significant collection management issue is how to best balance the needs of print-based and digital resources (blended collections). No one doubts that the shift to digital is permanent; however, it also appears likely that print is going to continue to be an element in collection decisions for at least the foreseeable future. Maria Anna Jankowska and James Marcum (2010) provided a concise summary of the challenges for libraries when it comes to handling the need for blended collections. They noted:

> Developing a blended model of print and digital resources supported by social networking services has raised a major concern that sustainable progress of academic libraries is threatened by a variety of factors such as: developing and preserving print and digital collections, supplying and supporting rapidly changing technological and networking infrastructure, providing free services to the public, maintaining growing costs of library buildings and lowering libraries' "ecological footprint." (pp. 160–161)

Stephen Abram (2013) took a slightly different slant on the digital/print issue. When asked to imagine the future of library collections in 2020, he noted: "In 2020, we are well beyond the debates about physical and digital collections. . . . There is growing understanding [of] the difference between entertainment-based collections like fiction, video, and music versus collections of nonfiction books and articles, podcasts, and digital-learning objects that support research, learning, decision making, discovery, culture, creativity and invention" (p. 42).

A balanced/blended collection is something of a challenge for public libraries, at least in terms of eBooks. It is not that libraries don't want to offer them. It is a matter of how to develop a model for doing so that works for both the library and the publishers. In 2014, Christopher Baker wrote, "The current climate for eBook collection development is not wholly inhospitable to public libraries but it does not support an expanded role for libraries beyond passive content licensee" (p. 202). Matters have improved somewhat since he wrote that; however, there are still significant challenges. We look at eBooks in more detail in chapter 13.

Access and Collaboration

Collaboration is something libraries have engaged in, to some extent, for many years. You could claim that the Library of Congress' practice of sharing cataloging data was an early cooperative venture that would push the starting point of collaboration back to the turn of the 20th century.

Library cooperation can and does take place in any area of library activity. Our interest lies with collection development. There have been a variety of such efforts over the years (see chapter 10 for a full discussion of such efforts). There is little debate that the most significant effort has been in the area of consortia programs. Kim Armstrong (2014) stated the case for the value of such endeavors, noting: "Libraries have leveraged participation in consortia as an effective means to save money, save time, mitigate risk, and co-invest to extend resources and services that would be inefficient or impossible for a single library to accomplish alone" (p. 271). Such efforts, almost inevitably, will increase in importance. Keep in mind such activities rarely reduce overall costs. Basically what they do is allow libraries to offer more resources and services for the funds they have available.

New Approaches

Thinking about and developing new ways of carrying out library services/activities is one thing. Getting those ideas funded and implemented is another matter. We believe that if librarians take a leadership role as "change agents" both in their library and parent institutions, they will be successful in getting the necessary funding and implementation support. Library leaders in the 21st century must be able to present compelling visions of the future in nonconfrontational terms—as advocates. As Pamela Kramer and Linda Diekman (2010) noted, "Advocacy is about educating stakeholders using the best available evidence and it is an ongoing process" (p. 27).

What are some of the reimaging/rethinking activities that libraries are currently engaging in? Public libraries, in some instances, are shifting to an ever greater position of being a community center while maintaining their role of community information resource. Some include some form of food service such as Nordic public libraries have offered for some time. Many are placing increased emphasis on local history, adding increased access to those resources and preserving them. Creation space is another expansion of the community participation concept—such as 3D "makerspaces," and writing and visual material workshops, for example. Academic libraries, as the result of more and more "large-scale digitization indicatives," will reduce floor space for print storage and increase space for more and new

---

Check This Out

A book that explores many of the topics we mentioned in this chapter in greater depth is G. Edward Evans, Margaret Zarnosky Saponaro, Holland Christie, and Carol Sinwell's *Library Programs and Services: The Fundamentals* (Santa Barbara, CA: Libraries Unlimited, 2015).

---

services such as learning commons. With more and more print resources converted to a digital form, preservation concerns will shift to maintain the new format(s). Perhaps the idea, which started in 2005, of "One Laptop per Child" will become reality. Peter Fernandez (2015) suggested about low-cost computers: "Although limited in some important ways, these extremely small, inexpensive computers can be used by libraries to expand access to educational opportunities, as well as make libraries more efficient" (p. 5). The potential for school libraries seems even greater.

Assuming the field achieves some, if not most, of the above, the future will indeed be bright. It will also mean those of us working in libraries will need more and new skills in order to be effective. Libraries will have to find a method of providing training in the new skills as well as greater depth in existing ones. Professional schools will need to rethink their curriculums and offer a variety of new subjects. For individuals in collection management, one can see a hint of what is to come in Sarah Pomerantz's (2010) comments: "In recent years, there has been a proliferation of new library positions, such as electronic resources (ER) librarian, licensing librarian, and digital collections librarian which include responsibilities related to acquiring electronic resources and maintaining, troubleshooting, and training users of these collections" (p. 40). We cover the issues related to such positions in various chapters throughout the book.

Points to Keep in Mind

- Libraries have had a very long history as part of society's institutional fabric.

- Libraries have also had a solid track record of being able to adapt to changing societal conditions as well as to technological developments.

- While long-term preservation has been, and is likely to continue to be, an important component of libraries' worth to society, they also have other immediate tangible values as well.

- Another factor that suggests that public libraries have a long-term future is the growing body of data that demonstrates society receives an excellent return on its investment in public library operations, as much as $12 for every $1 spent.

- What everyone, the general public and the profession alike, must keep in mind is that it is the content rather than the package that is of greatest importance. The idea of content rather than the package sometimes is overlooked with the image of libraries as a "book place." This occurs when the general public and the profession's focus is on technology at the expense of content.

References

Abram, Stephen. 2013. "Chapter Six." In *Library 2020: Today's Leading Visionaries Describe Tomorrow's Library,* edited by Joseph James, 41–48. Lanham, MD: Scarecrow Press.

Armstrong, Kim. 2014. "Consortia Services in Collection Management." In *Rethinking Collection Development and Management*, edited by Becky Albitz, Christine Avery, and Diane Zabel, 271–79. Santa Barbara, CA: Libraries Unlimited.

Baker, Christopher. 2014. "EBook Collection Development in Public Libraries." In *Rethinking Collection Development and Management*, edited by Becky Albitz, Christine Avery, and Diane Zabel, 199–213. Santa Barbara, CA: Libraries Unlimited.

Brogan, Mark, Philip Hingston, and Vicky Wilson. 2002. "A Rich Storehouse for the Relief of Man's Estate: Education for Knowledge Management." *Advances in Library Administration and Organization* 19: 1–26.

Bryant, Bonita. 1987. "The Organizational Structure of Collection Development." *Library Resources & Technical Services* 31, no. 2: 111–22.

Budd, John. 2014. "Education for Collection Development and Management." In *Rethinking Collection Development and Management*, edited by Becky Albitz, Christine Avery, and Diane Zabel, 89–99. Santa Barbara, CA: Libraries Unlimited.

Fernandez, Peter. 2015. "'Through the Looking Glass: Envisioning New Library Technologies,' How Inexpensive Computers Can Transform Information Access and Literacy." *Library Hi Tech News* 32, no. 7: 4–7.

Grogg. Jill E. 2009. "Economic Hard Times and Electronic Resources." *Journal of Electronic Resources Librarianship* 21, no. 2: 127–30.

International Federation of Library Associations and Institutions. 2016. *IFLA Trend Report: 2016 Update.* Updated January 25, 2018. http://trends.ifla.org/update-2016.

Jankowska, Maria Anna, and James W. Marcum. 2010. "Sustainability Challenge for Academic Libraries: Planning for the Future." *College & Research Libraries* 71, no. 2: 160–70.

Jones, Elisabeth A. 2013. "Chapter Three." In *Library 2020: Today's Leading Visionaries Describe Tomorrow's Library,* edited by Joseph James, 15–24. Lanham, MD: Scarecrow Press.

Jose, Verlon. 2017. "Finding Great Truths in Words Preserved in Libraries and Land." *Arizona Republic,* January 16, 2017, 10A.

Kramer, Pamela K., and Linda Diekman. 2010. "Evidence = Assessment = Advocacy." *Teacher Librarian* 37, no. 3: 27–30.

Pomerantz, Sarah B. 2010. "The Role of the Acquisition Librarian in Electronic Resources Management." *Journal of Electronic Resources Librarianship* 22, no. 1/2: 40–48.

Ptacek, Bill. 2013. "Chapter Eighteen." In *Library 2020: Today's Leading Visionaries Describe Tomorrow's Library*, edited by Joseph James, 117–20. Lanham, MD: Scarecrow Press.

Sass, Rivkah. 2017. "Forward." In *Yes! On Demand: How to Create Winning, Customized Library Services,* edited by Kathy L. Middleton, xi. Santa Barbara, CA: Libraries Unlimited.

Swift, Art, and Steve Ander. 2017. "Rumors of the Demise of Books Greatly Exaggerated." Gallup. http://www.gallup.com/poll/201644/rumors-demise-books-greatly-exaggerated.aspx.

Tenopir, Carol. 2009. "The Value Gap." *Library Journal* 134, no. 12: 20.

White, Martin. 2002. "Content Management." *Online* 26, no. 6: 20–22, 24.

Zurinski, Stephanie. 2007. "The Impact of Small Community Libraries." *Texas Library Journal* 83, no. 3: 126–27.

2
Intellectual Freedom and Ethics

To the librarian, intellectual freedom takes the form of the right to receive ideas, that is, to access information.
—Tami Echavarria Robinson, 2014

[Today's] realities create a setting that is ripe with temptations that can obfuscate and darken pathways for consistent ethical action.
—Brian N. Williams, 2015

Ethical dilemmas in libraries are difficult and complex and must be confronted on a routine basis. Library professionals often find themselves in potential ethical dilemmas and need the guidance and support of their organization and/or their professional (library) association.
—James H. Walther, 2016

Intellectual freedom (IF) is a complex concept in the real world. Library staff confronting an IF situation for the first time usually find it to be intimidating, worrisome, stressful, and perhaps a little scary. One way to prepare yourself for that time (and it is likely to occur at some time in your career) is to think about what you would do when it does happen beforehand. Case studies, in the safety of the classroom or workshop, are one method for thinking about what to do and how to handle such an event and hear from others about how they would approach the matter (more about cases/situations to ponder later in the chapter).

One convenient approach to thinking about the issues is to view IF as the overarching concept with other topics, such as ethics, access, privacy, and censorship, as different but linked issues. In predigital days, these concepts seemed highly complex; little did we know how complicated they would become with the arrival of the Internet and other technology developments. We do indeed live in interesting times; especially in the area of intellectual freedom.

Clearly, IF is far greater than a library matter; it is a basic concern for society. It is also more than censorship and libraries, although most library censorship more often than not involves some IF elements. There is a link between IF and the First Amendment of the Constitution that goes well beyond collection content challenges. Some examples of noncollection library-related IF issues that have led to court cases are library meeting rooms being used for religious services, type and level of Internet access, and parents' rights to see their children's library usage information.

Intellectual freedom is about people's right to know. That right underlies effective democratic decision making. As David O'Brien (1981) wrote, "The political ideal of the public's right to know has been enhanced by the Supreme Court's broad interpretation of the First Amendment as securing the conditions for an informed people and electorate" (p. 166). David Moshman (2003) made a case for IF being an essential element in the intellectual development of people to assess, process, discuss, refine, and defend concepts and ideas. He delineated a set of IF freedoms that are necessary for intellectual development—freedom of belief and identity, expression and discussion and inquiry, and freedom from indoctrination, quality, privacy, and due process (p. 36). As you will see as you read this chapter, several of these freedoms are related to libraries and their collections.

Libraries, the First Amendment, and Intellectual Freedom

We suggested in the last chapter that the American Library Association's (ALA) *Library Bill of Rights* was part of the basic philosophy/belief of today's librarianship. That document's statements are the foundation for CM activities. Two other significant CM documents from ALA are the *Freedom to Read* and the *Freedom to View*. ALA and its many divisions, sections, and interest groups have issued a number of additional documents related to CM. Among the most relevant are:

Labeling and Rating Systems—1951; amended 1971, 1981, 1990, 2009, 2014 (http://www.ala.org/advocacy/intfreedom/librarybill/interpretations /labelingrating),

Diversity in Collection Development—1982; amended 1990, 2008, 2014 (http://www.ala.org/advocacy/intfreedom/librarybill/interpretations /diversitycollection),

Access to Resources and Services in the School Library Media Program—1986; amended 1990, 2000, 2005, 2008, 2014 (http://www.ala.org/ala/issues advocacy/intfreedom/librarybill/interpretations/accessresources.cfm),

Code of Ethics of the American Library Association—1997; amended 2008 (http://www.ala.org/tools/ethics),

Schools and the Children's Internet Protection Act—2001 (http://www.ala.org /advocacy/advleg/federallegislation/cipa/schoolsandcipa), and

---

> ## Check These Out
>
> A number of other resources related to the topics in this chapter are available from ALA and are well worth a look. These include "The Children's Internet Protection Act (CIPA)" resource page: http://www.ala.org/advocacy/advleg/federallegislation/cipa, and "Libraries and the Internet Toolkit": http://www.ala.org/advocacy/intfreedom/iftoolkits /litoolkit/librariesinternet.

Minors' Rights to Receive Information Under the First Amendment—2004 (http://www.ala.org/Template.cfm?Section=issuesrelatedlinks& Template=/ContentManagement/ContentDisplay.cfm&ContentID= 28210).

The *Freedom to Read Statement* (FR) links the concept of unfettered reading to FR's seven "propositions" calling for libraries, publishers, and booksellers to collaborate in assuring that both the freedom of expression and the freedom to access those expressions are protected. Most, if not all, censorship challenges are related to FR and its links to the First Amendment. ALA's *Freedom to View Statement* expands the idea beyond print collection resources (http://www.ala.org/vrt/professionalresources/vrtresources /freedomtoview).

The *Code of Ethics of the American Library Association* acknowledges that "Ethical dilemmas occur when values conflict." Nevertheless, it delineates eight guiding principles for the ethical behavior of librarians. The first three on the list and the seventh are all related to CM activities to a greater or lesser degree. Many of the documents listed above have ethical issues built into them, although they do not always employ the words ethics or ethical. We explore CM ethics later in this chapter.

The ALA's organizational structure for dealing with intellectual freedom concerns is not clear-cut. The Intellectual Freedom Committee (IFC; http://www.ala.org/groups/committees/ala/ala-if) is responsible for making recommendations to the association regarding matters of intellectual freedom. The Office for Intellectual Freedom (OIF; http://www.ala.org/offices /oif), which has a full-time staff, has the charge of educating librarians and others about intellectual freedom and censorship matters. It is also the support service for the IFC, and it implements the association's policies related to intellectual freedom. As part of its educational function, the OIF produces several publications: *Journal of Intellectual Freedom and Privacy* (http:// www.ala.org/aboutala/offices/oif/JIFP, news and current developments relating to intellectual freedom), *Intellectual Freedom* News (a free weekly compilation of news by the ALA Office for Intellectual Freedom), and the *Intellectual Freedom Manual*.

Although the OIF does not provide legal assistance when a library faces a complaint, it does provide telephone consultation (occasionally with the addition of written statements or names of persons who might be able to testify in support of intellectual freedom). Very rarely does the OIF staff come to the library to provide moral and professional support.

Often, librarians are surprised to learn that the OIF does not provide legal aid. Instead, legal assistance might be available from the Freedom to Read Foundation (FRF; http://www.ftrf.org/). The FRF is not part of the ALA (it is a separate legal entity), but the two are so closely affiliated that many people have difficulty drawing the line between the two. The executive

---

Check This Out

While OIF exists at the national level, some state-level organizations may also provide support. For example, the Children's Cooperative Book Center (CCBC) assists Wisconsin librarians and teachers with dealing with challenges to materials. Like OIF, they do not provide legal assistance, but they will provide background information on the title being challenged (http://www.education.wisc.edu/ccbc/freedom/ifServices.asp).

---

director of the FRF is also the director of the OIF; with such an arrangement, it is not surprising that people think the FRF is part of the ALA. Be aware that there is no assurance of receiving financial or legal aid from the FRF; there are too many cases and insufficient funds to assist everyone. Anyone interested in becoming involved in intellectual freedom activities should consider joining ALA's Intellectual Freedom Round Table (http://www.ala.org/rt/ifrt), which is the general membership unit related to intellectual freedom. Although the ALA offers a variety of support services for handling censors' complaints, the best support is local preparation before the need arises.

Anne Klinefelter (2010), in discussing CM and the First Amendment, noted, "Selectivity in library collections, though, is unavoidable given scarcity of resources for collections, staff, facilities, and technology. . . . Given this selectivity, and given the general societal consensus that libraries are an overall benefit, courts are wary of applying standard First Amendment

---

Check These Out

We mentioned earlier in this chapter that it is a good idea to spend some time before facing your first IF challenge working with others on potential situations. Cases and scenarios are one good means of doing this.

Joyce Brooks and Jody Howard (2002) provide four "scenes" in which IF is in play in their article "What Would You Do? School Library Media Centers and Intellectual Freedom" (*Colorado Libraries* 28, no. 3: 17–19). School library media centers serve as the setting for these scenarios; however, it is easy to see how these cases could just as well happen in the academic or public library environment. (Most special libraries do not face very many IF issues as they are rarely open to the public and have a rather narrow focus in terms of CM work.)

Two titles published by ALA Editions (Chicago, 2009) and well worth a review are *Protecting Intellectual Freedom in Your School Library* by Pat R. Scales for the Office for Intellectual Freedom (OIF) and *Protecting Intellectual Freedom in Your Academic Library* by Barbara M. Jones for OIF. The Scales title includes a chapter on "Materials Selection" (pp. 1–34) that contains a series of case studies on selection issues, ranging from electronic database selection to curriculum demands. The Jones title contains a similar chapter on "Collection Development" (pp. 63–100) that includes case studies as well as a checklist of intellectual freedom tools for CM librarians. A third volume, *Protecting Intellectual Freedom in Your Public Library* by June Pinnell-Stephens, appeared in 2012 (Chicago: ALA Editions).

An additional title to consult is *Protecting Intellectual Freedom and Privacy in Your School Library* by Helen R. Adams (Santa Barbara, CA: Libraries Unlimited, 2013). In it, Adams covers such issues as challenges to school library resources and serving students with special needs.

analysis in library cases for fear the entire library system could be found in violation of the First Amendment" (pp. 347–48).

What is the "standard First Amendment analysis"? Usually, the courts require that there be total neutrality (*no* abridgment of freedom of speech) for there to be First Amendment protection. (Note: generally any library receiving government funds could look for First Amendment protection as a government agent/agency.) Selectivity is clearly not neutral. For example, in a public library setting selecting on the basis of quality would mean items of lesser quality would have little chance of being in the collection—that could translate into an abridgment of free speech case against a government agency. Under a strict constitutional interpretation/standard analysis of the First Amendment, quality selection would be unconstitutional. Fortunately, at least to date, no court has applied the strict interpretation to library cases. Klinefelter's article is one we believe anyone going into librarianship should read as it examines a variety of library-related court cases and goes beyond just CM issues. With that background on IF and the First Amendment in mind, we turn to questions of choices.

Ethics, Personal Beliefs, Biases, and Collection Management

Jean Preer (2008) once noted, "Ethics is about choices" (p. 1). We might reword her definition to say "Selection is about choices." What we elect to add, or not to add, to our collections has an impact upon our users' access to information as well as on their freedom to explore ideas, topics, and even recreational enjoyment without restriction. Collection managers are, in a very real sense, "gatekeepers" to knowledge for their clientele. Yes, users may be able to find the desired material elsewhere, especially in today's digital world, but through our choices we can make that access easy or hard. There are few hard and fast "rules" for how to handle these complex interrelated issues. In what follows, we attempt to outline some of the issues involved and how CM officers and libraries have from time to time addressed them.

In writing about ethics, integrity, and leadership Ann M. Martin (2009) stated, "social behavior adapts to the times, resulting in new dilemmas for school library media specialists. As a result, ethics adapt to social change, while the concept of integrity remains constant. . . . Library media specialists are obliged to know, understand, and adhere to the ethical principles that are the foundation of our profession" (p. 6). Although her statement addressed school library media specialists, we believe it applies to anyone in the profession, regardless of the library environment.

CM is always a matter of choices, some easy, some not so easy, some of an ethical nature, and many that are not. The ALA *Code of Ethics* is a starting rather than an ending point in CM choice making. We are, in theory, supposed to build collections that reflect the needs and interests of our service community. We are supposed to reflect all points of view in terms of controversial topics. We are supposed to be thoughtful and careful stewards of the monies we have available to create such collections. With just those three points in mind you can probably imagine where some dilemmas (ethical, personal integrity, and personal values for example) might arise. Just one example: what would you do if just one person—user or not—held a view contrary to everyone else in the service community and asked that her or his view be reflected in the collection? That would be easy to answer in a world of infinite financial resources—in our experience a nonexistent world—but it is not so easy in the real world. You might think just one person is an unlikely situation, and we agree, but does it matter, from an ethical perspective, if it is just 1, 100, or 1,000 out of a great many more?

There is a side to choice making that is sometimes labeled the "affective" side of collection building. Brian Quinn (2007) made the point that selection is not just a rational process: "The psychological literature indicates that decision making is not simply a cognitive process. . . . Making a decision about whether to purchase a book, cancel a journal, or add a database or aggregated package is fraught with uncertainly and ambiguity" (pp. 5, 7). How we go about our CM work activities reflect a variety of factors, some of which are psychological in nature. Looking at the management and psychology literature, you find ample evidence that those involved in decision-making processes are almost never 100 percent certain as to a decision outcome. Almost every decision carries with it some degree of uncertainty. The greater the level of uncertainty, the more stress the decision maker(s) is/are likely to experience.

Certainly the vast majority of library selection decisions are straightforward and the degree of uncertainty is almost nonexistent. However, even the most apparently simple selection decision may well carry some unacknowledged baggage with it. Everyone has a belief system, biases, and a set of values. All of these may color our choices, but most are not always at the forefront of our cognitive behaviors. Can we really shut these out when doing our selection work? Do we even think about them from time to time and perhaps reflect on the collection choices we have made? The answer is probably somewhere between once or twice (when someone has brought the matter up) to never. The fact is, we cannot shut our beliefs on and off like a light bulb. Thus, keeping in mind that we may, subconsciously, be building a collection that matches our values and beliefs is important in building a balanced collection.

One potential bias, and one that gets media attention from time to time, is political beliefs. Questions about the political bias of library collections are raised occasionally by those with conservative views. Will Manley (2010) did an opinion piece in which he wrote, "Despite our core value of intellectual freedom, librarians are not very tolerant of listening to points of view that stray from the basic liberal agenda. That is why conservative librarians are afraid to speak out: They fear professional ostracism" (p. 56). He went on to suggest there are several values that both the political Left and the Right have in common and the importance of using these commonalities to benefit everyone.

John Budd (2006/2007) commented, "The collections of public libraries are sometimes used as evidence for political stances of librarians who select materials for the collections" (p. 78). In the article, Budd looked at a set of

---

Check This Out

The following is an example of an article by Denise Rachel Gehring that illustrates to some degree Manley's point. The author of the piece began with, "The purpose of this annotated bibliography is to show perspectives on intellectual freedom from literature that provides approaches for librarians in faith-based institutions" (p. 48 in "Faith-Formed Intellectual Freedom: An Annotated Bibliography," *Collection Building* 2016, 35, no. 2: 48–53).

Check This Out

Questioning Library Neutrality, edited by Alison Lewis (Duluth, MN: Library Juice Press, 2008), contains 12 essays that address various aspects of attempts by libraries to maintain balanced collections and services. Topics range across the spectrum of concerns, such as policy issues, myths about library neutrality, and librarian activism. It is worth the effort to track down a copy.

---

political titles that had over 900 circulations between 2003 and 2005. His data set was 416 libraries that employed the same ILS system. The vendor had a database that served as a "union catalog" for the libraries. Thirty titles met the 900 circulation threshold. Of that number, 10 were "right leaning," seven "left leaning," and the balance fell somewhere in the middle (p. 86). For the group, those numbers would suggest there is a balance nationwide, at least for his sample libraries. What the article did not or could not answer was, how balanced is an individual library's collection? It is likely there was a mixed pattern—some rights, some lefts, and some in between—just like the overall sample results. It also seems likely that those on the Right or Left of the center point were, to some degree, a function of selector beliefs/values. Some may have been the result of the service communities' primary reading interest—which is not inappropriate by itself. The question would be, from an ALA *Code of Ethics* point of view, were contrary views reasonably well represented?

The point of the above discussion is not to illustrate a right or wrong issue, but rather to highlight the fact that not all of selection work is based on cognitive factors alone. We could have just as easily chosen topics such as religious beliefs, attitudes regarding gender issues, or rights of illegal immigrants—all of which have been debated by librarians in terms of services and collections.

Factors other than our beliefs, values, and philosophy of life can and do influence our selection decisions. Psychological and management literature on decision making show that something as simple as our mood at the time can play a role in what we decide. Very happy or unhappy moods reduce our focus on the task at hand. When the work environment is unsettled or stressful, we also have a tendency not to focus as sharply on the decision-making activity. Anything that distracts us from our selection has the potential to make our choices a little less sound than they might otherwise be.

Self-Censorship

We turn now to another affective issue that is widely acknowledged, at least by public and school librarians, when selecting collection items—"self-censorship." Whether it arises from discomfort with confrontation, economic fear (job loss), fear of physical violence (yes, it has happened), or some other reason, the result is the same; IF rights of one or more people may be impeded or even lost.

Is librarian censorship something new? Not at all. In 1908, Arthur E. Bostwick gave a speech to the ALA convention, "Librarian as Censor," in which he made the case that librarians should *not* select certain materials. There are still a few librarians who (long, long ago) in their youth encountered a public or school librarian who believed that "quality" was *the* basis for having an item in the collection. Often they went further, as "reader

---

From the Authors' Experience

One example from Evans' experience, when he was in sixth grade, revolved around a 500-page book of letters from the U.S. Civil War. (He had become fascinated with the war.) He had checked the book out from the main library and was working his way through it when it had to be returned or renewed. His branch librarian was upset he had "an adult book" and quizzed him as to how much he had read, why he wanted to read the rest of the book, and what he had "learned." At the end of day the book was renewed.

From the Advisory Board

Advisory Board member Susan Koutsky relates her experiences with self-censorship in school libraries:

Two instances of self-censorship I have seen in school libraries are where the librarian has chosen not to have graphic novels as part of the collection, and certain parts of the collection being designated for certain grade levels so that, for example, a kindergartener was not allowed to check out a "fifth-grade" book. In the case of the former, I can understand not buying certain classifications of books if budget is a restraining factor (it wasn't in this case). In the case of the latter, my philosophy has been if the child is interested and can access the information through his own reading or someone reading it to him, he can check out the book. I would leave it up to the parent to censor the book by having the child return it.

---

advisors," to get children and young people to read only quality items (quality based on their value system) and occasionally not allow the individual to check out an item.

One of the first major studies of self-censorship was Marjorie Fiske's 1959 book, *Book Selection and Censorship*. At that time, laws existed in California that required state employees to sign loyalty oaths. In terms of libraries, this translated into pressure to have only "patriotic" materials in library collections. One case arose from schools teaching the principles of the United Nations, as well as having materials in the library supporting those principles and, for that matter, teaching the subject. There was great pressure not to have such material in school libraries. The California Library Association became so concerned about the situation and its commitment to IF that it commissioned a study of the matter, administered by Fiske. One of the oldest favorite test questions in a collection development class was some version of "is selection a form of censorship?" Librarians often waffle or weasel-word their view about such a question as Fiske illustrated in a quotation from a librarian in her study: "We haven't been censoring but we have been 'conservative.' After all, this is a conservative community and that is how parents want it to be" (Fiske, 1959, p. 62).

Fiske's overall findings were, among other things, that two thirds of the librarians admitted they self-censored some of the time and 20 percent did so regularly (p. 68). Two good articles about the events and the Fiske study are Cindy Mediavilla's (1997) "The War on Books and Ideas: The California Library Association and Anti-Communist Censorship in the 1940s

---

Something to Ponder

A question for you: didn't the statement quoted from Fiske's report reflect the view that collections reflect local interests? Another question: how far should you go to provide materials that do not appear to reflect local interests in the name of balance and IF?

Check These Out

The following are some relatively recent publications related to the topics of ethics and censorship:

Melodie J. Fox and Austin Reece's 2012 article "Which Ethics? Whose Morality? An Analysis of Ethical Standards for the Information Organization" (*Knowledge Organization* 39, no. 5: 377–383).

Emily Knox's 2015 work entitled *Book Banning in the 21st Century* (Lanham, MD: Scarecrow Press).

Lili Luo's 2016 article "Ethical Issues in Reference: An In-depth View from the Librarians' Perspective" (*Reference & User Services Quarterly* 55, no. 1: 189–198).

Lauren L. McMullen's 2015 piece "Conscience and Conduct: Ethics in the Library" (*PNLA Quarterly* 79, no. 2: 35–38).

---

and 1950s" (*Library Trends* 46, no. 2: 331–47) and Joyce M. Latham's (2014) "Heat, Humility and Hubris: The Conundrum of the Fiske Report" (*Library Trends* 65, no. 1: 57–74). Ethics, integrity, professional positions, and the real world do not always come together neatly or easily, at least not in terms of CM activities.

Being Challenged

How warranted is the concern about being challenged on a selection decision? (Almost all challenges are a matter of differing opinions.) In an academic or special library environment, the chances are small to almost nonexistent. However, in the public and school library setting there is a reasonably high probability that sometime during your career one of your choices will be challenged. Some sense of the frequency of reported challenges appeared in a 2002 article by Nicolle Steffen regarding challenges to material in Colorado public libraries. For 2001, 11 percent (13 libraries) of the public libraries reported one or more challenges (50 challenges for the year). The challenges were a mix of materials and activities—50 percent were for books, 30.6 percent were for videos, and the balance were for Internet, music, periodicals, and exhibits/events (p. 9). She also looked at data from 1998 to 2001 and reported that 43.9 percent of the challenges were for adult materials and 42.7 percent were for children's items (p. 10). On the school library front, Linda Jacobson reported that over 40 percent of school librarians who responded to a 2016 *School Library Journal* survey indicated they have personally faced a book challenge, with 92 percent of challenges coming from parents. As noted by Jacobson, 10 percent of elementary schools

---

Check This Out

The complete survey results and supporting materials referenced in the Jacobson article are available on the *School Library Journal* Self-Censorship site, http://www.slj .com/features/self-censorship/.

---

and 12 percent of high schools include a restricted book section, and "many libraries that don't officially 'restrict' books shelve them by age of reader and sometimes require a parent's OK" (2016, p. 23).

Although very much related, challenges and censorship are not identical. One way to think about challenges is in terms of five levels. An "expression of concern" is the lowest level and most common occurrence. This happens when a person asks about an item and the person's comments/question is judgmental in tone, but the matter goes no further. An "oral complaint" is the second stage, but again there is no follow-up by the person complaining. The third level is "written complaint." The fourth level is "public attack" in which there are efforts to get press attention, as well as gaining other people's support. This is a tactic most often employed by an organized group rather than a single person. "Censorship," the end of the process, is where there is a successful effort to remove or change the access status of the item challenged

Just because an item is challenged does not mean that censorship will necessarily be the outcome. For example, using the 2009 Colorado State Library data, of the 48 challenged materials, 6 percent were dropped for some reason; 71 percent resulted in no change of the item's status; 10 percent were "moved"—reclassified, say from YA to the adult collection, or access changed (some form of controlled access); and 13 percent were removed from the collection. Where you place "moved" on the scale of successful censorship efforts does not change the fact that, at least for that year, such efforts succeeded in restricting access no more than 20 percent of the time (Colorado State Library, 2010).

The failure to succeed more often than not does not make the concern, pressure, or stress of going through such a challenge any less. There will be meetings, reports, etc. that will be required in order to resolve oral and written complaints, and if there are public attacks the stress level will increase. In all but the smallest public libraries, the person that selected an item will not be alone—senior managers will carry much, but not all, of the burden of addressing the concern. In a school setting, there are rarely other professionals to share the load. Handling a challenge takes time, effort, and willingness to work extra time—the other duties do not go away just because of a challenge. Is it any wonder school media specialists admit they sometimes don't select something they think has the potential for generating a challenge?

There are some steps to take to prepare for and, to some degree, reduce the chances of a full-blown challenge. Knowing the dangers of censorship and having a commitment to avoid it is not enough in today's world. Librarians must prepare for challenges long, long before there is a complaint. The first step in preparing for the eventual challenge is to prepare a policy statement about how to handle complaints and have the policy approved by all the appropriate authorities. There is a rather high degree of stress when you face your first challenge if you have no idea of what to do when facing an angry person who is complaining about an item. Even with policies and procedures in place, there is a chance your first encounter could escalate into physical violence (from a few bruises up to broken bones—it has happened).

From the Advisory Board

Advisory board member Susan Koutsky notes:

Many schools are in districts that have already developed policies regarding challenges. The district will often support the librarian, thus sharing the load.
    For example, the regulation for Montgomery County (Maryland) Public Schools (MCPS; *Regulation IIB-RA, Evaluation and Selection of Instructional Materials and Library Books*) is public (http://www.montgomeryschoolsmd.org /departments/policy/pdf/iibra.pdf) and available on the School Library Media Programs Evaluation and Selection web page: http://montgomeryschoolsmd .org/departments/media/evaluation.aspx. See specifically page 6 of the regulation, bullet F: "Reconsideration of Instructional Materials and Library Books."

From the Advisory Board

Advisory Board member Wendy Bartlett had the following observation with regard to up-to-date policies:

I stress to my classes that you get this out and revise it every year. My staff and I do so every February. Things change that fast, and it looks better to an irate customer or flustered Board member if the revision date isn't ten years ago! A current date within the last year says, "Hey, we're careful about this issue, and we just looked at it, so let's have a calm discussion based on this relevant and up to date info." I tell my students, "Your director will LOVE you for it!"

The odds of violence occurring are very low, but lack of training in policies and procedures increases the risk.
    A typical procedure is to have the individual(s) file a formal complaint by filling out a form that specifies what is at issue. For some individuals, just filling out the form reduces their concern(s) and the prospect of going through a formal process causes them not to go any further. Several organizations, such as ALA (http://www.ala.org/tools/challengesupport) and the National Council of Teachers of English (http://www2.ncte.org/resources /ncte-intellectual-freedom-center/) have recommended forms that are somewhat effective in defusing the immediate anger.
    After the library develops the policies and procedures and they are approved, everyone working in public services needs to understand the procedure(s) and receive training in implementing the system. Sometimes role-playing is helpful in reinforcing the training. The ALA Office of Intellectual Freedom site includes a series of materials available with suggestions for what to do before a potential censor arrives (http://www.ala.org/offices /oif). Two additional resources are Frances Jones' (1983) classic text *Defusing Censorship: The Librarian's Guide to Handling Censorship Conflicts* and Kristin Fletcher-Spear and Kelly Tyler's (2014) *Intellectual Freedom for Teens: A Practical Guide for Young Adults and School Librarians*. Unlike many other topics, challenges to library materials are neither new nor have they changed much over time.
    Major challenges usually involve an organized group which, in turn, involve interpretations of points of law and often highly charged emotional

---

Something to Ponder

What follows draws on an *Arizona Republic* newspaper headline ("Women's Effort Stocks Library Shelves with Marathi Books," February 4, 2017, pp. 3A, 9A). The story was about a public library accepting 150 books in Marathi (1 of India's 22 official languages). There was no clear statement regarding the library's gift policy; however, given that it accepted the gift as going into the collection, it seems likely the gift policy is rather open. (We look at collection policies in some depth in chapter 6.)

Would you have accepted such a gift? There are some long-term as well as short-term considerations as well as ethical/IF issues to consider when making the decision:

- equitability
- greatest good for the greatest number
- finite shelf space for collections
- cost to catalog and process the items

- social justice
- common good
- collection usage
- integrate or special section

A rather basic long-term consideration is, if you accept the books, what grounds will you have to turn down other offers, requests, and perhaps even demands from other groups wishing to promote their interests with collections?

The above are issues that arise in the selection process regardless of its nature—library acquisition or a user donation—to some degree.

---

issues. Therefore, a challenge that gets to the attack level normally involves attorneys and judges rather than just librarians and the community. We hear about the cases that reach the courts, but seldom about daily local problems. (The Office of Intellectual Freedom often suggests the vast majority of an objection to a collection item is never reported as it never goes beyond the first level.) All challenges start as local problems between the library and an individual or group from the community and are usually settled quickly. Depending on the nature of the material, the level of emotional involvement, and the prior administrative actions (that is, policies), the library may be able to quickly resolve the issue, or the problem may escalate until it reaches the courtroom.

Check These Out

You can read about a variety of challenges and censorship cases in chapter 18 ("Censorship, Intellectual Freedom, and Collection Development") in the fifth edition of *Developing Library and Information Collections* by Evans and Saponaro (Westport, CT: Libraries Unlimited, 2005). The types of challenges and censorship concerns are surprisingly constant through time.

You may also wish to consult *Public Library Collections in the Balance: Censorship, Inclusivity, and Truth* by Jennifer Downey (Santa Barbara, CA: Libraries Unlimited, 2017). Although the focus of the work is predominantly on public libraries, the issues of censorship it covers are also seen in school, academic, and even special libraries. It is worth a look.

You can understand why ethics and bias interact in complex ways with intellectual freedom and how the staff may at times be conflicted regarding how to react. Our best advice is to have some time devoted to discussing various situations that may generate stress or conflict in a group session before they become challenges "on the floor." Several of the resources mentioned earlier in the chapter can be useful for ideas for such discussions.

Access—Filtering

Filtering access to the Internet has been and remains something of a "hot topic" for the public, government officials, and libraries. The topic arose only after Internet access became widespread. Public and school libraries have faced complex issues of access, freedom to read and view, and protection of children. The primary reason given for filtering is to keep children from having access to "unacceptable" sites. Needless to say, there are differing views of what constitutes "unacceptable." Libraries were/are caught between the proverbial "rock and a hard place" on this issue with the public on one side and professional values on the other. As long as libraries offer Internet access to the public and are short of funds for providing that access, the professional position is given less weight in many instances.

The Children's Internet Protection Act (CIPA), enacted in 2000, requires libraries and schools to install filters on their Internet computers, and have an "Internet Safety" statement (an acceptable use policy) in place, if they want to receive federal funds for Internet connectivity (E-Rate funds). The penalty for not doing so is loss of federal funding. The intent of the law is to protect minors from pornography and other questionable websites. However, implementing the law challenges the principle of intellectual freedom and hampers the effectiveness of the Web as a reference source. Public and school libraries have developed various policies on implementing CIPA, from installing filters on all public stations, installing filters on some stations designated for children, and declining to install filters at all. While some libraries have gone to the extreme and practice what Kristen Batch (2015) called "overfiltering," some public libraries take a middle ground, either designating certain stations without filters as "adults only" or filtering and then disabling filters upon the request of an adult (allowed by CIPA). A rather large number have chosen to forgo E-rate funds in the name of IF and professional ethics.

What is the filtering environment like today? Essentially the dilemmas related to IF, filtering, and public libraries still bedevil both librarians and some members of their service community. A good article that covers the history of CIPA is by Paul Jaeger and Zhang Yan (2009). In their article, the authors made the point that public libraries and schools were singled out in CIPA in part because they provide children with Internet access. More

---

Check These Out

Two excellent and basic items that describe how filtering software works are Paul Resnick's 1997 *Scientific American* article "Filtering Information on the Internet" (276, no. 3: 62–64) and Steven J. Murdoch and Ross Anderson's chapter "Tools and Technology of Internet Filtering" in *Access Denied: The Practice and Policy of Global Internet Filtering*, edited by Ronald Deibert, John Palfrey, Rafal Rohozinski, and Jonathan Zittrain (Cambridge: MIT Press, 2008, 57–73).

From the Advisory Board

Advisory Board member Susan Koutsky noted that for public libraries in particular,

Adhering to CIPA regulations can be tricky, as patrons are all ages. Some computers and databases may need to be designated for adults only. In the Montgomery County (MD) Public School system, we are using the Common Sense Education curriculum to teach children about Internet safety and digital citizenship issues (https://www.commonsense.org/education/).

Check This Out

ALA adopted a statement entitled *Internet Filtering: An Interpretation of the Library Bill of Rights* in 2015 (http://www.ala.org/advocacy/intfreedom/librarybill /interpretations/internet-filtering). The statement reads in part, "Because adults and, to a lesser degree minors, have First Amendment rights, libraries and schools that choose to use content filters should implement policies and procedures that mitigate the negative effects of filtering to the greatest extent possible." It is well worth a look.

importantly, earlier efforts to regulate Internet content only dealt with controlling Internet access by children (for example, COPA, the Child Internet Online Protection Act) and were ruled unconstitutional and a violation of the First Amendment (pp. 8–9).

In between children and adults is a large group of library users—young adults. What about their IF rights in the CIPA environment? As Barbara A. Jansen (2010) wrote, "the landscape of Web 2.0 offers various viewpoints, original information from many sources, and means to express ideas and share results with a wide audience" (p. 49). She also noted, "In addition to blocking access to educationally viable resources . . . restricting access to social media sites in schools also calls into question the erosion of the principles of intellectual freedom for youth" (p. 48).

Check These Out

Helen R. Adams (2009) provided "Reflections on Ethics in Practice" (*Knowledge Quest* 37, no. 3: 66–69), giving some additional "how would you handle this" scenarios, most of which relate to privacy and access.

Trina Magi (2015) provides sound advice for libraries who must install filtering software in her article "I'm Being Required to Install an Internet Filter. What Should I Do?" (*Knowledge Quest* 44, no. 1: 63), while Lizabeth Elaine Stem's (2017) "Censorship: Filtering Content on the Web" (*The Southeastern Librarian*, 64, no. 4: 17–20) gives a useful overview of how filters work, as well as posing arguments for and against filtering.

A 2016 article that looks at the legal, professional, and ethics of filtering is Adrienne Muir, Rachel Spacey, Louise Cooke, and Claire Creaser's "Regulating Internet Access in UK Public Libraries: Legal Compliance and Ethical Dilemmas" (*Journal of Information, Communication and Ethics in Society* 11, no. 1: 87–104).

Bibliotherapy—Readers' Advisory Activities

Bibliotherapy is not an IF, access, or filtering issue as such, but it does have some of those elements associated with it. As such it is marginally related to what we do or do not select for the collection. A standard definition of the term is the "use of literature to bring about a therapeutic interaction between participant and facilitator" (Hynes and Hynes-Berry, 1986, p. 10).

Libraries frequently take the position in censorship challenges that reading or viewing something from a library collection does no harm. Yet there is evidence reading can have a therapeutic impact on people and their behavior. The issue is complicated. To a degree, both positions have some merit. Some years ago John Berry (1992) explored the question of the impact of reading on people in a *Library Journal* editorial, noting:

> If words don't incite action, I'm in the wrong line of work. . . . If they don't motivate people to act, antisocially or otherwise, then our First Amendment is of little value and less importance. This is a tough contradiction for those of us who must argue the case against censorship. . . .We can't support free expression by saying it won't do any harm. It is obvious that the action triggered by words and pictures can do harm and often does. (p. 6)

The profession should devote more time to learning about the circumstances in which reading or viewing may cause someone to harm themselves, others, or property. Perhaps a course or two in bibliotherapy should be required of any professional working in public service areas and CM personnel, especially school librarians and public library children's services staff.

Bibliotherapy is not a new concept; it is almost 100 years old in terms of its acknowledged application. Certainly almost all children's books written prior to the 1850s were didactic and written to teach certain values and behaviors. Perhaps such material should not be considered therapeutic; however, the intent was to achieve a desired behavior or value system.

Perhaps the first use of the term bibliotherapy was by Samuel Crothers (1916) in an article about using books to help "troubled" individuals. In the early 1920s, Sadie Peterson Delaney, chief librarian at the Tuskegee Veterans Administration Hospital, was using books to help World War I veterans regain mental and physical abilities. For more than 34 years she was a leading spokesperson for and teacher of bibliotherapy (Gubert, 1993).

In the late 1930s, Dr. W. C. Menninger, founder of the Menninger Psychiatric Clinic, incorporated bibliotherapy into his therapeutic treatment program. Until the post–World War II period, the therapy was focused on adults (Jones, 2006). Mental health professionals have established that in certain circumstances bibliotherapy is an effective treatment option in conjunction with other treatments (for example, see Timothy Apodaca and William R. Miller, 2003; Pieter Cuijpers, 1997; and Mark Floyd, 2003). Most bibliotherapists operate on the basis of several assumptions:

- The process is interactive; it involves both participant and facilitator.
- Literature encompasses all forms of communication, not just books.
- The process is both clinical and developmental.
- The process can be one-on-one or group-based.

- The outcome is improved self-esteem and better assimilation of appropriate psychological or social values for the participant(s).
- The process is a therapy but draws heavily on the healthy aspects of the mind.
- The process depends on the facilitator's ability to select the appropriate material for the participant to read and consider.

The important key to the concept is to know the medical diagnosis and the content of useful materials. It is *not* thinking you know what is amiss and recommending something; that is tempting for all of us, but especially for librarians working with children and youth. It is also about working with mental health professionals. Jami L. Jones (2006) gave some sound advice to librarians regarding mixing developmental reading, reader advisory/"coping" activities, and bibliotherapy, noting, "Even recommending a book as part of reader's advisory may touch on bibliotherapy if the book is used to heal. . . . Concern kicks in when giving someone a book who has mental health issues morphs into therapy. . . . Perhaps one role for librarians in the science of bibliotherapy is to partner with mental health specialists to provide the names of books as well as specific passages that could be useful in therapy" (p. 26).

Jarrett Dapier (2016) made the case for this type of bibiliotherapy when he wrote, "Hospitalized children and their families have particular information needs. Through the establishment of carefully curated library collections, hospital staff and libraries can provide children and their families with invaluable resources and programs to help them cognitively and emotionally" (p. 26).

There is much we do not know about the relationship between reading or viewing something and later behavior. Perhaps when we know more, our freedom-to-read statements may need revision. In many ways, the issues of filtering are rather like this as well. If we need to protect children from Internet materials, is it not also likely that we need to protect them from other materials as well? Determining the effect, or lack of, of reading, viewing, and listening on behavior should be a high priority. Our field makes the case for free and open access to all material for anyone at any time, yet

---

From the Authors' Experience

Evans was a library intern in a Veterans Administration hospital while in library school. At that time, he had not heard of bibliotherapy. As part of his duties he took books and magazines to the locked psychiatric ward for patients.

About halfway through his internship he was given some background by the ward staff in what to put on the truck prior to going to the ward. He became a marginal team member in the sense that doctors and nurses asked him to inform them of any patient requests for specific items, and he was frequently asked to provide a detailed description of the title's content. That assistance reduced the number of items the staff removed, but it never reduced the incorrect items to zero for any visit. The issue was, of course, that there was always patient progress (or lack of) as well as patient turnover, which, in the absence of being involved on a day-to-day basis with the ward, meant he had incomplete information about what to bring on a given day.

That experience made Evans reluctant to suggest items to people with the idea the material would help them.

there is evidence that reading, viewing, and listening to certain material by certain people at certain times does affect behavior in a positive or negative way. Reading and viewing materials can have a positive as well as negative role to play. Thus the process of creating an ethical collection that effectively serves users' needs can be very challenging.

Points to Keep in Mind

- Intellectual freedom is an important concept to think about and understand when you become engaged in CM activities.

- The American Library Association has a number of position documents that relate to IF, ethics, privacy, and access that provide sound starting points for your thinking.

- Selection decisions are a combination of both cognitive and affective factors.

- Ethical dilemmas are not uncommon in selection activities as you must try to balance personal beliefs and values with those of your profession.

- Because of CIPA, filtering is a given for school library media centers.

- CIPA and public libraries are uncomfortable bedfellows. The number of public libraries forgoing federal funds for Internet connectivity is greater than those who accept the CIPA terms. However, it seems likely there will be ongoing issues between libraries that do not filter and some of its service community constituents that engage in filtering Internet access.

- Bibliotherapy does work in certain circumstances, and the library profession does not yet have a sound understanding of the relationship between reading or viewing something and later behavior.

References

Apodaca, Timothy R., and William R. Miller. 2003. "A Meta-Analysis of the Effectiveness of Bibliotherapy for Alcohol Problems." *Journal of Clinical Psychology* 59, no. 3: 289–304.

Batch, Kristen R. 2015. "Filtering Beyond CIPA: Consequences of and Alternatives to Overfiltering in Schools." *Knowledge Quest* 44, no. 1: 60–6.

Berry III, John N. 1992. "If Words Will Never Hurt Me, Then . . ." *Library Journal* 117, no. 1: 6.

Bostwick, Arthur E. 1908. "The Librarian as Censor." *ALA Bulletin* 2 (September): 113.

Budd, John M. 2006/2007. "Politics & Public Library Collections." *Progressive Librarian* 28 (Winter): 78–86.

Colorado State Library. 2010. "Challenged Materials in Colorado Public Libraries." *Fast Facts*. ED3/110.10/No. 289. http://www.lrs.org/documents/fastfacts/289 _Challenges_Public_Libraries_2009.pdf.

Crothers, Samuel M. 1916. "A Literary Clinic." *Atlantic Monthly* 118, no. 3: 291–301.

Cuijpers, Pieter. 1997. "Bibliotherapy in Unipolar Depression: A Meta-Analysis." *Journal of Behavior Therapy and Experimental Psychiatry* 28, no. 2: 139–47.

Dapier, Jarrett. 2016. "Prescriptions for Joy: Libraries, Collections, and Bibliotherapy in Pediatric Hospital Settings." *Public Libraries* 55, no. 4: 24–27.

Echavarria Robinson, Tami. 2014. "Academic Freedom: The Role of Librarians in What Universities Contribute to Intellectual Freedom." *ALKI* 30, no. 3: 11–12, 14.

Fiske, Marjorie. 1959. *Book Selection and Censorship*. Berkeley, CA: University of California Press.

Fletcher-Spear, Kristin, and Kelly Tyler. 2014. *Intellectual Freedom for Teens: A Practical Guide for Young Adults and School Librarians*. Chicago: ALA Editions.

Floyd, Mark. 2003. "Bibliotherapy as an Adjunct to Psychotherapy for Depression in Older Adults." *Journal of Clinical Psychology* 59, no. 2: 187–95.

Gubert, Betty K. 1993. "Sadie Peterson Delaney: Pioneer Bibliotherapist." *American Libraries* 24, no. 2: 124–25, 127, 129–30.

Hynes, Arleen M., and Mary Hynes-Berry. 1986. *Bibliotherapy—The Interactive Process: A Handbook*. Boulder, CO: Westview Press.

Jacobson, Linda. 2016. "Unnatural Selection." *School Library Journal* 62, no. 10: 20–4.

Jaeger, Paul, and Zhang Yan. 2009. "One Law with Two Outcomes: Comparing the Implementation of CIPA in Public Libraries and Schools." *Information Technology and Libraries* 25, no. 1: 6–14.

Jansen, Barbara A. 2010. "Internet Filtering 2.0: Checking Intellectual Freedom and Participative Practices at the Schoolhouse Door." *Knowledge Quest* 39, no. 1: 46–53.

Jones, Frances M. 1983. *Defusing Censorship: The Librarian's Guide to Handling Censorship Conflicts*. Phoenix, AZ: Oryx Press.

Jones, Jami L. 2006. "A Closer Look at Bibliotherapy." *Young Adult Library Services* 5, no. 1: 24–7.

Klinefelter, Anne. 2010. "First Amendment Limits on Library Collection Management." *Law Library Journal* 102, no. 3: 343–74.

Manley, Will. 2010. "Conservatives Among Us." *American Libraries* 41, no. 10: 56.

Martin, Ann M. 2009. "Leadership: Integrity and the ALA Code of Ethics." *Knowledge Quest* 37, no. 3: 6–11.

Moshman, David. 2003. "Intellectual Freedom for Intellectual Development." *Liberal Education* 89, no. 3: 30–7.

O'Brien, David. 1981. *The Public's Right to Know: The Supreme Court and First Amendment*. New York: Praeger.

Preer, Jean, 2008. *Library Ethics*. Westport, CT: Libraries Unlimited.

Quinn, Brian. 2007. "Cognitive and Affective Process in Collection Development." *Library Resources & Technical Services* 51, no. 1: 5–15.

Steffen, Nicolle O. 2002. "Challenging Times: Challenged Materials in Colorado Public Libraries." *Colorado Libraries* 28, no. 3: 9–12.

Walther, James H. 2016. "Teaching Ethical Dilemmas in LIS Coursework." *The Bottom Line* 29, no. 3: 180–90.

Williams, Brian N. 2015. "Embracing Ethical Practices in Public Action." In *Handbook of Public Administration,* 3rd ed., edited by James L. Perry and Robert Christensen, 583–97. New York: Wiley.

3
Collection Management

Some time ago, a colleague was asked by a library board member when the staff would be "done" buying books for the library. He was under the impression that the library added materials until the shelves were full, and then they were finished. The truth is that library collections have a life cycle that is never finished.

—Holly Hibner and Mary Kelly, 2013

It is a safe bet that the collection budget in any library looks quite different in structure and scope today than 20 years ago. And this is a very good thing—it means there is flexibility and innovation in how we respond to the rapidly transforming world of knowledge, scholarship and information technology that is still in its infancy.

—Tony Horava, 2015

Floating [collections] has emerged as an attractive option for contemporary libraries for one very simple reason: it saves money. . . . Items can go where they are needed and wanted, creating an efficiency over the "just-in-case" model of a traditional collection, wherein items are purchased for every branch, large or small, on the chance a patron might want them.

—Wendy K. Bartlett, 2014a

The experience Hibner and Kelly related in the opening quote above is really not that unique. Many times, individuals think of libraries—public, academic, or school—as a "warehouse" for books only, and that the collections they contain are static. (There are differences of opinion, however. One of the authors recalls overhearing a remark made on a field trip to a newly opened public library facility: "It's a shame they spent all this money on a new facility and had to put back in all the old books." The assumption was that if there was a new facility, that would equate to all new books, not retaining the existing—although presumably useful—collection.) How libraries and their collections are accessed has evolved over time and along with it, the concept of how libraries have approached the creation and preservation of collections.

As Horava's quote alludes, there are a great deal of changes in collections, with new resources and formats becoming available almost daily. Today's libraries are more expansive in content and format (and expense) than in the days when collections were literally chained to the tables. It is doubtful the monks and others who managed the very first library collections would have envisioned a time when not only books would be available 24/7 online, but video, data, and audio content would be as well. With the increasing variety of information available in a variety of formats, price becomes a major concern. Budgeting is a major component of collections work, and funding sources are almost always stable at best, while costs are anything but static. The 2018 *Serials Price Projection Report* released by EBSCO Information Services confirmed the long-standing trend of annual serial price increases to be between 5 and 6 percent (EBSCO, 2017). For institutions with flat budgets, this has made for some tough decisions. As we will discuss in chapter 12, serials subscriptions can consume a majority of the available budget, depending on the type of library.

Components of Collection Management

Regardless of their type, one of the primary purposes of libraries is to assist people in locating and accessing useful information. Figure 3.1 illustrates the process involved in accomplishing that purpose. Institutions of all sizes and organizational format follow these steps—although they may have different labels for the same functions.

The process begins at the *identification* stage, during which designated personnel sort through available information resources to identify appropriate from inappropriate resources. In most instances, there is vastly more appropriate information available than the library can acquire with its available resources, much less house. Thus, there is a need to *select* the most useful or otherwise needed information to *acquire*. After acquisition, the library adds value to that information by *organizing* it in some manner. That process is followed by some form of the physical or digital *preparation* of the resource for *storage* and *access*; the goal of organizing and preparation activities is to assure the easiest possible access for the end users. Users often need assistance in identifying and accessing desired information from staff members (*interpretation*). Finally, users draw upon the accessed material to assist them in their activities/work (*utilization*), and on occasion *dissemination* of the outcome of their work to the internal or external environment, or both. If the transfer process is to function properly, there must be procedures, policies, and people in place to carry out the necessary *operational* steps. As always, there must be coordination and money for the staff to operate as effectively as possible; this is the administrative/managerial aspect of information work.

Collection management (CM), as defined in chapter 1, is a universal process for libraries. Figure 3.2 illustrates the major components of the process. One can see a relationship between figures 3.1 and 3.2, in that CM

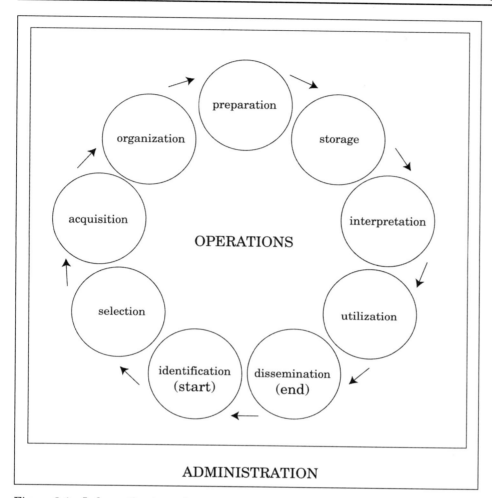

Figure 3.1   Information transfer process

involves three of the nine information transfer elements (identification, selection, acquisition). As implied by the circles in both figures, both the information transfer process and CM are constant cycles that continue as long as the library exists. All of the elements in the CM cycle are discussed in subsequent chapters.

Because our philosophy of CM focuses on meeting the information needs of the service community, we begin our discussion with the needs assessment element. The terms *needs assessment, community analysis,* or *user/service community,* as used throughout this text, mean the group of persons that the library exists to serve. They do *not* refer only to the active users, but include everyone within the library's defined service parameters. Thus, a community might be an entire political unit (i.e., a nation, region, state, province, county, city, or town). Alternatively, a community may be a more specialized grouping or association (i.e., a university, college, school, government agency, or private organization). Also, the number of people that the library serves may range from a very few to millions. Data for the analysis comes from a variety of sources and is not limited to staff-generated material. For CM

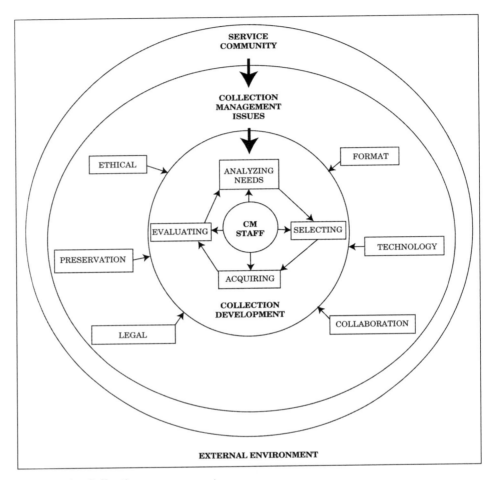

Figure 3.2   Collection management process

personnel, the assessment process provides data on what information the clientele needs. It also establishes a valuable mechanism for user input into the process of collection development. (Note the size of the arrow in figure 3.2 from the community to collection development; the size indicates the level of "community" input appropriate for each element.)

One use for the data collected in needs assessment is in the preparation of a collection policy(ies). Clearly delineated policies on both collection development and selection (covered in chapter 4) provide the CM staff with guidelines for deciding which resources are most appropriate for the collection. Some libraries call the document an *acquisitions* policy, some a *selection* policy, some a *collection management* policy, and others simply a *statement*. Whatever the local label, the intent is the same: to define the library's goals for its collection(s) and to help staff members select and acquire the most appropriate materials.

For many people, selection is the most interesting element in the CM process. One constant factor is that there is never enough money available to buy everything that might be of value to the service community. Naturally, this means that someone, usually one or more professional staff members, must decide which items to buy. This may mean choosing among items that provide information about the same subject, deciding whether the information contained in an item is worth the price, deciding upon a format for the information, or determining whether an item could stand up to its projected use. In essence, it is a matter of systematically determining quality and value—and varies with the setting. For example, in public libraries, purchases may focus on usefulness and popularity, with selectors asking themselves "will it circulate?" or "do people want it?"—while in academic settings, selectors may be more likely to ask "does this support X program?" Most of the time it is not just a matter of identifying appropriate materials, but of deciding among items that are essential, important, needed, marginal, nice, or luxurious. Where to place any item in the sequence from essential to luxurious depends, of course, on the individual selector's point of view. Its placement on such a continuum is a matter of perception and is an area where differing views regarding that placement can be problematic for the library.

Individuals buying an item for themselves normally do not have to justify the expenditure to anyone. However, when it is a question of spending the community's money, whether derived from taxes or an organization's budget, the decision may be debatable. The question of whose perception of value to employ is one of the challenges. Needs assessments and policies help determine the answer, but there is a long-standing question in the field: how much emphasis should selectors place on clientele demand, how much to place on what selectors *think* their clientele want, and how much on content quality?

Acquisition work is the process of securing materials for the library's collection, whether by purchase, as gifts, or through exchange programs. This is the only point in the collection development process that involves little or no community input; it is a fairly straightforward business operation. Often the individuals who have selection duties are not directly involved in the work of acquiring the selected material. In those cases, once the CM staff decides to purchase/lease an item, the acquisition department staff proceeds with the preparation of an order, the selection of a vendor, eventually recording the receipt of the item, and finally, paying the bill (invoice). (In school library/media centers, for example, these duties are often performed by the same person who selects the items.) Although details vary, the basic routines remain the same around the world, just as they do in either a manual or automated work environment.

Evaluating is the last element in the collection management process, and it can serve many different purposes, both inside and outside the library. For example, it may help to increase funding for the library. Certainly it will be an element in any library accreditation process. Occasionally, it may help in assessing the quality of the work done by CM staff. For effective evaluation to occur, the service community's needs must be considered, which leads back to community analysis.

The most common internal reason for evaluating items/resources in a collection is the fact that all resources have a finite period of high use, or even useful, life span. Frequently the driving force behind such assessments relates to the fact that libraries have limited shelf/storage space, or more commonly, limited funds with which to continue subscriptions to such online resources as databases or journal packages. In the case of physical objects, eventually the library will have to address the inevitable situation of having to secure additional collection space, stop acquiring new material, or withdraw items occupying existing space. Most libraries will engage in the last activity. Public, school, and special libraries rarely, if ever, have the

---

From the Advisory Board

Advisory Board member Wendy Bartlett notes that in the public library setting, there is not the same expectation that multiple copies of titles—including videos—are kept long-term. She observes: "They peak and they go. One way we maintain the integrity of our collection is to have a 'core collection.' We assign a 'CORE' designation to the 590 field of the MARC record for items like *On the Road* or *Pride and Prejudice*. That way, we can exclude them from weeding reports, and check on them periodically to ensure we have sufficient copies. This is [particularly] important in a floating collection where staff may not notice that we need more copies of *As the Caged Bird Sings* or what have you. Each selector assigns this designation as needed from the *Bible* to *The Joy of Cooking*. It's been very successful for us."

Check This Out

One title that visually explains the "life cycle" of an item in a collection is Holly Hibner and Mary Kelly's *Making a Collection Count: A Holistic Approach to Library Collection Management* (2nd ed. Chandos Information Professional Series. Oxford: Chandos Publishing, 2014), authors of one of the opening quotes for this chapter. Each of the eight stages in their "life cycle" model give, as they indicate, an "opportunity to survey the collection and evaluate it for quality" (p. 1). Their work is well worth the look.

---

opportunity to select either of the first options. Larger academic and some very large public libraries may have additional options available—by storing low-use items in compact shelving units installed within the facility or sending items to a remote (lower cost) facility and providing delayed access. The withdrawal process has several labels, the oldest being *weeding*, with *deselection* or *deaccessioning* or even *collection rightsizing* used at times. Regardless of the label, the end result is the same; when a library decides to withdraw a physical item, it will dispose of the item (by selling it, giving it away, or even discarding it).

Beyond the four core CM activities (covered in chapters 4–7), there are a host of issues that impact those activities in some manner. We have grouped those issues into six very broad categories (the first of which was addressed in the previous chapter; the remainder will be addressed in chapters 7–15):

- Ethical/intellectual freedom
- Formats
- Technology
- Preservation
- Legal issues
- Collaboration

Collection Management and Library Types

In figure 3.2, the outermost area is labeled "external environment." It is that external environment/service community that determines library type. The concepts discussed above are generic in character regardless of type.

How the concepts are translated into the real world of library operations arise from the library's external milieu.

One important fact to understand about libraries is that there are very, very few standalone operations. Libraries are almost always a component of a larger parent organization, whether that be a city, county, school system, or academic institution. That organization is also surrounded by external events, pressures, expectations, values, and so on. Those external elements eventually become factors for the library. Earlier in this chapter we noted the current serials price projection. This is a very real external environment issue that impacts all types of libraries.

We should also mention three other "generic" aspects of CM. The size of a library's service community has a definite bearing on collection development. Three facts of collection development are universal:

1. As the size of the service community increases, the degree of divergence in individual information needs increases.

2. As the degree of divergence in individual information needs increases, the need for resource sharing increases.

3. It will never be possible to satisfy *all* of the information needs of any individual or class of clientele in the service community from locally held/leased resources.

This third factor is particularly relevant in today's information infrastructure.

Institutional Libraries

Libraries, as most people in the U.S. think of them today, first came into existence in the mid-17th century. (Although earlier libraries existed, they had little resemblance to today's libraries.) They also shared many similar startup experiences, such as their early collections consisted of donated books from well-to-do individuals. One of the first, if not the first, U.S. institutional libraries resulted from a gift of several hundred books and a small endowment to an—at the time—unnamed college in Cambridge, Massachusetts, from one John Harvard (1636). Clearly, the notion of giving personal books and magazines to nearby libraries has a very long tradition in the U.S.—more about gifts and CM in chapter 8.

The notion of purchasing books (in the early days it was just books; other formats came later) for the academic library was not widespread until near the middle of the 19th century. The concept of actively developing, much less managing, a collection did not come about until the 20th century. College library collections were small and narrow in scope and depth until well into the 19th century, as most early colleges were affiliated with religious denominations and their curricula was normally restricted to selected texts. (Note: Universities did not come about in the U.S. until the late 19th century.) Keep in mind that until the early 19th century students were only expected to master prescribed texts—there was really no need for student access to collections. At that point, it was common for highly trusted faculty members to have the authority to decide what books should be in the library collection as well as who might read them. Some colleges provided some student library access for a few hours a week, but only under the watchful eyes of one or more trusted faculty members.

By the mid-19th century, students began establishing local literary/debating societies off campus with libraries with books, journals, and newspapers of interest to members. Often these collections had far greater depth and scope than did their college library; certainly hours of access were far greater and a person could explore any topic of interest without faculty approval and oversight.

In the later 20th century academic librarians began playing a major role in how campus libraries created and maintained their collections. The shift from faculty to librarian control came about for several reasons that were indirect outcomes of World War II. Because thousands of war veterans took advantage of a federal government program for higher education enrollment, colleges and universities were swamped with students. Increased enrollments meant there were more sections of more courses offered as well as students requiring advisement/assistance. This created a strain on faculty members' time to attend to what had been traditional faculty responsibilities. A further factor and time commitment for faculty was research. The success scientists had realized in helping to solve wartime problems led to the U.S. government offering a host of research grant opportunities. Since the institution received a share of each grant in the form of "overhead," there was institutional pressure on faculty to apply for such grants. The end result was faculty slowly gave up their collection development responsibilities to librarians. This trend has continued to this day; however, where there once were dedicated positions for collection development (subject bibliographers), that model has shifted in recent years to a liaison model where a librarian is given responsibility for collection management for one or more subject areas in addition to such responsibilities as reference, liaison work, and instruction.

Public Libraries

The origin of "public libraries" is often a point of debate. Some Greek and Roman communities had places where people could read scrolls. In fact, in some Roman public baths there were "dry rooms" filled with scrolls that people could read. However, there is no indication that such rooms were government supported but rather were a service that some baths offered.

It was not until 1731 that Benjamin Franklin organized what he called a subscription (social) library—individuals had to pay a fee to have access. Franklin's idea was that people would greatly benefit from pooling their money and could purchase a greater quantity and variety of material than they could on their own. The concept spread rather quickly; it was this idea that college students drew upon when they started their literary/debating libraries.

Although their size and service communities differ vastly, there are at least four attributes public libraries hold in common. First, they are supported by a government body—usually a municipality or county—with tax revenues. These may include a special levy/tax for library services. Second, the library is freely available to all residents within the taxing jurisdiction,

---

Check This Out

Benjamin Franklin's library still exists today as the Library Company of Philadelphia, focusing on society and culture from the 17th through the 19th centuries. See http://www.librarycompany.org/.

Check These Out

One article that describes the background and use of customer advisory committees (CAC) is Michael Kerr's "Customer Advisory Committees: Giving a Voice to Library Users" (*Feliciter*, 2012, 58, no. 3: 113–15), while Janie Pickett shares her experience with building an advisory committee at her high school in her article "First Steps with a Library Advisory Committee" (*Knowledge Quest*, 2013, 42, no. 1: pp. 14–17).

---

and it may also be available to neighboring community members via reciprocal agreements. Third, the collection is often wide-ranging in scope, catering to interests of the community from children's picture books to scholarly monographs. An additional attribute is that registered borrowers may check out a majority of the items in the collection for a period of time.

Unlike other library types, public library collection building has always been in the hands of the library staff. Initially selection was the director's responsibility, but as the collections and staffing patterns grew, librarians at lower administrative levels took over the work. The early textbooks about creating a library collection arose from the need in public libraries for people trained in book selection. One of the very first such books is Lionel McColvin's *The Theory of Book Selection for Public Libraries* (London, Grafton & Company, 1925). Two other early texts on book selection, both focusing on the public library environment, were Arthur Bostwick's *The American Public Library* (4th edition; New York: Appleton, 1929) and Francis Drury's *Book Selection* (Chicago: American Library Association, 1930). Over time, many large public library systems have centralized their collection/selection activities. However, advisory boards are often utilized by public library systems or branches in order to seek user input on a number of library issues, including collections.

School Libraries

School libraries also have their origins in the 19th century; however, their development has been considerably choppier than other library types. Even today, as communities struggle to address economic conditions, school libraries are often categorized as one of the "nice," but not essential, elements of elementary and secondary education (along with school nurses, counselors, art, and music instruction).

Unlike academic and public libraries, school libraries have some basis in state legislation as well as occasional regulations. New York governor DeWitt Clinton recommended the creation of school libraries in 1827. Over the next 50 or so years 21 other states passed legislation, often as part of an omnibus education bill, that included authorization of school libraries. Unfortunately, recommending and authorizing does not always translate into something happening. Certainly that was, and still is, the case for school libraries.

An interesting government document was published in 1876 by the Department of Interior, Bureau of Education. Its title was *Public Libraries in the United States of America: Their History, Condition, and Management.* The "public libraries" in the title referred to any library that was open to the public and/or funded in part by tax monies. The usual label at that time, for what we think of as public libraries, was free library. (There are chapters on college, law, medical, and many other library types in the 39-chapter and over 1,200-page document.)

Check This Out

A good article that discusses several key principles of intellectual freedom for school librarians and provides suggested resources for further consultation is Helen R. Adams' 2013 piece "Intellectual Freedom 101: Core Principles for School Librarians" (*School Library Monthly* 30, no. 2: 33–34).

At the time of the report, communities had yet to see an advantage of combining public and school library operations into a single system. Certainly many had done this by the mid-20th century. Later, during good economic times, some communities dismantled their combined systems. Although some communities may continue to have combined school-public libraries today, they are not widely popular. One notable exception is the Back of the Yards branch of Chicago Public Library, which was opened in 2013 in order to serve the high school next door (https://www.chipublib.org/about-back-of-the-yards-branch/). Most jurisdictions, however, adopt the mindset of the New Jersey Library Association (NJLA), which indicated in its *Statement on School/Public Library Joint Use Standards*, "although at first glance this may seem simple, experience in other states has demonstrated that this is a very difficult process and should only be undertaken after careful consideration" (NJLA, 2003).

School library funding is normally in the hands of local school districts or even the state superintendent of education (sometimes the sole book selector for the state's school libraries). In the past, those funds for libraries were often diverted to other uses. The New York section of the aforementioned 1876 *Public Libraries in the United States* report indicated, "The diversion of the library fund to other purposes continues, and all the official reports indicate that, in the majority of the districts, the people have come to accept the diversion as a matter of course, and that in some of the very existence of the library at any time is rather a matter of tradition than to knowledge" (p. 41).

Aside from funding issues, the issue of what is appropriate for children and young adults to read has probably been with us for as long as the printed books have existed. Certainly there was a general thought in the profession at the time that libraries had a moral obligation to control access to some books regardless of the reader's age. However, the concern regarding children's reading matter is perhaps as strong today as it ever was. George Hardy's (1889) comment would still resonate with many people today. He noted: "In your collection of books remember that it is important to guard against not only those books that mislead the conscience and studiously present ideas that are fundamentally false, but also against those that merely interest and consume time, but neither elevate the taste nor brighten life" (p. 347). Without question, one of the most challenging CM tasks is creating collections for children and young adults regardless of library type.

Special Libraries

This category of libraries is so diverse that few generalizations are possible. Broadly speaking, there are two types of operating environment for libraries: for-profit or nonprofit. Examples of for-profit are corporate libraries—an oil company library, for example—and partnerships—such as a library in a law firm. Examples of nonprofit libraries are museum, medical, and observatory. One generalization rests in the label for such libraries: their collections focus on a limited number of topics.

Another generalization that is more or less accurate is one or more of the library staff has in-depth knowledge of the library's subject(s) focus, especially when the person is involved in acquisition decisions. The special library environment is very much about "just in time" collection building rather than "just in case." The idea of information is paramount, especially in the for-profit settings, and cost is a distant second place (if it even comes up). "Newsletters" that cost thousands of dollars to access are not uncommon in for-profit libraries.

The literature on special libraries is sparse in comparison to that for other library types. One reason for this, especially for libraries in for-profit organizations, is the idea of proprietary information. How an organization goes about generating profit, what areas are deemed to be of interest, are no one's business but that of the organization. There is a field called "competitive intelligence" that is often of interest to professional staff in the for-profit libraries.

Today's selection process is most varied among and within library types. We explore the issues involved in the selection phase of collection management in chapter 6. Because of those many variations, it is difficult to make many generalizations. However, with that in mind, the following are some general statements about the variations:

1. Public libraries emphasize title-by-title selection, and librarians have traditionally done the selecting. (The concept of patron-initiated selection will be covered in chapter 8.)

2. School libraries select based upon subject areas/topics for educational purposes as well as recreational reading. Although the media specialist may make the final decision, a committee composed of librarians, teachers, administrators, and parents may have a strong voice in the process.

3. Academic libraries select materials in subject areas for educational and research purposes, with selection done by several different methods: faculty only, joint faculty/library committees, librarians, or subject specialists.

4. Special libraries generally select items from a range of topics. Selection decisions are primarily driven by user requests. Cost of material is rarely a feature in the acquisition decision in the for-profit setting.

Collection management is a dynamic process that should involve both the professional staff and the service community. Few information professionals question the need or value of client input; the question is how much there should be. The best answer is, as much as the organization can handle and still carry out its basic functions, and as much as the community is willing to provide.

Standards and Guidelines

This is as reasonable a place as any to briefly discuss guidelines and standards in terms of collection management. There are a number of professional organizations, both within the field of librarianship and beyond, that have guidelines or standards that may influence CM work. A few of the standards are focused just on CM issues such as those found on the ALA *Standards and Guidelines* web page (http://www.ala.org/tools/guidelines /standardsguidelines). This page lists 43 broad categories of standards and guidelines, with the number of standards and guidelines appearing under each of the categories being many times greater. Certainly not all of those categories apply in any direct way to CM work; however, 11 of the categories are applicable. The most obvious category is "Collection Development and Management," which lists six separate standards and guidelines.

Collection-related guidelines cover almost every area of CM activities. Knowing the standards/guidelines pertinent to one's library environment is obviously important; however, they are not the driving force behind daily CM work. They most often come into play during assessment activities and/or accountability activities. They can, however, be helpful in efforts to address budgetary issues and occasionally staffing concerns. The majority of today's standards and guidelines are qualitative rather than quantitative in character, which generally requires more time and effort when making a case for more resources. Nevertheless, they can be useful.

Library organizations are not the only ones to have created standards that relate to libraries and their collections. Perhaps the most important group of organizations are those that accredit educational institutions or some component within such institutions. There are literally hundreds of such agencies whose scope of interest may be national, regional, or statewide in nature. One very important group of agencies is the six regional accrediting agencies. These agencies look at educational institutions (K through postsecondary) to essentially give a "stamp of approval" that an institution is meeting established quality criteria. Going through the accreditation process is voluntary; however, most institutions do so for two major reasons. The first reason is "accredited status" is very often essential when seeking federal funds; lacking such status generally means there is no reason to even attempt to request such funds. The second reason is, in the minds of the general public, being accredited means the institution is of high quality, even if people have no idea of what criteria were employed to determine such status.

We will use the Northwest Commission on Colleges and Universities (NWCCU) as a brief example of the role of accrediting agencies on library collections. NWCCU covers Alaska, Montana, Idaho, Nevada, Oregon, Utah, and Washington. It has a section of its standards (2.E) devoted to "Library and Information Resources." The standards read in part, "Consistent with its

---

Check These Out

Accreditation for higher education institutions occurs at both the institutional and program level, with different agencies responsible for the processes at each level. Tom Schmiedl provides a succinct overview of the accreditation process and agencies associated with it in his 2017 article "Library Support for Accreditation: A Guide to Online Resources" (*College & Research Libraries News* 78, no. 2: 96–100).

A more detailed overview of the accreditation process is found in *Reviewing the Academic Library: A Guide to Self-Study and External Review*, edited by Eleanor Mitchell and Peggy Seiden (Chicago: American Library Association, 2015). Their work is divided into three sections, focusing on why libraries may be subject to review, approaches to the process, and gathering supporting data. The volume is well worth a look.

mission and core themes, the institution holds or provides access to library and information resources with an appropriate level of currency, depth, and breadth to support the institution's mission, core themes, programs, and services, wherever offered and however delivered" (NWCCU, 2010). Failure to meet those criteria will have a negative impact on the institution's accredited status. Regional accreditation agencies have a variety of categories for institutions they review, ranging from fully accredited to nonaccreditation.

Emerging Trends in Collection Management

Library collections, whether they are found in schools, institutions, public facilities, or other organizations, are not static entities. As noted in our opening quote by Horava, the composition of library collections and the types of resources available to users have significantly changed over the past 20 years, or even since the last edition of this text. Although it is not always possible to have a crystal ball handy to stay ahead of the changes in the collection development game, Lisa Peet (2015) provides some sage advice, noting: "When it comes to formats, though, librarians . . . need to be trend-watchers. . . . While no one can perfectly predict the growth or decline of a given format, there are indicators everywhere" (p. 34). Some of the key trends emerging or prevalent at the time this text was being prepared include evidence-based collection building, patron-driven acquisition, open access models, weeding, and pop-up and floating collections.

Patron-driven acquisition or demand-driven acquisition (PDA/DDA, described more in chapter 8) is one method of collection management that is now prevalent in most academic institutions, and represents a major shift from the traditional "just in case" method of collection development to "just in time." The first applications of PDA were for journal articles and eBooks. Now, however, even print books and video titles have been brought into the PDA mix. Fulton (2014) noted that records for print titles can be loaded into a catalog for discovery by users, with a request triggering a purchase, the same as with an e-version (p. 23). Additionally, vendors such as Kanopy and Alexander Street Press have made inroads in DDA services for video titles (covered in chapter 13). A 2017 *Library Journal* survey indicated that print material expenses still made up over 56 percent of average materials budgets for public libraries, but other formats, including audiobooks, downloadable audio, DVD/Blu-ray, music, and eBooks also claimed a piece of the collection "pie" (Hoffert, 2016, p. 33). With the variety of delivery modes

---

Check This Out

In 2018, Matt Enis reported on the results of a survey of academic libraries conducted by the *Library Journal* research staff and funded by EBSCO ("E-Resources Continue Academic Gains," *Library Journal* 143, no. 6: 16–18). Survey results indicated that 60.3 percent of current academic collections were comprised of print materials, with the expectation being that print books would only account for 16 percent of budgets within five years (p. 15). If projections are accurate, this would represent a significant shift in purchasing trends and practices within a relatively short period of time. An infographic describing survey results and a link to the full survey itself is available from the *Library Journal.Com* website (https://www.ebsco.com/blog/article /collection-development-trends-in-academic-libraries).

From the Authors' Experience

Saponaro worked at an institution that briefly toyed with the idea of purchasing a print-on-demand machine, only to ultimately decide to dedicate those funds instead toward more traditional DDA/PDA activities. The Expresso Book Machine® (EBM®) service was still available at the time this volume was being prepared as an offering of On Demand Books (http://ondemandbooks.com/ebm_overview.php), a company established by the founders of the EBM®.

---

multiplying, user expectations for materials in these formats are likewise increasing. However, those expectations must be managed against what is available and affordable. We cover selection decisions in chapter 6.

Other factors to consider when trend-watching are the role of shared collection building (covered in chapter 10), as well as the impact of open access (covered in chapter 13) and repurposing space via weeding (covered in chapter 9). One additional collection trend worth mentioning is the concept of Print-On-Demand (POD). In her review of the collection management literature, Lehman (2014) remarked on POD models of acquisition, which in some institutions was made possible via a specialized machine purchased and available in-house to meet that need (p. 171). Due to the price of the machine itself and relatively low return on investment, POD in library settings has not to date gained the foothold expected by its developers. However, commercial publishers have welcomed the concept and, as noted by Kelly Gallagher (2014), "Gone are the days of printing speculative stock, and hoping it will sell. POD has fundamentally changed the very essence of the publishing model that has, since the days of Gutenberg, been premised on printing a book first and then trying to sell it" (p. 244).

Floating Collections

One additional trend in libraries worth exploring a bit more is the concept of floating collections. Although the name may conjure the image of some sort of "bewitched" collection levitating through a library, or one housed on a cruise ship, the reality is floating collections represent a type of patron-driven collection management where patron requests drive the location and subsequent return and housing of a title. Floating titles are requested at one branch or facility and delivered to the requesting patron at a different facility. When the patron is finished with the title, it remains at the current facility, rather than being returned to the loaning library, as is the norm with such requests. The title remains at the "borrowing" institution until it is requested again by someone at that same institution or another library in the participating system.

Wendy Bartlett (2014a) outlined several reasons for the popularity of floating collections, beyond those noted in her quotation opening this chapter. These benefits can include an increase in circulation, less wear and tear on the items themselves, and a savings in processing time (p. 6). Not all types of materials in a collection are necessarily open to, or good candidates for, floating—such as reference materials or serials. However, libraries are free to determine what portion of their collections are allowed to float. For their advantages, floating collections do represent a change in workflow for technical and public services staff, and several considerations must be made before launching a floating collection. These include ensuring the collection

to be floated is weeded before the floating project begins, assessing the availability of hold shelves and bookdrops, understanding service needs and
patterns, and providing ample communication with both library staff and
constituents (Bartlett, 2014b, pp. 291–292). Perhaps the last factor is the
most important as all staff, not just those in circulation and access services,
need to be well versed on the goals of the program and its mechanics.

At the time this volume was being prepared, floating collections are
predominantly found in public libraries, such as New York Public Library
(NYPL, https://www.nypl.org/blog/2011/03/19/sneaky-ways-you-can-shape
-our-collections), although some academic institutions such as Penn State
(Coopey, Eshbach, and Notartomas, 2016), Denison University, and Kenyon College (Greever, 2014) have successfully experimented with floating
their collections. The Penn State "experiment" in particular provides a good
roadmap for any institution contemplating a floating project. Their process
began in 2010 as the concept was initially examined and key questions were
assessed, such as whether or not the ILS in use could support the program.
A small pilot was crafted for a specific format (monographs) at specific institutions within the system. Although the pilot was relatively small given the
overall size of the collections, time and energy was spent addressing such
issues as adapting catalog displays to account for changes in actual item
location, and identifying a process to keep items secure despite varying security systems in use at the participating libraries. Ultimately, the decision
was made to continue the floating project, slowly adding items in phases
(ibid., pp. 171, 176). At the time Bartlett wrote her work, school library and
media centers had not yet jointed the floating bandwagon, mainly because
of the challenges of materials crossing jurisdictions, as well as differences in
curriculum and populations (Bartlett, 2014a, p. 10).

As seen in the Penn State example, in order for such collections to be
of use, they need to be discoverable by users and supported by integrated
library systems (Bartlett, 2014a, p. 2). A key component in the continuing
use of floating collections is use analysis. Tools such as the floating collections modules available via Decision Center from Innovative Interfaces
(https://www.iii.com/products/sierra-ils/decision-center/) and collectionHQ
(http://www.collectionhq.com/) facilitate such analysis. Use analysis results,
such as one conducted by Nashville Public Library (NPL), have shown that
the choice to float collections can lead to understocked and unbalanced
collections in participating libraries (Rutherford, 2016, p. 47). At least in
NPL's case, the decision was made to discontinue floating (ibid., p. 48). This
should not to be considered a weakness in the floating model. Instead it is
yet another reminder that "one solution or method or practice does not by
any means fit all" (Bartlett, 2014b, p. 290). The same can be said for any
emerging trend. You need to understand your users, as we will discuss in
the next chapter.

Check This Out

While print monographs make up the majority of floating collections, the Kansas
State Library developed a floating program whereby preloaded audiobook and video
players for kids, read-along audiobooks, and preloaded learning tablets for kids were
made available to libraries throughout the state. The collection also included "Story-
Packs"—backpacks containing games, puzzles, and puppets along with a guidebook
and suggested lesson plans (https://kslib.info/389/Floating-Collections).

A Word About: Pop-Up Libraries

Pop-up libraries are another emerging trend in collections that are worth mentioning. These temporary collections are generally tailored to a specific event or theme, and provide the source library with an outlet for sharing its collections with a wider audience. Pop-up installations have been used in both public and academic settings. For example, Medina Public Library advertises a pop-up service available for community events and programs (http://mcdl.info/m/outreach/), while the Houston Public Library partnered with the Children's Museum of Houston for its pop-up installations (http://houstonlibrary.org/get-involved/community-engagement/pop -library). In 2016, the University of Maryland (UMD) Art Library first established pop-up installations in the student union gallery (Stamp Gallery), as well as the UMD Art Gallery. Some of the advantages of the pop-ups included fostering partnerships across campus, as well as bringing materials into the galleries where students studying the specific artists profiled would better be able to access them. In the case of the UMD libraries, the collections did not circulate; however, user feedback continued to be positive.

A review of the University of Maryland Libraries experience is provided in Johnnieque B. (Johnnie) Love's "Pop-Up Libraries in Academic Settings: Taking It to the People" from the *Proceedings of the 2016 Canadian Association of Professional Academic Librarians* (CAPAL) conference: http://capalibrarians.org/wp/wp-content /uploads/2016/08/5C_Love_paper.pdf.

Another good article on pop-up installations is Asha Davis, Celia Rice, Deanne Spagnolo, Josephine Struck, and Suzie Bull's "Exploring Pop-up Libraries in Practice" (*Australian Library Journal*, 2015, 64, 2: 94–104).

Taking on Collection Management Responsibilities

Although several of the emerging trends covered in the previous section highlight resources that are made available to library users electronically, print materials still play a role in the collections of all libraries, regardless of type, and will continue to do so for the foreseeable future. While that aspect may remain relatively stable to some degree, policies and procedures are very likely to change over the career lifetime of anyone assuming CM work. CM personnel must understand and consider both the print and electronic world, at least for the present, in order to focus on the overall collection. One way to develop excellent collections, both print and digital, is to always keep in mind content is the most important concern, after which comes such issues such as format and cost.

What exactly is involved when taking on responsibilities in collection management? From our own experience, and in broad terms, there are 14 areas that CM personnel must master:

- Differentiating between the responsibilities of CM librarians from other interested parties (faculty, parents, governing boards, for example).

- Determining/assessing the service community's information needs.

- Understanding local collection development policy issues.

- Learning the locally used selection sources (reviews, publishers, etc.).
- Comprehending how the library balances its collections between print, other media, and digital resources.
- Gaining an awareness of the local acquisitions system(s), existing approval plans, and standing or blanket order plans.
- Discerning and understanding local CM collaborative initiatives.
- Learning local standards for assessing the collections and CM in accreditation projects.
- Knowing local storage/deselection issues, concerns, and practices.
- Understanding how the library handles preservation issues.
- Participating in discussions regarding legal issues related to collection access and use.
- Investigating and understanding how the library handles intellectual freedom issues and any library policies regarding ethical interaction with vendors.
- Ascertaining how collection development fiscal issues/allocations are addressed.
- Developing skills to function as an effective liaison/advocate for the library and its collections.

These last two bullet points are key challenges for CM today. Budgeting and allocations are often at the forefront of every CM decision. Additionally, both authors have experience taking over subject areas for which they were not necessarily experts. Wray (2016) likewise encountered a similar experience, noting one of the key stumbling blocks for new librarians is overcoming a "crisis of confidence" and developing those skills (p. 105). It can, however, be done with some time and persistence.

While Graduate Library and Information Science (GLIS) courses are excellent at providing the basics of the areas a graduate may find her/himself working in, coursework is not always a substitute for hands-on experience in a work setting, nor does it necessarily provide subject-specific background. It is highly unlikely that any two libraries are identical in all respects; if for no other reason than their external environments are different, which in turn requires adjustments in practices. Thus, this book will provide a good exposure to the basics, while the Author and Advisory Board Experience boxes illustrate some real-world examples. Nevertheless, there will still be much to learn. This learning can certainly begin in any field studies/practicum opportunities that are available/required during the library program and will continue well into the formal job setting and throughout your career.

Some libraries, recognizing the critical importance of CM, provide incoming librarians who will have some CM responsibility with an in-depth orientation to local practices. Such orientation is very valuable for all new individuals—recent graduates or long-time professionals—as the local variations must be mastered before one's performance is as effective as possible. The University of Maryland Libraries (UMD) has created an orientation checklist for new subject specialists that includes a section for collection management along with the other core areas of responsibility (outreach/liaison services, reference, instruction, scholarly communication/open access, and research data services). Additionally, UMD has developed a *Collection*

Table 3.1   UMD Libraries Collection Development Training Manual Outline

---

I. Resources for New Selectors

Designed as a starting point for new selectors. Section includes an overview of duties of selectors and links to resources and tools found elsewhere in the Manual.

II. Overview of the Collection Development Unit

Unit overview and links to key committees and task forces.

III. Policies and Procedures

Links to key policies and procedures in collection development—including working with gift items and licensing.

IV. Tools for Selectors

Includes links to such resources as information on using the online ordering system and acquisitions module of the integrated library system, preparing collection assessments, and a listing of selection resources and tools developed by subject specialists at UMD.

V. Helpful Resources/Appendices

Departmental and vendor contact information and a glossary of terms.

Development Training Manual to assist both new and seasoned staff with their CM responsibilities. Table 3.1 provides an outline of the manual, which is available on the staff intranet.

The UMD example provides options for individuals with collection development responsibilities and is not meant to be prescriptive, much like the tone of this work. In the end, CM work is individualized, and as noted by Christina Wray, "The most important thing to remember is that you should choose tools that support your process" (2016, p. 114).

Points to Keep in Mind

- Library collections are by no means static in either size or format—a fact that may take some constituents by surprise. However, collections are the cornerstone of a library's service program.

- Although library types differ, all libraries follow the same basic cycle starting with identification and ending with utilization and dissemination of information.

- There is almost always more information available for acquisition than a library can afford to purchase or house. For this reason, selection is a key step in the collection management process.

- Collections should be geared toward all users and responsive to all needs, not just those of current users.

- Much of collection development is learned on the job, and the process of learning about and evaluating new trends in collection development is never-ending.

References

Bartlett, Wendy K. 2014a. *Floating Collections: A Collection Development Model for Long-Term Success*. Santa Barbara, CA: Libraries Unlimited.

Bartlett, Wendy K. 2014b. "Floating Collections: Perspectives from a Public Librarian." In *Rethinking Collection Development and Management*, edited by Rebecca Albitz, Christine Avery, and Diane Zabel, 289–96. Santa Barbara, CA: Libraries Unlimited.

Coopey, Barbara, Barbara Eshbach, and Trish Notartomas. 2016. "Floating Collection in an Academic Library: An Audacious Experiment That Succeeded." *Journal of Access Services* 13, no. 3: 166–178.

EBSCO Information Services. 2017. *2018 Serials Price Projection Report*. https://www.ebscohost.com/promoMaterials/EBSCO_2018_Serials_Price_Projections.pdf.

Fulton, Karin J. 2014. "The Rise of Patron-Driven Acquisitions: A Literature Review." *Georgia Library Quarterly* 51, no. 3: 22–30.

Gallagher, Kelly. 2014. "Print-on-Demand: New Models and Value Creation." *Publishing Research Quarterly* 30, no. 2: 244-48.

Greever, Karen E. 2014. "Floating Collections: Perspectives from an Academic Library." In *Rethinking Collection Development and Management*, edited by Rebecca Albitz, Christine Avery, and Diane Zabel, 281–87. Santa Barbara, CA: Libraries Unlimited.

Hardy, George E. 1889. "The School Library a Factor in Education." *Library Journal* 14, no. 8: 342–47.

Hibner, Holly, and Mary Kelly. 2013. *Making a Collection Count: A Holistic Approach to Library Collection Management*. 2nd ed. Oxford, UK: Chandos Pub.

Hoffert, Barbara. 2016. "Trend Turn Around." *Library Journal* 141, no. 3: 34–6.

Horava, Tony. 2015. "Adventures in Collection Management: What Is a Collection Budget for Nowadays?" *Technicalities* 35, no. 6: 1–6.

Lehman, Kathleen A. 2014. "Collection Development and Management." *Library Resources & Technical Services* 58, no. 3: 169–77.

New Jersey Library Association. 2003. "Statement on School/Public Library Joint Use Standards." https://njla.org/content/njla-statement-schoolpublic-library-joint-use-standards.

Northwest Commission on Colleges and Universities. 2010. "Standard Two: Resources and Capacity." *NWCCU Standards*. http://www.nwccu.org/accreditation/standards-policies/standards/.

Peet, Lisa. 2015. "Format Follows Function." *Library Journal* 140, no. 14: 34–7.

Rutherford, Noel. 2016. "To Float or Not to Float." *Library Journal* 141, no. 6: 46–8.

United States. Department of Interior, Bureau of Education. 1876. *Public Libraries in the United States of America: Their History, Condition, and Management*. Washington, DC: Government Printing Office.

Wray, Christina C. 2016. "Learning Collection Development and Management on the Job." *Collection Management* 41, no. 2: 107–14.

4
Collection Management Policies

Policies may have been created some time ago, have not always been subject to review and renewal and largely represent a print-based view of library collections.

—Stuart Hunt, 2017

How do collection policies and practices exist in our libraries? What does this dynamic reveal about the state of innovation?

—Tony Horava and Michael Levine-Clark, 2016

Having a good collection management policy is the foundation of a quality collection. All collection decisions are driven by this policy.

—Holly Hibner and Mary Kelly, 2013

As strange as it might seem, all of the above rather different takes on collection management reflect today's reality regarding such policies. First and foremost, most libraries in the U.S. probably have some type of selection, collection development, or collection management policy. However, as suggested by Stuart Hunt's quotation, these policies may have been collecting dust on some shelf for years. Many years ago, a library school professor who taught collection development (and a friend of the authors) told her classes, "On the first day you go to work in collection development, ask to see the written policy so you can study it. When they tell you they don't have one, faint. By the way, you need to practice fainting and falling so you don't hurt yourselves; not many libraries have written collection development policies." Perhaps that was more or less the case for academic libraries in the middle to late 20th-century environment. Today there probably is a written statement; however, it may be more rooted in theory than in practice, as is suggested in the quotation by Horava and Levine-Clark.

There are many reasons why practice and theory are not congruent. Perhaps the overriding reason for the incongruity is the pressure of time. No matter what type of library you find yourself in, you will quickly learn that there are more demands for this or that responsibility than there are hours available. Anything that adds to the time pressure creates more stress. Few of us can memorize the entire contents of the collection policy as well as the many other policies that the library has in place. The result is a tendency to look at the policy only when there is a significant uncertainty as to the proper course of action. (Keep in mind the meaning of policy; from a management perspective, it is a *guide* to action, not a *rule*. You have some flexibility in terms of what actions are allowable; certainly that flexibility is not limitless—boundaries should be made clear in the policy.) A second significant reason is that over time, when making use of the flexibility, we slowly drift away from the policy intent without realizing that we have done so, in part due to a changing information environment.

Lois Cherepon and Andrew Sankowski (2003) made the following point:

> Collection development in the 21st century has become a balancing act for academic libraries. Deciding what to purchase in electronic format, what to continue to purchase in print, and what to purchase in both formats becomes increasingly difficult. . . . The answer involves compromise, keeping current with both technology and resources, [and] creating or recreating a collection development policy statement. (p. 64)

Although their focus was the academic library environment, the issues they raised concern all types of libraries. The Hunt quotation reinforces the notion that review and renewal are essential components of having a "living useful" policy. We would also suggest that effective collection development always has been a balancing act of formats. E-resources have added another layer of complexity to the process, albeit probably the most costly and complex layer. The complexity requires an up-to-date written policy statement for reasons we outline in this chapter.

Joseph Straw (2003) conducted a survey of Association of Research Libraries (ARL) library websites to determine how many had Web-based collection development statements. At the time of his study, 54 percent had no such Web statements and in all likelihood many of those institutions do not have a current written policy either. In the same issue of *Acquisition Librarian* as the Straw article, James Spohrer (2003) wrote about the fact that the University of California, Berkeley, library's collection development policy had not been revised since 1980—well over 20 years. Horava and Levine-Clark (2016) surveyed a group of academic CM managers regarding various aspects of their work, including the status of any collection policy. Less than half had a detailed policy in place.

When there is a revised policy in place it tends to focus on electronic resources due to the complexity arising from this format and the cost impact on collection development. Unfortunately, little attention is paid to other formats during the revision process.

This brings us to the last opening quotation. There is something of a sliding scale of how accurate the Hibner and Kelly (2013) statement is. For school library environments, the statement is almost always spot on. For public libraries, it is more often than not true. For academic libraries, the thought is, more often than not, less accurate.

What Is a Collection Management Policy?

Collection development policies, collection management policies, selection policies, acquisition policies—are they just different names for the same thing? They are different—the latter two would only address one aspect of managing a library's collection. However, the reality is people tend to use the labels interchangeably, which probably reflects the fact that regardless of the label, the policies cover a wide range of collection management topics.

Regardless of the library setting, there is an essential truth in the Hibner/Kelly statement. There are many uses for a well-crafted collection development policy:

- It informs everyone about the nature and scope of the collection.
- It informs everyone of collecting priorities.
- It forces thinking about organizational priorities for the collection.
- It generates some degree of commitment to meeting organizational goals.
- It sets standards for inclusion and exclusion.
- It reduces the influence of a single selector and personal biases.
- It provides a training and orientation tool for new staff.
- It helps ensure a degree of consistency over time and regardless of staff turnover.
- It guides staff in handling complaints. It also reassures board and staff members that the collection development team knows what they are doing and are consistent in handling complaints.
- It aids in weeding and evaluating the collection.
- It aids in rationalizing budget allocations.
- It provides a public relations document.
- It provides a means of assessing overall performance of the collection development program.
- It provides outsiders with information about the purpose of collection development (an accountability tool).

Some people suggest that rather than a comprehensive policy, it would be better and more practical to create "mini-policies" for subject areas and specialized service programs. Such policies could provide greater depth while being less cumbersome to use on a daily basis. They would also provide greater guidance for the stakeholders who have varied interest in this or that aspect of CM.

Creating a Policy

Creating, and *maintaining*, a sound CM policy takes more than a little time, thought, and effort. Perhaps just that time commitment plays an important role in why many policies fail to be regularly reviewed and revised. Many languish in the "when there is time" to do pile.

A reasonable question is, given the effort involved in developing a policy and getting it approved, "What purpose will the document serve?" There are a number of valuable purposes for such policies, especially for public and school libraries.

One purpose, regardless of library type, relates to the reason a library exists—largely, to meet the information needs of a particular service population. That is simple to state as an abstract proposition; however, translating that proposition into useful practice is not so simple. The information universe is immense and all libraries have minute resources (in comparison to the information universe) with which to build an effective collection.

Another broad-based value of having a policy lies within the word "guidance." A sound policy provides several types of guidance for several different stakeholders. Some of the stakeholders are internal to the library and others are external. The internal categories are staff members, especially newcomers, and, of course, those individual(s) who make collection decisions. Externally, there is the service population that has major interest in the collection content. Another group is composed of library board members—all libraries have some form of "board" oversight, be it governing or advisory in character. Such bodies have a more direct interest in library programs and services than does the overall service population. A third group, which may not come quickly to mind, is the body/person who supplies library funding (school district, city council, campus administration, for example) whose interest is always the bottom line and why there is always a request for more money to acquire material for the collection.

Beyond the guidance purpose there is the obvious utility of setting limits on the range of topics and formats to include in the collection. It also assists CM personnel in planning their work activities in terms of priorities. Such policies are also a component of any library public relations activities. Also, as we have noted from time to time, collaborative collection management activities are essential in today's world. The collection

From the Advisory Board

Advisory Board member Wendy Bartlett notes that with regard to creating policies:

A "best practice" that I **highly** recommend to my students is to revise the collection development policy every February. It is SO important if there is a challenge or complaint not to have to hand over to a Board member or an irate customer a policy that hasn't been revised for several years. A fresh, "Revised, February 2018" written in the corner assures the public, the staff, and the Board that the collection development staff is staying abreast of trends, and is on the ball. Additionally, it's an excellent way of getting the collection development team "in front" of administration and Board in a highly proactive "we've got this covered" kind of manner each year.

management policy plays an important function in formulating and informing such undertakings.

A central value for public and school libraries is the shield function of an approved policy. Challenges, in terms of collection content, arise more often than library staff would like and defending the content can be time consuming, stressful, and frustrating even when there is a policy. Not having one makes a successful outcome almost impossible.

Stages of the Policy Development Process

There are three major tasks in establishing a sound policy—determining the who and how, the what, and the when aspects. Each task requires thoughtful planning and implementation. The tasks are interrelated and often are a matter of organizational politics, library public relations, and service community relations.

The "who" to directly involve in the drafting process is perhaps the most complex to handle. Today's libraries try to be as participative and transparent as possible. One aspect of those efforts is allowing the community's voice to be heard on issues as early as feasible and likely to be forthcoming. The feasibility side of doing so is rarely a concern—essentially it is possible at the outset.

The "likely" component is problematic as the drafting process will take a substantial time commitment for those engaged in the writing process. Finding outsiders willing to make a commitment can be difficult. Further, identifying individuals with enough depth of knowledge in the field to be effective contributors while not actually in the field is even harder. The usual approach is to draft a policy "in-house" and then invite the service community to review and comment on the draft.

The feedback/review aspect is a major component in how valuable the policy is likely to be in the long-term for the library. It is not so much how much feedback occurs as it is that the opportunity to comment took place. When the policy development occurs with service community input, the usual outcome is a stronger collection and fewer content disputes. Thus, carrying out this step in the "who" drafted/created the policy is vital.

What to Include

Sound policies cover at least five broad areas: purpose/mission of the collection, topics and formats covered by the policy, selection criteria, assessment/evaluation of the collection, and how the library will handle complaints about collection items. Such sections usually contain some subtopics/details. CM policies must be relatively long and detailed if they are to meet the above goals.

Other sections in a policy might address collection preservation concerns (weeding, digitation, and storage, for example), handling of donations (in-kind), collaborative resource sharing activities (reciprocal borrowing and joint purchasing activities), and special collections (such as funds from the operating budget). Given the modern ubiquitous nature of online self-publishing, a modern policy should address whether self-published authors will be considered for the collection, whether through a donation or purchased. As we restate below, there is no such thing as a "free book." Almost any aspect of creating, maintaining, or accessing a collection can become a section in a comprehensive policy.

Details of a Basic Policy

The first element should consist of a clear statement of overall institutional objectives for the library. Statements such as "geared to serve the information needs of the community" have little value or concrete meaning. To ensure that the statement will help selectors and has specific meaning, all of the following factors should be present:

1. Organizational mission and goals. Having a short statement about parent organizational goals and how the policy links to the library's mission helps place the document into a larger context.

2. A brief general description of the service community (town, country, school, or business). What is the composition of the community and what changes are occurring? If you have done a thorough job of community analysis, this part of the policy will be easy to prepare.

3. Identification of the service clientele. Does this include anyone who walks in the door? Who are the primary clients? Does this group include all local citizens, all staff and students of the educational institution, all employees of the business? Will you serve others, and if so, to what degree? Will the service to others be free, or will there be a fee? Are there other differences in service to various groups (for example, adults, children, faculty, or students)? Will there be service for the disabled, the institutionalized, and users with below-average reading ability or other communication problems? These are but a sample of the questions one might ask about the service population. There are no universal answers; there is a right answer for a particular library at a particular time, and this answer will change over time.

4. A general statement regarding the parameters of the collection. What subject fields will the library collect? Are there any limitations on the types of format that the library will acquire? What are the limits in audiovisual areas? This section should provide an overview of the items covered in detail in the second major element of the policy.

5. A detailed description of the types of programs or patron needs that the collection must meet.

Providing information about the characteristics of the user population, in addition to simply identifying who the library serves, is essential for newly hired subject specialists in understanding the customer base. Data about what and how the primary customer groups use information materials aids in selecting the right material at the right time. Outlining the character of the various subject fields the library collects, as well as information about the major producers of the materials collected, will assist individuals taking over a new subject responsibility. Including data about review sources will further enhance the usefulness of the policy. Statements about subject and format priorities also are beneficial, especially when combined with an indication of the percentage of the materials budget normally expended on a subject.

Academic libraries need to consider how much emphasis to place on research material in comparison to instructional material. Again, statements about collection goals are appropriate.

A section outlining the general limitations and priorities for the collection addresses such topics as:

- To what degree the library will collect retrospective materials.

- If the library will buy duplicate copies of an item. If so, what determines the number of copies to acquire? What will be the retention period for duplicates?

- Whether the library will engage in collaborative collection development activities. This section must leave no doubt as to whether the library's basic philosophy is one of self-sufficiency or cooperation.

- Defining the service community. There are a variety of potential users to consider; the following is a sample of the possibilities:

Potential Users

Adults

Young adults

School-age children

Preschool children

Physically disabled (e.g., the blind, visually impaired, and persons who use wheelchairs)

Shut-ins and persons in institutions (e.g., hospitals, residential care facilities, and prisons)

Teaching faculty

Researchers

Staff and administrators

Undergraduate students

Graduate students

Postgraduate students

Alumni

- What formats the library will collect is another general topic to spell out. The following is a selective listing:

Formats

Books (hardbound, paperback, or electronic)

Databases

Newspapers

Periodicals (paper, microform, and electronic)

Microforms

Slides

Video recordings

Audio recordings

Online resources (Internet and other services)

Musical scores

Pamphlets

Manuscripts and archival materials

Maps

Realia

Specimens

Software formats

Subject Areas Collected

This section is the heart of the policy. Not only does it specify subject areas, it also defines the depth of collecting activities. Clearly the library's mission is *the* factor that determines the depth of collecting as well as assessing the reading level of the user (general reader, student, or scholar, for example). ALA guidelines suggest a five-level system for indicating depth: comprehensive, research, study, basic, and minimal. The Research Libraries Group (RLG) adopted a conspectus model that is similar in character. A 2003 article by Glen McGuigan and Gary White discussed the rationale and framework for the subject-specific section of the policy. Nonacademic groups have modified the conspectus concept to meet the needs of all types of libraries. The conspectus model has become the de facto standard for assigning a numerical value to the existing collections and the level of collecting the library wishes to maintain or achieve. It serves as a tool for both collection policy development and assessment.

In most of the models, a collection development officer assigns a numerical value to each subject area in terms of both current collecting levels and existing collection strength. With some models the library may also indicate the desired level of collecting, if it differs from existing values. The RLG system of coding employs five values: 0—out of scope; 1—minimal; 2—basic information; 3—instructional level; and 4—research level. The *Pacific Northwest Collection Assessment Manual* (1992) offers a seven division coding model: la, lb, 2a, 2b, 3a, 3b, and 3c.

One of the major concerns or criticisms about the conspectus method relates to how different selectors, in the same or different libraries, apply the codes. It is important that all selectors apply the codes in the same way to ensure some degree of consistency among libraries. Until the *Pacific Northwest Manual* appeared, the process of assigning values was highly subjective. However, the *Pacific Northwest Manual* offers quantitative guidelines to help selectors assign consistent values. The following are the major points:

Check This Out

A good article that provides an overview of the background and development of the RLG conspectus model is Richard J. Wood's 1996 piece "The Conspectus: A Collection Analysis and Development Success" (*Library Acquisitions: Practice & Theory* 20, no. 4: 429–453).

---

1. Monographic Coverage in a Division (will vary according to publishing output)

    la = out-of-scope

    lb = (or less) fewer than 2,500 titles

    2a = 2,500–5,000 titles

    2b = 5,000–8,000 titles

    3a = 8,000–12,000 titles representing a range of monographs

    3b = (or more) more than 12,000 titles representing a wider range than 3a

2. Percentage of Holdings in Major, Standard Subject Bibliographies

    lb (or less) = 5% or below

    2a = less than 10%

    2b = less than 15% holdings of major subject bibliographies

    3a = 15–20%

    3b = 30–40%

    3c = 50–70%

    4 (or more) = 75–80%

3. Periodical and Periodical Index Coverage

    lb = some general periodicals + *Readers' Guide to Periodical Literature* and/or other major general indexes

    2a = some general periodicals + *Readers' Guide to Periodical Literature* and other major general indexes

    2b = 2a + wider selection of general periodicals + 30% or more of the titles indexed in the appropriate Wilson subject index + access to the index

    3a = 50% of the titles indexed in the appropriate Wilson subject index and access to the index(es)

    3b = 75% of the titles indexed in the appropriate Wilson subject index and/or other appropriate major subject indexes + access to the indexes + a wide range of basic serials + access to nonbibliographic databases

    3c = 3b + 90% of the titles indexed in the appropriate Wilson subject indexes + access to the major indexing and abstracting services in the field.

The conspectus model does take time to develop and is another factor in why policies are rarely totally reviewed and revised on a regular basis. The conspectus model has other applications, and was incorporated into the design of the original Getting It System Toolkit (GIST, http://www .gistlibrary.org), an open source collection management tool that was developed at SUNY Geneseo (Bowersox, Oberlander, Pitcher, and Sullivan, 2014, p. 12). Elizabeth Futas (1993) published an interesting article about genre literature and a conspectus approach. She suggested that you might use categories such as recreational, informational, instructional, and reference for a genre materials policy statement.

Most subject areas fall into one of the middle intensity ranges. Few libraries have more than one or two topics at the upper levels; libraries usually restrict such categories to a person (e.g., Goethe or Sir Thomas More) or a narrow topic (e.g., local history or 19th-century Paris theater). The Robin Li and Melissa Ma Science Library at Stanford University has applied the conspectus to its chemistry collection (https://tinyurl.com/STANFORD -RLG), while Michigan State University Libraries have applied the model to their Iberian Studies collection (https://tinyurl.com/MSU-RLG).

Selection Responsibility

Who actually makes the acquisition decision for an item is a key part of any policy. While it is true that a library director is ultimately the final decision maker for everything that occurs in the library, the reality is that no one expects the head librarian to personally perform all library tasks, except in the smallest libraries. Because the collections are essential to the success of the library's mission, the question of who will actually develop them is vital. The answer requires a careful examination of the needs of the library and the nature of the service community. Outlining who selects and the basis for selecting an item is central to the policy's purpose.

School media center selection responsibility can be particularly troublesome because of possible conflicts about who controls collection content—parents, teachers, media specialists, principals, or the school board. The United States Supreme Court ruling in *Board of Education, Island Trees Union Free School District v. Pico* (1981) limited the power of school boards to add, remove, or limit access to materials.

There is a range of options for who selects, and often there is more than one category. For example, end users may be given a voice in selection activities, but more often than not a staff member makes the final choice. Therefore, the range can and often does include:

1. Independent selectors;

2. Faculty/teachers;

3. Committees; and

4. Individuals or groups using a centrally prepared list from which selections are made.

In an academic library setting, departmental faculty members may either have the sole responsibility for selection or are just one source, along with librarians.

There are a few generalizations regarding the differences in selection responsibility between different types of libraries. Educational institution libraries usually have more user (teachers and students) involvement and greater use of subject specialists than is seen in public libraries. Special or technical library staff often have advanced training in the field in which their library specializes. That staff, with substantial input from the primary customers, is responsible for selection. Public libraries normally use librarians, often department heads from public service areas, as selectors, working through selection committees or from lists prepared by a central agency.

In terms of library staff selectors, there are several possibilities and mixes, such as librarians from public service areas with no special CM background or training beyond basic library education, librarians from technical service areas with no special background or training beyond basic library education, subject specialists with advanced training in a subject, department heads, full-time CM individuals, and even the head librarian.

How to Select

In addition to specifying how selectors will select, this section of the policy should provide general guidelines concerning what, and what not, to select. Normally, such written guidelines are more important in public libraries and school library media centers than in academic or special libraries. This is because there are more groups with an interest in the content of the collection and concern about its impact upon the children and young adults using it. Following are some sample selection guideline statements:

- Select items useful to clients.
- Select and replace items found in standard lists and catalogs, including awards lists.
- Select only those items favorably reviewed in two or more selection aids.
- Do not select items that received a negative review.
- Try to provide both, or all, points of view on controversial subjects.
- Do not select textbooks or solutions manuals.
- Do not select items of a sensational, violent, or inflammatory nature.
- Select only items of lasting literary or social value.
- Select items that are of high demand/popularity.
- Avoid items that, though useful to a client, are more appropriately held by another local library.

The list could go on and on. See chapter 6 for additional discussion about selection criteria. Whatever criteria the library chooses, the collection development policy must clearly state the criteria in order to answer questions that may arise about why something is or is not in the collection.

Gifts and Deselection (Weeding)

A topic related to how to select items to acquire is the question of what to do with gifts. Do the guidelines for acquisition decisions also apply to gifts? Also, many gifts are not needed for the collection, which raises the question of the disposal of such items. A related concern is collection space is finite. What happens when the stacks are at capacity? Adding marginally useful gifts makes that event occur more quickly.

In our view, the golden rule for gifts is: Do not add a gift unless it is something the library would buy. Selectors must resist the temptation to add an item because it is free. No donated item is ever "free." Processing costs are the same for gifts and purchased materials. Expending library resources to add something to the collection just because it was a gift, when it does not match the library's collection profile, is a very poor practice. Applying the same standards to gifts as you do to purchased items will also reduce later weeding problems.

A written gift policy should make it clear whether the library accepts only items matching the collection profile or accepts anything with the proviso that the library may dispose of unwanted items in any manner deemed appropriate (such as selling or exchanging). Equally important is a statement regarding conditional gifts. Will the library accept a private collection and house it separately, if the donor provides the funds? Will it accept funds earmarked for certain classes of materials and use them to acquire new materials? If a donor wishes to provide a magazine, journal, or newspaper subscription, will they provide ongoing support and multiple copies for branches if required? These are some of the major questions that the policy writers should address in a section on gifts.

Gifts and endowment monies are excellent means of developing a collection, provided the library has maximum freedom in their use. Naturally, the library must answer an important public relations question regarding gifts: Is it better to accept all gifts, regardless of the conditions attached to them, or should the library avoid conditional gifts? If there is a clearly reasoned statement as to why the library does not accept conditional gifts, there should be fewer public relations problems.

Deselection/Discards

Deselection, or weeding, programs vary from library to library, but all libraries eventually must face the issue—there is no more space to house items. Even the largest libraries must decide what materials to store in less accessible facilities; most large libraries have some type of limited-access storage facility for their "legacy collections." A sound policy provides staff with guidelines regarding the criteria, scope, frequency, and purpose of a weeding program.

At present, such questions seldom arise for anything but print materials. In school media centers and public libraries where other formats are in high demand, especially audio and video recordings, there is a greater need for replacing worn-out items or replacing them with updated formats than for weeding unused materials. Needless to say, the policy should address the replacement process.

Multiple copies of best sellers and other books in high demand are issues in most public and educational libraries. The questions are, how many copies should the library purchase, and for how long should the library retain multiple copies? To some extent rental programs can help reduce the cost of purchasing popular titles and reduce long-term storage of books in high demand for a short time. However, rental plans do not resolve the question of how many extra copies to retain or what the retention period should be.

Questions about multiple copies are not limited to popular or mass-market titles in public libraries. Similar issues arise concerning textbooks in educational libraries. There are no easy solutions to the problem of extra textbooks in educational settings, unless the library operates a rental system. Some policy guidelines for academic libraries are:

- Buy 1 copy for every 10 potential readers during a six-month period.

- Buy 1 copy for the general collection and acquire one copy for every 5 readers during X months for the high-use or rental collection.

- Buy 1 copy for every 10 students for required reserve reading use.

The length of time, number of readers, nature of use, and local conditions influence how many textbooks are purchased and how long they are retained.

Collection Assessment/Evaluation

Evaluation is essential to collection development. Chapter 9 outlines the major issues and needs the policy should cover. The policy should indicate whether the evaluation process is for internal purposes (e.g., identifying collection strengths and weaknesses), for comparative purposes, or perhaps for reviewing selectors' job performance. Each purpose requires different evaluation techniques or emphases. Making decisions about the how and why of evaluation ahead of time, putting them in writing, and getting them approved will save time and trouble for staff, patrons, funding agencies, and governing bodies.

Complaints

The final section of a general collection development policy outlines the steps to be taken in handling complaints about the collection. Eventually, every library will receive complaints about collection content. It is easier to handle questions about what is not there (the library can always try to buy a missing item) than handling objections about items the library already owns. The other major problem will be questions as to why the policy limits collecting areas in a certain way.

When faced with a borrower or parent who is livid because of an item's inclusion in the collection, how do you defuse the situation? Passing the buck to the supervisor will only increase the person's frustration. However, without guidelines for handling this type of situation, it is dangerous to try to solve the problem alone.

It is important that the library establish procedures for handling complaints *before* the first complaint arises. Ad hoc decisions in this area can cause massive public relations problems. In this instance, the merits of consistency far outweigh the drawbacks. Whatever system for handling complaints the library chooses must become part of the written collection development policy. ALA provides a range of suggestions for handling complaints on its "Challenge Support" website (http://www.ala.org/tools /challengesupport). Of particular note is the series of suggestions for "How to Respond to Challenges and Concerns about Library Resources" (http:// www.ala.org/tools/challengesupport/respond) condensed from the ninth edition of the *Intellectual Freedom Manual* (Chicago: ALA Editions, 2015).

Electronic Resources

In many ways, the selection of e-resources is so sufficiently complex that it deserves to be a separate policy. One reason is a good collection policy for other formats can be lengthy, and additional complexity often makes for a document that is seldom consulted.

Second, and more notably, we believe the differences outweigh the similarities with other library-oriented formats. One difference, explored in chapters 12 and 13, is the issue of ownership (often the library does not actually own the material). Another issue is technological concerns that are generally absent from other formats. Yet another factor, for database packages, is the process is usually a consortia-based decision (group decision making by libraries rather than a single selector). For the individual library, it becomes a question of whether to join or not join in the licensing project. The local concern is often a matter of who makes that decision; for example, the director (cost and legal implication), the collection management staff, or the reference staff. Spelling out the local process in a policy is a sound practice.

Like the print policy, there ought to be an overview section that defines terms and outlines the context of the policy. What does the policy cover? Does it include one-time purchases of eBooks, ongoing subscription services, or both? What about data sets? Does it cover the library's linking to various websites?

When there is agreement on the scope of the policy, just as with the print policy, there should be a statement about users. There are some thorny issues related to Internet access for certain classes of users, in particular children (see chapters 2 and 15). There are also some user issues associated with some companies' license agreements. Any differences in service levels and, if appropriate, the type(s) of user eligible to receive the service should be in the policy.

Roger Durbin and his colleagues (2002) wrote an insightful and still cogent essay about the need for an eBook policy. Although policies are guidelines rather than ironclad rules, outlining expectations for electronic materials is often easier at the abstract policy level than in a heated debate about a given product. Related to the question of role is an assessment of how an electronic version of a title compares to a print version—is it a total or partial duplication, or is it complete with added features? If the e-version duplicates a paper one, is there a time delay between the availability of one of the formats? Sometimes (more often than you might expect based on the popular press about technology) the print version appears months ahead of the electronic one.

Getting the Policy Approved

Having invested considerable staff time, as well as gaining community input, in preparing a comprehensive collection development policy, it is essential that it is approved by senior management (such as a board—either advisory or governing). With such approval, everyone effectively agrees on ground rules for building a collection that will serve the community. An ideal policy approval process might consist of the following:

1. The director reviews and comments on the almost final draft and distributes it to the library staff for comments and suggestions.

2. If necessary, solicit additional community comments.

3. The original committee incorporates the comments and suggestions into an "approval" interim draft.

Check These Out

Collection management policy development is one of those areas in the field where the basics remain very constant and the age of the publication is less important than the content. Certainly all U.S. libraries should consult the many collection management guidelines available through the American Library Association (http://www.ala .org/alcts/resources/collect/collmgt/guides).

Two older but very detailed books on the subject are by Frank W. Hoffman and Richard J. Woods—*Library Collection Development Policies: Academic, Public, and Special Libraries* (Lanham, MD: Scarecrow Press, 2005) and *Library Collection Development Policies: School Libraries and Learning Resource Centers* (Lanham, MD: Scarecrow Press, 2007). These titles provide sound ideas for content as well as examples of polices.

---

4. The director presents the final draft statement to the approving body for review, possible revision, and approval.

5. Between board review and final approval, the library may have a final community feedback meeting.

6. Finally, prepare a condensed version for distribution to each new user of the library.

Following such steps ensures community, staff, and administrative consensus about issues before a problem arises. It is much easier to agree on evaluation procedures, review procedures, levels and areas of collecting, and so on in advance rather than to try to handle them in the heat of a specific disagreement. An approved policy makes it easier to resolve disagreements, because it provides a body of established and agreed-upon rules.

Collection development is a complex process that is highly subjective, rife with problems and traps for the unwary. A comprehensive written policy, developed with the advice and involvement of all parties concerned, helps regulate the process and makes it less problematic.

Points to Keep in Mind

- A well-written collection policy serves several functions, including informing users of the nature and scope of the collection, setting the standards for inclusion and exclusion, guiding staff in how to handle complaints, and providing a means of assessing overall performance of the collection.

- Tasks to be addressed in the development of a sound collection policy include determining the who, how, what, and when aspects of collection management.

- Five areas commonly included in policies are the mission of the collection, topics/formats collected, selection criteria, collection evaluation, and how to handle complaints.

- The final policy should be reviewed and approved by senior management and reviewed and updated on a regular basis.

References

Bowersox, Tim, Cyril Oberlander, Kate Pitcher, and Mark Sullivan. 2014. *Building Responsive Library Collections with the Getting It System Toolkit*. Geneseo, NY: IDS Project Press. http://hdl.handle.net/1957/55523.

Cherepon, Lois, and Andrew Sankowski. 2003. "Collection Development at SJU Libraries: Compromises, Missions, and Transitions." In *Collection Development Policies: New Directions for Changing Collections*, edited by Daniel C. Mack, 63–76. New York: Haworth Press.

Durbin, Roger, James Nalen, Diana Chlebek, and Nancy Pitre. 2002. "eBook Collection Development and Management: The Quandary of Establishing Policies and Guidelines for Academic Library Collections." In *Advances in Library Administration and Organization*, Vol. 19, edited by D. E. Williams and E. D. Gartan, 59–84. Amsterdam: JAI.

Futas, Elizabeth. 1993. "Collection Development of Genre Literature." *Collection Building* 12, nos. 3/4: 39–45.

Hibner, Holly, and Mary Kelly. 2013. *Making a Collection Count: A Holistic Approach to Collection Management*. 2nd ed. Chandos Information Professional Series. Oxford, UK: Chandos Pub.

Horava, Tony, and Michael Levine-Clark. 2016. "Current Trends in Collection Development Practices and Policies." *Collection Building* 35, no. 4: 97–102.

Hunt, Stuart. 2017. "Collection Development in U.K. University Libraries." *Collection Building* 36, no. 1: 29–34.

Island Trees decision. 1981. 457 U.S. 853, 102 S. Ct. 2799.

McGuigan, Glen S., and Gary White. 2003. "Subject-Specific Policy Statements: A Rationale and Framework for Collection Development." *Acquisitions Librarian* 15, no. 30: 15–32.

Pacific Northwest Collection Assessment Manual. 4th ed. Lacey, WA: Western Library Network, 1992.

Spohrer, James. 2003. "The End of an American (Library) Dream: The Rise and Decline of the Collection Development Policy Statement at Berkeley." *Acquisitions Librarian* 15, no. 30: 33–47.

Straw, Joseph. 2003. "Collection Management Statements on the World Wide Web." *Acquisitions Librarian* 15, no. 30: 77–86.

5
Assessing User Needs

There is also a renewed practical interest in the analysis and assessment of information needs of library clients because understanding such needs is essential to providing effective service and appropriate collections in both face-to-face and virtual library services.

—Reijo Savolainen, 2017

Libraries must acknowledge that they [now] reside in an increasingly competitive marketplace and should react accordingly. One form of response is the adoption of a more patron-centric, rather than collections-centric, orientation for a library. Traditional measures of libraries, such as size of collections and circulation statistics, fail to articulate or demonstrate the impact and value that an academic library offers its host institution.

—Susan Gibbons, 2013

Libraries will always need to meet the particular needs of their users. Using marketing segmentation is an effective way of being able to achieve this. Marketing segmentation is the process of getting to know and defining sub-groups of the community and their needs. Also, it involves assessing what needs are being met by the library and what needs are not being met yet.

—Zhixian Yi, 2016

It almost goes without saying, if libraries are to effectively provide their service populations with access to appropriate information resources, they must understand that population in its various forms and interests. Doing so requires time, patience, and an ongoing effort. Ongoing because service populations are never static, they change. Changes may be very rapid, and rather easy to spot, or may occur slowly over years, and thus much harder to identify. Missing a change, regardless of its speed, can cause serious problems for a library.

Successful organizations, regardless of sector, study and assess what their "target" populations need, want, demand, and expect in the way of service or products. They commit resources to monitoring that population in an effort to understand the areas they are doing well in and those areas requiring improvement from the target population's perspective. There are two general techniques that are useful in engaging in learning about and monitoring potential users of a service or product—environmental scanning and market research.

The terms "environmental scanning" and "market research" are relatively recent additions to the library lexicon. In the past other labels were more common; for example, public libraries employed the term "community analysis" for the process; some libraries still do. Business libraries often referred to the process as conducting an "information audit." Another common term, regardless of library type, is "needs assessment." School library media centers often use terms such as "curriculum mapping" and "collection mapping" for the activity. Today, more and more academic libraries have positions with the word "liaison" in the title—one responsibility of the position is to monitor faculty and student needs and interests.

Regardless of the label used, the goal was, and remains, similar—attempting to understand potential and actual users of their services and collections. Faye Chadwell (2009) highlighted the importance of understanding the service community when she wrote: "It is also going to be imperative that we keep our users' developmental, education, and entertainment needs in mind—more than we ever did in the print realm" (pp. 76–77).

Today, more and more libraries engage in long-term and strategic planning and employ both environmental scanning and market research as part of that process. Although the purpose of such data gathering is far broader than CM work, the results generally prove useful to CM personnel. A major advantage of conducting one broad-based analysis is that it will actually save time and effort in the long run. Any effort to examine a service population is time consuming and often the staff goes over much of the same ground with slight variations when doing single-focus projects.

Community analysis, market research, and environmental scanning all can produce information such as the following:

- Why a person does or does not use a particular product or service.

- How a person uses a product or service.

- Where a person gains access to a product or service (a library example would be in the library or via remote access).

- What a person's attitude is about the service or product.

- What, if any, new services or products are desired.

- How much a person is willing to "pay" (time, effort, money, for example) for a service or product.

You can see how each of the above might translate into CM work as well as other aspects of library programs and planning activities.

There are hundreds of reports and articles that contain information about users' information-seeking needs and use of information. However, there is little that is specific enough to be very useful to both library A and also library B. As a result, other than for very broad generalities such as "women tend to read more fiction than men," or "young people do not read anymore," each library must conduct its own study. Some in the profession have raised questions about the value of such studies given the time and effort involved.

Studies of library users and nonusers require the investment of considerable time and effort. Colin Mick and his colleagues (1980) suggested that user studies "provide little information which can be applied to problems involving either the management of information work or the design of information products or services" (p. 348). In their conclusions, they suggest a major factor that causes the lack of practicability or transferability to other libraries is that, "Information travels through diffuse, complex paths. Individual information behaviors are the product of complex interactions involving personal attitudes, backgrounds, role, function, specific task situation, environment, etc. It is highly unlikely that any two individuals would display the same information behaviors" (p. 354). Keep in mind the authors' interest was in how broadly applicable a study would be to any two libraries, not on how one library's study would be useful to that library.

It seems rather likely the authors would be in agreement with Faye Chadwell (2009) that to some extent "user information needs" is a library construct rather than a user perception. Librarians must keep this in mind. Asking a person, "Tell me about your information needs" will more often than not cause the person to stare blankly while attempting to understand just what you are asking.

Douglas Zweizig (1980) raised valid questions about the utility of many community studies as well as suggesting ways a library can get practical data for CM purposes. He noted that, "The use of community analysis data is a creative act, and one who expects findings to clearly suggest action will be disappointed" (p. 41). For all of his concerns regarding the challenges for translating data into decisions or plans, Zweizig ends his essay with a quotation from a Dylan Thomas poem in which a sheep herder is asked why he danced in a fairy ring to protect his sheep and who responded by saying, "I'd be [a] damn fool if I didn't" (p. 45). Libraries likewise would be foolish if they did not engage in community assessments. Understanding the limitations of such studies is one key to knowing how to construct useful studies. Zweizig's chapter is well worth reading as the basic issues of assessing the service community's interests and concerns remain unchanged. Further, he provides excellent advice on how to develop an effective instrument for data collecting.

Even individuals who raise concerns about the time, effort, and money that goes into such studies acknowledge that when they are carefully developed, carried out, and thoughtfully analyzed, they do provide valuable data for CM work. Those who have some doubts regarding value for time and effort rightly contend that there must be a clear goal(s) for the study and results should not be stretched beyond the original goal(s) after the data is collected.

Concepts and Terms

It is far beyond the scope of this chapter to address all the concepts that are employed in needs assessment studies. However, there are three we must define—needs, wants, and demands. We employ them not only in this chapter but several others as well:

- *Needs* are issues for the community, institution, or person that require one or more solutions; it does not always follow that a need is something the community, organization, or person wants.

- *Wants*, on the other hand, are things that the group or person is willing to expend time, effort, or money to acquire; it does not necessarily follow that the want is good for those wanting it.

- *Demands* are wants that a group or person is willing to take action to achieve (such as paying for it, writing letters requesting it, making telephone calls, testifying, or demonstrating). From a library perspective, the ideal outcome of a study is identification of needs that are wanted and demanded.

The above terms are generic in character. Because the literature of librarianship, including this book, makes frequent use of the term "need," the following breaks down that term into more discrete meanings. Jonathan Bradshaw (1972) discussed four types of social needs: normative, felt, expressed, and comparative, which have had wide acceptance within the social sciences.

Normative needs often are based on expert opinion. One commonly cited normative need is the need to increase the literacy level. Teachers, librarians, and others, in their professional roles, express this normative need. To some degree, the general public accepts this need; however, finding adequate funding to address the need is often a challenge. This is due to the fact the community/society does not perceive the importance of the normative need.

Felt needs (wants) come from the community based on its belief about a problem or issue. How appropriate or realistic felt needs may be is often debatable; nevertheless such needs are a reflection of a community's perception of a situation. Just as normative needs are not always what the community thinks is important, felt needs do not always reflect what is good for the community.

Expressed needs (demands) reflect behavior. Individuals often say they want or need something, but their behavior shows they really want or need something else. Libraries tend to respond well to expressed needs. That is, libraries are more likely to meet a greater percentage of the active customers' expressed needs than the needs of infrequent users. A needs assessment project can reveal whether the library is overresponding to active users' needs.

Comparative needs are the result of comparing the service population to other like populations. From the library perspective, one such comparison might be the number of items circulated per capita. When making such comparisons, the service level or collection relevance for the two groups must be the same. One advantage of focusing on comparative needs is that they usually result in some quantitative measures that can be useful in setting goals for new services or programs according to the results of the assessment project.

Another term that more accurately reflects the service community's view of what librarians are seeking when doing a community assessment is *interest*. That word is something that is easy to understand and reflects how a person thinks about what information they are looking for; a person rarely thinks "I have an information need for a recipe for chicken supreme." They might think "need" but not "information need."

It is useful to remember, both during the processes of data collecting and analysis, that as the importance of the information wants increase, so do the amounts of money, time, and other resources organizations or people are willing to expend to secure accurate information. From the individual to the largest organization, all information seekers place a value on each type of information used, often without being fully aware that they are doing so.

Several factors influence the information's value; one factor is its importance for pending decisions. The type and format of information wanted may also play a role in the valuation process. Another factor is accessibility and the effort required to gain access to information—sometimes labeled the "law of least effort."

According to the law of least effort, people and organizations expend as few resources as possible (time, money, or effort) to secure information. Frequently when a person is preparing a document, there is a need for more or updated information. A typical reaction is to turn first to materials at hand. Most people try this even when they know where they can secure the appropriate information, just because the known source is less convenient. Today, the process follows some variation of:

- Check the Internet.

- Check existing files/materials at hand (both physical and digital resources).

- Ask a friend or work colleague (the "invisible college").

- Check with the local library and its databases for resources available, preferably electronically or on-site.

- When all else fails and the need is great enough, request the library to secure the material from some other source (document delivery or, when available, purchase on demand).

Experienced CM personnel are well aware of a sequence such as the above. They factor that knowledge into their thinking and decision making regarding what resources to acquire or lease.

Why Spend the Time and Effort on Service Community Studies?

One reason to engage a service community study for CM purposes is the fact that the information world contains hundreds of millions of information sources. Only a tiny fraction of the universe is likely to be relevant to one's service community. Even that small fraction contains a rather large number of potentially relevant items and is far greater than any one library can hope to acquire/provide access to. Data from user studies can narrow the focus to a more manageable pool to consider.

We noted earlier that the data collected from a properly constructed study can meet a variety of library needs. Certainly the addition of each purpose adds to the time, effort, and cost of conducting the project; however, there will be substantial savings over undertaking a series of single-focus projects. A sampling of potential uses for service community studies are:

- Developing collections (assessing demographics changes or topics of high and low interest, for example)

- Planning new services (e.g., exploring the level of interest in some types of new services, or responding to rapidly changing platforms for accessing information)

- Locating service points (such as expanding or contracting service locations, including mobile service locations)

- Assessing physical facility requirements (such as complying with legal physical access as required in the Americans with Disabilities Act [ADA, 1990], creating group or quiet study areas, etc.)

- Adjusting staffing patterns (assessing the need for additional staff at service points, staff with different skill sets, or using staff at lower skill levels)

- Assessing collections and services (one typical example is addressing accreditation requirements)

- Planning budgets (for example, adjusting fund allocations)

Each of the above uses or goals does have some importance for those involved in CM work. One issue that you might not think had any implications is the example of Americans with Disabilities Act (ADA) compliance. Although the ADA does primarily focus on physical facilities, it also addresses other access issues that people with disabilities may face. A small example of the physical facility aspect is that when a library has an open stack collection, the aisles must be wide enough to accommodate wheelchairs or the library must provide someone to assist the person who uses a wheelchair in accessing the collection. (Collection growth and available space is a major challenge in academic libraries, and one of the first methods to gain more stack space is to look at narrowing aisle width to perhaps accommodate a few more stack ranges. ADA requirements limit that option.)

One obvious way ADA directly impacts collections is that the law mandates that all people have access to public resources regardless of physical impairment. One implication is that visually impaired individuals should have access to the collections in some manner. Some libraries purchase "Large Print" editions of titles that are also in standard print form. Educational libraries often do not have the option of enlarged print versions of their titles; however, they must provide access to that material for anyone requiring assistance. Again, that assistance may be mechanical (for example, reading machines) or human, but the assistance is nonetheless required. Digital

---

Check This Out

One example of a user study is described by Ian Rowlands and David Nicholas in their 2008 article "Understanding Information Behaviour: How Do Students and Faculty Find Books?" in the *Journal of Academic Librarianship* 34, no. 1: 3–15. The authors undertook a study of user information-seeking behavior in a UK university. (The issue of interest to them applies to any library providing access to eBooks regardless of type or country.) Rowlands and Nicholas provide an example of a focused study and its practical value for CM, the purpose being "to develop an initial baseline understanding of people's levels of awareness and previous experience of using eBooks so that the impact of different kinds of interventions (e.g., including or not including eBooks in the library catalogue) could be systematically explored" (p. 3).

materials and even library websites raise similar access issues. Knowing what percentage of the service community might call for such assistance helps plan fund allocations. A relatively recent article on this topic is Marcus Banks' 2017 piece, where he notes, "Providing this support in user centered and responsive ways fulfills the librarian's obligation to offer service to all users" (p. 24).

Conducting assessment studies is essential for effective collection management. One clear example of why it is imperative for libraries, especially public libraries, to have a regular community monitoring process in place can be seen in the demographic shifts that occurred in one service area in Los Angeles over a 50-year period, 1950–2000. Everyone knows communities change over time. How fast or dramatic such changes are is less well known in the absence of regular monitoring. Evans studied the U.S. Census tract data of the Los Angeles basin between the years in question. During this time period, a shift in demographics occurred, with ethnic populations changing from a predominantly single ethnic group to a more mixed population. Although the shifts were gradual, taken as a whole the shifts that did occur between the first year analyzed and the last were dramatic, and underscored a need for libraries serving these areas to adjust collections to better address current users' interests. Libraries also needed to deal with items that already existed in their collections that reflected the interests of a different population. In terms of CM, this creates some serious funding challenges, especially when attempting to meet new needs. To avoid unwelcome surprises, whether it is from a new program or course being implemented in an academic setting, or from a demographic shift in a public or school library setting, it is important to pay close attention and monitor developments in the surrounding community. (For a full review of the analysis and its implications, see chapter 3, "Assessing User Needs," in the sixth edition of this text.)

From the Authors' Experience

We provide the following as an example related to the importance of understanding one's service community:

Fairfax County Public Library (FCPL) is "market-driven and customer-driven" (i.e., how can and does the library system best serve its customers' needs in the community where they reside?). Those needs and interests determine how the individual branches of the library respond to their respective communities. Convenience for the patrons and providing what best serves the customer are the primary goals of FCPL—that the libraries "add value to and are valued by" the community.

One of the greatest challenges facing FCPL is the changing demographics and increasing numbers of languages used in Fairfax County. Although uncertain at this time as to the best way to encourage new Americans to use the system, the library intends to be proactive, not reactive, to the situation and the future. For instance, in order to assess how well the library has responded to patrons' needs, FCPL has conducted telephone surveys, in-branch user surveys, and online surveys. The telephone survey included questions that specifically related to how FCPL has responded to demographic changes such as cultural, lingual, and age-related fluctuations.

Practical Aspects

Regardless of its name (community analysis, needs assessment, collection mapping, information audit, market research, environmental scanning, and more), all assessment projects draw upon some of the following data collecting techniques. When considering an assessment project, careful planning is a must. A sample of the planning issues to consider includes the following:

1. What is/are your target population(s)?

2. What is the goal or purposed use of the data you hope to collect?

3. Is the target population knowledgeable, interested, or willing enough to respond to questions? Might there be a language problem that would require translations?

4. Is there staff available with the requisite skills to carry out the project?

5. Is a consultant necessary? Where would the funding come from to pay for such services?

6. How will you ensure the data collected accurately reflects the respondents' true thoughts rather than what they think the library wants to hear?

7. What methods for data analysis are most appropriate?

8. Will the data collecting/questions asked raise unrealistic expectations for both respondents and staff?

Assessment projects are most easily accomplished and useful when they have a relatively narrow focus. As noted above, the first step in a project is to identify the target population(s). "Target populations" or "market segments," to use terms from the business world, are essentially the same thing. That is, identifying a distinctive set of characteristics in the overall population to study, to communicate with, to provide service to, etc. Lea Bailey's (2009) article "Does Your Library Reflect the Hispanic Culture?" is an example of a "target population." Annie Armstrong, Catherine Lord, and Judith Zelter's (2000) article "Information Needs of Low-Income Residents in South King County" is an example of another target group, while a more recent example is EunYoung Yoo-Lee, Tamara Rhodes, and Gabriel Peterson's 2016 article "Hispanics and Public Libraries: Assessing Their Health Information Seeking Behaviors in the E-Health Environment." From a library point of view, the service population has two basic segments: users and nonusers. Clearly, from a CM perspective, what you would like to know about those segments is very different and would mean a general study of the total service population, producing very mixed results at best. The basic notion of "marketing segmenting" is to create smaller and smaller homogenous groups. Doing so assists in tightening the scope and focus of the project and improves your chances of good participation by the individuals asked to take part in the study. You can further tighten the undertaking by asking the following questions: "What are the interests of the segment?" "How do individuals in the segment seek and use information?" and "How well does the library address such interests?" Certainly there are more such questions to consider, but our point in asking such questions is that they can refine your final project.

Check This Out

Another example of a library-based project, but for a non-CM purpose, that may generate useful CM information is Sherri Jones and Jessica Kayongo's 2008 article "Identifying Student and Faculty Needs through LibQUAL+™: An Analysis of Qualitative Survey Comments" (*College & Research Libraries* 69, no. 6: 493–509).

Sometimes there are preexisting sources of data related to the proposed project, occasionally in sources that may appear to be unrelated to libraries. For example, marketing firms often collect "lifestyle" data and occasionally have a question or two about library usage such as asking how frequently respondents used the library in the last year. Because the organization asking the question is not a library, more people will answer more honestly than they would have had a library asked the question. (Respondents often attempt to please or not give a negative impression of themselves. Thus, they provide responses they think will give the questioner what is wanted rather than the truth.) Locating such studies can save time and effort and perhaps provide more reliable data.

Developing a set of questions to ask is not as simple as it might seem. Several resources exist that can assist in formulating project questions. Almost any basic textbook on research methods outlines the fundamental techniques of survey research, as do many marketing books. Beyond the fundamental research methodology level, some practical guides are available. Currency is less an issue than having guides with sound track records. Some useful titles include:

Boston College University Libraries—Community Analysis. http://libguides.bc.edu /communityanalysis

> An online guide with links to resources for community analysis. Although the focus is on Massachusetts, a number of resources are useful from any geographic location.

Henczel, Susan. 2001. *The Information Audit: A Practical Guide.* München: K.G. Saur.

> While the information audit is most often associated with the special library, this book has useful ideas for any type of library; it also contains three case studies.

Hughes-Hassell, Sandra, and Anne Wheelock, eds. 2001. *The Information-Powered School.* Chicago: American Library Association.

> This practical book provides tools and templates for conducting collection analysis and curriculum mapping in school libraries.

Kaufman, Roger, and Ingrid Guerra-López. 2013. *Needs Assessment for Organizational Success.* Alexandria, VA: ASTD Press.

> A useful book that provides an excellent overview of the process.

Lamb, Annette, and Larry Johnson. *The School Library Media Specialist: Collection Mapping.* http://eduscapes.com/sms/program/mapping.html.

> An online resource that provides a sound overview of collection mapping for the school library environment.

Lauffer, Armand. 1982. *Assessment Tools for Practitioners, Managers, and Trainers.* Newbury Park, CA: Sage Publications.

A practical guide to assessment methods.

Loertscher, David V., and Marc Crompton. 2018. *Collection Development Using the Collection Mapping Technique: A Guide for Librarians*. 3rd ed. Salt Lake City, UT: Learning Commons Press.

A well-respected discussion of collection mapping.

Nicholas, David, and Eti Herman. 2009. *Assessing Information Needs in the Age of the Digital Consumer*. 3rd ed. London: Routledge.

This is a concise guide to assessing information needs covering how to frame a project, how to choose methods of data collecting, and how to set realistic goals/outcomes.

Rossman, Marlene L. 1997. *Multicultural Marketing*. New York: American Management Association.

Written for businesses wishing to become more effective in marketing products to a wider base, this book provides excellent insights that apply to library needs assessments. Particularly good for public libraries.

Sleezer, Catherine, Darlene F. Russ-Eft, and Kavita Gupta. 2014. *A Practical Guide to Needs Assessment*. 3rd ed. San Francisco: Wiley.

A good work providing the fundamentals for a needs assessment project as well as sample tools.

Warren, Roland L. 1955. *Studying Your Community*. New York: Russell Sage Foundation.

This is a classic for anyone planning a public library assessment project.

Common Types of Data Collected

There are a host of data categories that may be useful for a library's assessment project, varying from library type to library type. We can only touch on a few of the many variations here. The resources provided above explore many more of the options that exist.

Historical data is useful in several ways. Understanding a community's historical development may lead to a better, and sometimes quicker, understanding of the current environment. Historical background information also provides clues about areas of the collection to weed or areas in which it is no longer necessary to acquire material.

Geographical information answers questions such as: In which physical directions is the community growing? (This is an issue for large academic campuses as well as for public libraries.) What is the distribution of population over the geographic area? (One example of where such information is useful is in schools where there is a busing program.) This type of information helps the library staff determine service points or other access points, which, in turn, may influence the number of duplicate titles they acquire or provide access to. Even in today's digital information world, geography matters. Two good articles regarding current geographical issues and libraries are by Julia Todd (2008) and Jeanine Scaramozzino and her colleagues (2014).

Transportation availability data, combined with geographic factors, is important in the library's decision-making process regarding how many service points to establish and where to locate them. The aforementioned "law of least effort" is a factor to keep in mind when thinking about "transportation." What service exists? What does it cost? What are its hours? Who uses the service? Answers to such questions play a role in planning service points, which can, in turn, impact CM decision making.

Legal issues will not be too difficult to determine, nor will the amount of data accumulated be large. Nevertheless, there may be legal implications for collection development. In some academic institutions, the teaching faculty has the legal right to expend all book funds. We explore legal issues and CM in more detail in chapter 15.

Political information, both formal and informal, has a relationship with legal data, much like the link between geographic and transportation information. Some questions are: To what extent is the library a political issue? How do the politics of the community work? What group of individuals or agency provides funding? Who influences fiscal decisions? Answers to most of these questions will not have a direct bearing on which titles go into the collection, but they may influence the way in which the library secures and allocates funds.

Demographic data is essential in formulating an effective collection development program regardless of library type. Academic and school libraries experience changes in student demographics just as public libraries must adjust to community changes. Waiting until change takes place creates an image of an institution that is slow to adapt.

Today, census data is easier to access through services such as the American Community Survey (ACS, https://www.census.gov/programs-surveys/acs/). Data from the U.S. Census long form (SF3, STF3, and STF3A) are the most commonly used data sets for library projects. The ACS is an *annual* survey that produces SF3-like data for the noninstitutionalized population. The sample methodology employed is the same as SF3's. The site includes data for places with populations of 20,000 or greater. The plan is that eventually ACS will report data at the tract level nationwide.

Economic data may help the library better plan its collection development activities. That is, anticipating increases or decreases in funding can lead to a more even collection. An economy based on semiskilled or unskilled workers calls for one type of collection, a skill-based economy calls for another, and an economy based on knowledge workers calls for still another. Communities with a seasonal economy or a predominantly migrant population face several problems. What type of service and which formats would best serve the seasonal population?

Social and educational organizations reflect community values. Although social patterns are slower to change than individual attitudes, the library must consider such pattern shifts in planning an integrated collection-building program. Social clubs, volunteer groups, and service organizations, for example, affect and reflect community interests. The most important group of organizations is educational. Academic institutions no longer offer only two-year, four-year, and postgraduate degree programs. Evening adult education classes, day and night degree programs, off-campus or online-only classes, and even some remedial high school–level courses create complex instructional programs, each facet having different collection needs. A public library's concern must be broader than public and private primary and secondary schools; it should also consider adult vocational programs and higher education.

Cultural and recreational organizations also reflect community interests. As with social organizations, these formal groups provide useful clues to highly specialized interest areas with enough community interest to sustain a formal group. Many of these groups, when given library service, join the library's most solid and influential supporters.

Other *community information services* are, in some respects, the most important CM issue. If the library identifies several community information sources, and if the various sources can develop a working cooperative agreement, everyone will benefit. All too often public, school, and academic libraries in the same political jurisdiction operate as if they existed in isolation. When a group of publicly supported libraries in a local area fails to develop cooperative programs, considerable resources and services go to waste. We explore collaborative issues in chapter 10.

Data Collecting and Analysis Techniques

A number of options exist for data collecting activities. As part of the planning process, a decision should be made as to what methodology (or methodologies) to employ as well as deciding how you intend to analyze the data. In this section, we cover a few of the options available, ranging from the very common survey method to focus groups to the less widely employed techniques such as the information audit.

Key informants and community forums primarily use some form of interview or focus group techniques. Social indicator and field survey projects, while using the interview method, often rely on questionnaire data and the results of behavior observations. Occasionally in educational situations, the diary method can be employed. Large-scale projects almost always use a combination of methods as each has certain strengths and weaknesses. Multicampus or multibranch sites need to be sure there is "buy-in" to use the same methodology at the same time in order to enhance validity and credibility. (However, this does not mean that individual sites cannot conduct their own supplemental user studies.)

Regardless of the method chosen, a challenge for gathering data is gaining community buy-in to the process. Often it is advisable to start with some small-scale data collecting activities that will assist in formulating larger scale efforts. One place to begin to gain some understanding of interests is with one or two people—key informants, gatekeepers, or community opinion makers.

Key Informants—Gatekeepers

Key informants are individuals who are in a position to be aware of community interests such as public officials, senior administrators, department chairs, community organization officers, or business leaders who are influential and whom other people view as knowledgeable about community affairs. Through interviewing such individuals, insights are gained into areas of interest and concern that ought to be explored in more depth. Another term that is sometimes used for key informant is *gatekeeper*.

One shortcoming of the key informant approach is the person does not fully represent the community. Such people are selected because of their presumed knowledge rather than being drawn from a statistical random sample. Therefore, you cannot assume the person's views necessarily reflect a broad spectrum of the community. The opinions of key informants will reflect personal biases and several such individuals should be interviewed. In essence, this type of data supplies subjective but useful information about how people of influence perceive the community's information needs.

Focus Groups and Community Forums

A *focus group* is a small-sized group drawn from the general community; however, having a number of sessions with different memberships

---

Check This Out

A comprehensive treatment of creating, implementing, and running focus groups is Richard A. Krueger and Mary Anne Casey's *Focus Groups: A Practical Guide for Applied Research,* 5th ed. (Los Angeles, CA: Sage Publications, 2015).

---

will provide some broad insights. The *community forum*, on the other hand, is a form of "town meeting." Focus group members are recruited/selected, whereas anyone is welcome at a community forum.

Advantages of the community forum are that it is easy to arrange, relatively inexpensive to hold, and may bring up a broad range of topics. Focus groups are more complicated to organize but, as the name implies, they are focused on topics of the library's choice rather than on open aspects. A major disadvantage of both methods is that the data obtained is impressionistic and subjective. This data may be extremely difficult to categorize and is not readily amenable to statistical analysis. Although these disadvantages are serious, both formats are useful as a "grassroots democratic process" for soliciting opinions, ideas, and criticism from the service community. When exploring options for starting a service to an underserved cultural or ethnic group, both options can be effective in securing otherwise difficult to secure data.

Social Indicators

Social scientists have developed a method (natural area) that makes use of *social indicators* to determine the needs of various segments of a community. A "natural area" is a unit within the community that can be set apart from other units or areas by certain characteristics. Those characteristics, or social indicators, may be geographical features, such as rivers or transportation patterns; sociodemographic characteristics, such as age, sex, income, education, and ethnicity; population factors, including distribution, density, mobility, and migration; the spatial arrangements of institutions; and health and social well-being characteristics, such as condition of housing or suicide rates.

By selecting factors that researchers think are highly correlated with those groups in need of information, the library may be able to extrapolate the information needs of the whole community. What these social indicators (also called factors, variables, or characteristics) may be is a point of much disagreement among researchers in library and information science. Some social indicators are age, health, sex, employment, education, marital status, income, and location of domicile or work site.

What are the implications of those indicators for the library? The following are some broad generalizations based on library research:

- Social media and the Internet have and are changing how people access information and the manner in which they use libraries.

- The digital world has made it possible for people to remotely access libraries 24/7.

- Use of libraries tends to decrease with age, especially among adults over the age of 55. (One reason for decreased use is deteriorating vision and other health problems.)

- Senior faculty, researchers, and organization officials tend to use libraries less as they increase in status and age. (They still use information; however, the actual gathering is usually done by junior or support staff, who tend to be younger.)

- Women make greater use of libraries than men, regardless of the library's institutional environment (public, academic, or corporate).

- As the number of years of education increases, so does use of libraries, up to about 16 years of formal education. After earning a bachelor's degree, a person's library use curves downward. (Apparently, graduate and postgraduate education moves the person into the invisible college network, so there is less need to use formal information systems.)

- Income level and use of formal information systems also show a J-shaped curve. That is, low income usually translates into low use; use rises through middle and upper-middle income levels; and use sharply decreases at high income. (Apparently, persons with high incomes can purchase a large percentage of the information they require.)

- Generally, as health declines, there is a decrease in the use of formal information systems. (However, with proper equipment and special services, libraries can reverse this tendency.)

- Persons employed in manual labor tend not to use formal information systems. Information use tends to increase in direct relationship to increased levels of skills required to perform the work.

- The so-called "Librarian's Axiom"—economic downturns result in an increased use of libraries and library materials.

- The "law of least effort" is clearly evident in the finding that as the distance of the residence or workstation from the information center increases, there is a corresponding drop in use.

- Single persons and married couples with no children tend to use formal information systems less than couples with children, and as the number of children rises, so does use.

Field Surveys

The field survey approach depends on the collection of data either from a sample or the entire service population. It is rare to attempt to survey every member of a service community, if for no other reason than the high cost in time and effort to do so. Thus, sampling and sample size become the keys to collecting valid and reliable data. Books on statistical methods will provide details about sampling techniques.

A goal of some field surveys is to contact nonusers as well as users. The most common means of collecting data is through interview schedules or questionnaires. The methods most frequently used are telephone interviews, person-to-person interviews, and mailed questionnaires. Some libraries have research offices available to them in order to help develop, execute, and analyze surveys. If such an office is not available, other resources, such as library associations, may provide suggestions for where to turn for assistance.

To be effective, the library must pretest survey questions whether they are to be used by interviewers or as a form from which a respondent works.

The library should test the proposed questions with individuals who have backgrounds or positions similar to the target population. The purpose of pretesting is to learn what responses the library might expect to receive and whether the answers will in fact address the project issues. People are often surprised to see just how many interpretations an apparently simple question can generate. The goal of pretesting is to reduce that variation to the smallest possible size. It is not at all uncommon for there to be several rounds of testing before achieving consistent results. Consistency in this case means having questions that respondents will interpret/understand in the same way.

One choice the library must make is between structured or unstructured questions for the survey. Open-ended questions (unstructured) take more time to answer than fixed-alternative, or closed, questions (structured). The type of question asked can affect both the response rate and data analysis. Open-ended questions are more difficult to code and analyze, and there are fewer methods of statistical analysis that one can apply to them. With the structured format, data is homogeneous and more easily coded and analyzed.

If some of the target population does not speak English, it is necessary to translate the questions into the language(s) of the target population, if one wants to understand all the information needs. Respondents should be offered both versions of the questionnaire; offering only the translated version may be interpreted as an insult. A local native speaker should do the translation; slang or local usage may not follow formal speech patterns that nonnative speakers tend to use.

The next step in the field survey is to select a sample. Cost is an important issue when selecting a sample size. A large sample may call for complex selection methods, which in turn add to the time and costs of a survey. An important element for gathering useful data is to have a statistically random sample of the proper size to ensure the data is both valid and reliable.

One survey method is *interviewing*. This approach permits face-to-face contact, may stimulate a free exchange of ideas, and usually has a high response rate. The drawback to this method is that for any large sample size, it becomes labor intensive. It also requires some thorough training in interviewing techniques for those conducting the interviews. The training is necessary to reduce the real risk that interviewers may not be absolutely consistent in how they ask the questions or respond to the interviewee's nonverbal behavior. Both of these actions will lead to less reliable data. Telephone or video call interviewing may save some staff time, but has the disadvantage of how long a respondent is willing to give to such calls. Pre-planned telephone/video interviews will work, but also take more time to schedule.

Mailed, emailed, or online surveys require less staffing and training than surveys that depend on in-person or telephone interviews. These two advantages can significantly reduce the cost, in both time and money, of

---

Check This Out

Robert V. Krejcie and Daryle W. Morgan (1970) outlined a method for determining sample size that is frequently referred to in the literature in their article "Determining Sample Size for Research Activities" in *Educational and Psychological Measurement* (30, no. 3: 607–610).

Check These Out

A good article about the process of using an online survey for collection building is Kristi Jensen's (2009) piece "Engaging Faculty Through Collection Development Utilizing Online Survey Tools" (*Collection Building* 28, no. 3: 117–121), which describes its use with students and faculty in an academic setting.

A good site that provides examples of survey instruments and how to develop them is "Library User Survey Templates and How-To's" from Library Research Service (LRS): https://www.lrs.org/library-user-surveys-on-the-web/.

---

conducting a survey. However, there are some significant disadvantages to such surveys. First, most mailed or emailed surveys have a low response rate (often the rate is less than 20 percent) and such low response rates can seriously affect the validity and reliability of the collected data. Even with repeated mailings the response rate is frequently low, and the cost of keeping track of who has or has not responded can be high if an online survey system does not automatically track responses. Additionally, unless extra steps are taken to limit access or track IP addresses, online surveys have the added disadvantage of perhaps having a few people with an "agenda" repeatedly filling out the survey.

Another issue is language(s), both in terms of literacy level and not being a native English-language speaker. With an interview, a trained interviewer can detect, from the respondent's verbal and nonverbal signals, when there is something not quite right about a question.

Because of these disadvantages, libraries using a mail or email survey method must carefully design the questionnaire and use the simplest and most succinct language possible while still meeting the established objectives. Libraries should also attempt to determine what an acceptable response rate will be before expending the time and money for a survey that could be of questionable value.

Some other data collecting techniques are observation, diaries, transaction logs, and citation analysis. *Observation* of user behavior can serve as a cross-check on what users report as their behavior in an interview, questionnaire, or diary. A concern about observation data is how much the observer's presence affects the observed behavior. *Diaries* can be excellent sources of detailed information about what, when, where, and how information was sought and used. Getting participant cooperation is an issue, as recording activities can be viewed as unnecessary extra work. In educational situations where the diary is linked to a classroom activity, it works well. One can also get satisfactory results in a corporate setting where only a few individuals participate. There is a concern that since the data is self-reported it would be biased toward making the reporter "look good" rather than reflecting actual behavior. This is where the observation method can come into play as a cross-check.

Electronic databases do or should provide *management reports* or *transaction logs* that can supply very important information about when and what was accessed. With cost of the resources being so high, checking such reports/logs should be a regularly scheduled activity. In most cases, one will not be able determine who (type of user) accessed the database, but there should be data on when, how (on- or off-site), and how often.

Citation analysis is a helpful tool for collection development. It can assist in identifying "core" collections, weaknesses, and strengths of an

> ### Check This Out
>
> One title that covers a number of assessment models is Denise Troll Covey's 2002 title *Usage and Usability Assessment: Library Practices and Concerns* (Washington, DC: Digital Library Federation, Council on Library and Information Resources, http://www.clir.org/pubs/reports/pub105/contents.html). Each method covered (such as focus groups, user protocols, etc.) includes a discussion of how assessment results can be applied, as well as challenges associated with using that particular assessment methodology.

existing collection. We explore this method in chapter 9. Below is a small sample of the ways in which libraries have employed some of the techniques we have covered.

Examples by Type of Library

Academic Libraries

One university library that engaged in studying its service population is the University of Michigan (Crist, Daub, and MacAdam, 1994). They employed the focus group as their data collecting method. At the University of Michigan, the focus group information led to the formulation of a telephone survey. With the assistance of a marketing firm, the library designed a study to ensure that there would be statistically reliable and valid data. They used open-ended questions related to course work and library use. In today's digital information world, academic libraries might specifically focus on aspects such as:

- What electronic databases do you use more than once a month?
- When preparing the results of your research, do you prefer print or electronic "notes" and resources?
- What are the major or critical problems you encounter when using digital resources?
- What type(s) of assistance would you like to have available when using electronic resources?

Public Libraries

King County Library System (KCLS) in Washington, with a service area of more than 2,000 square miles, has engaged in studying its service areas for some time. Between 1991 and 1997, 24 of 40 service areas had in-depth studies done (Thorsen, 1998). KCLS used a variation of a method Evans employed when consulting on needs assessment—a visualization of the service area. In their case, they drove the team through the area, making stops at various points. (Evans would also drive the area, then return to photograph "typical" areas. In working with the branch staff, he would mix the photographs with some from other service areas and determine just how well the staff knew their service area.) KCLS used its data for more than collection development purposes, just as suggested earlier in this chapter. They planned services, collections, hours, programs, etc. around, at least in part, the data gathered during the survey/assessment activities.

School Library Media Centers

In the school environment, a popular assessment tool is collection mapping. As with other methods that we covered in this chapter, the technique can be useful in a variety of planning activities, not just collection management. The technique assumes a person has also done a curriculum map. Such mapping can help answer such questions as:

- How well does the collection support the curriculum and meet the academic and recreational needs of the students?
- To what degree does it assist teachers in their class preparation activities?
- What is the right balance between print and media, and has it been achieved?
- How much of the budget can/should go toward e-resources?
- To what extent must students depend upon the public library collections and free Web resources to complete class assignments?

Jo Ann Everett (2003) provides an entertaining and informative essay about collection mapping. In the same volume, Charlotte C. Vlasis (2003) covers the techniques and issues in curriculum mapping. When combined with demographic data about students such as gender, socioeconomic level, ethnic, racial, and cultural background, learning differences, and native language, curriculum mapping and collection mapping enable school librarians to develop collections that address the information needs of the broader school community and fit the teaching-learning context.

Special Libraries/Information Centers

Special libraries tend to focus on small groups and individuals within an organization. Thus, the assessment techniques used by large libraries are seldom appropriate. Corporations, research institutes, professional organizations, and the like seldom have a sound knowledge of the basic issues related to acquisition and use of information within themselves, unless there are regular information audits. Some of the key issues are:

- What information resources are currently in use?
- How are these resources used?
- What are the outcomes, if any, of their use?
- What equipment is required to use the information, and who uses that information?
- What is the cost of the information and its associated equipment?
- What is the "value" of the results? That is, what is the cost/benefit of information acquisition and use within the organization?

Information audits are one assessment technique available for special or corporate libraries. Such audits can help ensure maximum value is realized from the organization's expenditures on information resources. They are usually company- or division-wide in scope and take into consideration all information resources, not just the resources housed or made available through the library. Susan DiMattia and Lynn Blumenstein (2000) reported on a survey they conducted about the value of information audits. They noted that the audits "often detected gaps and duplication in services and resources" (p. 48). Based on their study, DiMattia and Blumenstein identified four goals that information audits should help identify:

1. Information needs to meet organizational targets,

2. Overall information resources,

3. The knowledge and expertise resources of the organization, and

4. Where information resources reside, who uses it, the barriers to its use, and the gaps that need to be filled. (p. 48)

There are several other methods that are particularly good when addressing a small group environment such as found in the special library environment. Five such methods are activities, data analysis, decision making, problem solving, and empirical analysis.

The *activities* approach uses an in-depth interview with an individual or group and its objective is to outline of all the activities of a typical day or project. The focus is on decisions made, actions taken, topics discussed, letters or memos written and received, and forms processed. The approach assumes that daily activities fall into a regular pattern and once that pattern is clear, the librarian or information officer can translate these activities into information requirements. One problem with the method is that people often forget important but infrequently performed tasks. Another drawback is the tendency to overemphasize the most recent problems or activities.

Data analysis is a method in which the investigator examines information sources used and materials produced by the person or group. This approach circumvents the problems of forgetfulness and overemphasis on recent work. Reports, files, letters, and forms are the focal point of the study. The investigator examines the documents to determine what information was used in creating them. After finishing the examination, the researcher discusses each item in some depth with the person(s) concerned to determine which resources they consulted in preparing the documents. Through this process, it is possible to identify unnecessary information sources and to determine unmet needs.

The *decision-making* approach is similar to data analysis, but it focuses on the decision-making process. Again, the researcher is interested in the information used to formulate decisions and the origin of that information. The researcher also looks at the information received but not used. During the interview the researcher explores how the cost of not having the right information, or not having it as soon as required, affected the decision-making process. In the profit sector, either or both factors can have serious financial implications for the organization.

The *problem-solving* approach is similar to the decision-making approach, except the focus shifts to problem solving. Frequently, a problem-solving activity cuts across several departments or units and takes more time to complete than a decision-making process. The problem-solving approach provides a better organizational picture more quickly than the decision-making approach does.

All of the preceding approaches depend on the user providing accurate information about what she or he did or did not do. *Empirical studies*, in contrast, are based on observations of what is done (expressed needs), how users act, and what information sources were used. If a formal information center exists, it might conduct experiments, such as varying the location of information sources or removing them, to determine whether the users' perceptions of the value of an item translate into use.

Data Visualization

Conducting user assessment activities is only part of the process. Once the selected assessment tool is used, normally a great deal of data is amassed. This data must then be compiled, analyzed, and presented in order to be acted upon by the library and its administration. Although some have the ability and inherent skill to quickly and easily synthesize complex spreadsheets and determine their implications at a glance, this is not true across the board. Thus, when it comes to analyzing and presenting data, the saying that a picture is worth a thousand words often comes into play. Enter data visualization techniques. As noted by Hsuanwei Chen (2017), data visualization "can translate plain data into a graphical display that speaks to the audience in a more intuitive, powerful way" (p. 6). Thus, it allows the individual reviewing the graphic to better act upon the results presented.

Although it may be thought of as a relatively new concept, data visualization can be traced to the early days of map making. The famous cholera maps compiled by John Snow in 19th-century London can be seen as one early example of data visualization (Rogers, 2013). In addition to their usefulness for presenting the results of user needs assessment activities, visualization strategies and tools can also be useful in collection assessment activities. Tools for data visualization range from commercial products such as Tableau (http://www.tableau.com) or open source tools such as D3.js (https://d3js.org/) as well as resources developed in-house such as SeeCollections. In the case of SeeCollections, this tool was developed by the Kingsborough Community College Library (CUNY) specifically to visualize library holdings (Eaton, 2017). However, depending on the situation, data visualization may still be possible with nothing beyond the graphing functions of a spreadsheet program such as Excel. The University of California, Riverside used this very technique in its assessment of its Latin American Studies program (Haren, 2014). The resulting graphs were then available for use with stakeholders outside of the library.

A full discussion of data visualization is beyond the scope of this text, but the following resources are worth consulting:

Evergreen, Stephanie D. H. 2017. *Presenting Data Effectively: Communicating Your Findings for Maximum Impact.* 2nd ed. Los Angeles: Sage Publications.

> A thorough manual on developing data visualizations for research results, focusing on the areas of text, graphics, arrangement and color. A companion data visualization checklist Evergreen co-produced with Ann K. Emery is available online: http://stephanieevergreen.com/wp-content/uploads/2016/10/DataVizChecklist_May2016.pdf.

Friendly, Michael. 2008. "A Brief History of Data Visualization." In *Handbook of Data Visualization*, edited by Chun-houh Chen, Wolfgang Karl Härdle, and Antony Unwin 15–56. Heidelberg: Springer-Verlag.

An excellent article tracing the history of data visualization from its origins in the earliest mapmaking activities to the present.

Introduction to Data Visualization—Guide from the Duke University Libraries. http://guides.library.duke.edu/datavis/

Provides an overview of data visualization concepts and terms, as well as links to resources for designing visualizations. From the Data and Visualization Services unit of Duke University Libraries.

Points to Keep in Mind

- You must understand the service community's interests in order to create a valued and sustainable collection.

- Collecting data about community interests is essential to developing the necessary understanding.

- Periodic large-scale studies are necessary; however, ongoing monitoring of the library's environment is the key to effective needs assessment.

- Data required to assist in collection management activities varies by type of library; several obvious categories are demographic, economic, and geographic.

- Methods of data collecting are also varied. Focus groups, field surveys, collection mapping, and information audits are among the most common approaches.

- Regardless of the data collecting approach employed, the essential aspect of such projects is that if a sample rather than the entire service population represents the target study group, great care is taken to assure the sample will be statistically valid as a representation of the total.

- Once collected, the assessment data must be presented. Data visualization tools present one option for delivering results of needs assessment so that they can be acted upon.

References

Armstrong, Annie, Catherine Lord, and Judith Zelter. 2000. "Information Needs of Low-Income Residents in South King County." *Public Libraries* 39, 6: 330–35.

Bailey, Lea. 2009. "Does Your Library Reflect the Hispanic Culture? A Mapping Analysis." *Library Media Connection* 28, no. 3: 20–23.

Banks, Marcus. 2017. "Library Websites for All: Improving the Experience for Patrons with Visual Impairment." *American Libraries* 48, no. 6: 24–25.

Bradshaw, Jonathan E. 1972. "The Concept of Social Need." *New Society* 19, no. 496: 640–43.

Chadwell, Faye A. 2009. "What's Next for Collection Management and Managers? User-Centered Collection Management." *Collection Management* 34, no. 2: 69–78.

Chen, Hsuanwei Michelle. 2017. "Chapter 1: An Overview of Information Visualization." *Library Technology Reports* 53, no. 3: 5–7.

Crist, Margo, Peggy Daub, and Barbara MacAdam. 1994. "User Studies: Reality Check and Future Perfect." *Wilson Library Bulletin* 68, no. 6: 38–41.

DiMattia, Susan S., and Lynn Blumenstein. 2000. "In Search of the Information Audit: Essential Tool or Cumbersome Process?" *Library Journal* 125, no. 4: 48–50.

Eaton, Mark. 2017. "Seeing Library Data: A Prototype Data Visualization Application for Librarians." *Journal of Web Librarianship* 11, no. 1: 69–78.

Everett, Jo Ann. 2003. "Curriculum Mapping and Collection Mapping: Otherwise Known as 'The Camel with Two Humps.'" In *Curriculum Connections Through the Library*, edited by Barbara Stripling and Sandra Hughes-Hassell, 119–37. Westport, CT: Libraries Unlimited.

Gibbons, Susan. 2013. "Techniques to Understand the Changing Needs of Library Users." *IFLA* 39, no. 2: 162–67.

Haren, Shonn M. 2014. "Data Visualization as a Tool for Collection Assessment: Mapping the Latin American Studies Collection at University of California, Riverside." *Library Collections, Acquisitions, & Technical Services,* 38: 3–4, 70–81.

Mick, Colin, Georg N. Lindsey, and Daniel Callahan. 1980. "Toward Usable User Studies." *Journal of the American Society for Information Science* 31, no. 5: 347–56.

Rogers, Simon. 2013. "John Snow's Data Journalism: The Cholera Map That Changed the World." *The Guardian.* March 15. Online. https://www.theguardian.com/news/datablog/2013/mar/15/john-snow-cholera-map.

Savolainen, Reijo. 2017. "Information Need as Trigger and Driver of Information Seeking: A Conceptual Analysis." *ASLIB Journal of Information Management* 69, no. 1: 2–21.

Scaramozzino, Jeanine, Russell White, Jeff Essic, Lee Ann Fullington, Himanshu Mistry, Amanda Henley, and Miriam Olivares. 2014. "Map Room to Data and GIS Services: Five University Libraries Evolving to Meet Campus Needs and Changing Technologies." *Journal of Map & Geography Libraries* 10, no. 1: 6–47.

Thorsen, Jeanne. 1998. "Community Studies: Raising the Roof and Other Recommendations." *Acquisitions Librarian* 10, no: 20: 5–13.

Todd, Julia L. 2008. "GIS and Libraries: A Cross-Disciplinary Approach." *Online* 32, no. 5: 14–18.

Vlasis, Charlotte C. 2003. "Librarian Morphs into Curriculum Developer." In *Curriculum Connections Through the Library*, edited by Barbara Stripling and Sandra Hughes-Hassell, 105–19. Westport, CT: Libraries Unlimited.

Yi, Zhixian. 2016. "Effective Techniques for the Segmentation of Academic Library Users." *Library Management* 37, nos. 8/9: 454–64.

Yoo-Lee, EunYoung, Tamara Rhodes, and Gabriel M. Peterson. 2016. "Hispanics and Public Libraries." *Reference Services Review* 44, no. 2: 85–99.

Zweizig, Douglas. 1980. "Community Analysis." In *Local Public Library Administration*, 2nd ed., edited by E. Altman, 38–46. Chicago: American Library Association.

6
Selecting Materials

Good book selection will help increase the use made of the library. A library with 100 cheap but useful and used books is much more valuable than one with an unlimited number of costly but useless and neglected volumes.
—Lionel Roy McColvin, 1925

Librarians have become increasingly aware of their responsibilities to be attentive to both content and format in selection of library materials.
—Peggy Johnson, 2013

Collection development is often a question of balance; librarians must decide how many copies of one very popular item to buy without sacrificing diversity in the collection as a whole.
—Anna Mickelsen, 2016

Quality collections are those that fulfill users' needs.
—Laura Costello, 2017

As the McColvin quote above suggests, the concept of good selection has a 100-year-long history, and will continue for the foreseeable future. Careful selection is even more important in challenging budgetary times, as libraries of all types are more often required to demonstrate a return on investment. Selection work can be enjoyable—and selection is often what those responsible for adding materials to their collections think is *the* primary activity in collection management. Understandably, it is much more enjoyable to review titles and select a new resource than cancel a database or journal package, review a spreadsheet line by line, or scan a range of shelves to select titles for deselection. However, as we know, those are all important elements in the collection cycle.

The primary goal of selection is to create a cost-effective collection that meets the needs of the service population. Beyond the goal of creating collections matching the needs of users, collections should be sustainable. William Walters (2008) noted a goal of selection is that collections "can be maintained without significant degradation over time" (p. 576). The question is how to achieve such sustainability. Alyssa Vincent (2017) suggests several tactics can be employed simultaneously, including "encouraging budgeting models that prioritize interdisciplinary resources to come forward; literally building collections slowly in a way that acknowledges and respects the labour of library staff people, utilizing a variety of sources to determine the best resources in a field; and aligning new collections with institutional goals" (pp. 8–9).

Although collections contain a variety of material types and formats, the focus of this chapter is on the content element. Sometimes it is easy to lose sight of the fact that the content—not the "thing" (or package) it comes in—is what matters. In many cases, the variations in format still convey the same content. However, the cost to acquire and maintain a particular format can and does vary and should be assessed in terms of its purpose and potential usage. Ultimately, content, purpose, and cost are factors to consider when deciding what to add to the library's collection.

Aside from these factors, it is important to note that selection decisions can come down to making a choice from several possible options and thus are not always simple "yes/no" decisions. For example, there are times when selection decisions involve having to decide between two useful titles and knowing that one of them might generate complaints regarding its content or that the content relates to a topic of which you personally do not approve. These factors can complicate an otherwise straightforward selection decision, but still must be considered in the selection process.

Engaging in Selection Activities

It is true that selection work can be one of the most enjoyable and rewarding library duties. However, it is also true that it is challenging and, at times, a little stressful. Here we explore some of the things that lead to both the positive and negative sides of selection activities. Over time, we have made a list of "rational" factors involved in selection decision making. In this chapter we cover the factors that apply to items regardless of format (we review format-specific factors in chapters 11 and 13). None of what follows is original; the factors discussed have been explored by many writers on collection building for many years, as seen in the accompanying sidebar.

Here we present the factors that are scattered throughout the literature on collection management after grouping them into 12 broad categories, ordered more or less in the sequence of the selection decision process:

1. Institutional setting
2. User interests/needs
3. Resources to consult to identify potential items
4. What exists in the collection
5. Known collection gaps
6. Depth and breadth of subjects/topics based on library policy
7. Language of the material and local interest

8. Quality evaluation

9. Cost/usage assessment

10. Cost vis-à-vis available funds

11. Availability of items elsewhere (locally)

12. Prioritizing items to acquire

Collection Management Theory Reviewed

Over the years, a number of individuals have presented theories of collection management. Some of the key authors and their main concepts include:

McColvin, Lionel Roy. 1925. *The Theory of Book Selection for Public Libraries*. London: Grafton & Company.

- Information should be current. (Frequently this is *the* determining criterion for selection.)
- Consider physical characteristics when deciding between two books with similar content.

Drury, Francis K. W. 1930. *Book Selection*. Chicago: American Library Association.

- Establish suitable standards for judging all books.
- Apply criteria intelligently, evaluating the book's contents for inherent worth.
- Be broadminded and unprejudiced in selection.

Haines, Helen E. 1950. *Living with Books: The Art of Book Selection*. 2nd ed. New York: Columbia University Press.

- Know the community's character and interests.
- Be familiar with subjects of current interest and represent subjects applicable to these conditions.
- Practice impartiality in selection. Do not favor certain hobbies or opinions. In controversial or sectarian subjects, accept gifts if purchase is undesirable.

Ranganathan, S. R. 1952. *Library Book Selection*. Bombay/New York: Asia Publishing House. Rpt. 1990.

- Books are for use.
- Every reader his book.
- Every book its reader.
- Save the reader's time.
- A library is a growing organism.

Broadus, Robert N. *Selecting Materials for Libraries*. 2nd ed. New York: H. W. Wilson, 1981.

- Be aware of the impact of publicity that may stimulate demand.
- Make some provision for serving the needs of potential users in the community. Having made such a provision, advertise it.

(continued)

- Weigh the differences between true demand (which reflects individual needs) and artificial demand (resulting from organized propaganda efforts).

Curley, Arthur, Dorothy M. Broderick, and Wallace John Bonk. 1985. *Building Library Collections*. 6th ed. Metuchen, NJ: Scarecrow Press.

- Large public libraries have the largest amount of flexibility in terms of selection options, while small public libraries are the most limited in terms of resources and staff to make selection decisions.

- In most academic libraries, demand is the operative principle: college libraries acquire materials needed to support the instructional program. No one questions the quality of the material if the request originated with a faculty member or department.

Johnson, Peggy. 2013. *Fundamentals of Collection Development and Management*. 3rd rev. ed. Chicago: American Library Association.

- Collection development activities may be broadly grouped into the categories of selecting, budgeting, planning and organizing, and communicating and reporting.

- The library's internal and external environment plays an important role in collection activities.

- Factors such as the publishing industry, scholarly communication, copyright law and the reality of budgetary constraints, preservation needs, cooperation and retention decisions all impact current collection activities.

From the above it should be clear that selection practices can benefit from both past and current theory.

A more detailed outline of collection theories from the authors above, including a summary of the second edition of the Johnson text, may be found in the sixth edition of this title (G. Edward Evans and Margaret Zarnosky Saponaro. *Collection Management Basics*. 6th ed. Santa Barbara, CA: Libraries Unlimited, 2012).

Institutional Setting and User Interests

As we discussed in chapter 3, the library's parent organization creates its "type"—academic, public, school, or special. The type of library immediately reduces the size of the information universe upon which a selector has to focus. The scope is further influenced by the characteristics of the service community that the selector is working with, such as having the assignment to work on the needs in the subject areas of anthropology and sociology, to build the children's collection, provide curriculum support for grades K–4, etc. Only in the very largest libraries will the selector deal with a very broad range of topics and all classes of users.

User interests play a large role in the selection process. Such interests are often the deciding factor in the "buy or not" decision. Those interests are known though resource usage and, often, through user suggestions. We cover demand/patron-driven acquisitions in chapter 8.

Resources to Consult

Once you determine the selection "universe," you can then look for resources that are likely to provide information about materials in your assigned area(s). In today's digital world, the range of possible useful resources is much greater than they were in the print-only environment. Several of the most frequently used resources are:

- Bibliographies
- Vendor directories
- Vendor and association publications/lists
- Best, recommended, "core," or "standard" lists

Bibliographies have long served an important role in collection development. They come in a variety of forms ranging from very general to very narrow in scope. Such information may well impact your decision to add the item to your collection. In the past, print book-length bibliographies written by subject-matter experts in a specific field were a standard source for selectors to use when engaging in retrospective collection development. While extensive retrospective collection building occurs much less frequently today, such bibliographies are still used by those needing a comprehensive study of past publications available in a subject area. One of the most general "bibliographies" is OCLC's *WorldCat®* (https://www.worldcat.org/default.jsp). As of mid-2018, it contained over 2 billion bibliographic holdings, with more being added daily as libraries around the world add their new acquisitions to the database. As a supplement to the main *WorldCat®* catalog, OCLC Research and the WorldCat.org team developed *WorldCat Fiction Finder* (http://experimental.worldcat.org/xfinder/fictionfinder.html) as a means to help users identify fiction genres such as spy stories, mystery, and science fiction. Even with the *Fiction Finder* option in mind, given the breadth and depth of the *WorldCat®* database, it is not the best place to begin to look for new items that may be useful for your library. However, it is very useful when you need to verify some information about a known item such as which nearby or consortial partner libraries already hold the item. This information may impact your decision to add or not add a particular item to your collection.

An alternative to *WorldCat®* for identifying books (including eBooks, audiobooks, and multimedia titles) is *Books in Print®* (*BIP*) by R. R. Bowker (http://www.bowker.com/products/Books-In—Print.html). *BIP* is available in both U.S. and global editions and provides an opportunity to search by author, genre, subject, or even character. Lately many institutions, including those of the authors, have opted to forgo their subscription to *BIP* due to budgetary constraints or in light of the availability of other resources. However, it does remain one of the long-standing options available for such identification work and can be a useful tool if available.

Beyond bibliographies, each discipline has its own vendors for monographs, serials, and other materials that tailor to its research, and several sources exist to locate such vendors. One of the long-standing resources in the field is *Literary Market Place: Directory of the American Book Publishing Industry* or *LMP*. *LMP* is an annual print publication from Information Today (http://books.infotoday.com/directories/lmp.shtml), and can be useful for identifying vendors as well as agents and distributors. Cengage/Gale's *Publishers*

Directory (*PD*, https://tinyurl.com/GalePD41) is another long-standing resource, which includes information on small press and museum publishers as well as major publishing houses. While *LMP* and *PD* are subscription-based, *PublishersGlobal* (http://www.publishersglobal.com/directory/united -states/publishers-in-united-states/) is a free website that provides directory information for publishers by subject, media type, and language.

Both *PD* and *PublishersGlobal* include international as well as domestic publishers. However, another source for international vendors is the *Foreign Book Dealers Directory* (*FBDD*, http://www.ala.org/CFApps/bookdealers/). *FBDD* is produced and maintained by the Foreign Book Dealers Directories Subcommittee (FBDDS) of ALA's Association for Library Collections and Technical Services (ALCTS). *FBDD* was originally established to assist in locating book and serial vendors who provide materials from Asia, the Pacific, Africa, the Middle East, Eastern Europe, and the countries that comprise the former Soviet Union. As noted by FBDDS, the need to maintain the directory recognizes the current climate where "many colleges and universities have devoted greater attention to international events, and are developing programs that support study abroad and outreach to other countries; these demand the purchase of materials from varying regions of the world to support developing curricula" (http://www.ala.org/CFApps/bookdealers/about.cfm).

After identifying certain publishers as annually issuing a number of items that are of high interest, a selector will often find that going directly to those publishers' websites is a good method of identifying potentially useful items. Such sites usually provide information about released titles as well as titles scheduled to be released in the near future ("Forthcoming Titles" is a common label for such pages). Occasionally, sample chapters may be available online for reviewing. Almost every publisher of more than a dozen new titles per year has a backlist (items released in prior years but still in stock) and will issue print catalogs and promotional flyers, although e-flyers and catalogs are becoming a more popular (and environmentally conscious) means of marketing. It is easy for a selector to get on a print or online mailing list; it can be challenging to get off a print marketing list, although most email lists have an "unsubscribe" option available. Another option is to make a list of preferred publishers and visit their booths at library association meetings. Often display copies of newly released or forthcoming titles are available to refer to and consider.

While publisher descriptions of current and upcoming titles can provide useful information, selectors need to be cautious about any publishers' descriptions of their offerings. Needless to say, publishers rarely say anything bad about a title and often suggest the title is much better than it actually turns out to be. Further, there are some firms that libraries cannot trust—they simply put out totally misleading information. Another caution to keep in mind is that some announced forthcoming titles never do appear. Placing an order for such items may tie up much-needed funds for something that never materializes in the acquisitions receiving unit. There are several common reasons for this to happen—the author fails to deliver the expected material, or what is delivered in unacceptable. We explore such issues in more depth in chapter 8.

There are thousands of subject bibliographies, best, recommended, "core," or "standard" lists in existence. Two such items are *Children's Core Collection* (H. W. Wilson—print, and EBSCO—online, https://www.hwwilsoninprint .com/child_core.php) and *Resources for College Libraries*™ (ProQuest, https:// www.proquest.com/products-services/Resources-for-College-Libraries.html). Content of these identification tools varies from a single narrow topic to

---

Check These Out

While the above are some of the most frequently used standard sources for identifying forthcoming and existing publications in a specific subject area, the list of potential sources is limited by your imagination. Other potential sources to consider include:

- Social media (items shared by other people in your subject area and other libraries' Facebook pages)
- Auction catalogs
- Subject guides created by librarians at other systems or institutions
- Journals, magazines, or national newspapers with book reviews such as the *New York Times* or *Washington Post*
- Literary press catalogs
- Patron suggestions
- Class syllabi
- Amazon.Com or BN.Com
- Departmental newsletters

---

broad-based core lists that include fiction and nonfiction titles as well as a variety of formats. Other lists include the "Sudden Selectors Series" developed by ALCTS (http://www.ala.org/alcts/resources/collect/collmgt/ssg) and the list of recommended print and media maintained by ALA (http://www.ala .org/awardsgrants/awards/browse/rlist?showfilter=no). Online acquisition systems, such as *GOBI® Library Solutions* from EBSCO or Baker & Taylor, can also be a source of "best of" or other award-winning titles such as Pulitzer Prizes, National Book Awards, and National Book Critics Circle Awards. In addition, Follett's *Titlewave®* (http://www.titlewave.com/), which is also linked inside Follett's *Destiny* online catalog software, contains lists such as state award winners, titles recently reviewed in *School Library Journal*, Common Core materials, STEM (Science, Technology, Engineering, Mathematics) materials, etc.

When using such tools you want to ascertain at least four key points. First, what is the date when the tool first appeared? In a fast-changing world, what is "good" today may be useless in a year's time. Second, who produced the list, and what were the person's or persons' qualifications for doing the work? Third, what criteria were employed in making the judgment to include an item? Fourth, and most important, just how relevant is the list to your library situation? Determining the answers for the first three questions is often more challenging than you might think, and recommendations must still be weighed against local needs and availability of funds. However, such lists can serve as a valuable starting point for locating new titles.

What Is in the Collection/What Is Lacking

We covered collection policies at length in chapter 4. These policies are a key tool in the selection process by providing a framework for collection priorities while setting limits on the range of topics and formats to include in the collection. Such information supplies the broad context for your selection activities; what it does not do is tell you what already exists in the collection.

Two primary methods exist for determining what is currently in the collection. First and foremost is exploring the library's holdings through ILS (integrated library system) generated reports. You can generate such reports by call number, fund code, subject, format, or other parameters such as date acquired. Keep in mind that such reports will give you a snapshot of what was purchased and in theory available to users at one point in time, but may not guarantee that the title is still available (as seen in the discussion below about missing titles).

Another method is spending time in the stacks looking at the items on the shelves in your area(s) of responsibility. Factors to consider as you do this are what titles are there in this or that narrow topic, what these titles contain, how old they are, and what usage patterns are discernible. This may seem like extra work, especially as you likely have more job obligations than simply CM duties. However, doing this will save you more time than you spend in the stacks as you engage in your ongoing selection work—you will have less and less need to check to see if you have or need a particular item. Two side benefits of this method are that it can help with your work with patrons, as you will better be able to direct them to materials in their subject area, and it can help you determine if a weeding or deselection project may be called for in a specific area. (We cover deselection in chapter 9.)

As for gaps in the collection, information about what is lacking or missing can come from several sources. Certainly some information will come from your time in the stacks, but this is especially true if you know the subject area well and are actively following key publishers in the area(s) for which you select. Any appropriate core/best/recommended list may provide other clues to voids to fill. However, one in-library source will provide significant input—public service departments. Data from public services can include traditional "suggest a title" online or print forms as well as Interlibrary Loan (ILL) requests. ILL requests in particular can be very useful regarding current user interests that are unmet by the local resources. One caution, particularly in the academic library setting, is to make certain that a number of requests from one person reflects ongoing interest and not the needs of a one-time project.

In the late 1990s, some academic libraries started exploring a "books on demand" program that uses ILL requests as the basis for acquiring items for the collection (see Jennifer Perdue and James A. Van Fleet's 1999 article "Borrow or Buy?" for a discussion of the origins of the practice at Bucknell University). Selectors have voiced concern over such systems, such as those raised by Dracine Hodges and her colleagues (2010), who noted, "There is a real difference between building a balanced collection for the future and giving patrons what they want now" (p. 219). However, David Tyler and his associates (2010) noted in their study, "The UNL [University of Nebraska, Lincoln] project confirmed findings in the literature indicating that purchase-on-demand programs at libraries of several types have been very successful at obtaining cost-effective materials that are not only suitable for their collections but also meet the needs of multiple patrons" (p. 174). Responsiveness to user needs in a timely fashion is a primary draw of such systems, such as the program dubbed Next Gen ILL instituted by the University of California, Irvine (UCI). Becky Imamoto and Lisa Mackinder (2016) reported on the pilot program developed at UCI, designed to "enhance the delivery of ILL content to our users in an expeditious manner and save on costs" (p. 371).

From the Authors' Experience

In early 2018, the University of Maryland Libraries (UMD) embarked on a program to fill eBook ILL requests through the existing demand-driven DDA program. ILL staff reviewed requests received and if the title already existed in the DDA pool, they would activate the title and notify the patron. ILL staff forwarded requests requiring mediation to Collection Development on behalf of the patron, and only those requests that could not be filled due to cost or other restrictions would be redirected back to ILL for standard processing. The program will be assessed each semester to determine whether or not it will be continued.

From the Authors' Experience

Saponaro worked with both the Head of Resource Sharing and the Collection Maintenance Coordinator in public services at UMD to place listings of InterLibrary Loan (ILL) requests, Reported Missing (RM) and Missing titles (MI) on the library staff intranet twice yearly so that subject specialists could reference them. The ILL loan lists reflected both books and other items that were physically borrowed from other institutions to fill patron requests, as well as those items that were requested and borrowed by users from other institutions. While the first list gave a better snapshot of user needs at the local level, subject specialists appreciated knowing what materials in the collection were requested elsewhere. The RM list reflected those titles that were being actively searched by collection maintenance personnel, with the expectation the item could reappear. Items on the MI list had been searched for a longer period of time with little expectation that the item would be located again. These listings included circulation data and gave the selectors an opportunity to consider titles for replacement. A separate replacement fund was available for missing titles that subject specialists opted to replace, so that they did not need to use existing discretionary funds for this purpose. It was the responsibility of each subject specialist to review the lists and determine if any titles should be ordered for the collection.

Circulation department records are another resource. One obvious category of information comes from the "lost and paid for" file. While it may or may not be the selector's responsibility to handle a replacement, in any event there may be a pattern of lost and paid for items that reflects a high interest level about a topic or particular work that needs some attention. Almost every circulation department has a "search file," that is, records of items users could not locate and have no record of being charged out. Circulation staff searches for the missing items, and they often find the item misshelved, lying on a table, or on a book truck waiting to be reshelved. However, some items do seem to disappear and eventually a decision about replacing the item must take place. As with lost and paid for items, CM staff may see a pattern in what is missing and need to answer the question "what do we do about this?"

Language

In chapter 1, we mentioned ALA's *Diversity in Collection Development: An Interpretation of the Library Bill of Rights* (1982; amended 1990, 2008, 2014), developed in recognition of growing diversity in library communities.

Check These Out

Todd Quesada and Julia Stephens had a pointed exchange over the role of Spanish-language materials and services in public libraries. Their articles provide food for thought:

- Quesada, Todd Douglas. 2007. "Spanish Spoken Here." *American Libraries* 38, no. 10: 40, 42, 44.

- Stephens, Julia. 2007. "English Spoken Here." *American Libraries* 38, no. 10: 41, 43–44.

Juris Dilevko and Keren Dali discuss a variety of tools and measures taken to improve multilingual collections in the public library setting in their article "The Challenge of Building Multilingual Collections in Canadian Public Libraries" (*Library Resources & Technical Services* 2002, 46, no. 4: 116–37).

Brian LaVoie of OCLC provides an interesting state-level analysis of public library language collections in his November 24, 2014, blog post, "What Languages Do Public Library Collections Speak?" (https://hangingtogether.org/?p=4671).

In her 2017 article "From Hashtags to Better Readers' Advisory" (*ILA Reporter* 35, no. 1: 25–26), Hannah Rapp discusses the origins of the We Need Diverse Books (WNDB) movement—otherwise known as #WeNeedDiverseBooks. Two sites suggested in the article as sources of diverse materials, particularly in the area of young adult literature, are the aforementioned We Need Diverse Books (https://diversebooks.org/) as well as Rich In Color (http://richincolor.com/). Both sites include resource lists and are well worth a look.

As the statement indicates, library content "should represent the languages commonly used in the library's service community." Further, as Bisset noted, "A library, whether it is public or educational, is a central service point, not affiliated to one sector and can play a role in the concept of social inclusion by offering resources in the languages of its community" (2010, p. 12). However, such decisions are not always easy, particularly when faced with real-world budgetary limitations, competing needs, and selectors who may not have knowledge of a particular language or culture (Garrison, 2013).

For many selectors, the issue of adding items in languages other than English can cause some stress. When funding is limited, do you select an item in a language you know has few readers in the service community when you know those few are active users and supporters of the library? What about selecting materials in a language you know has potential users, but very few active? Some stress may surface as often the choice is between two or more equally good options.

Tools are available to assist selectors in locating and acquiring foreign language materials for the collection. These include the bibliographies, foreign press directories such as the *Foreign Book Dealers Directory*, as well as foreign language bookstores, staff who speak the language, and approval plans available to the library from international vendors such as Puvill (Spanish, Portuguese, and Latin American—http://www.puvill.com/), Harrassowitz (German—https://www.harrassowitz.de/), or MIPP International (Eastern European—http://www.mippbooks.com/). (Approval plans are discussed further in chapter 8.)

Quality

Determining quality is the center of the selection process and perhaps the most complex. In this section, we look at many of the elements that are part of estimating an item's quality. You rarely use all of the following quality factors for a single item, but you will need to use some of them. Different elements come into play as the character of the item changes (such as fiction or nonfiction, mass market or scholarly, adult or juvenile).

Reviews

One obvious, and likely the most frequently used, starting point for quality assessments are published reviews, when they exist. Reviews are very, very helpful; however, they do have their limitations. Perhaps the most significant limitation is the percentage of new titles that actually receive a review. One large category of new items not reviewed is new or revised editions of a work. As most of the titles in this group are textbooks, the lack of reviews is less important as many libraries exclude textbooks from their collections.

There are several factors that impact a title's review status. First and foremost is the volume of publishing occurring each year. For U.S. production, data from Bowker's *Library and Book Trade Almanac* (*LBTA*, formerly *The Bowker Annual*) provides some insights. Using 2014 preliminary data, one finds the reported U.S. production for the year was 200,768 titles (Bogart, 2015, p. 455) and 33,860 reviews (p. 478) published in the so-called "gatekeeper" review sources. Those figures suggest that 16.8 percent of the new titles received one review. The true number reviewed is far lower as the assumption of one review per title is not valid, as some titles get multiple reviews. (Note: The 2015 edition is the latest edition that posted review source data.)

Given the volume, it is no surprise editors of review columns or journals receive hundreds to thousands of items from which they must select only a few to review. From there, editors have to make decisions as to what to include. For example, *Choice*, long a tool used by academic selectors for materials for their collections, notes on its own website that, "Due to the high volume of materials received, *Choice* is able to review only 25 to 30 percent of the titles submitted" (http://www.ala.org/acrl/choice/publisherinfo).

The editors' primary limitation on the number of reviews for print publications is cost and the publication space they have for reviewing. Another limiting factor is having someone qualified and available to review an item within the required timeframe. (Good reviews require a person who knows the subject or genre well, who has no personal interest regarding the author/creator of the item, and has adequate time for writing the review. Keeping such people available and being able to give people proper time for producing a sound review, and usually for nothing more than "Thanks, you can keep the review copy," is a challenge.) One trait of good selectors is they keep in mind the names of reviewers and how well their reviews matched the items after receipt in the library.

It is important to keep in mind the absence of a review does *not* mean an item lacks quality. Liz Johnson and Linda Brown (2009) studied a number of review sources and found it difficult, if not impossible, to obtain an exact figure of the number of books reviewed annually. As they noted, "It is easy to see why there is no comprehensive data on the number of books reviewed each year, after considering what a mammoth undertaking it would be to track all media sources where books are reviewed" (p. 82). Their observation is even truer today when you consider the number of online review sources not included in their original study.

Starting Points for Reviews

Despite their limitations, reviews are a valid starting point for selectors, particularly for disciplines or genres that may be new or unfamiliar to the selector. Some of the most frequently used book review resources appear below. Almost all are subscription-based. However, most have selected reviews freely available on their sites:

- *Booklist* (https://www.booklistonline.com/)—Published by ALA for over 100 years, this reviewing source focuses on resources for public and school libraries.

- *BlueInk Review* (https://www.blueinkreview.com/)—A fee-based service for self-published titles.

- *Choice* (http://www.choice360.org/)—Published by the Association of College & Research Libraries division of ALA, *Choice* includes both a print and online offering. Both focus on titles recommended for college and university libraries.

- *The Horn Book* (http://www.hbook.com/) is published bimonthly while its sister publication, the *Horn Book Guide* (http://www.hbook.com/horn-book-guide/), is issued in digital PDF semiannually. Both focus on children's and young adult titles. The subscription-based *Horn Book Guide Online* provides access to reviews back to 1989 (http://www.hornbookguide.com/cgi-bin/hbonline.pl).

- *New York Times Book Review* (https://www.nytimes.com/section/books/review)—Contains reviews of new releases as well as best-seller lists for fiction, nonfiction, and paperbacks.

- *Publisher's Weekly* (https://www.publishersweekly.com/pw/reviews/index.html)—Includes reviews from adult and children's titles from the U.S. and Canada. Reviews include fiction and nonfiction titles, as well as audiobooks. The website also includes a "Best Books of the Year"—regular and summer editions (https://best-books.publishersweekly.com/pw/best-books/summer-reads-2018) with links to prior years.

- *School Library Journal* (https://www.slj.com/?subpage=Reviews%2B)—The research journal of the American Association of School Librarians division of ALA. Includes reviews of books, videos, audio recordings, and online resources for children and young adults.

- *SB&F* (*Science Books and Films*, https://www.aaas.org/program/science-books-films-sbf)—A journal from the American Association for the Advancement of Science devoted exclusively to print and nonprint science materials for all age groups.

Review sources for materials in other formats include:

- *AudioFile®* (https://www.audiofilemagazine.com/)—Published in print six times a year, with reviews also available online. *AudioFile* "Earphone" awards are identified annually for "truly exceptional

---

Check These Out

A good book that discusses U.S. book reviewing is Gail Pool's *In Faint Praise: The Plight of Book Reviewing in America* (Columbia: University of Missouri Press, 2007). Pool was a longtime book review editor for several journals and newspapers. Two very enlightening chapters are "Unnatural Selection" and "The Match." Unnatural selection deals with the issue of why the number of titles actually reviewed is so small, while the match chapter discusses the challenges in finding the right reviewer. The book is short, informative, and a "good read."

While one may think that only positive reviews appear, that is not always the case. Phillipa Brown (2015) discussed the issue of negative reviews in "Playing Nice, Being Mean, and the Space In Between: Book Critics and the Difficulties of Writing Bad Reviews," which appeared in *In Moments of Valuation: Exploring Sites of Dissonance* (ed. by Ariane Berthoin Antal, Michael Hutter, and David Stark, 133–147. London: Oxford University Press). Her chapter explores the subjective evaluations of critics, based on her interviews of 30 fiction review critics, and is an interesting read.

---

titles that excel in narrative voice and style, characterizations, suitability to audio, and enhancement of the text" (https://www.audiofilemagazine.com/reviews/earphones/).

- *ccAdvisor* (http://www.choice360.org/products/ccadvisor)—A joint product of the Charleston Company and *Choice*, this resource was launched in 2017 as a guide to academic databases and websites.

- *Video Librarian* (http://www.videolibrarian.com/index.html)—Covers both theatrical and nontheatrical new films for public, school, university, and special libraries. Available in print and online.

An excellent website for identifying hundreds of sources for book reviews is *The Complete Review* (http://www.complete-review.com/links/links.html). The site includes links to English and other foreign language review sites. In addition to individual review sources listed above, two aggregated sources for locating reviews are *Book Review Index* (Gale, online via *Book Review Index Plus*—https://www.gale.com/c/book-review-index-plus) and *Book Review Digest Plus* (H. W. Wilson, online via EBSCO—https://www.ebsco.com/products/research-databases/book-review-digest-plus). Additionally, as mentioned earlier, some acquisitions systems (such as *GOBI® Library Solutions* from EBSCO) include links to review sources within their systems, which is an obvious time-saver on the part of busy selectors.

Other Quality Factors

Reviews are one source of assessing quality, but they should not be the only one relied upon in the selection process. At the end of the day, selectors must exercise independent judgment before choosing a title—especially when faced with limited budgets and multiple possibilities. Some additional factors to take into account when assessing a title are:

- Type of material (fiction or nonfiction, for example)
- Subject matter and relevance to the collection

- Content
- Potential value for the service community
- Treatment/coverage (level and depth)
- Theme(s)
- Intended audience
- Presentation style (writing quality)
- Accuracy
- Utility/format (indexes, references, illustrations, platform features if online, etc.)
- Author's reputation
- Reputation of the publisher, producer, and/or advisory board
- Point of view (evidence to support a view)
- Fiction (plot, characterizations, realistic/fantasy, etc.)
- Selector's assessment of the title

The above factors are all useful when you have an item to examine, such as with approval plans (we discuss such plans in chapter 8) or when you visit a publisher's booth at a conference and can inspect newly published titles or galleys of forthcoming titles. The reality is that much of your assessment work will have to occur without having an opportunity to inspect/read the material.

Without an item in hand or a review, you will have to make some judgments on the basis of a bibliographic citation or material supplied by the publisher or producer. Assessing the suitability of an item for your collection based on limited information is a challenge. Essentially, it takes time, experience, and making some poor "calls" before you will get comfortable with this phase of collection development. It is also true that you will experience a similar learning curve when you change libraries. The following are a few tips that will help lessen the number of early "poor calls."

Even with the most basic citation—author, title and subtitle, date of publication, publisher/producer, and price—a number of clues still exist as to the item's quality; this is especially true in today's online world. Start with the author/creator. Ask yourself: "Do I know the name from prior selection activities?" and "Are there other items in the collection by this person?" (your discovery system or OPAC will quickly provide the answer to this question). If not, you can turn to the Web for information about the person and the individual's qualifications. You can check *WorldCat*® or your local acquisition system to see what other items the author is associated with, as well as which libraries hold copies of prior titles as well as the current item under consideration. Some acquisition systems will provide data on books shipped directly from approval plans and standing orders as well as those selected as firm orders. The more items the person has produced and that are widely held is a good clue to the general quality of the person's work. Another plus of such searches is you gain additional insight regarding the content from subject headings that have been assigned to the title and, on occasion, you can even see the table of contents.

You can also do the same type of checking regarding the publisher/producer, if you do not happen to know it. Some academic and large public

---

Check This Out

An older but still relevant article about using citation information in the selection process is Ross Atkinson's (1984) work "The Citation as Intertext: Toward a Theory of the Selection Process," in *Library Resources & Technical Services* (28, no. 2: 109–19). Atkinson was one of the best thinkers about collection management on both a theoretical and practical level.

From the Authors' Experience

For most of his "selector career" Evans was responsible for materials in anthropology, archaeology, and often sociology. One such assignment was at Tozzer Library (Harvard University's anthropology library), which had at the time over 100 years of attempting to be one of the world's foremost anthropology libraries. Most of the selection work had to be done from citation information in bibliographies and O.P. book dealer catalogs. Certainly teaching experience in both collection management and anthropology was a great help in making quality judgment calls. However, someone without such a background could also have done well using the ideas outlined above.

For example, reading a citation about conditions on the Lakota reservations in South Dakota, he had different expectations regarding the content of items with place of publication as "Washington, D.C., 1986" or "Pine Ridge, S.D., 1977." The latter would have a much different perspective than would the former and depending on the library's need for more information on the Lakota views, the latter would likely be the better choice. Another example of how a citation element could modify a judgment is a title implying comprehensive or comparative treatment of a broad or complex subject, with pagination indicating a much shorter book than would be reasonable for the topic.

When a citation string includes subject descriptors, profound modification in judgment can occur. An entry in a bibliography might seem appropriate for Tozzer Library until encountering the subject heading *juvenile*. Without the supplemental context, it is possible and even probable that the library would order some inappropriate items because of inadequate information—one of those "poor calls" that we all make.

Advisory Board member Susan Koutsky seconds the experience, noting:

I have definitely made the same mistake—ordering a book that sounded appropriate for elementary, but it was really for a higher age.

---

libraries have developed "reputation data" for publishers they use with great frequency. However, there is a necessity to reassess such data on a regular basis as the pace of change in the publishing industry is no less than that in librarianship. Past studies that have explored this concept include those of John Calhoun and James Bracken (1983), as well as Paul Metz and John Stemmer (1996). More recent studies include those of Tina Neville and Deborah Henry (2014) and Alesia Zuccala and her colleagues (2015).

Neville and Henry focused their research on book publishers in the field of journalism and suggested in part, "Librarians or faculty wishing to emphasize scholarly citations might find the publishers ranking highest in average Google Scholar cites or the h-index calculation to be the most helpful. For those concerned with profitability, the higher rankings for WorldCat holdings or for the RCIR [relative catalog inclusion rate] method might be useful" (2014, p. 384). Zuccala and her colleagues in turn studied materials in the discipline of history and suggested looking at total citation counts as one factor in evaluation. They also suggested some additional variables worth considering, albeit difficult to gather, including the annual sales figures for each publisher, how many books have been sold and distributed specifically for the subject in question and how many scholarly reviews have been written for the publishers' book titles (2015, p. 1340). The effort to collect the data to create the index, though considerable, would familiarize selectors with the publishers from which the library frequently buys as well as with the publishers' track records in producing highly recommended titles.

Cost Issues

If you review the list of quality factors to consider that appeared earlier, you will see the final element was "your assessment." When that assessment is that the item is a potential purchase for the collection, the selection decision is still not complete. There are still a few more factors to think about before making the final decision to acquire the item—price.

The first consideration is cost-benefit. At first it will be challenging to make a determination of the potential use of the item; however, it is important to make an estimate. Funds are limited and gaining maximum usage out of the items acquired demonstrates good stewardship. To do this, you can perform a cost-benefit analysis for each item to determine if usage will be proportional to cost. This will certainly not be a formal analysis, but you will make one in your mind based on your experience. Such analysis is worthwhile for, as noted by Doug Way (2017), "It's important to understand that . . . unused books are not just sunk costs" (p. 2). He went on to note that the cost of retaining books on open shelves averaged $4.26 per volume per year. This is certainly not a large figure in and of itself, but it becomes one when factoring in the number of volumes in a library collection and the recurring nature of this cost. Thus, a title purchased and sitting on the shelf unused has residual costs beyond its purchase price.

The second cost consideration is obvious: how much money is left to spend and how long must it last? (Most funding is by fiscal year—FY—and at a certain point in the year orders must be paused in order to "close" the books in preparation for the next FY.) The longer the timeframe before new funds are available, the more likely you will hold off on the "buy decision" as there is a chance even better items will appear later in the year. The question is—how long to wait? Near the end of a FY, you often face the issue of not having enough money to acquire all the items you want or need. Another factor, particularly in the world of e-resources, is that some e-titles are only available for an indefinite period of time, as vendors can and do remove titles from eBook platforms. (We discuss e-resources in chapter 13.) Which items can wait, which are "must acquire now," and how to make the call are questions that bedevil even the most experienced selectors.

Related to available funding is the cost of the resource itself. This will vary greatly depending on the format and subject matter of the item. In general, materials supporting science- and technology-related fields (STEM) are more expensive than those in the social sciences or humanities. The average costs of hardcover titles for several frequently purchased disciplines as reported in the 2017 edition of *LBTA* (Barr, 2017, pp. 314–315) are:

Art—$75.70

Business and Economics—$159.32

Children's Titles—$25.32

Fiction—$29.80

Health and Fitness—$72.94

Medical—$174.98

Science—$203.51

Travel—$40.36

Although the figures above are only averages, these examples show that item cost will vary depending upon the discipline. Another factor to keep in mind is that while there are certainly variations by discipline and publisher, in general the cost of materials has increased steadily each year (Barr, 2017, p. 312).

With your assessment of potential value, cost to usage, and available funding, you must prioritize the items—which titles should be acquired now, which ones can wait for a while, and which ones may never be acquired. There is a continuum of importance from absolutely essential to the ultimate luxury, with almost all of the items falling somewhere in the mid-range.

Another factor that may come into play in setting the priorities is the availability of the item locally and the existence of reciprocal borrowing or collection building agreements. There may be items that become essential due to more or less binding agreements, while items that would be nice to have in the collection are not purchased as they are available nearby or can be obtained quickly via consortial loan policies. (We cover collaborative CM in chapter 10.)

Variations in Selection by Library Type

Selection practices, policies, and procedures vary by individual institution. However, there are some generalizations that can be made. Purely for ease of presentation, we employ the traditional categories of libraries: academic, public, school, and special. Certainly, there are great differences even within each category, and what follows provides only a broad overview of the thousands of variations that exist.

Academic Libraries—Community Colleges

In the United States, there are two broad categories of postsecondary schools: vocational and academic. Publicly supported vocational programs in the United States are generally referred to as community colleges (CCs). However, the reality is that most CCs have both vocational and academic programs. The academic program in the CC setting is roughly equivalent to the first two years in a college or university and may lead to an associate of arts degree. Such programs can also serve as a transfer program to a four-year college or university. If the transfer program is to succeed in providing the equivalent of the first two years of a four-year undergraduate degree, then the scope of the program must be just as comprehensive as that of the university program. That in turn has library collection implications.

Collection management personnel in a community college library have a challenging job. Not only must they focus on the academic programs, but they must also give equal attention to a wide range of vocational programs—and do so with a modest budget. Unfortunately, from a cost perspective, it is seldom possible to find materials that are useful in both programs. As

---

From the Authors' Experience

Saponaro worked with several subject areas in the community college learning resource center (LRC) setting for a number of years and found that for the most part, her selection activities focused upon current resources to meet the needs of courses and curricula currently taught. Retrospective purchases, when made, tended to be for items declared as lost or for titles that were damaged beyond in-house repair capabilities. In both cases, an assessment was made before a replacement copy was ordered to determine if the item in question had potential future use to justify the replacement. General selection sources such as *Choice* and vendor catalogs were two frequently used selection tools, as were recommendations and suggestions from faculty members. Occasionally, gifts were offered for the collection. Such items were evaluated for inclusion based on their perceived utility to the curriculum.

---

we saw in the previous section, one factor is that the costs of materials to support some programs (such as health and medicine) tend to be higher than others (such as literature or history). Also, many vocational programs require more visual media than print-based materials (monographs, journals, serials, etc.), which accounts in part for the fact that U.S. community college libraries tend to be leaders in the use of media materials. Like other academic institutions, librarians at CCs must also factor in the purchase of materials that support online distance-learning programs and provide off-site access for users. Further, community college librarians normally have other duties assigned to them beyond their collection development responsibilities, such as reference and instruction (although this pattern is becoming more the norm for all types of libraries).

Beyond their vocational and academic offerings, CCs also offer extensive adult continuing education programs. These programs often have little or no relationship to the degree programs. In most CCs the library, or learning resource center (LRC), must handle all programmatic information needs. Given the diversity of subjects, program support needs, and levels of user ability, the community college library more resembles the public library than it does its larger relation, the university library. In addition to standard reference and reserve collections selected to support curricular programming, community college library collections can include career and leisure materials.

CC libraries serve a heterogeneous community, and their collections must reflect a diverse population with varying levels of language skills. Selection is usually item by item, with less use of blanket orders and approval plans than in other types of academic libraries. Collections generally contain at least a few items in all the standard educational formats. Selection personnel generally use a greater variety of selection aids than their colleagues in other types of libraries.

College Libraries

Although college libraries serving primarily bachelor's degree programs are diverse, each tends to serve a relatively homogeneous user group. (Only the small special library that caters to a company or research group is likely to have a more homogeneous service community.) One characteristic of bachelor's degree programs is that, within a particular college, all the students

---

Check These Out

Because of its widespread use as a selection aid, several librarians have studied *Choice* to determine its effectiveness. The studies listed below are a sample of the research done on the topic and are worth the read:

- Jobe, Margaret M., and Michael Levine-Clark. 2008. "Use and Non-Use of *Choice*-Reviewed Titles in Undergraduate Libraries." *Journal of Academic Librarianship* 34, no. 4: 295–304.

- Kousha, Kayvan, and Mike Thelwall. 2015. "Alternative Metrics for Book Impact Assessment: Can *Choice* Reviews be a Useful Source?" In *Proceedings of 15th International Conference. Society of Scientometrics and Informetrics Conference. Istanbul, Turkey. 29 June to 3 July 2015*, pp. 59–70. Istanbul: Boğaziçi University Printhouse. http://www.koosha.tripod.com/ChoiceReviews.pdf.

- Williams, Karen Carter, and Rickey Best. 2006. "E-book Usage and the *Choice* Outstanding Academic Book List: Is There a Correlation?" *Journal of Academic Librarianship* 32, no. 5: 474–78.

---

who graduate, regardless of their major, complete some type of general education program. A program of core courses means that students select from a limited number of courses during their first two years. Less variety in course offerings makes library selection work less complex. As was the case with community colleges, support of the curriculum is the primary objective of the college library collection. College libraries may offer some collection support for faculty research, but, unlike universities, colleges seldom emphasize research. With the curriculum as the focus for collection development activities, selectors have definite limits within which to work. Faculty members frequently play an active role in selection, more so than in the CC or university context.

Two frequently used tools designed to assist selectors in the college library setting are *Choice* (http://www.ala.org/acrl/choice/) and *Resources for College Libraries,* mentioned earlier. Both resources are published by the Association of College & Research Libraries branch of ALA and are both designed to meet the specific needs of college library collection development officers by reviewing publications aimed at the undergraduate market. *Choice* also offers webinars, white papers, and an online blog called *Open Stacks* (http://choice360.org/blog) as a means of further supporting the work of selectors.

University Libraries

University and research libraries have collections ranging from a few hundred thousand to many millions of volumes. Although these libraries are not as numerous as libraries of other types, the size of their collections and the number of their staff, as well as monies expended per year on operations, far surpass the combined totals for all the other types of libraries. Association of Research Library data for 2015–2016 (the latest available at the time this volume was being prepared) indicate that the costs of materials ranged from 28 percent to 66 percent of total spending in surveyed libraries (*Chronicle of Higher Education*, 2017, p. 79). This can, and does,

---

Check These Out

Two aspects of academic library selection are title-by-title versus approval plan selection and selection of titles for other than the general circulating collection (namely reference titles). Irene Ke, Wenli Gao, and Jackie Bronicki's (2017) article "Does Title by Title Selection Make a Difference? A Usage Analysis on Print Monograph Purchasing" (*Collection Management* 42, no. 1: 34–47) details a study of print materials selected for the collection at the MD Anderson Library at the University of Houston, comparing the usage of titles added via the approval plan to those selected as firm orders. Susan L. Collins (2016) provided an overview of the process developed at Carnegie Mellon University to select reference titles in her piece "The Votes Are In: A Process for Selecting Reference Books and Managing the Reference Budget" (*Collection Building* 35, no. 3, 61–63). Both are interesting reads worth a look.

---

amount to millions in collection costs. Of all the library types, university libraries are the most likely to engage in retrospective selection, as well as actively select resources in foreign languages for the collection. Traditionally, university library collections consisted predominantly of monographs and serials, with less use of audiovisual materials (depending on the focus of the collection) than other types of libraries. While print was long the dominant format selected in university libraries, Peter Monaghan notes that "at most academic libraries now, usage of digital and electronic materials surpasses—often, far surpasses—that of physical books, and expenditure follows usage" (2017, p. 80).

Traditionally, selection in university libraries was the job of subject specialists whose primary responsibility was to perform collection development activities. However, as noted by Sandra Barstow and her colleagues, this model is changing, with the workload of many subject specialists being skewed more toward instruction, data management, reference, and research support, leaving less and less time for selection activities (2016, p. 791). As a means of reducing workloads while ensuring adequate collection building, university libraries tend to depend heavily on standing and blanket orders as opposed to firm orders. Using such programs allows selectors more time for retrospective buying and for tracking down items from countries where the book trade is not well developed.

Purchase or licensing models in all library types have become more complex over time with the onset of options such as evidence-based, demand-driven, and open access publication models all vying for the attention of selectors. (We will discuss these models further in chapter 8.) While challenging to manage, these new access models also provide users more opportunities to get the information they need for their research and teaching. As noted by Tony Horava and Michael Levine-Clark, "in transforming the traditional, fixed concept of a collection to a fluid model of engagement and discovery, we are recognizing the transformative changes that have occurred in our environment and among our users" (2016, p. 101). All of these changes do result in "a vastly more complicated publication landscape to be navigated by selectors" (Barstow, Macaulay, and Tharp, 2016, p. 790). Add to this complex landscape that in the case of many academic libraries, collections budgets are often flat, receiving no annual increases to address inflation. How significant an issue is inflation? The Library Materials Price Index Editorial Board of ALA's ALCTS Publications Committee compiles data annually that

---

Check This Out

For an interesting perspective on academic libraries and the scholarly publishing field, see Albert N. Greco's 2015 piece "Academic Libraries and the Economics of Scholarly Publishing in the Twenty-First Century: Portfolio Theory, Product Differentiation, Economic Rent, Perfect Price Discrimination, and the Cost of Prestige" (*Journal of Scholarly Publishing* 47, no. 1: 1–43).

From the Authors' Experience

Despite budgetary challenges, university libraries still need to support the teaching and research missions of the institutions they serve and acquire new materials. Many of the tools used by subject specialists in university libraries are the same as those listed earlier in this chapter. At UMD, Saponaro once surveyed subject specialists as to which resources they indicated they personally used in their own selection activities. Their suggestions reflect a wide range of sources beyond those listed earlier in the chapter. Their suggestions included:

- Faculty and student requests
- Trade publications
- Social media (items shared by other people in my subject area and other libraries' Facebook pages)
- Auction catalogs
- Departmental newsletters
- Online discussion groups where materials are suggested
- Course syllabi
- EBay
- Vendor catalogs
- Subject guides created by librarians at other universities

---

is published in *LBTA*. Data for 2016 (the latest available as this volume was being prepared) indicates that serial prices on average increased at a rate of 7.1 percent, with eBook prices increasing at an average rate of 7.21 percent (Barr, 2017, p. 348). Libraries that do not see annual increases in their collections budget are then left with making difficult decisions in terms of what resources to purchase, as well as, in many cases, what existing resources to cancel.

Public Libraries

Public library selection practices are increasingly diverse. This diversity arises from a number of factors, ranging from the population size and geographic area covered and demographic composition of communities served to the collection sizes themselves that range from several hundred titles (Coalfield Public Library, TN, for example) to large research collections of millions of volumes (such as the New York City Public Library). Despite this variety, some generalizations apply to most public libraries. The service community normally consists of unrelated constituencies: persons from various ethnic groups, of all ages, with various educational backgrounds and levels of skill and knowledge, and with a variety of information needs. "Wants" are the dominant factor in selection. Although librarians make the final selection decision, they frequently employ a collection development committee that involves some users. Growth of the collection is modest because of limited stack space and weeding activities focus on the removal of worn-out or outdated materials. Most selections are current imprints, with retrospective buying generally limited to replacement titles.

Additionally, public libraries support a wide range of format options beyond traditional print books, magazines, and newspapers. Other formats found include eBooks, e-magazines, audiobooks, graphic novels, media resources, and streaming audio and video services as well as online databases available both onsite and to remote users. Perhaps the main difference in collection development between public libraries and libraries of other types is the strong emphasis on recreational needs, in addition to educational and informational materials. Trade publishers count on a strong public library market for most of their new releases. Without the library market, book buyers would see even higher prices, because only a fraction of the new books published would become strong sellers, much less bestsellers.

For larger libraries, there are two important issues in selection: speed and coordination. Most of the larger libraries are part of systems with a main library and several branches. The reading public likes to read new books while they are new, not six to nine months after interest wanes. Often interest is fleeting, especially in fiction. Thus, having the new books on the shelf or available electronically and ready to circulate when the demand arises is important. With several service points, a system must control costs. One way to help control cost is to place one order for multiple copies of desired items rather than ordering one now, another later, and still more even later. Multiple copy orders tend to receive a higher discount for the library—although e-resources are an exception to this, as "unlimited" access to titles is often much more expensive than single-user access.

Anticipating public interest is a challenge for the public library, and it probably would be impossible without several sources of information. Unquestionably, the most important source is the selector's inquiring, active mind and the commitment to read, read, read. Material requests and interlibrary loan reports can also provide useful data for selection. As noted by Brady Clemens, "while it is certainly true that not every item requested by a patron for purchase or interlibrary loan should be acquired, taken together the information from patron requests can reveal gaps in the collection that the selector may decide are areas of need" (2014, p. 72).

One of the most useful selection aids available for public libraries is *Publishers Weekly*. Reading each issue cover to cover provides a wealth of information about what publishers plan to do to market new titles. Clues such as "30,000 first printing; major ad promo; author tour"; "BOMC, Cooking and Crafts Club alternative"; "major national advertising"; "soon to be a Netflix miniseries"; or "author to appear on the *Today Show*" can help the selector to identify potentially high-interest items before demand arises. Additionally, *Library Journal* and *Booklist* provide "Prepub alerts" and "upfront preview" listings. All three publications include such information in both their print and online publications. The McNaughton Plan (rental plan) is one way to meet high, short-term demand for multiple copies of print, video, and audio titles—we discuss this plan in more detail in chapter 8.

Check This Out

Anna Mickelsen, the author of one of this chapter's opening quotations, provided several suggestions for additional sources of publication information ("Practice Makes Perfect," *Library Journal* 141, no. 14 [2016]: 34–36). These included:

- Edelweiss+—https://www.edelweiss.plus/—for publisher catalogs
- NPR Books—https://www.npr.org/books/
- NetGalley—https://www.netgalley.com/—access to prepublication galleys (p. 34)

In addition to these suggestions, Mickelsen provides advice on budgeting and collection analysis. Her article is well worth the read.

The need to coordinate order placement is one reason some public libraries use selection committees. Such committees, especially if they include a representative from each service location, reduce the problem of order coordination. In large systems with dozens of branches and mobile service points, such as the Los Angeles Public Library, total representation is impractical. In such cases, the selection committee develops a recommended buying list, and the service locations have a period of time to order from the list. Although it is not a perfect system, it does help achieve some degree of coordinated buying and cost control. Regardless of their library's size, librarians at public libraries all face the challenges of finding the money and time to buy materials. Reviews play a vital role in helping selectors locate the best possible buys with limited funds. *Booklist* is one selection aid to assist in this purpose. Although all the titles contained in *Booklist* are recommended, it also identifies highly recommended titles (called "the best buys"). *Booklist* also reviews a wide range of materials including reference titles. Free online newsletters offered on the *Booklist* website, such as *Online Video Review* (https://www.booklistonline.com/video-review) and *Top*

Check This Out

Abby Preschel Kalan provides advice for selection in the public library environment in her 2014 article "The Practical Librarian's Guide to Collection Development" (*American Libraries* 45, no. 5: 42–44). One of her pieces of advice worth considering concerns cost issues we covered earlier in this chapter:

> Know your budget for purchasing new materials and divide it by 12. This is your guideline for how much you can spend each month. Granted, there are months when you will spend more and others when you find you can spend less. And if you have trouble staying within your budget, look for grants, try to cajole your director into finding a pot of gold for you (show that director your great circ statistics), or excite your Friends group (if you have one) to raise funds for the collection you are hawking at the moment. (p. 43)

Her article is well worth the read.

Check This Out

The Pew Research Center issued a study in 2015 that sheds some light on how public libraries are viewed and used in their communities. The report, "Libraries at the Crossroads" edited by John Horrigan (http://www.pewinternet.org/2015/09/15/libraries-at-the-crossroads/), is an interesting and informative read.

Shelf Reference (https://www.booklistonline.com/top-shelf-reference), are one way of receiving insight on new titles directly in an email inbox.

Another distinctive feature of public library collection development is an emphasis on children's materials. In many public libraries, children's books get the highest use. Most libraries depend on positive reviews when making selection decisions about children's books. Children's collections in public libraries historically have not had a large overlap with collections in local school library media centers. The focus of school library media centers tends to be on curriculum support, while recreational materials have usually been the largest component of public library children's collections. This overlap may be growing, however, as homeschooling becomes more popular and public libraries find themselves needing to meet both the research and recreational needs of younger clientele. One frequently used review source is *School Library Journal* (http://www.slj.com/). Another resource that can be helpful in the selection of these materials is the *Bulletin of the Center for Children's Books*, a publication from Johns Hopkins Press and the Graduate School of Library and Information Science at the University of Illinois at Urbana-Champaign (http://bccb.lis.illinois.edu/).

Two other special features of public library collection development are noteworthy. First, the public library, historically, has been a place to which citizens turn for self-education materials. Self-education needs range from basic language and survival skills/knowledge for the recent immigrant, to improving skills gained in school, to maintaining current knowledge of a subject studied in college. In addition to the true educational function of the preceding, there is the self-help and education aspect exemplified by learning how to repair a car, how to fix a sticky door, how to win friends and

---

Check These Out

Two columns available on the *LibraryJournal.com* website that provide insight into readers' advisory (RA) activities are *RA Crossroads* (http://www.libraryjournal.com, search RA Crossroads) and *Wyatt's World* (http://www.libraryjournal.com, search Wyatt's World), both authored by RA librarian Neal Wyatt. Neal Wyatt and *Library Journal* also teamed together in fall 2017 to launch a daily update newsletter entitled *Book Pulse*. The service is free and can be subscribed to from the *LibraryJournal.com* website (http://www.libraryjournal.com, search Book Pulse). Subscription-based options for title suggestions are available via the suite of *NoveList*® products offered by EBSCO (https://www.ebscohost.com/novelist).

Print titles dealing with genre fiction include the *Genreflecting Advisory Series* produced by Libraries Unlimited. The series currently contains over 40 titles covering genre types (Latino literature, graphic novels, historical fiction, horror, etc.) and some that focus on an age group.

influence people, or how to write code for games or apps. Selecting materials for the varied educational wants and desires of a diverse population can be a real challenge and a specialty in itself.

The last feature of note is the selection of genre fiction, a staple in most public library collections. Most people read only a few types of fiction regularly. Some readers will devour any western about range wars but will not touch a title about mountain men. Learning about the different categories and their authors is not only fun, but useful for anyone developing a public library collection. Review sources such as *Library Journal*, *Booklist*, and *Publishers Weekly* provide coverage of such titles.

School Library Media Centers

Allison Zmuda and Michelle Luhtala observed that the focus of the school library media center (LMC) collection is that it "addresses the learning community's needs, reflects trends in publishing, and evolves with changing needs of learners" (2017, p. 22). While the same could be said of all library settings, Zmuda and Luhtala's remarks were specifically directed at LMC settings. Today's LMCs are very different from those in the past. They no longer are limited to books and other standard library materials, but frequently include media labs or even makerspaces. Some similarities exist among community college, college, and school media center selection and collection development. Each emphasizes providing materials directly tied to teaching requirements, and each uses instructor input in the selection process. Additionally, the emphasis is normally on current material, with limited retrospective buying.

Community college and school media centers share the distinction of having the greatest number and variety of media materials in their collections. Both school and community college media centers must serve an immense range of student abilities. Some LMCs integrate literacy programming into their offerings such as One School, One Book® or One District, One Book® (Read to Them® Foundation, http://readtothem.org/about/) or First Book (https://firstbook.org/) programs, and select titles accordingly for their collections.

Although similarities do exist, the differences between school media centers and other educational libraries far outweigh the similarities. Take curriculum support, for example. School media centers have very limited funding for collection building; in this area they resemble the small public library. With limited funds and limited staff (perhaps only a part-time professional with volunteers covering most of the work), most of the money goes to purchasing items that directly support specific instructional units. Information about grade level and effectiveness in the classroom are two crucial concerns for the media specialist. Grade level information is generally available, but it is very difficult to locate data about classroom effectiveness. Usually, the time involved in gathering effectiveness data is too great to make it useful in media center collection development.

School district or regional programs may impact selection activities. Approved buying lists created by a district selection committee or purchase agreements that require orders be made from specific vendors are not uncommon in the school library setting (Mardis, 2016). Normally, teachers and media specialists serve on committees that review and select items for purchase. Some parent representation on the committee is desirable. Whatever the committee composition, the media specialist must take the responsibility for identifying potentially useful items, preparing a list of suggestions, and securing examination or preview copies for group consideration. Most importantly, the committee must have a clear sense of collection emphasis, of how the items under consideration support current curriculum, and of how the collection will grow as the curriculum evolves. Some LMC specialists are moving toward models where students are involved in the purchase process. Zmuda and Luhtala described such a shift, while media specialist Andy Plemmons provided a concrete example. In his case, students at the elementary school where he worked were given a budget and accompanied him to a local bookshop to select titles for the media center. He noted, "this group of students has a library budget that they have complete control over. Through surveys, they have set purchasing goals to buy new books for the library that kids want to read" (2017). Students at the New Milford (NJ) High School media center have also experienced the same student-curated collecting. A group of students selected by teachers accompanies the media specialist to a local Barnes and Noble to purchase titles for the collection, with Kara Yorio noting, "The student curation has been an un-qualified success—with just a few books seeing a decline in interest" (2018, p. 15).

Published reviews play a significant role in media center selection. Often, school districts secure published reviews and also inspect items before making purchase decisions. The reasons for this are a result of parental and school board interest in the collection's content and the need to spend limited funds on materials that will actually meet teachers' specific needs. The most widely used review sources are *Booklist, Horn Book, School Library Journal, Voice of Youth Advocates, Teacher Librarian,* and resources available through H. W. Wilson such as the *Children's Core Collection.* Online tools such as Follett's *Titlewave®* (https://www.titlewave.com/) or Baker & Taylor's *FirstLook™ for Schools* (http://www.btol.com/pdfs/FirstLook_Schools .pdf) are additional options.

As student body diversity continues to increase in schools, the collection must reflect these changes. Two tools available to assist in creating collections reflective of the population are *MultiCultural Review* and the Children's Book Council's *Goodreads Bookshelf* (https://www.goodreads.com /review/list/7947376-cbc-diversity?shelf=read). *MultiCultural Review* is a journal focused on race, ethnicity, and religious diversity that provides reviews of books and other media with multicultural themes and topics. The Children's Book Council (CBC) founded the CBC Diversity Initiative in 2012

From the Advisory Board

Advisory Board member Susan Koutsky provides her process when selecting materials:

I start building my order by looking at lists of award winners such as the Caldecott Medal, Newbery Award, Pura Bel Pré Award, Geisel Award, the Children's Notable Lists, and others on the ALA/ALSC website (http://www .ala.org/alsc/awardsgrants/bookmedia). The winners of the Coretta Scott King Book Award (http://www.ala.org/rt/emiert/cskbookawards) and my state award winner lists are also important. *Children and Libraries* published a list of awards, with a theme of diversity (Vol. 13, no. 3/Fall 2015). Another important resource is my district colleagues. We have book sharing sessions periodically throughout the year, and a spreadsheet is maintained, so that we can review and select resources recommended by fellow media specialists.

to promote diversity in children's literature. The *Goodreads Bookshelf* is one of the resources they sponsor to provide access to current and backlist titles by CBC-member publishers. Another more general resource is Colorín Colorado (http://www.colorincolorado.org/), a bilingual website with activities, resources, and advice for educators and families of English-language learners.

Special Libraries

There is a saying: "if you've seen one, you've seen them all." That is definitely not true when it comes to special libraries and information centers. In fact, the opposite is more likely the case in that if you have seen one special library, then very likely you have only seen *one*. This class of library (also referred to as corporate libraries or information centers) is the least homogenous of all library types and includes everything from corporate and association, law, government, medical, and museum libraries to centers found in correctional institutions and even theological libraries.

Dividing this category into three subclasses—scientific and technical, corporate and industrial, and subject and research—allows some useful generalizations. However, even these subclasses are not always mutually exclusive. A hospital library can have both a scientific and a corporate orientation if it has a responsibility to support both the medical and the administrative staff. In teaching hospitals, there is an educational aspect to collection building as well. There may even be a flavor of a public library, if the library offers a patient-service program. Some corporations establish two types of information centers, technical and management; others have a single facility to serve both activities. A geology library in a large research university may have more in common with an energy corporation library than it does with other libraries in its own institution. Large, independent, specialized research libraries, such as the Newberry, Linda Hall, or Folger libraries fall into a class by themselves, yet they have many of the characteristics of the research university library.

Despite the wide range of constituencies they serve, special libraries have not influenced professional practice as much as you might expect. This does not mean that special libraries have not made important contributions or developed innovative practices; it merely means that circumstances often make it difficult or impossible for special libraries to share information about their activities in the same manner as other libraries. Their diversity in character and operational environment is one reason for special libraries' modest influence. Another reason is that libraries and information centers in profit-oriented organizations frequently limit the reporting of activities and new systems for proprietary reasons; knowing what a competitor is working on may provide a company with an advantage. Such concerns often limit the amount of cooperative activities in which corporate libraries may engage. One way to learn about an organization's current interests is to study the materials in its library.

As noted by Tara Murray, special librarians "must take an interest in the organization's goals, not just those obviously related to information needs, and they must be able to answer questions in language easily understood by those who control the budget" (2017, pp. 253–254). Most special libraries have very current collections and, in terms of collection policy, would match those of comprehensive research libraries, but without the retrospective element. Despite the heavy emphasis on current materials, virtually none of the best-known selection aids are of help to persons responsible for collection building in special libraries. Most of the material acquired for special libraries is very technical and of interest to only a few specialists; as a result, no meaningful market exists for review services. Recommendations of clients and knowledge of their information needs become the key elements in deciding what to acquire.

Needs assessment activities are also a regular part of the special library program, to a greater degree than in other types of libraries. Selective dissemination of information (SDI) is a technique often used in special libraries. By developing and maintaining user interest profiles, the library can continually monitor the information needs and interests of its service population, allowing more effective collection building. The technique also serves as a public relations activity. Every SDI notification serves as a reminder of the library's existence and value. Usually, SDI services are ineffective for large service populations, because the services are too costly to operate; however, several commercial firms offer SDI-like services. Further, many database services including Elsevier's *ScienceDirect* allow users to create their own SDI services.

Quality or Demand

Librarians have been debating the question of what factor should be the primary driver of collection building—quality or demand—for over 100 years. As we saw in chapter 2, there was a very strong sentiment within the profession in the 19th century in favor of quality. Throughout the 20th century, the trend shifted toward demand driving the selection decisions so that "just in time" collection building (demand driven, or patron driven) started to take hold over traditional "just in case" (arguably quality-based) selection methods. Probably all librarians in the 21st century and perhaps even some in the 20th century would have agreed it would be desirable to have both items of quality and material that reflected what people wanted to read, view, or listen to. The unfortunate reality is a library rarely has such luxurious funding for collections to be able to fully indulge both desires. For most, if not all libraries, demand is the dominant factor. Add to this that "an arguably fine (i.e. high-quality, well-organized, and reasonably comprehensive) collection that fails to meet the actual real-life needs of the scholarly population it is supposed to serve is not a 'good' collection in any meaningful sense" (Anderson, 2011). This sentiment echoes the words of one of our opening quotations by Laura Costello.

The quality issue is still relevant to an extent when it comes to children's selection work. In most cases, this is more theoretical than actual. There are very few, if any, purely quality children's collections any longer. However, some still believe that it is their responsibility to lead children to books of some literary quality. They will use the more popular books as "bait" to get the kids into the library and then try to gently urge the award winners and other "good" books on the children. At the other end of the spectrum are librarians who say it is a triumph to get kids to read anything these days or that children have as much right to read works of less than stellar literary merit as adults do. The authors of this text agree with this latter view, perhaps best summarized by Jennifer Downey (2017), who noted that when it comes to selecting materials,

> Librarians and other bookish types have long had a tendency to look down their noses at less-than-serious genres such as street lit and romance fiction, although this only serves to alienate

potential patrons. Remember that some genres tend to serve as gateway reading for readers working their way up the ladder of serious reading. Also keep in mind that there are those patrons who simply like what they like and don't have a desire to move on to more serious literature—and this is perfectly fine. (p. 176)

Points to Keep in Mind

- Selecting materials for a library collection is often one of the most enjoyable and satisfying activities a librarian performs, even if it is at times complex and difficult.

- Selection decisions are primarily based on rational information; however, there are times when emotional factors come into play.

- Selection decisions rest on a number of factors related to the environment selected for or the resource being evaluated; most of the rest will call for you to make a judgment.

- Factors up to the point of making the quality judgment are straightforward.

- Quality "calls" are the center of the selection decision-making process.

- Reviews are a help in making quality decisions, especially in smaller library settings, but keep in mind only a very small percentage of the annual output of new materials ever get a review.

- Assessing quality effectively takes time, but with practice it is possible to do so even from a basic citation string.

- Perhaps the most difficult "call" is the setting of priorities for acquiring an item—buy now, wait a while, put into the "someday file."

- Time, experience, and making some poor calls are what it takes to become an effective selector. The best of us had to learn from our mistakes. Enjoy the work.

References

American Library Association. 1982. *Diversity in Collection Development: An Interpretation on the Library Bill of Rights*. Chicago: American Library Association. Adopted July 14, 1982, by the ALA Council; amended January 10, 1990; July 2, 2008; and July 1, 2014. http://www.ala.org/advocacy/intfreedom/librarybill/interpretations/diversitycollection.

Anderson, Rick. 2011. "What Patron-Driven Acquisition (PDA) Does and Doesn't Mean: An FAQ." *The Scholarly Kitchen*. May 31, 2011. https://scholarlykitchen.sspnet.org/2011/05/31/what-patron-driven-acquisition-pda-does-and-doesnt-mean-an-faq/.

Barr, Catherine, ed. 2017. *Library and Book Trade Almanac*. 62nd ed. Medford, NJ: Information Today.

Barstow, Sandra, David Macaulay, and Shannon Tharp. 2016. "How to Build a High-Quality Library Collection in a Multi-Format Environment: Centralized Selection at University of Wyoming Libraries." *Journal of Library Administration* 56, no. 7: 790–809.

Bissett, Cindy. 2010. "Developing a Foreign Language Fiction Collection on a Limited Budget." *Australian Library Journal* 59, no. 1/2: 12–22.

Bogart, Dave, ed. 2015. *Library and Book Trade Almanac*. 60th ed. Medford, NJ: Information Today.

Calhoun, John, and James K. Bracken. 1983. "An Index of Publisher Quality for the Academic Library." *College & Research Libraries* 44, no. 3: 257–59.

Chronicle of Higher Education. 2017. "Spending by University Research Libraries." 63, no. 43 (August 18): 79.

Clemens, Brady A. 2014. "Collection Management in Small Public Libraries." In *Creative Management of Small Public Libraries in the 21st Century*, edited by Carol Smallwood, 71–78. Lanham, MD: Rowman & Littlefield.

Costello, Laura. 2017. *Evaluating Demand-Driven Acquisitions*. Cambridge, MA: Chandos Publishing.

Downey, Jennifer. 2017. *Public Library Collections in the Balance*. Santa Barbara, CA: ABC-CLIO.

Garrison, Kasey L. 2013. *"This Intense Desire to Know the World": Cultural Competency as a Personal and Professional Disposition in Collection Development Practices*. Paper presented at: IFLA WLIC 2013—Singapore—Future Libraries: Infinite Possibilities in Session 101—Library Theory and Research. http://library.ifla.org/id/eprint/66.

Hodges, Dracine, Cyndi Preston, and Marsha J. Hamilton. 2010. "Patron-Initiated Collection Development: Progress of a Paradigm Shift." *Collection Management* 35, no. 3/4: 208–21.

Horava, Tony, and Michael Levine-Clark. 2016. "Current Trends in Collection Development Practices and Policies." *Collection Building* 35, no. 4: 97–102.

Imamoto, Becky, and Lisa Mackinder. 2016. "Neither Beg, Borrow, Nor Steal: Purchasing Interlibrary Loan Requests at an Academic Library." *Technical Services Quarterly* 33, no. 4: 371–385.

Johnson, Liz, and Linda A. Brown. 2009. "Book Reviews by the Numbers." In *Assessment of Library Collections in a Consortial Environment: Experiences from Ohio*, edited by George Lupone, 80–110. London: Routledge.

Johnson, Peggy. 2013. *Fundamentals of Collection Development and Management*. 3rd rev. ed. Chicago: American Library Association.

Mardis, Marcia A. 2016. *The Collection Program in Schools: Concepts and Practices*. 6th ed. Santa Barbara, CA: Libraries Unlimited.

McColvin, Lionel Roy. 1925. *The Theory of Book Selection for Public Libraries*. London: Grafton & Company.

Metz, Paul, and John Stemmer. 1996. "A Reputational Study of Academic Publishers." *College & Research Libraries* 57, no. 3: 234–47.

Mickelsen, Anna. 2016. "Practice Makes Perfect." *Library Journal* 141, no. 14: 34–36.

Monaghan, Peter. 2017. "As Libraries Go Digital, Costs Remain Tangible." *Chronicle of Higher Education* 63, no. 43: 80.

Murray, Tara E. 2017. "An Unlikely Collaboration: How Academic and Special Libraries Can Help Each Other Survive." *Journal of Library Administration* 57, no. 2: 249–58.

Neville, Tina M., and Deborah B. Henry. 2014. "Evaluating Scholarly Book Publishers: A Case Study in the Field of Journalism." *Journal of Academic Librarianship* 40, no. 3/4: 379–87.

Perdue, Jennifer, and James A. Van Fleet. 1999. "Borrow or Buy? Cost-Effective Delivery of Monographs." *Journal of Interlibrary Loan, Document Delivery & Information Supply* 9, no. 4: 19–28.

Plemmons, Andy. 2017. "Student Book Budgets: A Walk to Avid Bookshop." *Expect the Miraculous: Barrow Media Center*. Athens, GA: David C. Barrow Elementary Media Center. February 3, 2017. https://expectmiraculous.com/2017/02/03/student-book-budgets-a-walk-to-avid-bookshop/.

Tyler, David C., Yang Xu, Joyce C. Melvin, Marylou Epp, and Anita M. Kreps. 2010. "Just How Right Are the Customers? An Analysis of the Relative Performance of Patron-Initiated Interlibrary Loan Monograph Purchases." *Collection Management* 35, no. 3/4: 162–79.

Vincent, Alyssa. 2017. "Breaking the Cycle: How Slow Fashion Can Inspire Sustainable Collection Development." *Art Libraries Journal* 42, no. 1: 7–12.

Walters, William H. 2008. "Journal Prices, Book Acquisitions, and Sustainable College Library Collections." *College & Research Libraries* 69, no. 6: 576–86.

Way, Doug, 2017. "The Shifting Nature of Academic Library Collections." *Library Connect: Modern World Trends in Development of Academic Libraries*. http://nur.nu.edu.kz/handle/123456789/2515.

Yorio, Kara. 2018. "Success of Student-Curated Collection." *School Library Journal* 64, no. 3: 15.

Zmuda, Allison, and Michelle Luhtala. 2017. "Turn Up the Volume in the Library through Personalization." *Teacher Librarian* 45, no. 1: 21–25.

Zuccala, Alesia, Raf Guns, Roberto Cornaccia, and Rens Bod. 2015. "Can We Rank Scholarly Book Publishers? A Bibliometric Experiment with the Field of History." *Journal of the Association for Information Science & Technology* 66, no. 7: 1333–347.

7
Collection Management and Technical Services

Selecting, purchasing, and receiving are functions that exist within the realm of collection development. However, how those services are organized varies from library to library.
—Laurel Tarulli, 2014

For many years, when a library needed additional staff and there was no funding for new positions, staff were reassigned from technical services to other areas of the library.
—John Sandstrom and Liz Miller, 2015

The major shift from print to electronic resources (e-resources), including born-digital resources, in library collections over the last decade has impacted every area in academic libraries. While anecdotal evidence is shared with regard to the ways in which certain specific functions in technical services is changing, it is much more of a challenge to grasp the big picture of the various changes transpiring in technical services.
—Jeehyun Yun Davis, 2016

Two main reasons for shelf-ready implementation across libraries of all sizes are: (1) the need to improve materials turnaround time and (2) the desire to redeploy staff for other projects or tasks.
—Consortium of Academic and Research Libraries in Illinois (CARLI), 2015

Providing access to "information" is a multifaceted undertaking, especially for libraries. Today's information environment is vast in terms of content and formats. Libraries face informational needs both educational and recreational in character. As we saw in chapter 3, technical services plays a key role in the CM life cycle. CM is about identifying appropriate materials, within funding limits, that address the service population's wants and needs. However, acquiring the material does very little to provide effective access to the content of those items. Doing nothing more than acquiring materials and making them available to people is a little akin to a poorly organized book sale. That is, lots of items, perhaps sorted into broad topics—with people having to spend substantial time determining if there is something of interest.

To provide effective (well, more effective) access to content, libraries "add value" to the materials they make available. That activity requires substantial staff efforts and some funding that goes beyond salaries. Those efforts take place in the part of the library organizational structure that the profession labels *technical services*. Traditionally the profession divides library functions into three broad categories—administration, public services, and technical services. As information technology (IT) services and support play an increasing role in libraries, this function can be considered a fourth function, if it is not grouped within technical services.

Certainly today, the labels and organizational structure differ among libraries. Whatever the label, the reality is the tripartite aspect remains. There is a fundamental requirement to administer library activities—such as secure funding, oversee the safety and maintenance of the facility, and handle personnel matters. Then there are activities that require the staff to directly interact with members of the service population—public services. There are also activities that allow the library to attract people to use its services and programs (the value-added function), which rarely requires direct interaction with the public—technical services. For a library to be effective and provide high-quality service, all three basic functions are essential and they must interact harmoniously with one another, no matter what label the library applies to them. Harmony is not always easy to achieve.

Technical services (TS) and collection management, as the opening Tarulli quotation suggests, have always been interlinked. The relationship has not always been the easiest of internal library relationships—occasionally there is some disharmony. When selectors are not part of technical service personnel, minor issues of who does what and when can, over time, become operational roadblocks. Perhaps the most common issues relate to money (no surprise there)—how much was allocated, how much remains—does that include encumbered funds, what is the last date to submit an order request, what is the status of a request made, and the like.

Another factor is there is often a dual reporting relationship in terms of CM and TS staff. That is, people who are trying to interact effectively, but who have different direct supervisors who may have different priorities, can find the relationship waters muddy at times. These have been potential concerns for years. In addition, the increasing prevalence of electronic resources and how they are acquired has added more potential challenges to work relationships. (See chapter 10 for a discussion of the nature and challenges of consortial decision making.)

Collection management involves some elements of all three basic library functions—funding requirements (administrative), user needs assessment (public services), and acquiring appropriated items (technical services)—making it something of a challenge to place structurally. Traditionally, technical

---

From the Authors' Experience

As an example of how labels for technical services units can change, in early 2017, the Acquisition and Metadata Services departments of the University of Maryland, College Park (units formerly composing Technical Services) were reorganized into four departments under the unit heading of Collection Services:

- Acquisitions and Data Services (ADS)
- Continuing Resources and Database Management (CRDM)
- Discovery and Metadata Services (DMS)
- Original and Special Collections Cataloging (OSCC)

Although some of the unit titles are very different from their earlier versions, the mission of the unit remains to acquire, describe, provide access to, maintain, and enhance the discovery of collections and support the research and teaching goals of the university.

---

service operations had four broad categories of activity: acquisitions (securing resources), cataloging/metadata services (adding value to those resources), preparation (processing physical items for use by the public), and bindery (a preservation process). The first and last categories are part of effective collection management. Staffing of these functions can be a challenge, even with advances in technology. Sandstrom and Miller, in one of our opening quotations, noted the shifting staff from technical service to other areas. Certainly budget issues have played some role in the reduction in staff. However, technology and shared technical service activities are the primary causes for the changes.

Given the ongoing transforming impact of technology on technical services, libraries have been applying different labels to their "backroom" activities. Some libraries are employing Collection Management as the overall label, as CM plays a role in those backroom functions to a greater or lesser degree. Another factor for finding a new label for such activities is the rather common linkage in people's minds that technical implies technology. Thus in a library there can be the notion that technical services and information technology are the same thing. How the changes will play out long-term is impossible to predict beyond the idea there will be a continuing evolution in terminology.

Technical Services Functions

There are three core activities that you found and still find in the "backroom" of most libraries—acquisitions, cataloging, and physical processing. A fourth common unit is a bindery/repair unit. Increasingly, there may be an independent "electronic resources" unit or perhaps "system development" or information technology department included as a part of TS (perhaps including the library technology support personnel). Neither CM nor electronic resources/system/information technology support fit comfortably into either technical or public services. Before exploring some of the reasons for the discomfort, we will look briefly at the character of core technical services functions and how they have changed relatively recently.

From the Advisory Board

Advisory Board member Wendy Bartlett notes that many TSD departments in public libraries increasingly include Information Technology departments, becoming the "ITSD," or Information and Technical Services Department.

Cataloging and Metadata Services

Over time, there has been a change in the nature of "backroom" operations. Cataloging—adding value to information resources through enhancing accessibility in various ways—is one of these activities that has undergone significant change over time. Cataloging was once a very labor-intensive activity for a library before there were efforts to share cataloging work among libraries. Over the past 100+ years, those sharing activities have increased to the point that for the majority of U.S. libraries, cataloging is something they purchase rather than doing the work in-house. A number of libraries even purchase their physical resources (books and media) "shelf ready" (a catalog record ready to add to a database and processed ready to shelve in the public stacks).

Whether the work is done in-house or not, cataloging plays a major role in the value-added operations of a library. It produces a record for each item in the library's collection. (Those records are part of what is now called metadata—data about data/information.) In the distant past, that record took the form of a 3x5-inch card with a hole punched in the bottom center. In actuality, there were a number of cards for each item that provided access to the item's content. In today's digital world, that record is a MARC record (machine-readable cataloging) that serves the same function, but with more means of access to item content.

One factor in the reduction of staffing in a cataloging department was the shift from a card to a digital format. Cards were filed in the "public card catalog"—cabinets with drawers specifically designed to house the cards. "Cards" is the appropriate word, as each item added to the collection had a set of cards. At a minimum there were three cards: an author card, a title card, and a shelf-list card. Nonfiction items had several cards indicating subjects covered by the item. Public catalogs were usually divided into two broad categories—author/title and subject. There was a shelf-list catalog as well in the technical service area more often than not, and the shelf-list catalog contained one card for each item filed by call number (in shelf order). Obviously the library staff filed the cards, which was a labor-intensive and rather complex activity. ALA originally published a 50-page book on rules for proper catalog card filing in 1968, which was most recently updated in 2002

Check This Out

The standard online catalog or OPAC is a well-known feature in libraries. However, another tool for libraries to manage access to resources is the knowledge base or KB. Kristen Wilson provides an in-depth exploration of knowledge bases in the 2016 *Library Technology Report* issue "The Knowledge Base at the Center of the Universe" (52, no. 6; https://journals.ala.org/index.php/ltr/issue/view/606) devoted to the topic. It is well worth the read.

(American Library Association, 2002), showing that the practice was long-lived in libraries. For most libraries, such filing activity was a two-person process (it was very complex). One person would file the card where that person thought was the correct location ("above the rod"). A second person then checked the location and, if the card was properly located, "pulled the rod," dropping the card in place and reinserting the rod that held the cards in the drawer. When the shift to digital records occurred, this labor-intensive activity was no longer necessary and perhaps the equivalent of several full-time staff positions became available for other tasks.

Shared cataloging is another factor in the attrition of a library's cataloging staffing pattern. The notion of sharing such work is far from new—the Library of Congress (LC) started offering printed card sets to other libraries in 1901. Over the next 60-plus years a variety of projects were created to share cataloging information as well as other technical service activities (acquisition, for example). Today's largest online public access catalog (*WorldCat®*) came into existence in 1967. Certainly it was a far cry from today's giant as it was focused on Ohio academic libraries (its first name was the Ohio College Library Center).

During the card catalog days, LC's card sets were a boon for many libraries. Creating a "bib record" for an item took time (again there was a large body of rules for creating a proper record). In addition there was the matter of creating the necessary additional cards (typist pools were rather large). Thus, if you could identify an LC card set, staff time was saved. The challenge was finding the set. LC might be one of the largest libraries in the world, but it takes time for it to process all its acquisitions and it has different priorities for processing items than other libraries, especially public and school libraries. Thus, in pre-OPAC times, there was a substantial amount of local cataloging taking place that duplicated the efforts of many other libraries acquiring the same item.

Providing subject access was another complicated task in pre-OPAC times. While it still takes time and thought to select the best subjects for inputting in a digital record, the process is faster than when subject cards were part of a set—gone is the typing of such headings on cards. One reason for the time needed for assigning subjects is the goal of being as consistent as possible in those assignments and terminology. Libraries do this by using "controlled vocabularies" (thesaurus is another label) as the source of a subject heading. Perhaps the world's largest subject thesaurus is the Library of Congress's *Library of Congress Subject Headings* (you can gain a sense of both the size of the list and its complexity by visiting http://loc.gov/aba /publications/FreeLCSH/freelcsh.html). A less complex list of subject headings is *Sears Subject Headings* (http://www.hwwilsoninprint.com/sears.php).

A final element in how cataloging enhances users' access to collection content is the creation of a "call number." (We must note that there are other cataloging activities that we will not cover—authority files, which still exist digitally, and "tracings," for example—that contributed to the staff workload in the card set days.) A call number places like items together in the public area as well as providing an order for items within a topic. This "number" is what allows public service staff to shelve items in a manner that makes it easier for the public to locate items of interest.

Works of fiction have a call number that reflects the author, title, and perhaps the copy number (popular titles often have several copies and the copy number is what identifies the specific copy). Nonfiction call numbers have a classification code (first line), author code (second line), and perhaps publication date and/or copy number. (The call number is what the public and staff see on the spines of bound items on the library's shelves. Placement of call number labels on other formats can present challenges in terms of visibility.)

The classification code for an item in the U.S. almost always comes from one of two sources: either the Library of Congress Classification (LCC) or the Dewey Decimal Classification (DDC) system. The LC system is alphanumeric in character (https://www.loc.gov/catdir/cpso/lcc.html) and is designed for larger institutions needing greater flexibility in placing items into their collections, while the DDC (https://www.oclc.org/en/dewey/features/summaries .html) is numeric-based and has been adopted by many public and school libraries. Once again in the card catalog days, call numbers had to appear on every card and someone had to type that number. This is another task that is no longer necessary; however, that does not take away the need to generate call number labels for items going into collections today.

Metadata

We have relatedly made the point libraries are about enhancing people's ability to gain access to information resources for learning purposes or for personal enjoyment. In the days of predominantly print resources, physical card catalogs were the primary access to such library resources; less than perfect certainly but very useful. If nothing else in those days a person could physically browse the collection in the stacks. Online catalogs with features such as keyword searching further improved "findability" or "discoverability." Today, however, the variety of formats available has made the landscape much more complex. Unlike physical copies, e-resources are not easily physically browse-able and this is where metadata comes into play.

What is metadata? At its most basic library meaning, metadata is data that increases a user's ability to identify and gain insight about a collection item regardless of its format (analog or digital). Although the idea and term came about due to the advent of digital formats, the fact of the matter is the card catalog was/is a metadata system. It provides information about a resource—author and title, for example; metadata just greatly expands that description detail, if you will. Thus, the idea of providing details about a resource is not new to librarianship. What is new is the depth of analysis that is possible and the ways in which you can apply that information for library purposes as well as creating greater user access.

Metadata applications are varied, with most industries having their own approaches (information producers, libraries, music, motion picture and television, and museums, for example). They also have varying labels for the components of their application. For libraries, we believe the best component labels are those of the NISO (National Information Standards Organization, https://www.niso.org/). NISO's purpose is to provide a place where "publishers, libraries, and software developers turn for information industry standards that allow them to work together"—http://www.niso.org/home). There are three major components to the NISO metadata standards—descriptive, structural, and administrative.

As you would expect, the first component provides guidance for how to describe an item, such as the old familiar author and title information. It goes far beyond the cataloging rules of the past. (You can gain a sense of the depth of possible analysis by reviewing *Understanding Metadata: What Is Metadata, and What Is It For?* written by Jenn Riley for NISO [2017], which defines metadata and describes how it is stored and shared, as well as reviewing notable languages and tools and future directions for metadata.)

Structural metadata identifies information about the organization of the item, such as the order of a soundtrack or chapters in a book, which can also be useful to the end user. It also can provide linkages/relationships among resources. A library special collection example might be the relationship(s) between manuscript folders, print resources, and images. Another feature is it can link related files such as JPEG.

On the administrative side, the process handles such concerns as date of creation and how it was created—essential technical data like resolution or compression, for example. It is about long- and short-term issues related to digital files. One area of concern for CM personnel is this is where information about intellectual property rights resides as well as limitations on usage of the item (DRM—digital rights management). We look at DRM concerns in chapters 12 and 15. This is also where preservation issues are recorded, such as "refreshing cycles" and possible migration concerns. (Most digital records require some "refreshing," e.g., reviewing to ensure that they still operate properly.) In the days of videocassettes, libraries with large collections of such items actually played the tapes at least once a year. Another example is NASA found over 12 percent of their early computer files had corrupted over time, which might have been avoided had the tapes been refreshed more often.

This book will not go into more detail about cataloging and metadata, but before we move on, we do want to recognize the timing implications associated with materials that undergo these processes. As Knowlton (2017) observed, there is a need to balance the creation of metadata with the accessibility of items for users. He stressed that "the longer a book waits for cataloging, the less likely it is to circulate. What may have been a 'hot' book when it was first acquired 'cools off' as it waits to be cataloged. The implications for cataloging workflow management are many and profound" (p. 6).

Check These Out

It goes almost without saying: there are a host of online resources to learn about various aspects of cataloging and metadata. We offer just a couple of sites you may wish to visit:

For those of you with more than a passing interest in library history, a fun resource to learn more about the card catalog is *Evolution of the Library Card Catalog* (http://libraryhistorybuff.org/cardcatalog-evolution.htm), while LC's "What Is a MARC Record and Why Is It Important?" (https://www.loc.gov/marc/umb/um01to06.html) provides an overview of the history of MARC records and their significance.

The American Library Association has an online guide to cataloging resources available (http://libguides.ala.org/catalogingtools/classification) that provides links to standards and tools for cataloging and classification.

Karen Coyle's 2005 "Understanding Metadata and Its Purpose" (*Journal of Academic Librarianship* 31, no. 2: 160–63) looks at metadata for document-like objects and introduces Dublin Core, Metadata Object Description Standard, and Metadata Encoding and Transmission Standard. She then discusses the meaning of metadata for library cataloging.

Another title that fully explains the concept of metadata in nontechnical terms is Jeffrey Pomerantz's 2015 *Metadata* (Cambridge, MA: MIT Press). In it, he explains metadata's role and purpose in our digital world.

Acquisitions

We will only briefly mention acquisition processes here, as we have a full chapter on the topic (chapter 8). Normally, acquisition units are very much a "backroom" activity, with very little direct contact with the public, unless they run a "help desk" service for resource access questions. However, it is a TS unit where there is ongoing interaction with collection management personnel. Once an item is selected there are many steps to secure the item for the library. This is where collection development funds are controlled and spent. We explore all these concerns and much more in the next chapter.

Serials Control

Serials are a staple component of all library collections (academic to special library) regardless of the serial's format (analog or digital). Further, even in today's digital environment most libraries still subscribe to print versions of some serial titles. People still enjoy sitting and reading a print magazine or newspaper. Thus, almost all public libraries have a selection of paper-based serials. Some libraries, particularly larger research and public libraries, also maintain microfilm collections of selected titles that were originally received by the library in print. Newspaper collections, if not duplicated online, are the titles frequently held in microfilm, but the format itself is not without its drawbacks—such as users' unwillingness to learn how to use microform readers.

Just what is a serial? Like breakfast cereals, they come in several varieties as well as variations within a variety. (We explore the concept of serials in more detail in chapter 12.) The major commonality is they are ongoing publications—no "one and done" for such materials. One variety of serial is the magazine—the type of publication we all encounter at retail checkout counters, especially in grocery stores. The intended audience is rather substantial; some titles are truly mass market in scope while others may be narrow in subject focus but still have a wide readership. Newspapers are another mass market serial that almost all academic and public libraries make available to their service populations. Related to magazines is the journal, and while the two terms are frequently used interchangeably, there are important differences.

The three most important differences between journals and magazines are size of audience, cost, and preservation concerns. Journals focus on a relatively narrow topic and have an equally narrow potential readership—essentially scholars or very well-informed readers. Given those two facts, it probably is not surprising that journal subscriptions are substantially higher than magazines. Since scholarship advancements are at least partially dependent upon what has gone before and one characteristic of serials is distributing information quickly in modest length, maintaining back files of journals is important to both scholars and society. There are some lesser recognized serial materials, at least on the part of the general public. The varieties of serial publications are covered in chapter 12.

Cost, unpredictability, as well as the library's need to be accountable for how it manages all its resources, create a need to manage serials. There are a number of serial-related questions that management/control systems can answer. Perhaps the most common question is, "Has the current issue of __ arrived yet?" Another very common question is, "Is it time to bind/store __ last complete volume?" While fewer and fewer libraries are maintaining microfilm back files of serial titles, the arrival of microfilm reels and when

---

Check This Out

Gary W. Ives provided a very thorough review of serial management functions and needs in his 2013 work *Electronic Journal Management Systems: Experiences from the Field* (Hoboken, NJ: Taylor and Francis).

---

to replace print copies with the microfilm is another issue. When to renew a subscription is another question most effectively answered by the control system.

Unpredictability is a serious challenge for libraries and is a key factor in serials work. It takes time and energy to ensure all the issues paid for have in fact arrived and to decide how long to wait for a missing issue. In the manual system days, the person doing the check-in routines was expected to also "keep an eye open" for missing issues. When there was a problem, a decision to "file a claim" or not took time. One of the staff time-saving features of an integrated library system (ILS) serial control module is it can generate claim forms automatically when an issue fails to arrive when predicted. There is still staff required to review the forms and make the appropriate decision regarding sending the claim, but that is far less than in pretechnology days.

The check-in process is also faster as a result of having an ILS serials control system, but only by a little. A person can more quickly locate the appropriate check-in record; however, the process of property marking and adding a security tag has not changed for hard copy issues. Paper issues of a magazine or journal lacking those two features essentially means whoever is holding it "owns it." The retail trade has a concept called "shrinkage" that applies to merchandise unaccounted for. Libraries have a similar problem, even with a materials security system in place. (See below for a discussion of physical processing for collection materials.)

Preservation is a CM/TS concern, especially in academic libraries. Serial preservation can be a significant cost as well as physical space concern, especially for academic libraries, as is availability of the material itself. (For example, in summer 2018, libraries received notice a major microfilm publisher was undergoing reorganization, leaving libraries wondering if they would receive issues they had paid for and if alternatives existed for materials they once received in microfilm.) School and special libraries rarely face major preservation concerns for serials. It is the larger public and most academic libraries that need to address how to handle quantities of lost issues of serials of various types. Such libraries have some obligation to preserve information for future users, even something that may seem of little interest beyond today. We explore this topic in more depth in chapter 14.

Physical Processing

While much has changed in technical services over the past 60-plus years, the basic components still exist, if in a rather different form. As long as libraries acquire physical formats for their collections, there will be a backroom process that physically prepares such items for public use.

The key purpose of processing activities is to provide a link between the bibliographic record and the physical item. The linkage takes several forms. In most cases today, the main link is a barcode label. A second link is a label attached to the item that reflects the call number associated with the bib record. The barcode provides a unique number for an item and is also used on library cards. A barcode for each authorized user allows the item to circulate and the library to know who has the item. (In the days of manual systems, the process was more complicated—labels, book pockets, book cards, all with the attendant author, title, and call number. This is another example of a TS labor-intensive activity.)

In our digital library world, most physical items going into the collection have at least two electronic tags affixed to them in addition to the call number label. One is the barcode mentioned above. The other is a security tag of some type, most commonly a strip, placed out of view. Another e-tag that is becoming more common is an RFID (Radio Frequency Identification) tag. The barcode allows for the linkage of the item to a borrower's record. The security strip helps control the "shrinkage" mentioned above, that is, the disappearance of items from inventory. Such strips will not deter a committed thief—all systems have some weaknesses, but what they are most effective for is keeping honest people honest. An RFID tag can perform all of the above tasks; however, at least today, they are more often less comprehensive in character.

If you were to create a library from scratch today, the comprehensive RFID would be a sound choice—one tag does the work of three. However, given the cost considerations for RFID, that is not something you are likely to do and you will almost always be in an environment where there are legacy collections with their dual tagging systems. Two of the most common reasons for moving to RFID tags for selected collections (local history, reference, etc.) is to enhance the speed of the self-checkout (for both the staff assisting and those using self-checkout procedures) and to more effectively handle inventory activities. One example of the inventory aspect is searching for misplaced books—a rather common occurrence when users "help" the staff by reshelving items they examined but did not check out. A staff member, using an RFID wand, can just walk through the stacks and the radio frequency tag will signal the item's presence—assuming the item has not truly gone missing.

When it comes to physical processing, like cataloging, the process remains a library necessity. Both are required to build an accessible collection of information resources for the library's service population. As noted in the opening quotation from the Consortium of Academic and Research Libraries in Illinois (CARLI) report, "shelf-ready" is one of the more recent

Check These Out

A very good and concise overview of RFID written by a long-term expert on library technology issues is Richard Boss' 2003 "RFID Technologies for Libraries" (*Library Technology Reports* 39, no. 6: 6–58), while ALA maintains an online guide to RFID technology (https://libguides.ala.org/rfid-libraries).

Another sound overview is Yogesh K. Dwivedi, Kawaljeet Kaur Kapoor, Michael D. Williams, and Janet Williams' 2013 piece "RFID Systems in Libraries: An Empirical Examination of Factors Affecting System Use and User Satisfaction" in the *International Journal of Information Management* (33, no. 2: 367–77).

A good survey that discusses the benefits and challenges of implementing RFID is Mohd Kamir Yusof and Md Yazid Saman's 2016 article "The Adoption and Implementation of RFID: A Literature Survey" in *LIBRES: Library & Information Science Research Electronic Journal* (26, no. 1: 31–52.)

changes to how a library may handle backroom activities. Perhaps the most succinct definition of "shelf-ready" is "a collection of materials received from a vendor or publisher that comes with catalog records and physical processing already in place" (2015, p. 1). The CARLI report noted that the two most common reasons libraries opt to implement such a program are to speed up the process from the time the library places an order until it is available to users, and to free up staffing FTEs for reassignment.

A shelf-ready program can help the library free up some staff time for reassignment. Most such programs start small and slowly build up. Both the library and vendor need some time to work through the inevitable glitches that are common in two-party projects. The most common starting point is with a few firm orders (see chapter 8 for a discussion of order types). Another option is continuation or series order—both would bring in only modest numbers of items while working out the details for a more full-blown program. Shelf-ready may free up some staff time but it *will not* save money. The library essentially trades cash for time.

Shelf-ready is a concept rather than one specific package; you customize it for your library with a vendor. Packages range from loadable bib records to what is almost as simple as ordering the item, taking it out of the box, and putting it onto the shelf. (Two such vendors are *GOBI® Library Solutions* from EBSCO, https://gobi.ebsco.com/, and Baker & Taylor's *TechXpress,* http://www.baker-taylor.com/ps_details.cfm?id=339).

Box-to-shelf is more a theoretical idea than a practical matter. Prudent libraries engage in monitoring activities; regardless of the complexity of the shelf-ready program, mistakes can and do happen even in a long-standing program. There probably will be some staff time savings, but not as much as perhaps projected. You can gain a sense of the staff efforts involved in such programs by visiting Michigan State University library's "Shelf-Ready Processing" (https://www.lib.msu.edu/techservices/procedures/shelfready/). A Web search will produce many more examples.

Bindery/Repair

In the above sections we have noted how technological developments have affected technical service operations and its staffing patterns. Bindery and repair activities have not experienced as much change—it was, and still is, very much a local hands-on operation. There has been a decline in the volume of bindery work in some libraries as digital versions replace some former print subscriptions, or as funding constraints require libraries to adopt a "do not bind" policy. Based on the authors' experience, that decline has not been as great as libraries had thought would occur.

In terms of repairs, little has changed and it would be the rare library that did not do some in-house repair work from time to time. Repairs require that some decision take place—repair, replace, discard, or preserve in present condition, for example. Who makes such calls? Certainly CM staff will be involved, since there may be costs to consider. Perhaps a senior staff member will have some input as well as the acquisitions department. Probably the factor that carries the most weight in the decision-making process is potential future use, followed closely by cost considerations.

While repair work is an in-house activity, bindery processes are almost always done by a commercial bindery. There is an exception to that when the item needing treatment is valuable. In such cases, a conservation/preservation specialist does the custom work in order to maintain the most value for the item in question. Commercial binderies do the bulk of the general

---

From the Authors' Experience

The following is a minor personal example, but one that helps you understand why we noted that bindery work is not inexpensive. Evans planned on giving five family members a special gift: a bound copy of his father's college graduation yearbook (back then departments issued yearbooks). Evans had a PDF of the original volume (96 pages), which he took to a local printer for an estimate. The printing cost for what would be the "text block" was just over $80, including taxes. The print shop said they would secure an estimate for the binding. Sometime later, the printer called to say the estimate was in and that Evans might like to sit down. The cost to bind the five 96 pages would be $879 and change.

There are two important points to note about this example. First and foremost, certainly the per volume cost would drop as more copies were added—essentially the primary cost is the set-up charge. In essence, the process was a small custom job. The point to keep in mind is library binding is also more or less custom work—yes, many items are sent to the bindery in one shipment, but rarely more than two of the same title in a shipment. (Most libraries employ a different color "cloth" for titles shelved near one another and each volume has different spine information, which makes the process close to "custom" processing.)

The second point is that libraries almost always have a contract with the bindery firm, which ensures some level of ongoing work for the firm. The higher the expected volume of work, the greater the discount off the "list price" the library receives. While there is an initial setup cost as indicated above, once the bindery is aware of the parameters for a library, those remain standard and sending volume information can be automated.

Our basic point is that traditional library binding practices cost a substantial amount of money, and such costs should not be ignored when developing a collections budget.

---

bindery work for libraries. The Library Binding Council and NISO have established library binding standards.

Without doubt, preserving serial titles represents a cost/space concern for many libraries, especially academic. There are several options for resolving the question of what to do with serial titles. The traditional approach has been to bind issues in physical works containing one or more volumes of a serial title. This approach is not inexpensive and represents a potential ongoing annual expense. In general, school libraries do not do a large amount of outside bindery work since it is often easier to replace volumes than prepare and send them to a bindery, while public libraries may choose to selectively bind such items as genealogical materials, reference works, or local history titles.

Boxing loose serials is another option. Although this practice is not frequently used today, it is still seen in public and school libraries. As you might expect, there are tradeoffs involved with each option. (Traditional binding is the most secure and long-term preservation alternative, but at a high cost.) Enclosed boxes (string ties or Velcro® closures, for example) provide protection at a far lower cost than binding. One of the major downsides to this option is that issues can be and frequently are misfiled by both staff (especially when there are multiple volumes of a title in a single box) and well-meaning users who believe they are helping. Another concern is it is easier to remove an article from a single issue than it is from a bound book. (There is a problem of "mutilation" that almost all libraries face.)

From the Authors' Experience

The University of Maryland Libraries, recognizing both finite shelf space and funding, enacted a policy for subscribed journal titles in *JSTOR* so that print *JSTOR* titles received at campus libraries would be retained only until they appeared in the online database. At that point, print copies would be discarded. Exceptions were made case-by-case for titles such as those in Art and Music, which would require continued availability of the print edition. (See: https://www.lib.umd.edu/collections/policies/jstor -retention-policy).

Check This Out

There is an "industry" serial that covers library bindery interests that has existed under several titles over the years. (Title changes were and are common with serials and present CM staff with some challenges in how to handle such changes.) Older titles were *Library Scene* and *New Library Scene*, and since 2006 the title has been *ShelfLife* (Jupiter, FL: Library Binding Institute, and Book Manufacturers' Institute 2006–). It is a publication that is worth looking at from time to time, especially if the library has a traditional bindery program.

A related and even less expensive option is to store issues in open-sided plastic or metal containers (sometimes referred to as Princeton files). Being open on one side makes them quicker to use, but it also makes them even more susceptible to misfiling concerns. Another concern is that unless the file is at or near capacity, individual issues can be damaged.

Some libraries have opted to do nothing about back issue retention. We are unaware of any academic library to do this, but for mass market serials there is little need for all libraries to preserve back issues of, say, *TV Guide* or the now-defunct *Cat Fancy*. Deciding what to do with serial back files is certainly a CM concern, especially as print magazine titles continue to become less and less frequently issued. However, it probably will involve input from various stakeholders as it involves costs and library mission and goals.

Serial preservation activities, assuming there is an effort to do so, is a labor-intensive activity. An ILS serial module can alert the staff when a title's volume is complete, but it cannot provide information that the library still has all the issues and certainly is unable to gather the issues from the shelves. All the issues may or may not be on the shelf. Missing issues raise several questions—how long do we search for the items, do we try to locate a replacement copy, and should we leave the issues that are present in the public area or place them in a holding location? (RFID tags will help speed the search and save some staff time but the questions will remain.) To answer such questions the staff needs to know the importance of the title as well as its usage. These are things CM staff is most likely to know.

Shipping and Receiving

Shipping and receiving is perhaps the most overlooked backroom activity in libraries. Frequently it is a subunit in the acquisitions department because acquisitions generates the highest volume of work. It is also an area that you seldom hear about except when items go missing ("It must have gone missing in the mail room"). We all have had the experience when we are certain we mailed something, yet an item fails to arrive where we thought it would. There are times we are right and times when we are wrong. The point is, you need to carefully plan shipping and receiving activities as they are the starting and, sometimes, the ending point for technical service activities.

In middle- and large-size libraries it is not uncommon to receive a number of boxes from several vendors on the same day, and perhaps have some material to pack and ship back. Without a carefully designed work space and work plan, it is possible to create problems for the library. Items vendors claim were shipped and items the library claim never arrived, vendor shipments mixed up, missing invoices, and the like can and do arise, even in well-planned units. How well the unit performs will have an impact on technical services workflow.

You might think that shipping is not a significant library activity beyond outgoing first-class mail. Certainly smaller public libraries, school media centers, and special libraries have low levels of shipping; however, they often engage in ILL activities that do involve shipping and receiving. Most medium-size academic and public libraries have a rather active shipping operation that is more complex than just ILL transactions.

There are two major categories beyond ILL that are rather common—leased material and approval plan material. (We discuss these programs in more detail in chapter 8.) Leased material, which allows libraries to stretch limited funds, come in and are returned on schedule. Approval plans, as the name suggests, arrive for the staff to review to keep some items and return the remaining items.

Keeping ILL, leased, and approval items separated from one another and from firm order materials is critical for the library. Any mixing of the items causes delays, claims, extra work, and, occasionally, money. Effective shipping and receiving, although not often thought of as a major player in library operations, is, in fact, very important. One primary reason is that it is the unit that begins the workflow for technical services.

Technical Services Workflow

When you think about the above activities you might well think all the work takes time. Indeed it does take time; exactly how much time is an important consideration for both the library and the service population. Certainly performance times are important in terms of all library activities; however, the technical service workflow and the time it takes between requesting an item and having it available to the end user is perhaps the most important one.

Initially you might think that the time an item takes to end up on the shelf doesn't have an impact on the library's public image. The fact of the matter is it does play a surprisingly large role. When the time is reasonably short—a month or so—most people rarely think about the issue. When the timeframe runs to months they do notice. If the library does not correct the problem(s), its public image will suffer. Why would this be the case?

Providing access to information resources is the fundamental purpose of libraries. Another purpose is to make the resources available in a timely manner—time of need. It really does not matter what type of library you consider; timing matters. Teachers and professors have time constraints (topics to cover within a term) and if a requested item arrives after the point of need, the library's image will take a hit (at least in the point of view of the

Check These Out

Rhonda Glazier and Sommer Browning published an article in 2017 about coordinating the place where bottlenecks in workflow most often arise—"Acquisitions to Cataloging: Examining the Handoff in Electronic Resources Workflow" (*Against the Grain* 29, no. 1:40–43).

Gwen M. Gregory discusses how she developed the Resource Acquisition and Management Department at the University of Illinois–Chicago Library in her article "For the Duration: Creating a Collection Maintenance Unit in Technical Services" (*College & Research Libraries News* 78, no. 8: 440–43).

Kari Schmidt and Christine Korytnyk-Dulaney wrote about the issues of rethinking technical services in a digital environment in their 2014 piece "From Print to Online: Revamping Technical Services with Centralized and Distributed Workflow Models" (*Serials Librarian* 66, no. 1: 65–75).

One article on workflow that had a special connection with one of this book's authors was Sally Gibson's 2015 "Utilizing a Time to Shelf Study to Start a Conversation on Change" (*Performance Measurement and Metrics* 16, no. 1: 28–33). The reason for the connection was her article was about how Milner Library (Illinois State University) engaged in studying and shortening the time it took to get items through technical services. Evans had been a cataloger at Milner Library many years ago. The day he started as cataloger his workspace had eight standard single-faced library shelving defining the area—filled with books to be cataloged. There was a three-year backlog on those shelves. The fact of the matter was such backlogs were the norm in academic libraries at the time. Current technologies and sharing work efforts have allowed a great reduction in time to shelf from years to weeks to days.

person requesting something). Public libraries also face pressure to have a short time to shelf period, particularly for a new bestseller title or one about a "hot" current topic. The point is people do tend to share their negative experiences with an organization more often than they share the positive ones. Time to shelf is a small but important part of the library's public image.

Technical services has an overall workflow rate as well as internal workflow rates for each of its units. A sound, coordinated flow is essential in order to avoid having a series of peaks of high volume followed by very slow periods. A steady flow can help reduce staff stress, assure the budget is neither over nor under spent, and make materials available to the public in a timely manner. As you might guess, having three or more units, each with an internal system for handling its workload, can make coordinating those flows into a single overall effective flow a challenge.

If the library makes use of a management tool kit known as work analysis or "scientific management," coordinating the various flows will be easier. Work analysis is a set of tools that allows you to review and assess work activities. There are methods of charting workflow, for charting decisions, charting the relationship of people and equipment, assessing how a task is best carried out (time and motion), as well as a number of other aspects of how, when, and where a task takes place. (This book will not explore these various tools; however, there is an excellent book that does so: Richard Dougherty's 2008 *Streamlining Library Services: What We Do, How Much Time It Takes, What It Costs, and How We Can Do Better*, Lanham, MD: Scarecrow Press.) Workflows require monitoring and controlling as circumstance, technology, and corporative activities evolve. There is no such thing as one and done when it comes to workflows; if nothing more, personnel will change over time.

Collection Management and Technical Services

We opened this chapter with a brief discussion of where CM fits into the structure of a library. There is little consensus as to what the best structural placement may be, but what is clear is there *must be* solid working relationships between all the working parts.

Some years ago management consultants were charging substantial fees for presentations on how to avoid having organizational "silos." Silos are the organizational structures that foster unit independence while not encouraging cooperation, coordination, and sharing. From a library historical perspective, traditional library structures can create, even if unintentionally, an environment that can lead to silos. All of us, practitioners and soon to be practitioners, understand the primary purpose of libraries—to provide a designated service population (a public) with access to information. However, a basic fact of library life is that very rarely do all the resources that are desirable to provide the best possible access exist. Further, all too often, the available resources are barely adequate to do more than provide a marginally acceptable level of service. Libraries must constantly try to "do more, better, and faster, and with fewer resources." Such an environment can lead to the creation of silos.

Labels/words do matter when it comes to thinking about organizational unit status. If the library's primary purpose is to provide access to information for its public, there is at least a hint of importance in the "pecking order" of units in public services versus technical services. That order can become a factor in how much true cooperation, coordination, and sharing will occur.

Collection management can be a force in reducing potential silo building in libraries. To be effective, CM *must* draw upon information/work activities from both public and technical service units. This chapter has illustrated the linkage between CM and backroom functions. It is a truism that in order to create useful collections CM personnel *must* understand who uses what, when, and how. Further, it is also essential to have information about what the library's public wants, needs, and, perhaps, demands (chapter 5 dealt with understanding the library's service population). CM is an effective bridge between units.

Another element that has and can help reduce library silos is technology. The starting point might reasonably be placed when the ILS became commonplace. The online catalog was and is very different from the card catalog.

Check These Out

You can find a thorough review of all the technical services functions, including in-depth information about cataloging in G. Edward Evans, Shelia S. Inter, and Jean Weihs' *Introduction to Technical Services,* 8th ed. (Santa Barbara, CA: Libraries Unlimited, 2011).

A good article covering how technical services has evolved and is changing is Jeehyun Yun Davis' 2016 piece "Transforming Technical Services: Evolving Functions in Large Research University Libraries" (*Library Resources and Technical Services* 60, no. 1: 52–65). Davis provided one of the opening quotations for this chapter, and her article provides good food for thought. The article includes an illustration showing the overlap that occurs between technical services functions and other key library services such as scholarly communication, collection development, and digital initiatives (p. 59).

OPACs have made for a much more interactive environment between library staff, regardless of where they are placed in the library's operational structure, and the library's public. Real-time information about order status, tags, bindery status, etc. are possible. From a CM perspective, perhaps "patron driven selection" is the most interactive possibility (see chapter 8 for a discussion of this concept).

In other chapters throughout the book, we look at examples of where cooperation, coordination, and information sharing is critical to a library's success.

Points to Keep in Mind

- Traditionally there was a three-part structure for libraries that consisted of administration, public services, and technical services. In some libraries, information technology has become a fourth major function.

- Over the past 30-plus years the structure has flattened in many libraries and that, along with technological developments in the field, has caused some rethinking of labels for the component parts of the structure.

- Although technical services functions are often behind the scenes (literally in the basement or backroom of libraries), the functions they perform are an essential part of the CM life cycle.

- In today's changing digital world there are four units you can expect to find in most libraries' backroom operations: acquisitions, cataloging/metadata, serials, and processing (including bindery).

- There is little doubt that in the library world traditional technical services have experienced the highest degree of change.

- The workflow within technical service units has a substantial impact on the library's image—time to shelf.

- Collection management can be a bridge between the traditional labels and the changing thought about library structure as its effectiveness is dependent upon close cooperation and coordination on the part of all units.

References

American Library Association. 2002. *ALA Rules for Filing Catalog Cards.* 2nd ed., edited by Pauline A. Seely. Chicago: ALA.

Consortium of Academic and Research Libraries in Illinois (CARLI). 2015. *Exploring Shelf-Ready Services: Technical Services Committee's 2015 Annual Project.* https://www.carli.illinois.edu/exploring-shelf-ready-services.

Davis, Jeehyun Yun. 2016. "Transforming Technical Services: Evolving Functions in Large Research Libraries." *Library Resources and Technical Services* 60, no. 1: 52–65.

Knowlton, Steven A. 2017. "The Older It Gets, the Colder It Gets: Time Required for Cataloging of a Book Affects the Likelihood of Its Circulation." *Technicalities* 37, no. 5: 1–6.

Riley, Jenn. 2017. *Understanding Metadata: What Is Metadata, And What Is It For?* Baltimore, MD: NISO. January 1, 2017. https://www.niso.org/publications/understanding-metadata-2017.

Sandstrom, John, and Liz Miller. 2015. *Fundamentals of Technical Services.* Chicago: American Library Association.

Tarulli, Laurel. 2014. "Who Does What? Building Relationships Between Technical and Public Services Staff." In *Rethinking Collection Development and Management,* edited by Becky Albitz, Christine Avery, and Diane Zabel, 31–40. Santa Barbara, CA: Libraries Unlimited.

8
Acquisitions

Acquisitions librarians have the unenviable task of balancing and stretching the budget between print sources that remain popular and the explosion of electronic resources while maintaining a balanced collection that meet or exceed our patrons' needs.

—John Ballestro, 2012

The name "acquisitions" itself is a little misleading today. While librarians still purchase print materials that have dedicated shelf space and collection counts in general go up rather than down, many of the resources obtained are not only not physical, but also not permanent.

—Frances C. Wilkinson, Linda K. Lewis,
and Rebecca L. Lubas, 2015

While most people intuit that one or more professionals within a library select those resources to which the library provides access, rarely is much thought given to the process by which this takes place.

—Jesse Holden, 2017

We have seen in prior chapters how collection management (selectors) have the responsibility of analyzing the user community, developing the collection policy, and identifying materials for selection in alignment with both user needs and the policy in place. Once these steps are complete, the collection management cycle continues and the work is carried on through acquiring identified resources. In the past, most acquisitions work was done mainly behind closed doors (which perhaps should have had a sign on it that read "magic happens here," as evidenced in the opening quote by Jesse Holden). However, in today's complex budgetary and information resources environment, acquisitions and collection management staff increasingly must work hand in hand in order to ensure selection decisions become reality in both a timely and cost-effective manner.

There are three broad categories of acquisition work—making decisions regarding how to acquire an item, working with vendors/suppliers to secure the desired materials, and maintaining the appropriate financial and other records related to each acquisition transaction. Although perhaps not as enjoyable as seeking out new items for the collection and at times extremely challenging, acquisitions work can be rewarding for those up to the challenge.

In the past, an acquisitions librarian needed basic skills including rapid decision making and fiscal management. Today, those skills are still important. However, acquisitions staff must also be good communicators, be technologically savvy, be able to deal with the "legalese" found in licensing/leasing agreements, and be more and more a diplomat when dealing with colleagues and consortia members. NASIG, an independent organization focusing on information resources management, developed a series of competencies for librarians whose work focuses on print and electronic resources management. Core competencies for electronic resources librarians as identified by the NASIG Core Competencies Task Force (NCCTF) included the aforementioned fiscal management and licensing knowledge, but also an understanding of metadata, standards, and emerging practices (NCCTF, 2013, pp. 2–3). Add to these skills those identified by the NCCTF (2015) for print resources management, which include the ability to troubleshoot problems and evaluate workflows (p. 1). Since most collections include both print and online components, it is safe to say that those involved in acquisitions work must have an increasingly broad set of skills, perhaps none more important than "[f]lexibility, open-mindedness and the ability to function in a dynamic, rapidly changing environment" (NCCTF, 2015, p. 10).

To be fully effective, all those involved in collection management (including selectors) and acquisitions personnel must have a very cooperative working relationship. Poor coordination can and does result in duplication of effort, slow response time, and high unit costs. Achieving coordination requires that all parties understand the work processes, problems, and the value of one another's work. As noted by the authors of one of the opening quotations of this chapter (Wilkinson, Lewis, and Lubas, 2015), "Acquisitions personnel increasingly have the opportunity to work across the library organization in more dynamic and proactive ways. These personnel are playing an expanding role in the shaping of the library's collection of information" (p. 3).

Acquisitions departments have several broad goals. Five common goals are:

1. To acquire materials in as timely and cost-effective a manner as possible.

2. To maintain a high level of accuracy in all work procedures.

3. To keep workflows simple, in order to achieve the lowest possible unit cost.

4. To provide data on items acquired to collection management and administration.

5. To develop close, friendly working relationships with other library units and with vendors.

Speed is a significant factor in meeting user demands as well as improving user satisfaction. An acquisitions workflow that requires three or four months to secure items available locally in bookstores or that is not able to take advantage of short-term vendor discounts on packages or resources will create a serious public relations problem and will not generate goodwill among public services or collection management staff, not to mention users. A system that is very fast but has a high error rate will increase operating costs, and will waste time and energy for both departmental staff and suppliers. Studies have shown that, in many medium-sized and large libraries, the costs of acquiring and processing an item are equal to or greater than the price of the item. (See Edna Laughrey, 1987; David C. Fowler and Janet Arcand, 2003; and Kate-Riin Kont, 2015 as examples.) By keeping procedures simple, and by periodically reviewing workflow processes, the department can help the library provide better service. Speed, accuracy, and thrift should be the watchwords of acquisitions departments. Certainly, online ordering, electronic invoicing, and credit card payments greatly enhance the speed with which the department can handle much of the traditional paperwork.

Acquisitions is often turned to by collection management and library administration to provide the data required for a number of reporting requirements, usually in a short timeframe. This data can include order reports by subject area for discipline accreditation evaluations, cost per use data for subscriptions to electronic resources, reports on the number of gift items received or microformats held, or the number of turnaways (access rejections) received by eBooks in a specified time period. All of these require the ability of acquisitions personnel to interpret the information request and provide a response in a timely manner. While some data requests, such as those needed for serials review and cancellation projects, may have a long lead time, this is usually not the case. In truth, time is of the essence for most data requests, and the characteristic highlighted earlier of flexibility on behalf of acquisitions staff comes into play.

The underlying key to successful acquisitions programs is developing and maintaining good relationships both within and outside the library. Good internal working relationships with the entire library staff are of course important; however, there are three areas where these relationships are of special importance—with public services staff, the cataloging/metadata services department, and with library and organizational budget and administrative offices.

Needless to say, public services staff, including selectors, are the most important group for the department to establish positive relationships with, as it is their input that generates primary work activities for acquisitions units. Librarian selectors, reserves and interlibrary loan units, and teaching faculty are generally good at accurately supplying 80 to 90 percent of the information necessary to order an item. However, tensions can develop if that percentage drops by very much and the department staff has to spend more time tracking down or verifying required information, including licensing requirements or fund codes to use for the acquired item. When users submit requests, the amount of time establishing what is really wanted and the library's need for the item goes up dramatically. The flow of material into and out of the department can become an issue in technical services, especially the metadata services/cataloging department. Both acquisitions and metadata/cataloging seek to have a reasonably smooth flow throughout the year—with few peaks and valleys. However, the incoming requests are the driving force behind that flow, and keeping that flow constant is often a challenge, especially near the end of the fiscal year (FY).

Another tension point that is becoming more and more common is the use of outsourcing for a substantial amount of technical service processes. That is, ordering items to arrive shelf-ready and with the cataloging record already loaded or ready to be loaded into the library's ILS or discovery system. This is the theory, but in reality it does not always work out this way. John Ballestro, one of the authors of our opening quotations, detailed an outsourcing pilot undertaken at Southern Illinois University Library. Due to technological constraints and the resulting impact on other technical services units, the pilot was not as successful as hoped, leading Ballestro to remark, "What is frustrating from an acquisitions standpoint is the workflow and workload seem to be dependent on outside forces that we cannot control" (2012, p. 121). One tension arises over whose responsibility it is to check on the quality of the incoming material. Catalogers generally do not have the background to deal with the financial aspect of the "preprocessed" material while acquisitions personnel rarely have the background to verify the cataloging data. Working out a reasonable solution may take time and cause tensions in previously good relationships.

Senior administrators are another group with a vested interest in the department's operation, especially its fiscal management. The most senior administrator (director) is responsible for everything that takes place in the library. For almost all libraries, the two top components in the operating expense (OE) budget are salaries and the funds for collection development. The two categories often represent 80 percent or more of the OE. Needless to say, senior administrators must closely monitor those expenditures. In some larger libraries, the administrative office has taken on handling the acquisition unit's financial recordkeeping in order to have a better day-to-day picture of the total budget situation.

Beyond the senior administration there are outside groups that have an interest in the department's fiscal activities. Certainly the most prominent of those is the business office of the library's parent institution. Its interest is in ensuring that the acquisitions department's financial recordkeeping is in compliance with its regulations as well as maintaining proper accounting practices. It does not have an interest in what materials are acquired for the collection as long as the purchases fall within the permitted categories—books, journals, etc. Normally there is at least a monthly interaction between the units as the parent business office sends out a monthly report on what it has on record as the expended and unexpended library funds.

Other business offices that the department interacts with fairly frequently are the vendors and acquisition departments in libraries in a consortium that acquires material for the group. Perhaps the more challenging of the two are the other libraries where the sharing of the payment to the vendor of the product has to be coordinated. It is likely that a consortium with more than a dozen members will have libraries operating on different FY (fiscal year) calendars. Making a payment for a shared purchase may be a challenge for a member or two near the end of their FY. We explore consortial activities in more detail in chapter 10.

Acquiring Materials

There are five steps in the overall acquisitions process:

- Request processing
- Verification

- Ordering
- Reporting (fiscal management)
- Receiving orders

The first four phases of the process are described in this chapter. The process of receiving orders is described in more detail in *The Complete Guide to Acquisitions Management* (Frances C. Wilkinson, Linda K. Lewis, and Rebecca L. Lubas, 2nd ed. Santa Barbara, CA: ABC-CLIO, 2015).

At the start of the acquisitions process (request processing), before the departmental staff can decide on what method to employ to acquire an item, they must engage in some preliminary sorting and checking activities. Incoming requests must be reviewed, be they paper or virtual in format, to establish both the need for the item and that all of the required ordering information is there. (This is not to suggest the department will override selectors' decisions when we say "the need for the item.")

Requests for the library to acquire an item for the collection can arrive in print or electronic format. The library may have a standard print or online suggestion or order form available, or orders can be submitted directly by selectors via an online acquisitions system. Items may also be brought to the attention of the acquisitions unit via an email or telephone call with a selector/faculty member. In these cases, such requests must be translated into a standard format. If the selector does not do so themselves, a staff member converts such requests to the department's standard format and the verification work begins. Verification is perhaps the most interesting and challenging duty in this department. The attempt to establish an item's existence when there is very little information is similar to detective work.

When the requests are from CM personnel, there is normally only a modest need for verification work. Orders submitted outside of an automated acquisition system via a paper form may have some missing ordering information such as the ISBN (International Standard Book Number, a unique number for each title and its format—paperback, eBook, or hard cover) because the source the selector used did not contain the information. The department must also check to determine if the item is already on order or owned. Many, if not most, nonfiction works cover more than one topic. For example, for a book with the title *History of the Political Impact of the Women's Movement in the United States*, three or more selectors might have seen information about this title at nearly the same time and each submitted a request. Even when the ILS or acquisitions system allows selectors to see the status of an on-order title, it is possible that an earlier request for the item has not been entered, so no record exists and the selector submits a duplicate request. In addition, there are times when announcement of a new release does not mention it is part of series to which the library has a standing order. If the item is online and requires a license, this must be verified as well (we cover licensing of e-resources in chapter 13). Last but not least, there may be times that a legitimate request for a duplicate copy will be made—such as in the case of ordering an online version of an older print title in order to facilitate class use. Thus, the department checks all requests to determine the need for the item (not to second guess selectors, but to avoid unwanted duplication and waste limited funds). Pre-order checking is facilitated by online acquisitions systems or through such tools as ProQuest's *OASIS®* (Online Acquisitions and Selection Information System), the Library Corporation's Online Selection & Acquisitions system (*OSA*™), or *GOBI® Library Solutions* from EBSCO.

When the request is from users, such as through a mediated Demand-Driven Acquisition (DDA) program (further discussed later in this chapter), the department must not only check to see if the item is in the queue to be ordered, on order, or received and being processed, but also if it is already in the collection in another format. If the order is to be rejected for any one of these reasons, the user must be notified in a timely manner.

Acquisition Methods

Once details of the order are verified, three important decisions must be made before the order is placed:

- Which acquisition method to use.
- What vendor to use.
- What funding source to use.

There are eight standard methods of acquisition—firm order, standing order, approval plans, blanket order, subscriptions (for serials departments), leases, gifts, and exchange. Regardless of the acquisition method chosen, one thing to keep in mind is that an order is a legal contract between the library and the vendor. This means a vendor could force payment even if the library experiences a financial setback. The all too common setback is for the parent institution to "take back" some of the funds allocated to the library. The parent body does not usually specify where the library finds the required amount, merely that it deliver the required funds. Unless the collections budget is specifically exempt from the "take back," most of the time the only uncommitted funds in the amount required are those in the collections budget. Most library vendors are well aware of this type of event and almost never press their legal right to payment for items that were on order when the financial "claw back" occurred.

Firm Orders

A firm order is the usual method of acquisition for titles that the library *knows* it wants. Such orders are normally one-time purchases, and a majority are for print or electronic monographs, DVDs/videos, maps, scores, or other similar formats. This method is also used for other resources such as journal back files or some primary source databases where no future additions or updates are expected. Firm orders are also the best method to use for the first volume in a series, even if it is possible that the entire series may be ordered at a later date. Firm orders can be sent directly to a specific publisher, but for the most part, online acquisitions systems such as those mentioned earlier can manage both firm and approval plan orders. Occasionally, firm order titles are not available via the online system, or cannot otherwise be fulfilled by that system in a time frame needed (as in the case of "rush" orders). In these situations, acquisitions personnel may select either a physical or online retail outlet (discussed later in this chapter) for the item in question.

Standing Orders

Unlike firm orders that are intended to be one-time purchases, standing orders are an open order for all titles fitting a particular category. They are best suited for items that are serial in character and for which the library is confident it wants all the publications as they appear. Some examples are a numbered or unnumbered series from a publisher that deal with a single subject area (for example, titles in the *Animation: Key Films / Film-makers* series by Bloomsbury Publishing—https://www.bloomsbury.com /uk/series/animation-key-filmsfilmmakers/). Often publishers issue annual volumes that the library knows it will want on an ongoing basis. Other broad categories are the irregular publications of a professional society, memoirs, or special commemorative volumes, for example. Vendors offering standing order services include Brodart, whose *FASTips* service focuses on authors, series, or bestsellers (http://www.brodartbooks.com/library -collection-development/fastips/page.aspx?id=261), and ProQuest's Standing Order program (http://www.proquest.com/products-services/Standing -Orders.html). Of note is that Brodart's program includes both English- and Spanish-language materials.

An advantage of using the standing order method is that the library places the order for the series/items rather like it places a journal subscription, saving the time and energy of library staff. Once the standing order is placed, the supplier (vendor or producer) automatically sends the items as they appear along with an invoice, so there is no need to place individual orders for each title in the series. As they are an ongoing commitment much like a serials subscription, some thought should go into the decision process when considering series items. When the selector knows that the reputation of the publisher or editor of the series is sound, it is probably best to place a standing order. However, especially in academic libraries, existing standing orders can be the result of a faculty member's request from long ago, and if the library does not periodically review its standing orders, it may find that there is no longer an interest in the series' subject. The result is money being spent on less useful items.

The greatest drawback to standing orders is their unpredictable nature in terms of both numbers and cost. Since production rates cannot be predicted, standing orders cannot be paid for in advance as can be done with a subscription. Certainly there are fewer problems about numbers for regular series, but their cost per item may vary. When it comes to publishers' series or irregular series, a library may go years without receiving a title, then receive several volumes in one year. Looking at past experience and using an average amount is a safe approach; however, the library is seldom able to set aside exactly the right amount. Committing (encumbering) too much money for too long may result in lost opportunities to acquire other useful items. Committing too little can result in having invoices arrive and not having the funds available to pay them. Standing orders are a valuable acquisition method, but one that requires careful monitoring throughout the year.

Approval Plans

Approval plans are closely related to standing orders in that they involve automatic shipment of items to the library from a vendor along with automatic invoicing, after acceptance by the receiving library. The differences are that the approval plan normally covers a number of subject areas and the library has the right to return titles it does not want within a contractually specified timeframe (unless the approval plan items arrive preprocessed or shelf-ready, in which case returns are normally not permitted). Although viewed by some as a way of bypassing title-by-title selection and the expertise of the selector (see, for example, John Stephen Brantley, 2010), as noted

---

Check This Out

While approval plans are normally associated with print or electronic monographs, Lisa Hooper describes the process of creating an approval plan for music scores in her 2016 article "The Art of Crafting Music Score Approval Plans: An Ongoing Process" (*Collection Management* 41, no. 4: 228–35). It is an interesting read.

---

by Alison Griffin and Sarah Forzetting (2012), "the sheer volume of tasks that today's . . . librarians face makes them a necessity" (p. 17).

Approval plans can be established for print or electronic titles, or a combination of both. In the past, most academic libraries made it a regular weekly "event" for selectors to review and sign off on print approval plan titles received. While this practice is not as widespread today, or may be required only for titles from specialized foreign language or arts materials, the underlying assumption was that selectors or collection management staff can make better decisions about an item's appropriateness by looking at the item before committing to its purchase.

Advantages of approval plans are that they can save staff time and effort when properly implemented, and can allow libraries to collect materials as they are published. However, if they are not thoughtfully established or carefully monitored, they can be costly. There is research evidence that indicates the approval plan can result in a substantially higher number of very low or no-use items being added to the collection. (For examples of research in this area, see: Evans, 1970; Evans and Argyres, 1974; Tyler et al., 2013; and Ke et al., 2017). Further, as noted by Johnson (2016), "While approval plans have the benefit of automating the decision-making and purchasing process, there may be some subjects where the research and teaching needs of an area can't be appropriately supported through an approval plan" (pp. 492–493).

The key element in making the approval plan a cost-effective acquisition method is creating a sound "profile" with the plan vendor. The profile can be created by the subject selector alone, or can also be created in conjunction with the acquisition librarian. It is also important to consult with those parties interested in CM, such as teaching faculty or selectors from related fields/subjects. A profile outlines the parameters of the plan and covers issues such as subjects desired, levels of treatment (undergraduate, graduate, etc.), languages/countries coverage, no reprints, no collections of

---

Check This Out

Sarah Tudesco and her colleagues Julie Linden and Daniel Dollar from Yale University created a method that would not only allow assessment of approval plan purchases, but also enable data to be manipulated by such factors as purchase order type, fiscal year, or library. Their process is described in "Do We Approve? New Models for Assessing Approval Plans" (in *Proceedings of the 2016 Library Assessment Conference: Building Effective, Sustainable, Practical Assessment—October 31–November 2, 2016*, edited by Sue Baughman, Steve Hiller, Katie Monroe, and Angela Pappalardo, 157–165. Washington, DC: Association of Research Libraries. http://old.libraryassessment.org/bm~doc/30-tudesco-2016.pdf).

reprinted articles, no consumables or spiral-bound titles, and so forth. The more time devoted to profile definition, as well as monitoring the actual operation of the plan and making adjustments, the greater the value of an approval plan to the library and the acquisitions department.

Demand-Driven and Evidence-Based Acquisitions

A growing subset of approval plan work are the concepts of demand-driven (DDA) and evidence-based acquisitions. As Karin Fulton (2014) noted, "Dwindling budgetary resources across the board for all types of libraries have necessitated more creative approaches for acquisition and increased emphasis on meeting the immediate needs of the patron" (p. 22). Both public and academic libraries have addressed these needs through implementing patron-driven (PDA) or demand-driven (DDA) selection processes for eBooks and, to a lesser extent, streaming media. In demand-driven models, patrons ultimately make the decision to "trigger" or purchase a title that appears in the local catalog or discovery system. Just as with their print approval plan predecessor, DDA programs are built upon profiles targeted to a specific library. Unlike approval titles, which are normally physical books sent to a library, DDA title records are loaded into the catalog or discovery system at predetermined intervals. To the patron, the title appears as if it is "owned" by the library—with perhaps the only indication that is not the case being a "DDA title" tag next to the online access link in the item record.

Once a DDA title is located by a patron, most are accessible for the first few minutes for free (known as a "short-term loan"), after which point a small charge is incurred by the library. After a specified number of uses, a "trigger" is achieved and the title is automatically purchased at full price. Any use after the purchase is free. Ann Roll observed that "current DDA practices in some libraries demonstrate that DDA is actually returning the approval aspect of approval plans. However, users, rather than librarians, approve the titles" (2016, p. 5). As such, DDA marks the gradual shift away from the traditional model of "librarian as selector."

One of the most concerning aspects of DDA/PDA models is budgeting. Robert Cleary (2015) noted, "Demand-Driven or Patron-Driven Acquisitions (DDA/PDA) present budgeting challenges and require some measure of control, either through limiting available records to a single subject collection or setting dollar limits with vendors" (p. 163). Unlike print titles, DDA titles can be available in one of several user models, including one-user, three-user, unlimited, and nonlinear lending. Each model has its own price point, with unlimited use generally the highest cost. Libraries who set their

---

Check This Out

PDA/DDA programs are not limited to eBook, audio, or video formats. The University Library at the University of Illinois at Urbana-Champaign developed a DPP (Data Purchase Program) as a means of acquiring data sets requested by students and faculty with the goal of making the data available for future campus use. Details of the program are outlined in Beth Sheehan and Karen Hogenboom's 2017 article "Assessing a Patron-Driven, Library-Funded Data Purchase Program" (*Journal of Academic Librarianship* 43, no. 1: 49–56), and at https://www.library.illinois.edu/sc/purchase/.

default DDA purchase as unlimited may find their budget rapidly spent. Another unanticipated expense is staff time. Some titles in the DDA pool may have publisher restrictions associated with them or are otherwise ineligible for a short-term loan. These titles then may become mediated requests, where information is sent to the library—generally the acquisitions unit—to review and approve or reject. Such reviews, particularly if they require input from a selector, take time. Tony Horava (2017) summed up the implications of entering into a DDA program when he observed, "[T]here are philosophical issues, budgetary issues, and logistical/workflow issues that all need to be addressed" (p. 16).

Evidence-based acquisition (EBA) is another form of patron-driven acquisition that is beginning to grow in popularity. The evidence-based concept first appeared in medicine in the 1990s and since that point has appeared in other fields including nursing, management, and librarianship. In this model, decisions are based upon "finding, appraising and implementing the evidence" based on professional judgment (Koufogiannakis and Brettle, 2016, p. 6). EBA is an access-to-own model where funds are paid upfront for a specific collection of materials for a specified time period (fiscal year or semester). The amount paid is generally less than the full cost of the collection. During the length of the examination period, all titles in the collection are available to patrons via the catalog or discovery system, as if they were owned by the library. Patrons access the titles the same way they would in a regular DDA program. The difference, however, is that at the end of the access period, the list of title use is reviewed by the library. Those titles that showed high use are purchased using the prepaid funds and remain in the library's permanent collection, while access to other titles is removed. As noted by Ying Zhang, "In a nutshell, libraries eventually only acquire what users need. The expenditures are easier for the libraries to predict and access easier to manage. On the other hand, because of the upfront access fees, the publishers realise a faster cost-recovery and more accurate profit forecast than the PDA model. In concept, evidence-based acquisitions appears a win-win for both libraries and publishers" (2014). To date, major publishers such as Cambridge (https://www.cambridge.org/core/services/librarians/evidence-based-acquisition), Elsevier (https://www.elsevier.com/librarians/article-news/evidence-based-ebook-purchasing), and JSTOR (https://www.jstor.org/librarians/products/books/acquisition-models) have started evidence-based programs, while consortia such as Orbis Cascade have entered into evidence-based agreements for member libraries (https://www.orbiscascade.org/evidence-based-acquisitions). EBA is a model worth watching.

Blanket Orders

A blanket order is a combination of a firm order and an approval plan. It is a commitment on the library's part to purchase all of something, usually the output of a publisher, or a limited subject area, or from a country. In the case of a subject area or country, there is a profile developed between the library and the blanket order vendor. The materials arrive automatically along with the invoice, thus saving staff time. Another advantage for country blanket order plans is that they ensure the library acquires a copy of limited print runs. (It is not uncommon to have very limited print runs of scholarly items in many countries, where print on demand is also not an option. Waiting for an email or print announcement may mean that there are no copies available to purchase.) One example of a blanket plan is the Cooperative Acquisitions Program for international materials administered by the Library of Congress (LC; https://www.loc.gov/acq/ovop/). Any library that wishes to acquire materials from a specific country covered by the program deposits funds with LC annually to cover the projected cost of materials.

Like the standing order, the major drawback of blanket order plans is predicting how much money the library will need to reserve to cover the invoices. There is even less predictability with blanket order plans because there are more variables. Another drawback is that blanket order agreements may include an option to return unwanted titles, but generally it is too expensive or time consuming to do so, and libraries keep all titles received via the plan. Further, some blanket orders may outlive their original intended purpose and thus not continue to be an effective use of funds. Pongracz Sennyey advocated that libraries regularly assess the performance of blanket orders much as they do standing or other subscription orders. He suggested two methods by which to do so, monitoring "the quantity of books received, both in their totality as well as within the different subject areas stipulated by the profile; and [assessing] the quality of the books received" (1997, p. 446).

Subscriptions

Subscriptions refer to any resource with an annual payment to retain access. Journals, magazines, newspapers, and databases all fall into this category. Some types of resources, such as streaming media, can be either firm orders or subscriptions, depending on the content and the pricing model. Subscriptions are a combination of standing and blanket orders, and a library may enter a subscription for a given timeframe just as an individual does for personal magazines. Managing a half dozen or so personal subscriptions is not difficult for an individual. However, when a library subscribes to hundreds or even thousands of journal titles, services of a subscription agent are a necessity. Susan Davis and her colleagues conducted a study of library practices when it came to subscription agents. Their survey included academic, public, corporate, and school libraries and results indicated 96.3 percent of survey respondents used a subscription agent, while 75 percent of respondents also managed some subscriptions directly with the publisher (2015, p. 244).

The advantage of a subscription agent is that rather than going through an annual renewal process, many libraries enter into an agreement to automatically renew subscriptions until the library requests a cancellation (known as 'til forbidden orders). This saves both the library and agent/vendor staff time and paperwork. This is a cost-effective system for those titles the library is *certain* are of long-term interest to end-users. (We discuss bundled subscriptions or "big deals" in chapter 12.)

Check This Out

For all the service they provide, subscription agencies are currently facing challenges to remain relevant. David Stuart discusses the future of subscription agents in the era of open access in his 2016 article "A Changing Role in a Changing Market" (*Research Information,* Feb/Mar, no. 82: 4–6). It is an interesting read.

Leases

Leases are now the primary means for handling e-resources (aside from journal back file sets or other primary source materials that are one-time purchases). The decision to lease is almost always in the hands of the supplier rather than the library, although sometimes a library can "buy" the product, usually at a substantially higher price. The difference between buying and leasing has significant implications for the library and its users. Essentially the library pays for *access* to the information for only as long as it pays the annual fee. At the end of a lease, the library generally loses all access to the material it was paying for, although some suppliers will provide long-term access to the material that was available during the lease period (otherwise known as perpetual rights). Chapters 12 and 13 provide more information about this and other issues related to electronic resources.

Most public libraries face the challenge of having a high demand for popular titles; however, that high demand only lasts a short time. The challenge is how to meet the demand and yet not spend too much money on short-term interest items. One solution libraries employ is to buy two or three copies and set up a reservation/request queue for those wishing to read/listen to the item. The public understands the challenge, but still do express frustration with the reservation system. Both Brodart and Baker & Taylor provide another method of leasing (renting) popular materials in formats such as print, audiobook and DVD. Brodart's McNaughton® program offers plans for adult and young adult titles (http://www.brodartbooks.com /subscription-services/page.aspx?id=100226). A similar program is offered by Baker & Taylor's Book Leasing service (http://www.baker-taylor.com/pdfs /Book_Leasing.pdf). In either case, libraries rent multiple copies of an item for the duration of the title's popularity and return the unneeded copies. Both plans offer high-demand items that the vendor staff selects. A library cannot order just any book; it must be on the vendor's list of high-demand titles. There are advantages to a lease program for popular materials. First off, items are received are shelf-ready—and can go directly to users. Further, users are happy because of shorter waiting times for the latest bestseller or popular film. Also, at the end of the time frame determined by the lease,

---

Check These Out

Leased collections are not limited to public libraries. Some academic libraries also provide popular collections via Brodart or Baker & Taylor's leasing services. One of the most comprehensive articles on the topic of leased services in academic libraries, including suggestions for funding such services, is Janelle M. Zauha's "Options for Fiction Provision in Academic Libraries" (*The Acquisitions Librarian*, 1998, 10, no. 19: 45–54). More recently Kat Landry, Michael Hanson, Michelle Martinez, and Linda Meyer described a survey they conducted at Sam Houston State University to determine the feasibility of a popular reading collection in their 2017 article "Patron Preferences: Recreational Reading in an Academic Library" (*Journal of Academic Librarianship* 43, no. 1: 72–81). Their methodology and results make the article well worth the read.

Saponaro worked at a library that had a leased collection that included DVDs and audiobooks as well as print titles. Due to budgetary restrictions, the program was phased out after five years, but use statistics indicated the program was popular during its run.

titles the library does not wish to retain are shipped directly back to the vendor. They do not need to be discarded by the subscribing library.

For their advantages, there are some drawbacks to these lease programs. Parameters of the lease may not allow titles to be loaned to other libraries and may stipulate a specific loan period per item. An additional drawback of lease programs is that such preselected collections cannot address all local needs. However, anyone involved in meeting recreational reading needs will still find such programs worth investigating.

Gifts

In addition to licensed, firm-order, or approval content, the acquisitions department usually becomes the home for unsolicited gifts of books, serials, and other materials that well-meaning people give to the library. Both solicited and unsolicited gifts can be a source of important out-of-print materials for replacement, extra copies, and to fill gaps in the collection. Being able to point to the section of the collection development policy statement that covers gifts can be extremely useful when faced with a patron onsite who is insistent that the library accept their material on the spot. The policy will also help acquisitions personnel process accepted material quickly.

Reviewing gifts is important, as a library cannot afford to discard valuable or needed items that arrive as gifts. In the case of a large donation (upwards of hundreds of volumes), it is normally best to require the donor to provide a list for review prior to the acceptance of items into the collection—so as only to receive and process the desired titles at the outset. Selectors normally make the call to keep or dispose of gift items, whether or not they are a single title or a large collection. Selectors ought to keep in mind that they should not add an item just because it is "free." Rachel Kennedy and Peter Macauley wisely observed that

> Whether . . . resources are sold to an institution or donated free of charge, this is rarely an entirely selfless act on the part of the donor. In fact, it may be the case that gifted items present more problems for staff negotiating with donors, particularly if the donor holds the belief that they have generously given "something for nothing." (2015, p. 43)

Processing and storage costs are the same for a gift as for a purchased item. Older books require careful checking, as variations in printings and editions may determine whether an item is valuable or worthless. (Usually, a second or third printing is less valuable than the first work.) Not to mention, depending on the source of the donation, the items may come with unwanted mold, mildew, or insects—none of which belong in the library environment, no matter how well-meaning the donor.

Steven Carrico provided an excellent summary of the advantages and disadvantages of gift programs:

Positive Points of Gifts

1. Gifts can replace worn and missing items in a library.

2. Out-of-print desiderata often surface from gift donations.

3. Gifts can foster communication and goodwill in a library community.

4. Gifts may become heavily used or important research additions to a collection.

5. Some titles that are not available by purchase are available as gifts.

6. Worthwhile gift material not selected for a library collection can be put in a book sale, sold to dealers, or given away to underfunded libraries and institutions.

Negative Points

1. Gifts require staff time and are costly to process.

2. Dealing with even well-meaning gift donors is frequently an aggravation to staff.

3. Gifts take up precious space in a library.

4. Many collection managers give gifts low priority, so they may sit on review shelves for a long time.

5. A large percentage of most gifts are not added to a collection, which creates disposal problems.

6. Overall, since most gift books added to a collection are older editions, they will be less frequently used by library patrons. (1999, p. 210)

In addition to the workload and processing issues associated with gifts, there are some legal aspects about gifts that staff must understand. The IRS (Internal Revenue Service) requires a library, or its parent institution, that receives a gift in-kind (books, journals, manuscripts, and so forth) worth over $250 to issue a receipt to the donor. Additionally, the IRS forbids the receiving party (in this case the library) from providing an estimated value for the gift in-kind. A disinterested third party or organization must make the valuation (https://www.irs.gov/publications/p561). Normally, an appraiser charges a fee for valuing gifts, and the donor is supposed to pay the fee. Most often, the appraisers are antiquarian dealers who charge a flat fee for the service unless the collection is large or complex. If the appraisal is complex, the appraiser either charges a percentage of the appraised value or an hourly fee.

Donations and gifts also present an acquisitions option that can be appropriate at times. Sometimes a library user or board member donates certain materials on a regular basis, making it unnecessary to order the item if there is no immediate demand for the material. Occasionally, an appropriate series or set costs so much a library cannot buy it with regular funding sources. Seeking a donor to assist with funding or to pay for the purchase is not unheard of,

---

Check This Out

Joseph A. Williams reported on a study he conducted with public and academic libraries throughout New York State in his 2014 article "Is Trash a Library's Treasure? A Study of Gifts-in-Kind Practices and Policies Among New York State Libraries" (*Library Collections, Acquisitions, & Technical Services* 38, nos. 1/2: 1–9). He found that public and academic libraries had different motivations for accepting donations, but for the most part, libraries were selective in their acceptance of gifts. His article is an interesting read.

From the Advisory Board

Advisory Board member Susan Koutsky notes that some school libraries have used a wish list set up on Amazon.com, a book fair website, or other means to obtain materials they want via gift donation. Of course, promotion of the wish list program is essential to its success. Digital fundraising for collections, via a website such as GoFundMe, is another possible option for obtaining needed gift funds for collections.

but again, there may be substantial delays in acquiring the item. Most often, this takes place with rare books and special collections items. An active (and well-to-do) Friends of the Library group may be the answer to a special purchase situation. Friends groups, used judiciously, can significantly expand the collection and stretch funds. Deciding to use the gift method of acquisition will almost always result in a long delay in receiving the desired item.

Exchanges

Exchange programs come in two basic forms: the exchange of unwanted duplicate or gift materials and the exchange of new materials between libraries. The Library of Congress (LC) administers an extensive exchange program with over 5,000 institutions worldwide (http://www.loc.gov/acq/exchange.html). Usually, only research libraries at institutions with publication programs engage in exchange of new materials. Occasionally, libraries use this system to acquire materials from countries in which there are commercial trade restrictions. Where government trade restrictions make buying and selling of publications from certain countries difficult or impossible, the cooperating libraries acquire (buy) their local publications for exchange.

A variation on the exchange method is barter. For years, libraries have from time to time offered exchange lists whereby a library offers to another library anything on the list for the cost of shipping. Handling unneeded material this way was/is labor intensive—creating the list, distributing/posting the list, monitoring the requests, shipping the material, and finally collecting the shipping cost. LC administers a variation of barter in its surplus books program for eligible U.S. organizations (http://www.loc.gov/acq/surplus.html). One of the program requirements is that participating organizations must select materials in person at LC, although arrangements can be made to have a local individual act on their behalf (LC staff members are prohibited from serving in this role). Given the complexities of barter and exchange programs, these acquisition methods are rarely used outside of large research libraries.

From the Authors' Experience

Evans had the opportunity to work at a small research library at the Museum of Northern Arizona. The museum has a publication program that includes both popular and research report publications. The library had over 60 exchange partners in the U.S. and Europe. Given its very tight economic conditions, which was reflected in an almost nonexistent acquisitions budget, if it were not for the exchange program, the library would have been able to add very few newly published items to the collection.

Vendor Selection

An important part of the acquisitions process is selecting the appropriate vendor. There are six broad factors that come into play in making a selection:

- What is commonly carried (normal stock),
- The firm's technological capabilities,
- How quickly the firm is likely to deliver material(s) (order fulfillment),
- The firm's financial condition and discounts offered,
- The range of services available, and
- Customer service.

It is essential to remember that in almost every instance there will be a contract prepared, with all the legalities that such documents entail, once a choice is made. The contract will specify all the terms and conditions, many of which could have serious financial consequences for the library should the library wish to cancel or otherwise modify the agreement.

What the Firm Stocks

When looking for a source for collection items a key concern is what the company usually carries in stock. The important word here is *usually*. You see statements on vendors' websites that read "Over xxx million items in our warehouse" or something very similar. That is not useful information; it could mean there are many copies of a few thousand titles. What is useful is having a list of all the producers/publishers the firm regularly carries in its warehouse(s), as well as what series/producers/publishers they do *not* carry—such a listing may be surprisingly long and have unexpected names. What are the vendor's specialties, if any? For example, Baker & Taylor (a subsidiary of Follett) specializes in public and school library markets, Midwest Library Service focuses on academic and public libraries, while *GOBI®* *Library Solutions* from EBSCO (formerly YBP) focuses on academic and special libraries. Sales representatives often say the firm can supply *any* title from *any* publisher, with only minor exceptions. While it may be possible for a general (primarily mass market titles) book supplier to secure STM (Scientific, Technical, Medical) titles, the delays in delivery may be excessive. Knowing which publishers the vendor does not handle helps maintain good working relations in the long run, although securing that information may prove to be challenging.

Vendor Technological Capabilities

In this category, probably the key question is, does the firm's system have an interface that will work effectively with the library's ILS? If the answer is yes, may the library have a free test period to determine those capabilities prior to signing a contract? Other technology concerns are, does the firm offer free online pre-order checking, electronic ordering, invoicing, payments, claiming, technology support/troubleshooting, and what are the hours of availability, etc.? As noted by Joseph Thomas, "While the librarians in charge of working with vendors to provide content may or may not be familiar with the subjects treated in their journals or databases, they should certainly take advantage of opportunities to become familiar with the management tools that the vendors can provide" (2008, p. 4).

Speed of Delivery

We have mentioned several times that how quickly patrons receive the item they request is one measure by which the user community judges the quality of the library's service. Thus, it is not surprising that vendor fulfillment speed is a factor in making a final decision on which vendor to employ. Information about the average delivery time from the vendor ought to be cross-checked with some of the vendor's current customers. There should be no hesitation on the vendor's part in supplying a list of current customers. It also often pays to contact customers not on the list as a further cross-check.

Many vendors promise 24-hour shipment of items in stock. Do they make good on such claims? Generally, yes; however, the key phrase is *in stock*. Frequently, there can be delays of three to four months in receiving a complete order because one or more titles are not in the warehouse ready to be shipped. In addition to any patron goodwill issues that may arise, delays in receiving materials can also impact budgeting and encumbering (covered later in this chapter). For this reason, it is important that selectors understand the difference between such terms as "in stock" and "orders accepted" that may appear in the online acquisitions system used by the library.

Financial Considerations

One of the main financial considerations focused upon is if the vendor offers any discount rate for purchases. However, there is more to the story than this one factor. Certainly the discount rate is important; however, what is equally important is to what percentage of the items that discount rate applies. A related issue is, are there classes of material that carry service charges rather than a discount? There is also the possibility the rate will be dependent upon the contracted dollar amount spent with the firm within a specified period (normally the greater the amount spent, the higher the discount).

Discounting is a complicated issue in the book trade. The discount the library receives is dependent upon the discount the vendor receives from the producers/publishers, and normally only applies to print resources. Because vendors buy print titles in volume, they receive a substantial discount from producers. When they sell a copy of the highly discounted title to the library, the library receives a discount off the producer's list price. However, that is substantially lower than the vendor received. Clearly there must be a profit margin for the firm to stay in business. For example, if the vendor received a 40 percent discount from the producer, the discount given the library is likely to be 15 to 20 percent. If the library ordered the title directly from the producer, there is a slight chance the discount may be about the same level (10 to 15 percent). The advantage for the library of going with a vendor rather than ordering directly comes about from staff savings. That is, being able to send the vendor one order for titles from dozens of producers rather than creating dozens of orders going to each producer.

Every publisher's discount schedule is slightly different, if not unique. Some items are *net* (no discount); usually these are eBooks, textbooks, STM titles, or items of limited sales appeal. *Short discounts* are normally 20

Check This Out

The Swets Information Services bankruptcy and its impact is reviewed in Katar-zyna Stasik's 2015 article "Prelude, Tumult, Aftermath: A Subscription Agent Perspective on the Swets B.V. Bankruptcy" (*The Serials Librarian* 69, nos. 3/4: 267–76).

---

percent or less; these are items the producers expect will have limited appeal but that have more potential than the net titles. *Trade discounts* range from 30 to 60 percent or more; items in this category are high-demand items or high-risk popular fiction such as first-time authors. Publishers believe that by giving a high discount for fiction, bookstores will stock more copies and thus help promote the title. Vendors normally receive 40 to 50 percent discounts, primarily because of their high-volume orders (hundreds of copies per title rather than the tens that most libraries and independent bookstore owners order).

Another financial concern is with the firm's financial stability. Like other businesses, library vendors have encountered financial problems. In some extreme cases, firms declare bankruptcy and leave their clients without a source of material, as was seen when Swets Information Services declared bankruptcy in 2014 and NA Publishing and its parent Image Data Conversion, LLC announced bankruptcy in mid-2018 (Kelly, 2018). Further, even solvent publishers are requiring prepayment or have placed vendors on a pro forma status. Pro forma status requires prepayment, and suppliers extend credit on the basis of the current performance in payment of bills. Much of the credit and order fulfillment extended by publishers depends on an almost personal relationship with the buyer and the ability of the library to enter into such agreements. That in turn impacts the vendor's ability to fulfill orders as quickly as it did in the past. Thus libraries must select a vendor with care. It is not inappropriate to check a prospective vendor's financial status through a rating service, such as Dun and Bradstreet.

Additional Vendors' Services

Many of today's major vendors offer a variety of services that go beyond supplying items for the collection. They offer almost one-stop technical services, from pre-order checking to cataloging to shelf-ready (processed) material. Baker & Taylor, Brodart, Midwest Library Services, and *GOBI® Library Solutions* from EBSCO are some of the larger firms available that work with print and eBooks, while EBSCO Subscription Services (serials) and Harrassowitz are two options for serials subscriptions. In addition, there are smaller firms that provide good-quality service either for a specific subject area or region (such as Panmun Academic Services—Korea, or Ross Publishing—Eastern Europe); however, their numbers are decreasing in tight economic times.

Almost all vendors offer some combination, if not all, of the following in addition to their basic order fulfillment service:

- Pre-order searching and verification—many allow a search and direct downloading into an order form.

- Selection assistance such as access to reviews of items from major review journals.

Check These Out

Below are some sources to consult when trying to locate vendor products and services:

- *American Libraries Buyers Guide*—http://americanlibrariesbuyersguide .com/—Maintained by the American Library Association. Searchable by category keyword, with the ability to limit by state.
- *FEDLINK Vendor Services Directory*—https://www.loc.gov/flicc/contracts /vendorservicedir.html—A list of service descriptions and vendor links from the Federal Library and Information Network.
- *Librarians Yellow Pages*—http://www.librariansyellowpages.com/—From LibraryWorks. Once a subject category is selected, searches can be narrowed by facets such as type of library or service provided.

- More than one type of format (printed books, eBooks, audio/video recordings, for example).
- Electronic table of contents (TOC) and/or book jacket art for ordered titles. Academic libraries like the TOC service as it becomes searchable in the OPAC/discovery system and is a valued service by researchers. For a public or school library, the cover art, attached to the OPAC record, helps attract a reader to the item, rather like bookstores displaying many titles with the jacket facing out rather than having the spine showing.
- Cataloging and "shelf-ready" processing. Cataloging can take the form of downloading a MARC record into the library's ILS for catalogers to modify as necessary or having the vendor actually do the cataloging and forwarding the final record. Shelf-ready means the items arrive with labels and any necessary book pockets, property stamps, date due slips, etc. in place and ready to go into the collection.
- Customized management data.

In addition to serving as a vendor for collection materials, Brodart is a major resource for library furniture and equipment (book trucks, step stools, shelving units, etc.) as well as supplies (barcodes, date due slips, for example).

Customer Service Considerations

Customer service is no small issue for libraries. Acquisitions staff have a long list of customer service issues when it comes to vendors, including but not limited to resolving problems with online access—both on and off-site—claiming missing serial issues, obtaining price quotes and negotiating licensing agreements, canceling standing orders and subscriptions, replacing lost items, and making billing inquiries. Long-term relationships are the result of respectful dealings by both parties as well as taking some time to learn about the other party's challenges and needs. It is also based on having realistic expectations of one another.

Acquisition departments have a right to expect that a vendor will provide:

- A large inventory of titles in appropriate formats,

- Prompt and accurate order fulfillment,

- Prompt and accurate reporting on items not in stock,

- Personal service at a reasonable price,

- Prompt technical support for problems with shared technology, and

- Timely correction of faulty services such as incorrect cataloging or incorrectly processed shelf-ready items.

Most vendors are reasonably good at meeting those expectations once they become aware of the library's specific issues. Getting to that "once they become aware" point, however, is sometimes a challenge. Unanswered emails or unreturned phone calls to vendors are annoying to say the least, as is establishing a relationship with a specific representative only to have them reassigned, or worse, leave the firm or be laid off. (The flipside is equally annoying—when vendors repeatedly contact a library they know is under-going budgetary constraints with a request to start a new subscription or license.) In defense of the vendors, current economic conditions have caused them as many staffing issues as libraries. Layoffs, furloughs, and frozen vacant positions force organizations to employ technology to help address some of the personnel shortfalls, and often require vendors to "stretch" their service area—leading to the possibility of delayed responses to questions posed of vendor representatives. One point to keep in mind is that

> Vendors have their own sets of pressures which may be largely unknown to, unrecognized by, or of no concern to libraries. An inherent tension exists with libraries serving in a service model and as a customer to vendors, while vendors have expectations from the corporate environment, which may be foreign to the . . . library world. (Ostergaard and Rossmann, 2017, p. 22)

Patience truly is a key to maintaining civil working relationships with vendors. Vendors, on their part, have a right to expect the following from their library clients:

- A reasonable time to gain an understanding of the library's needs,

- Cooperation in placing orders using the firm's system rather than "we did it this way with our former vendor,"

- Keeping paperwork to a minimum and attempting to streamline operations,

- Prompt payment for services, and

- Not requiring too many exceptions to the firm's normal processes.

Unfortunately, libraries sometimes employ practices that are somewhat outmoded and reflect an attitude of "we always do it this way" and expect the vendor to change its practices to conform to the library's approach. Unless there is a parent institutional requirement involved (as in the case of licensing restrictions), the library should be open to at least considering modifying its practices. Being open about the average invoice payment cycle, ability to authorize partial payments, and similar matters from the start will also create a more positive library/vendor relationship.

Vendor Evaluation

Even the longest-held vendor/library relationships should not be taken for granted. Vendor evaluation should not only occur at the time a contract is being renegotiated or if a vendor is performing poorly; instead, it should be a regular process. If the relationship is solid and the vendor is providing what the library needs and when and how it needs it, the evaluation will indicate this. However, as noted by Susan Davis and her colleagues, "If an agent is underperforming, actions libraries undertake include requesting a change of service representative, transferring select titles to another agent, ordering direct from the publisher, and—if a situation warrants—a change of agent" (2015, p. 247). In the past, monitoring vendors was time-consuming and difficult. However, automated acquisitions systems produce a variety of useful management and vendor reports very quickly and in various formats. Knowing what to do with the quantity of data the systems can produce is another matter.

There are two types of evaluation acquisitions staff undertake. One is more of a monitoring of vendor performance with an eye to identifying small concerns that if left unmonitored could become a major issue. The other is a formal assessment of the vendor with an eye toward changing vendors or renewing a contract.

One obvious issue that arises in the evaluation process is which vendor performs best on a given type of order (such as conference proceedings, music scores, or streaming media). The first step is to decide what *best* means. Does it mean highest discount? Fastest delivery? Most accurate reports? Best customer service? Highest percentage of the order filled with the first shipment? All of the above? The answer varies from library to library depending on local needs and conditions. Once the library defines *best*, it knows what data to get from the system. Other evaluation issues to consider with both existing and new vendors include:

- How effective is the firm at handling rush orders (if applicable)?
- What additional services or added value to the content offered does the vendor offer?
- Is the vendor able to handle specialties (such as international materials, if it is a general dealer)?
- What is the pricing structure—including discounts and service fees?
- What is the return policy?
- How quickly are claims handled?
- Is Electronic Data Interchange (EDI) available for direct transmission of business data, such as orders, invoices, and claims?
- For e-resources in particular, how is the vendor addressing or planning to address accessibility issues?
- What is the financial status of the vendor?

Check These Out

Changing vendors is not an easy task, and involves many of the questions listed above. One method for identifying potential vendors is through issuing a request for proposal (RFP). Three sources for information on RFPs worth consulting are:

- American Library Association's "Implementing Library Technology: Request for Proposal (RFP) Writing" LibGuide (2018, http://libguides.ala.org/librarytech /rfp-writing).

- Chris Peters' "An Overview of the RFP Process for Nonprofits, Charities, and Libraries" *TechSoup* entry (2011. https://www.techsoup.org/support/articles -and-how-tos/overview-of-the-rfp-process).

- Micheline Westfall, Justin Clarke, and Jeanne M. Langendorfer's "Selecting a Vendor: The Request for Proposal (RFP) from Library and Vendor Perspectives" (*Serials Librarian*, 2013, 64, nos. 1–4: 188–95).

We have mentioned speed of acquisitions as one measure users take into consideration when judging library quality. It pays to keep in mind that "[p]atrons can get almost any book from Amazon in a matter of days. It doesn't make sense to them that the library cannot. In addition, libraries run the risk of seeming obsolete or ineffective when they cannot deliver readily obtainable materials quickly" (Ferris and Buck, 2014, p. 140). The same holds true for judging the effectiveness of a vendor. Typically a 30-day window for delivery is standard for vendors, after which the library may reasonably start a claiming process.

Libraries expect vendors to report the status of titles not delivered upon receipt of a claim. Most ILS acquisitions modules have the ability to generate claim forms based on the order and expected delivery date that the department establishes. Vendors should respond with a meaningful report within a reasonable period. Most vendors are quick to report because they understand most libraries cannot authorize any payment until the full order is in the library. In addition, the sooner the selector learns that a requested title is not available, the better, as this allows the selector to decide whether or not they wish to find an alternative title or pursue other means of acquiring it (such as through the out-of-print market, discussed later).

When dealing with U.S. publishers, allowing for the normal "snail mail" time, it is reasonable to send in a second claim 60 days after the first claim, if there has been no status report. Many order forms carry a statement reading "cancel after x days." Although such statements are legally binding, most libraries send a separate cancellation notice. Vendors that are consistently late with their deliveries or who are slow to respond to claims should raise a red flag for libraries.

A common occurrence is budget cuts; unfortunately, in the past and certainly recently, such cuts have occurred with some frequency. Most vendors are cooperative about making the adjustments. By establishing a regular cancellation date, libraries that must expend funds within their FY can avoid or reduce the last-minute scramble of canceling outstanding orders and ordering materials that the vendor can deliver in time to expend the funds.

Retail Outlets

Retail outlets can be a source of some materials for libraries. While they are an option, retail outlets are generally less able to accommodate the special fiscal requirements that most libraries must follow. Libraries in large metropolitan areas generally have a good bookstore nearby. Although most libraries will spend only a small portion of the materials budget in such stores, the possibility is worth exploring. One thing to keep in mind is that a large chain such as Barnes & Noble operates very differently from local stores and is not likely to be able to accommodate library needs beyond occasionally allowing a "corporate" or "educational" discount on some of the titles they carry.

Amazon.com or BarnesandNoble.com are used by libraries that need a quick turnaround time when it comes to popular titles. One challenge for libraries can be developing a workable means of payment, as online sites are based on credit card payments. Libraries and their parent organizations generally operate on a purchase order/invoice system. Libraries that cannot get a credit card in the departmental name due to regulations/reluctance on the part of the library's parent organization may encounter some challenges going the route of online outlets. Some departments will use a personal card and go through a reimbursement process; however, this is not a long-term or high-volume solution.

Orkiszewski (2005) conducted a comparative study of Amazon and a traditional library book and media vendor. He found on average that the Amazon discount was lower (8.75 percent) compared to the traditional vendors' 15.24 percent. One of his conclusions was, "Libraries interested in using Amazon should find it useful for trade and popular press books, DVDs, and book and media items that need to be acquired quickly" (p. 208). Some institutions, such as Columbia Gorge Community College (CGCC), have turned away from traditional acquisitions vendors, with Amazon filling this role. CGCC set up a credit account with Amazon to allow for monthly invoices (as opposed to item-by-item bills), and subscribed to the Amazon Prime service for expedited and free shipping. CGCC's experience through Amazon resulted in improved patron relations at the library, and as noted by Brian Greene, "Being responsive to our patrons' needs and fulfilling their requests quickly helped to cement the library in their consciousness as a viable option for obtaining materials" (2014). Although CGCC's move in entirety to Amazon for its acquisitions may be the exception more than the

---

Check This Out

In September 2017, Ithaka S+R announced it received funding from the Andrew W. Mellon Foundation to gather data on acquisitions models in libraries. Katherine Daniel, Joseph J. Esposito, and Roger C. Schonfeld conducted the research and part of their examination was the use of Amazon.com in library acquisitions. Preliminary results released in July 2018 (http://www.sr.ithaka.org/publications/library-acquisition-patterns-preliminary-findings/) indicated Amazon.com was the second largest book distributor behind *GOBI® Library Solutions* from EBSCO. The final report was issued in January 2019 (https://sr.ithaka.org/publications/2019-report-library-acquisition-patterns/) and it confirmed the use of Amazon for acquisitions. The report is well worth the read.

rule, their experience shows that e-stores can be of assistance and should not be dismissed out-of-hand as an acquisitions option.

Out-of-Print and Antiquarian Dealers

Libraries buy retrospectively for two reasons: to fill in gaps in the collection and to replace worn out or lost copies of titles. Given budget limitations of late as well as the need to increase purchases of nonprint and electronic resources, there has been a steady decline in retrospective buying on the part of libraries. Another factor in the decline is that it is now fairly easy to locate a copy of an out-of-print title in the catalog or discovery system, which then can be borrowed through ILL. As a result, acquisitions staff and selectors have decreasing experience to draw upon when they need to work in this field.

One outcome of the decline is that the field itself, which has always been very dependent on collectors, is even more driven today by collector interests than by library needs. Allowing for overlap, there are two broad categories of out-of-print (OP) dealers. One category focuses primarily on general OP books, that is, on buying and selling relatively recent OP books. Often, these books sell at prices that are the same as, or only slightly higher than, their publication price. The other category of dealer focuses on rare, antiquarian, and special (for example, fore-edged painted, miniature, or private press) books. Prices for this type of book can range from around US$10 to thousands of dollars.

Many acquisitions librarians and book dealers classify OP book distribution services into three general types: (1) a complete book service, (2) a complete sales service, and (3) a complete bookstore. The first two may operate in a manner that does not allow, or at least require, customers to come to the seller's location and all contact is by email or telephone. The owner may maintain only a small stock of choice items in a garage or basement. In a *complete book service*, a dealer actively searches for items for a customer even if the items are not in stock. In the past this was the standard approach for serious retrospective collection development. Today resources such as Marketplace in *GOBI® Library Solutions* from EBSCO and iFound in *OASIS®* via ProQuest provide integrated OP searching and fulfillment within the acquisition system itself. Given the availability of such services, many libraries handle all the work themselves.

A *sales service* is just what the name implies: A dealer reads the "wanted" sections of book trade websites and publications and sends off quotes on

---

Check These Out

Aside from services incorporated into acquisitions systems, other options to locate OP titles include:

- AbeBooks.Com—http://www.abebooks.com—Originally a source of OP books, this site now includes fine art and collectibles.

- Alibris for Libraries—https://library.alibris.com—Includes options for libraries to create want and wish lists of desired titles.

- BookFinder.com—http://www.bookfinder.com—A general search engine for OP titles.

Check This Out

For an interesting look into the life of an OP dealer, see Carol Apollo Kennedy's 2016 article "Random Ramblings—The Out-of-Print Book Market: Some Personal Perspectives" (*Against the Grain* 28, no. 5: 69–70).

items in his or her stock. Such services seldom place ads or conduct searches for a customer. The *complete bookstore* is a store operation that depends on in-person trade. Stores of this type often engage in book service and sales service activities as well.

The OP trade is very dependent upon the Web, with thousands of dealers having a Web presence. To some degree the Web has kept prices down, or slowed their increase, as comparing prices through an online site is very easy. Before OP online searching was possible, searching could have progressed for years before there was success. Now in a matter of minutes you can have rather definitive results. If you don't get a hit, in most cases dozens of hits, you can be reasonably sure the item is not available or you are lacking some critical data about the title. One reason for suspecting the item is not available is that sites have tens of thousands of dealer/members worldwide and the Web has become their major source of business.

Before deciding on a title, one must be careful to read the description provided online with a critical mind, at least for the rare book purchases. Dealer descriptions/condition statements can be very idiosyncratic and one must read them with a degree of caution. There are no official standards for such information. Some years ago *AB Bookman's Weekly* put forward some suggested terms and their definitions. What follows can only be thought of as broad meanings to help assess what a dealer may be describing.

Two of the top-level condition terms you may see are *as new* and *fine*. Presumably "as new" implies a flawless item—the identical condition as when published—including a perfect dust jacket, if that was part of the original. Sometimes a dealer will use *mint* for this state. *Fine* is a slightly less perfect state; perhaps there is a little evidence of shelf wear and use but of a very minor nature. *Very good* and *good* are conditions that most libraries find acceptable for general collection replacement copies—there is evidence of wear. *Fair* and *poor* condition states probably are not suitable for libraries except when nothing else is available and the need is very strong as they imply some defects in the item. *Ex-library,* as the term indicates, means the copy has the usual stamping, perforations, spindling, and other mutilations that libraries use to property mark an item.

A library may assume that most OP dealers sell their stock as described or "as is." If there is no statement about the item's condition, it should be in good or better condition. A common statement seen on websites is "terms—all books in original binding and in good or better condition unless otherwise stated." The OP dealer's reputation for honesty, service, and fair prices is important. To gain such a reputation requires a considerable period of time in this field, which can be an issue for libraries. If one is only purchasing a US$20/$30 replacement copy, the risks of dealing with an unknown dealer are not all that high. For higher-priced materials, there are real risks and the ease of posting an item for sale online has magnified the opportunities for less than honest sellers to make a sale. One clue to a good reputation is membership in organizations such as Antiquarian Booksellers Association of America (http://www.abaa.org) and/or International League of Antiquarian

Booksellers, (http://www.ilab.org); members usually have that information on their website.

One element in the OP trade is very mysterious to the outsider and even to librarians who have had years of experience with dealers: How do dealers determine the asking price?

Several interrelated factors come into play:

1. How much it costs to acquire the item.

2. The amount of current interest in collecting a particular subject or author.

3. The number of copies printed and the number of copies still in existence.

4. The physical condition of the copy.

5. Any special features of the particular copy (autographed by the author or signed or owned by a famous person, for example).

6. What other dealers are asking for copies of the same edition in the same condition.

To a large degree, dealers set prices after they know the answers to the questions of supply and demand. Without question, the current asking price is the major determining factor—given equal conditions in the other five areas. Thanks to online services available, determining how many copies are available and what their asking price is has simplified pricing for both the dealer and the buyer.

Fiscal Management

Record keeping and fiscal management are the key components of the next phase of acquisitions work. For a variety of reasons, careful record keeping of orders placed, items received, and amounts paid are essential. Acquisitions records are essential for providing the necessary accountability during audits, and stewardship activities frequently require reports generated by acquisitions. In addition, two other monetary related activities involve projecting/estimating price increases for materials and allocating the available funds for acquiring materials.

Tight economic times translate into tight collection funding for libraries. Lea Currie and Sara E. Morris observed, "No librarian charged with stewarding collections has ever had too large a budget. However, many in the last decade have survived with far too little" (2017, p. 47). For years, incremental drops on overall and collections funding, while not dramatic, have had a cumulative impact that shows in ways that service communities are noticing. Factors such as the Great Recession in the late 2000s and early 2010s and the rise in popularity of eBooks and their often expensive licenses contributed to public and academic libraries realizing real constraints with collections budgeting. While some modest increases in funding for library budgets were reported in a 2018 *Library Journal* budget survey, concerns over tax laws and their impact on libraries remain (Peet, 2018, p. 21). "Making do" with less has become a fact of life for most U.S. libraries and it seems likely to continue for some time. This in turn impacts future budgeting considerations. Brandi Scardilli (2015) noted, "[B]ecause most libraries are asking for funding for 5-plus years into the future, they have to consider inflation, new formats such as eBooks, and other issues that may arise" (p. 26). Thus, understanding the issues of financial control and making the most effective use of the available funds is critical. With collection funds usually being the second largest component in a library's budget, acquisitions staff must commit themselves to handling the funds properly and thoughtfully.

Estimating Costs

The collections budget plays a significant role in terms of the overall library budget. Because of this fact, funding projections for at least maintaining the current level of purchasing in the next budget cycle are an important factor for senior administrators as they formulate the overall budget request. Thus it is incumbent on the department to provide the most accurate estimates as possible. Libraries often have difficulty establishing credibility with funding authorities regarding the different nature of the materials purchased with collection funds. While library administration usually understands the peculiarities of pricing of library materials, funding authorities at higher levels may have difficulty accepting the fact that the CPI (Consumer Price Index) numbers do not apply to library materials. The notion that each item is one-of-a-kind—almost monopolistic in nature— seems hard to get across. In reality, library collection items do not fit the classic economic pricing model where there is competition between similar products. As a result, the producers of the materials can and do set their prices with only modest thought about competitive prices. For many years there was a double-digit percentage price increase for library material when the CPI was a modest single digit. Today the increases are not double-digit, but still well above the CPI rate.

U.S. librarians have created library price indexes that measure rates of change as one way to assist in estimating costs. A subcommittee of the National Information Standards Organization, the Z39 Committee (1974), developed guidelines for price indexes that were published as Z39.20 (National Information Standards Organization, 1999). Additionally, members of the Library Materials Price Index (LMPI) Editorial Board of the Association for Library Collections and Technical Services division of ALA compile the "Prices of U.S. and Foreign Published Materials." This listing appears in the *Library and Book Trade Almanac* and also on the LMPI website (http://www.ala.org/alcts/resources/collect/serials/spi). Such efforts provide data on price changes over a long period, which, when averaged, is as close as anyone can come to predicting future price changes. *Library Journal* also provides annual updates on periodical prices for all library markets (for example, see Stephen Bosch, Barbara Albee, and Kittie Henderson, 2018). The major problem with the published indexes is that when preparing a budget request, up-to-date information may not be readily available. The challenge is to find the most current data, which may determine the library's success in securing the requested funding.

Libraries that purchase a significant number of foreign publications also need to estimate the impact of exchange rates. Volatile exchange rates affect buying power almost as much as inflation. Although it is impossible to accurately forecast the direction and amount of fluctuation in the exchange rates 12 months in the future, some effort should go into studying the previous 12 months and attempting to predict future trends. A number

---

Check These Out

Exchange rates are not only of concern to U.S. libraries, as libraries worldwide encounter similar challenges. Some articles that provide the perspective from other countries include:

Mapulanga, Patrick. 2012. "Structural Adjustment Policies, Currency Devaluation and Liberalised Exchange Rate on Library Acquisitions in the University of Malawi Libraries" (*Bottom Line: Managing Library Finances* 25, no. 3: 123-34).

Scott, David R., and Nicole Eva. 2017. "The Canadian Dollar Versus the Collection: How Canadian University Libraries Are Coping" (*Partnership: The Canadian Journal of Library and Information Practice and Research* 11, no. 2. Online. http://dx.doi.org/10.21083/partnership.v11i2.3771).

---

of sources exist for monitoring exchange rates, including XE.Com (http://www.xe.com) and the Federal Reserve Foreign Exchange Rates (https://www.federalreserve.gov/releases/h10/current/). It is important to have good data about the amounts spent in various countries during the previous year. The country of publication is less important than the vendor's country. For example, if the library uses the vendor Harrassowitz, prices will be in euros regardless of the country of origin of the items purchased. After collecting the data, the library can use them as factors in estimating the cost of continuing the current acquisition levels from the countries from which the library normally buys.

Allocating the Budget

You would be correct to think dividing up the materials budget is a rather complicated process. Generally, the materials budget "pie" is divided into three main slices—books, serials, and e-resources (including eBooks, e-serials, and databases). Media can fall in the e-resources category or physical DVDs/Blu-rays, or CDs can be considered its own "slice." The "pie" scenario is a valid descriptor for the way materials budgets work, and one that administrators and vendors alike can understand. Mark Estes once explained to a library vendor, "My library book and computer research budget is a pie—for me to give you some more of my pie I must make another information vendor's piece smaller" (2009, p. 1). And, just as in Estes' vendor scenario, when one slice of the allocation increases, more often than not all of the other slices get smaller.

As noted by Jesse Holden, "The budget determines *how* much is to be spent, while fund allocations focus on *what* is purchased" (2017, p. 200). Ordinarily, the method of allocation reflects, at least to some degree, the library's collection development policy statement priorities. If the library employs a collecting intensity ranking system in the collection development policy, it is reasonable to expect to find those levels reflected in the amount of money allocated to the subject or format. Almost all allocation methods are complex, and matching the needs and monies available requires that the library consider several factors.

From the funding authority's point of view, it has no interest in how the library decides to allocate the funds provided they purchase material for the collection. However, except in the smallest library, there are usually several staff members who would like to have a voice in the allocation discussion/ debate. Each person will come to the table with her/his case for why "this year" their area must receive a bigger slice of the pie. Just as the library's budget request to the funding authority(ies) is a political process, so is the internal materials budget allocation process.

As no two collections are the same, each library will have its own categories for allocation. However, some of the more common categories are:

- Adult monographs (fiction/nonfiction)
- Adult serials
- Adult media
- Children's books
- Children's magazines
- Children's media
- Young adult (YA) books
- YA magazines
- YA media
- Reference materials
- Replacement items
- Rental/lease titles
- E-resources

The above reflects a public library environment. When it comes to academic and school libraries, the list of categories becomes even more complex, with allocations also managed by additional factors such as subject area (e.g., history, engineering) or funding source (e.g., gift funds). It may seem overly complicated the greater the number of fund lines developed and utilized. This is usually the case. However, as noted by Wayne Disher (2014), "Basically, if you have only a few budget allocation funds, your ability to gain a sense of how and where you spent your money diminishes as does your ability to articulate the effectiveness of your collection in meeting and responding to community needs" (p. 49). That articulation is in the way of budget reports prepared by the acquisitions unit.

Among the issues that factor into the allocation process are past practices, differential publication rates, unit cost and inflation rates, level of demand, and actual usage of the material. Implementing a formal allocation system takes time and effort, and opponents claim it is difficult to develop a fair allocation model. Certainly allocations add to the workload in the acquisitions department as they have to track more expenditure categories. Those opposed to the process also claim that, because the models are difficult to develop, libraries tend to leave the allocation percentages/ratios in place for too long and either add in the next year's percentage increase (if the collections budget even receives an increase) or keep things the same rather than recalculating the figures annually. Proponents of allocation claim that it provides better control of collection development and it is a more effective way to monitor expenditures.

A number of allocation models exist—and many libraries are examining the methods they currently use for determining allocations, especially in light of the impact electronic resources have on their collection budgets. (For example, some academic libraries take interdisciplinary databases and electronic serial costs "off the top" before allocating the remainder of the budget.) Regardless of the specific method used, a good allocation process provides at least four outcomes. First and foremost, it matches, or should, available funds with actual funding needs. Depending on the situation, a majority of the budget may be allocated at the start of the fiscal year, but part of the budget (generally less than 2 percent) may be set aside in a reserve fund. As Steven Sowards and Joseph Harzbecker (2018) noted, having such

---

Check These Out

Several resources worth consulting on the topic of collection budget allocations include:

Jeff Bailey and Linda Creibaum. 2015. "Developing a Weighted Collection Development Allocation Formula." *Proceedings of the Charleston Library Conference.* Online. http://dx.doi.org/10.5703/1288284316301. An overview of a workshop conducted at the Charleston Conference including factors in developing a weighted formula.

Meredith Schwartz. 2014. "Big Spender." *Library Journal* 139, no. 8: 24. An interview with Advisory Board member Wendy Bartlett and her process for allocating the budget at the public library system in Cuyahoga County, Ohio.

Cindy D. Shirkey and Lisa Sheets Baricella. 2014. "Employing a Use Factor to Distribute Monographic Funds." *Proceedings of the Charleston Library Conference.* Online. http://dx.doi.org/10.5703/1288284315593. Discusses the allocation model developed at East Carolina University that incorporates Bonn's use factor and the average price paid per title.

George Stachokas and Tim Gritten. 2013. "Adapting to Scarcity: Developing an Integrated Allocation Formula." *Collection Management* 38, no. 1: 33–50). Discusses the process followed at the Cunningham Memorial Library at Indiana State University to develop an allocation formula for print and electronic materials based on student enrollment, faculty FTE, and interlibrary loan requests.

---

a fund available can be useful as it is often difficult to determine the exact cost of a resource at the outset of the year and provides flexibility so that, "At some point later in the year, when the real cost becomes clear, excess contingency funds can be spent as 'free' reserves, perhaps for end-of-year one-time purchases" (p. 107). Second, the allocation process provides selectors with guidelines for how they should allocate their time as they track their expenditures throughout the year. That is, if someone is responsible for three selection areas with funding allocations of US$15,000, $5,000, and $500, it is clear which area requires the most attention. (In many cases, it is more difficult to spend the smaller amount, because one must be careful to spend it wisely.) Since almost no library has unlimited funds for materials, it is also important for selectors to be able to prioritize resources into those that must be acquired now in order to meet specific patron or programmatic needs and those that can be held aside for future purchase should funds become available.

An additional outcome is that the allocation process provides a means of assessing the selector's work at the end of the fiscal year. Finally, allocations provide the service community with a sense of collecting priorities, assuming the allocation information is made available to them. The library can communicate the information in terms of percentages rather than specific monetary amounts if there is a concern about divulging budgetary data.

Financial Records

We noted earlier that much of the acquisition department's work involves financial record keeping. As noted by Robert Cleary (2015), "If

---

Check These Out

Two recent resources for gaining an understanding of library accounting and budgetary practices are:

Robert Burger's *Financial Management of Libraries and Information Centers* (Santa Barbara, CA: ABC-CLIO, 2016).

Rachel A. Kirk's *Balancing the Books: Accounting for Librarians* (Santa Barbara, CA: Libraries Unlimited, 2012).

An older but still useful title is:

Anne M. Turner's *Managing Money: A Guide for Librarians* (Jefferson, NC: McFarland, 2007).

---

an invoice for an unpaid subscription arrives after the renewal period has begun, the opportunity to cancel and get a refund may be missed, if that was the intent. Another consequence of not paying close attention is that the funds may have been spent on other resources, and payment will be delayed until the next budget is available" (p. 164). One of the key people in the department making sure these things do not happen is the bookkeeper or accounting associate. This person may or may not have a background in library work, but regardless of their background, they will quickly pick up the requisite knowledge as most of the work follows standard accounting practices. One important part of their job is to be able to accurately track which invoices are truly those appropriate for the library. Although it does not happen often, as noted by Jesse Holden (2017), "Sometimes unscrupulous publishers will send content that was not ordered in the hopes of being able to invoice for it at a later time. Occasionally, an invoice will be included in hopes of tricking the person receiving the content at the library into paying for something that was not formally selected" (p. 107).

Encumbering

Whether the individual responsible for managing the acquisitions bookkeeping has a library background or not, there is one library related process that is unlike most business bookkeeping practice—encumbering. Encumbering allows the library to set aside monies to pay for ordered items. Selectors may not realize it, but when the library waits 60, 90, or 120 days or more for orders, it is possible that the monies available will be over or under spent, if there is no system that allows for setting aside funds.

The following chart shows how the process works. Day 1, the first day of the fiscal year, shows the library with an annual allocation of $1,000 for a particular subject area. On day 2, the library orders an item with a list price of $24.95. Although there may be shipping and handling charges, there probably will be a discount. Because none of the costs and credits are known at the time, the list price is the amount a staff member records as encumbered. (Some departments add a fixed percentage of the list price in order to more closely match what will be the invoice price.) The unexpended column reflects the $24.95 deduction, with zero showing in the expended category. Sixty-two days later, the item and invoice arrive; the invoice reflects a 15 percent discount ($3.74) and no shipping or handling charges. The accounting associate or bookkeeper records the actual cost ($21.21) under expended and adds the $3.74 to the unexpended amount. The amount encumbered now is zero.

	Unexpended	Encumbered	Expended
Day 1	$1,000.00	0	0
Day 2	$975.05	$24.95	0
Day 62	$978.79	0	$21.21

This system is much more complex than the example suggests, because libraries place and receive multiple orders every day. With each transaction the amounts in each column change. *Neither the acquisitions department nor the selectors know the precise unexpended balance, except on the first and last day of the fiscal year.* If the funding body takes back all unexpended funds at the end of the fiscal year (a *cash accounting* system), the acquisitions department staff must know the fund(s) balances as they enter the final quarter of the year.

Several factors make it difficult to learn the exact status of the funds, even when encumbering funds. One factor is delivery of orders. Vendors may assure customers they will deliver before the end of the fiscal year, but fail to do so. This is particularly true in cases of orders from international vendors. Such a failure can result in the encumbered money being lost. With a cash system, the acquisitions department staff must make some choices at the end of the fiscal year if there are funds in the encumbered category. The main issue is determining if the items still on order are important enough to leave on order. An affirmative answer has substantial implications for collection development.

Using the foregoing example and assuming that day 62 comes after the start of a new fiscal year and the new allocation is $1,000, on day 1 of the new fiscal year, the amount unexpended would be $975.05 ($1,000 minus $24.95), encumbered $24.95, and expended zero. In essence, there is a reduction in the amount available for new orders and the library lost $24.95 from the prior year's allocation. (One of the authors once took over as head of a library on June 25, and the system's financial officer reported the entire acquisitions allocation was encumbered for the coming fiscal year, starting July 1. To have some funds for collection development over the next 12 months, it was necessary to cancel 347 orders.) With an *accrual system*, the unexpended funds carry forward into the next fiscal year. Under such a system, using the previous example, the day 1 figures would be unexpended $1,000, encumbered $24.95, and expended zero.

There is a problem in leaving funds encumbered for long periods under either system, especially when there is rapid inflation or exchange rates are unfavorable. The latter are two reasons why a firm but reasonable date for automatic cancellation of unfilled orders is important.

The point of all this work is to allow the library to expend all the materials funds available in a timely manner without overordering. Remember that an order is a legal contract between the library and the supplier. Certainly most suppliers who have a long-standing relationship with libraries will understand an occasional overcommitment of funds, but they have a legal right to full, prompt payment for all orders placed. One way they allow libraries to address the problem is to ship the order on time but hold the invoice until the start of the next fiscal year.

A major problem confronting acquisitions staff is the number of allocation accounts to monitor and manage. In some libraries, the number may run over 400. Restricted funds are especially problematic because the library may charge only certain types of materials to such accounts. Although the bookkeeper or accounting associate's job may be to assign charges to the various accounts, that person also must know approximately how much money remains as free balance, as encumbered, and as expended. As the number of accounts goes up, so does the workload of those monitoring the accounts.

Stewardship

In addition to the regular funds provided by the parent institution, many libraries are able to acquire items for their collections via "special" funds available for that purpose. The two most common sources are grant money and endowment funds. Grants almost always have clearly specified reporting requirements regarding how the library used the money. However, endowment/gift funds may or may not have such requirements.

With grants, you may be expected to provide detailed information on items acquired (list price, discount, tax if any, etc.). The reason is that some categories of cost (such as overhead charged by the institution) may not be allowed under the terms of the grant. In other cases, all that you need to report is the number of items acquired. We would recommend generating a detailed accounting, even if it is not required, as there is always a chance the grant usage may be audited.

Endowments and special gifts, such as for memorial purposes, are another matter when it comes to ordering and reporting. They may or may not call for informing the donor what was acquired. However, it is a best practice to send such a report regardless of the necessity. Orders for materials from foundation or endowment accounts can present a challenge for acquisitions staff as foundation funds may need to be transferred into operating accounts by another office (usually a separate business office). In some cases acquisitions units place ordering deadlines for purchases that use foundation or endowment funds so that transfers can successfully be made during the same fiscal year.

Special gifts may be annual or one-time in character. Memorial gift funds can call for acknowledgment to a donor by placing a physical or virtual

---

Check This Out

Sherry Foster and Jennifer Robinson described how the Western Libraries at Western University, Ontario, Canada, worked with the development officer to implement a digital bookplate program in their 2012 article "Donor Recognition and Cultivation Through the Use of Digital Bookplates" (*Journal of Library Innovation* 3, no. 2: 43–49). They stressed the importance of collaboration with other units. At the time of the publication of the article the program had attracted over 200 donors. Although not frequently seen, libraries with digital bookplate programs include Brown University (https://library.brown.edu/bookplates/) and Fresno State (https://library.fresnostate .edu/find/bookplate).

book plate in the item indicating the name of the person being memorialized, or by acknowledging the item in some other way, such as on a library donor list. The same is often the case with endowed funds. Many academic libraries have numerous endowed book accounts, most of which specify a subject area where you may use the monies. In the case of narrowly defined topics, you may not identify an appropriate item for a year or more.

Telling donors, whether required or not, not only what was acquired but where to find it in the collection—call number—offers the donor(s) a chance to look at the items and judge your stewardship of their monies. That "extra" step can result in additional gifts for collection building. It does mean that acquisitions and cataloging departments must keep good records of what was selected and processed for several, if not dozens, of separate accounts.

Audits

Are audits really necessary in libraries? Must we remember how, where, when, and on what we spent every cent? Unfortunately, the answer is *yes* when it comes to library funds. Holly Hibner and Mary Kelly remind us that, "Library staff need to be careful, especially when spending [taxpayers'] money, to carefully and clearly document what they spent money on. Accountability is important to a transparent and trustworthy organization" (2013, p. 37). Embezzlement is not unheard of in libraries, as described by Herbert Snyder and Julia Hersberger (1997) and Nancy Hurst (2013). These articles make it clear why regular financial audits are necessary.

There are three basic audit types. *Operational audits* examine an organization's procedures and practices, usually with the goal of making improvements. *Compliance audits* examine how well an organization is following procedures established by some higher level body. An example might be to determine if the acquisitions department has followed the procedures for funds received through a federal government LSTA (Library Services and Technology Act) or Institute of Museum and Library Services (IMLS) grants. (See https://www.imls.gov/grants/manage-your-award/grant-administration for an example of the reporting requirements for an institution receiving an IMLS grant.) The *financial audit* is what comes to people's minds when they hear "audit"—usually with a sense of dread. It is often a yearly event for the acquisitions department wherein its records are examined by nonlibrary personnel to assure the funding authority, as well as other parties, that the monies were in fact expended in the expected way and that the records of those transactions comply with standard accounting practices and guidelines. One aspect of having the power to manage and expend substantial amounts of money is fiscal accountability. The amount of money does not need to be "substantial" if it involves public or private funds. For acquisitions departments, the auditor's visit is probably second only to the annual performance appraisal process in terms of worry and stress for the staff. The worry is not that they have done something wrong, but rather their not being able to find some type of documentation that an auditor wishes to check.

Check This Out

An enjoyable short poem by Robert Frost entitled "The Hardship of Accounting" addresses the issue of accounting and audits—http://varietyreading.carlsguides.com /forwards/hardship.php.

A legalistic definition of an *audit* is the process of accumulation and evaluation of evidence about quantifiable information of an economic entity to determine and report on the degree of correspondence between the information and established criteria. More simply put, it is the process of ensuring that the financial records are accurate and that the information is presented correctly using accepted accounting practices, and of making recommendations for improvements in how the process is carried out. The basic questions and required records relate to whether a purchase was made with proper authorization, was received, and was paid for in an appropriate manner, and whether the item is still available. (If the item is not still available, there should be appropriate records regarding its disposal.)

Although most audits are done annually, sometimes "spot checks" can occur. Some "red flags" that may trigger an audit include such things as duplicate payments, large payments—especially to foreign vendors—and payments made on behalf of another entity, or anything that looks odd or doesn't match up (such as an invoice for one amount but a payment for a lesser or higher amount).Who conducts the audit normally depends on the type of institution. For example, for public universities in the State of Maryland, audits are performed by the Maryland Office of Legislative Audits—a completely separate entity from the university. With automated acquisitions systems, undergoing an audit is considerably less time-consuming than in the past, where the "paper trail" was in fact a number of different paper records that had to be gathered and compared. Now, acquisitions systems and the ILS pull up the necessary information fairly quickly.

Points to Keep in Mind

- Acquisition departments secure the items that selectors identify as important to add to the collection.

- Three key areas of acquisitions work are determining how to acquire an item, acquiring the items, and creating and maintaining the financial records associated with the acquisition activities.

- There are eight broad methods for acquiring collection materials— firm order, standing order, blanket order, approval plan, subscriptions, leases, gifts, and exchanges.

- Demand-driven and evidence-based models of acquisition are emerging as options to standard approval plans.

- One of the keys to a successful acquisitions program is developing and maintaining good working relationships with vendors.

- Vendor evaluation should be a regular process, not done just when a vendor is performing poorly.

- Encumbering is a method that assists the library in not over or under expending the funds available for collection development.

- As libraries face budgetary challenges, careful stewardship of gift and foundation funds becomes more important.

- Audits and accountability go hand in hand; the audits demonstrate to funding authorities and other stakeholders that the library expended the funds entrusted to it in an appropriate manner.

References

Ballestro, John. 2012. "Losing Your Control: Acquisitions and Outsourcing." *Technical Services Quarterly* 29, no. 3: 113–21.

Bosch, Stephen, Barbara Albee, and Kittie Henderson. 2018. "Death by 1,000 Cuts." *Library Journal* 143, no. 7: 28–33.

Brantley, John Stephen. 2010. "Approval Plans, Discipline Change, and the Importance of Human Mediated Book Selection." *Library Collections Acquisitions & Technical Services* 34, no. 1: 11–24.

Carrico, Steven. 1999. "Gifts and Exchanges." In *Understanding the Business of Acquisitions,* 2nd ed., edited by Karen A. Schmidt, 205–23. Chicago: American Library Association.

Cleary, Robert M. 2015. "The Commitment Problem: Spending to Zero to Maximize the Efficiency of the Collections Budget." *Library Resources & Technical Services* 59, no. 4: 162–71.

Currie, Lea, and Sara E. Morris. 2017. "Maintaining Collections with a Flat Budget." *Insights: The UKSG Journal* 30, no. 1: 47–52.

Davis, Susan, Deberah England, Tina Feick, and Kimberly Steinle. 2015. "Minding the Store; Insights and Perceptions on the Role of the Subscription Agent in Today's Scholarly Resources Marketplace." *Serials Librarian* 69, nos. 3/4: 240–66.

Disher, Wayne. 2014. *Crash Course in Collection Development.* Santa Barbara, CA: ABC-CLIO.

Estes, Mark E. 2009. "Slicing Your Pieces of the Pie." *AALL Spectrum* 13, no. 4: 1.

Evans, G. Edward. 1970. "Book Selection and Book Collection Usage in Academic Libraries." *Library Quarterly* 40, no. 3: 297–308.

Evans, G. Edward, and Claudia White Argyres. 1974. "Approval Plans and Collection Development in Academic Libraries." *Library Resources and Technical Services* 8, no. 1: 35–50.

Ferris, Kady, and Tina Herman Buck. 2014. "An Ethos of Access: How a Small Academic Library Transformed Its Collection-Building Processes." *Collection Management* 39, nos. 2-3: 127–44.

Fowler David C., and Janet Arcand. 2003. "Monographs Acquisitions Time and Cost Studies: The Next Generation." *Library Resources & Technical Services* 47, no. 3: 109–24.

Fulton, Karin J. 2014. "The Rise of Patron-Driven Acquisitions: A Literature Review." *Georgia Library Quarterly* 51, no. 3: 22–30.

Greene, Brian. 2014. "Responsive Acquisitions: A Case Study on Improved Workflow at a Small Academic Library." *In the Library with the Lead Pipe.* November 5. http://www.inthelibrarywiththeleadpipe.org/2014/responsive-acquisitions-a-case-study-on-improved-workflow-at-a-small-academic-library/.

Griffin, Alison, and Sarah Forzetting. 2012. "Behind the Scenes: Approval Profiles from a Vendor's Perspective." In *Library Collection Development for Professional Programs: Trends and Best Practices*, edited by Sara Holder, 16–31. Hershey, PA: IGI Global.

Hibner, Holly, and Mary Kelly. 2013. *Making a Collection Count: A Holistic Approach to Library Collection Management.* 2nd ed. Chandos Information Professional Series. Oxford, UK: Chandos Pub.

Holden, Jesse. 2017. *Acquisitions: Core Concepts and Practices.* 2nd ed. Chicago: Neal-Schuman.

Horava, Tony. 2017. "Demand-Driven Acquisition and Collection Management." *Technicalities* 37, no. 4: 15–18.

Hurst, Nancy. 2013. "The Book Stops Here." *Public Libraries* 52, no. 5: 36–42.

Johnson, Qiana. 2016. "Moving from Analysis to Assessment: Strategic Assessment of Library Collections." *Journal of Library Administration* 56: 488–98.

Ke, Irene, Wenli Gao, and Jackie Bronicki. 2017. "Does Title-By-Title Selection Make a Difference? A Usage Analysis on Print Monograph Purchasing." *Collection Management* 42, no. 1: 34–47.

Kelly, Robert. 2018. "NA Publishing, Image Data Conversion, Announce Bankruptcy." Two-Year Talk. June 19, 2018. https://twoyeartalk.wordpress.com /2018/06/19/na-publishing-image-data-conversion-announce-bankruptcy/.

Kennedy, Rachel, and Peter Macauley. 2015. "Large-scale Acquisitions: The Story of Ian McLaren's Collection." *Australian Academic & Research Libraries* 46, no. 1: 39–51.

Kont, Kate-Riin. 2015. "How to Optimize the Cost and Time of the Acquisitions Process?" *Collection Building* 34, no. 2: 41–50.

Koufogiannakis, Denise, and Alison Brettle, eds. 2016. *Being Evidence Based in Library and Information Practice*. Chicago: Neal-Schuman.

Laughrey, Edna. 1987. "Acquisitions Costs: How the Selection of a Purchasing Source Affects the Cost of Processing Materials." In *Pricing and Costs of Monographs and Serials: National and International Issues*, edited by Sul H. Lee, 53–66. New York: Haworth.

Orkiszewski, Paul. 2005. "A Comparative Study of Amazon.com as a Library Book and Media Vendor." *Library Resources & Technical Services* 49, no. 3: 204-9.

Ostergaard, Kirsten, and Doralyn Rossmann. 2017. "There's Work to Be Done: Exploring Library-Vendor Relations." *Technical Services Quarterly* 34, no. 1: 13–33.

NASIG Core Competencies Task Force. 2013. *NASIG Core Competencies for E-Resources Librarians*. Rev. January 26, 2016. NASIG. http://www.nasig.org/site _page.cfm?pk_association_webpage_menu=310&pk_association_webpage=7802.

NASIG. 2015. *NASIG Core Competencies for Print Serials Management*. Rev. April 25, 2016. NASIG. http://www.nasig.org/site_page.cfm?pk_association_webpage _menu=310&pk_association_webpage=8576.

National Information Standards Organization. 1999. *Criteria for Price Indexes for Printed Library Materials*. ANSI/NISO Z39.20-1999. Bethesda, MD: National Information Standards Organization.

Peet, Lisa. 2018. "Holding Pattern." *Library Journal* 143, no. 3: 21–23.

Roll, Ann. 2016. "Both Just-in-Time and Just-in-Case." *Library Resources & Technical Services* 60, no. 1: 4–11.

Scardilli, Brandi. 2015. "Stormy Seas: The State of Library Budgets." *Information Today* 32, no. 10: 1, 26–27.

Sennyey, Pongracz. 1997. "Assessing Blanket Order Effectiveness: A Neglected Task in Collection Development." *Library Acquisitions: Practice & Theory*, no. 4: 445-54.

Snyder, Herbert, and Julia Hersberger. 1997. "Public Libraries and Embezzlement: An Examination of Internal Control and Financial Misconduct." *Library Quarterly* 67, no. 1: 1–3.

Sowards, Steven W., and Joseph J. Harzbecker, Jr. 2018. "Managing a Collection Budget." In *Health Sciences Collection Management for the Twenty-First Century*, ed. Susan K. Kendall, 83–120. Lanham, MD: Rowman & Littlefield.

Thomas, Joseph. 2008. "A Beginner's Guide to Working with Vendors." In *The E-Resources Management Handbook*, ed. Graham Stone. Online. UKSG. http://dx.doi.org/10.1629/9552448-0-3.19.1.

Tyler, David C., Christina Falci, Joyce C. Melvin, MaryLou Epp, and Anita M. Kreps. 2013. "Patron-Driven Acquisition and Circulation at an Academic Library: Interaction Effects and Circulation Performance of Print Books Acquired via Librarians' Orders, Approval Plans, and Patrons' Interlibrary Loan Requests." *Collection Management* 38, no. 1: 3–32.

Wilkinson, Frances C., Linda K. Lewis, and Rebecca L. Lubas. 2015. *The Complete Guide to Acquisitions Management*. 2nd ed. Santa Barbara, CA: ABC-CLIO.

Zhang, Ying. 2014. "Evidence Based Acquisitions—A Win-Win?" *Information Today Europe*. 6 August. http://www.infotoday.eu/Articles/Editorial/Featured-Articles/Evidence-based-acquisitions-a-win-win-98610.aspx.

9
Assessing Collections and the Library

Assessment tools and strategies have received considerable focus in our professional discussions.
—Anne Johnsonville Graf and Benjamin R. Harris, 2016

One way to determine the value of anything is to determine its usefulness. Nowhere is this truer than in libraries and, in turn, their collections. More and more, libraries are encompassing large percentages of their collections as electronic, and this begs the question about its value.
—Douglas King, 2009

The explosive growth of assessment programs in academic libraries over the last decade is well established now.
—Michelle H. Brannen, Sojourna J. Cunningham, and Regina Mays, 2016

Traditionally, an effective way to assess a diverse physical library was to focus on two collection indicators, capacity and use. The transition period from primarily print formats to primarily digital formats required researchers to take account of this shifting landscape in collection evaluation.
—Joy M. Perrin, Le Yang, Shelly Barba, and Heidi Winkler, 2017

Assessment, accountability, and outcomes are words that have become very familiar to library staff, even if they are not totally clear about what is required, over the past 20-plus years. Phrases such as "we are a culture

179

of assessment," "funders are demanding accountability," and "stakeholders want to know what the outcomes were," or some variation on such themes, have become fairly commonplace in the library world. Almost every library activity may be called upon to help meet the demand for answers. Of the three concepts, the one that is probably the most difficult to provide satisfactory data for is outcomes. Certainly, data such as items acquired or circulated rarely will suffice as an outcome measure (although such data may be part of a satisfactory response for other assessment questions).

Collections are not exempt from the demands for accountability, assessment, and outcomes. They also play a significant role in any overall assessment/evaluation of the quality of the library. Collection evaluation is not new; it has been something librarians and others have done for the better part of 100 years. What has changed is what library stakeholders expect as proof that they are indeed receiving real value for the support provided.

Providing the highest quality service is a key component in demonstrating value for money spent and for gaining user support. Brian Quinn's 1997 comment is as true today as when he wrote it:

> The concept of service quality is somewhat elusive and resists easy definition, but essentially it emphasizes gap reduction—reducing any gap that may exist between a customer's expectations and the customer's perception of the quality of service provided. More traditional measures of academic library quality such as collection size are considered to be of secondary importance. (p. 359)

More recently the term assessment has become almost a buzzword in both the professional and popular press. People apply it to almost every type of organization and activity. People also tend to use assessment and accountability interchangeably. Although the two terms are related, they are not identical (except in the very broadest meaning).

One way to think about the differences is that *assessment* is a process that an organization undertakes to look at its own activities, services, and/or operations. *Accountability*, on the other hand, is when an outside agency or group looks at an organization's activities, services, and/or operations. For libraries, there is almost always a parent body to which it is accountable. The parent body can and occasionally does look at some or all of the library's activities. The most common occurrence is the one we discussed in the last chapter—fiscal management and conducting audits of the library's financial transactions. For educational libraries, there is another outside group that engages in examining a library's activities—accreditation groups. Accrediting agencies represent one of the largest stakeholder groups with an interest in library service/quality—the general public.

In 2005, John B. Harer and Bryan R. Cole published an article on the importance of stakeholders' interest in measuring performance/service. They engaged in a Delphi study "to determine the importance of a list of critical processes and performance measures relevant to measuring quality in academic libraries" (p. 149). Their results suggested that, in an academic context, students, faculty, and the general public, at least in terms of publicly financed institutions' interests, were a significant factor in assessing quality (p. 160). Other types of libraries have equally diverse stakeholders with similar quality expectations.

There are a variety of reasons for a library to undertake collection assessment projects. Some are internal and others are external in character. At other times, both become factors. The following are some of the factors that come into play from time to time:

Collection Development Needs

- What is the true scope of the collections (that is, what is the subject coverage)?
- What is the depth of the collections (that is, what amount and type of material comprise the collection)?
- What are the ratios between print, media, and e-collections (are they appropriate for current user needs)?
- How does the service community use the collection (that is, what is the circulation and use within the library)?
- What is the collection's monetary value (which must be known for insurance and capital assessment reasons)?
- What are the strong areas of the collection (in quantitative and qualitative terms)?
- What are the weak areas of the collection (in quantitative and qualitative terms)?
- What problems exist in the collection policy and program?
- What changes should be made in the existing program?
- How well are collection development officers carrying out their duties?
- Provide data for possible cooperative collection development programs.
- Provide data for deselection (weeding) projects.
- Provide data to determine the need for a full inventory.

Budgetary Needs

- Assist in determining allocations needed to strengthen weak areas.
- Assist in determining allocations needed to maintain areas of strength.
- Assist in determining allocations needed for retrospective collection development.
- Assist in determining overall allocations.

Local Institutional Needs

- Determine if the library's performance is marginal, adequate, or above average.
- Determine if the budget request for materials is reasonable.
- Determine if the budget provides the appropriate level of support.

- Determine if the library is comparable to others serving similar communities.

- Determine if there are alternatives to space expansion (for example, weeding).

- Determine if the collection is outdated.

- Determine if there is sufficient coordination in the collection program (that is, does the library really need all those separate collections).

- Determine if the level of duplication is appropriate.

- Determine if the cost/benefit ratio is reasonable.

Extraorganizational Needs

- Provide data for accreditation groups.

- Provide data for funding agencies.

- Provide data for various networks, consortia, and other cooperative programs.

- Provide data to donors.

More often than not, collection assessment projects address several of the above factors, if for no other reason than doing a project takes significant time and effort, so meeting more than one objective makes good sense. There are times when projects provide unexpected dividends by providing information about a factor that was not part of the original project goals.

When an assessment project is undertaken for accreditation purposes, the initial work is straightforward as there is a clear goal—address the

---

From the Authors' Experience

One of Evans' consulting projects was at a private university where student complaints about the campus library became a concern of senior campus administrators. Although the objections raised by on-campus students covered a wide range of issues concerning the quality of library service, the collection was the most often mentioned issue.

The students complained about lack of material without being more specific. Thus, the initial focus was on collection depth, breadth, and usage patterns, and a request for a random sample of the collection base for analysis. The request for the sample was intended to look at holdings by subject areas and the institution's degree programs and determine some ratios of holdings to usage on the chance that it was just a few areas that were causing the complaints. The surprise finding was the fact that there was a 13-year "hole" in the collection in which no (or very few at best) new monographs had been added to the collection. Students tend to want the newest information for their course assignments. What the analysis showed was the holdings prior to 1984 were balanced across the degree program areas, but were totally skewed toward later material.

Perhaps the outcome of an increase in the budget for on-campus library resources would have been the same; however, the dramatic nature of the totally unexpected data very likely made the increases larger and quicker than might have happened otherwise. Unexpected findings are not all that rare.

areas of interest to the accrediting body. A challenge in this area is when the visiting team is "onsite" and requests information immediately (often the timeframe is less than 24 hours). (Visiting teams are rarely onsite for more than five days and a rough average is closer to three days.) To address such requests, those who conduct the collection assessments for the library must understand the pros and cons of the various methods available for conducting such work.

No one suggests that it is possible to determine the adequacy of a library's collection solely in quantitative terms. However, in the absence of quantitative guidelines, budgeting officers, who cannot avoid the use of quantitative data—such as volumes added—for decision making, adopt measures that seem to have the virtue of simplicity but are essentially irrelevant to the library's function. Therefore, it is necessary to develop quantitative approaches for evaluating collections that are useful in official decision making and that retain the virtue of simplicity while being relevant to the library's programs and services.

Collection Assessment Methodologies

Some years ago, ALA issued the *Guide to the Evaluation of Library Collections* (Lockett, 1989). Although this title has not been updated, it continues to provide a useful framework for collection assessment by dividing evaluation methods into two broad categories: collection-centered measures and use-centered measures. Each category consists of several evaluative methods. The methods focus on print resources, but there are some that can be employed with e-resources as well. The categories, along with their associated methodologies, are:

Collection-Centered Methods

- List checking, bibliographies, and catalogs
- Expert opinion
- Comparative use statistics
- Collection standards

Use-Centered Methods

- Circulation studies
- User opinion/studies
- Analysis of ILL statistics
- Citation studies
- In-house use studies
- Shelf availability
- Simulated use studies
- Document delivery tests

Each method has its advantages and disadvantages. A good approach to an assessment project is to employ several methods that will counterbalance one another's weaknesses. (We cover e-resource assessment in chapter 13.)

Check This Out

One study that explores combining methodologies of data collection is Rachel Kirkwood's 2016 piece "Collection Development or Data-Driven Content Curation? An Exploratory Project in Manchester" (*Library Management* 37, nos. 4/5: 275–84). In her review of the process used at the University of Manchester Library, she notes one of the key "lessons learned" when it comes to collection assessment projects is that the "data-driven approach will always be constrained by the quality and availability of data and metadata" (p. 282).

Additionally, combining assessment methods provides still more evidence for data-driven decisions, which are the expectation in many libraries today. As noted by Ian Chant and Matt Enis, "Data can help to confirm suspicions, prove hypotheses, and offer evidence for the success of library programs. It can also dash expectations or surprise sleeping biases, forcing the rethinking or reinvention of a program that isn't living up to its potential" (2014, p. 38).

Collection-Centered Methods

List Checking

List checking is an old standby for collection evaluators; it may well be the first method that libraries employed after recognizing the need to assess their collections. It can serve a variety of purposes. Used alone or in combination with other techniques—usually with the goal of coming up with some numerically based statement, such as "We (or they) have X percentage of the books on this list"—one of its advantages is that it provides objective data. Consultants may check holdings against standard bibliographies (or suggest that the library do it). Doing this allows for comparisons between the local collection and bibliographies that provide some insight about collection quality.

Another recent addition to this form of assessment is a product from OCLC's Sustainable Collection Services® (SCS) called *GreenGlass*®. With *GreenGlass*®, libraries, usually as part of a consortia, receive reports that allow them to compare print monograph holdings as a means of determining collection strengths and gaps (http://www.oclc.org/en/sustainable-collections /features.html). With this information, libraries can work together as a group

---

From the Advisory Board

Advisory Board member Wendy Bartlett suggests one way of creating a customized bibliography for a library:

Creating a "Core Collection" is a great idea for public libraries, particularly ones that float. Selectors build a core collection by choosing ten titles each month to make "core," and a note is added to the 560 field in the ILS. Then, once a quarter, the core list can be printed and checked against holdings to ensure there are enough copies of *The House of the Seven Gables* or *The Joy of Cooking* or what have you on the shelf. Then you are essentially creating your own "standard bibliography" that is tailored to your service community.

From the Authors' Experience

The University System of Maryland and Affiliated Institutions (USMAI) worked with SCS for a system-wide evaluation of print monographs (https://www.oclc.org/en /news/releases/2017/201712dublin.html). Although project parameters were such that the *GreenGlass*® data set did not include materials from special collections at the University of Maryland Libraries (UMD), data did include holdings information for Big Ten Academic Alliance libraries, as well as other regional consortia. The data was useful for deselection projects conducted in the general collections at UMD.

---

to build retention models to support shared collection development. The Eastern Academic Scholars' Trust (EAST) is one consortia that used data from SCS to develop an extensive retention model (https://eastlibraries.org /process). *GreenGlass*® data is also used by individual libraries to create customized reports to support local deselection activities for print monographs.

Regardless of collection size, it is worthwhile to take time to review some of the best-of-the-year lists published by various associations and journals. Such reviews will help selectors spot titles missed during the year and serve as a check against personal biases playing too great a role in the selection process.

List checking rests on several assumptions; one is that the selected list reflects the goals and purposes of the checking institution. A second assumption is that the sample size, assuming that entire list is not checked, is such that it is both valid and reliable. That is, the data are only as good as the sampling method employed. Another assumption is there is some correlation between the percentage of listed books held by a library and the percentage of quality books in the library's collection. This assumption may or may not be warranted. An equally questionable assumption is that listed books not held necessarily constitute desiderata, and that the proportion of items held to items needed (as represented on the list) constitutes an effective measure of a library's adequacy.

Certainly there are shortcomings of the checklist method. Eight criticisms that appear repeatedly in the literature are:

- Checklists are developed for a broad range of libraries and are never a complete match for any particular library.

- Almost all lists are selective and omit many worthwhile titles.

- Many titles have little relevance for a specific library's community.

- Lists may be out of date.

- A library may own many titles that are not on the checklist but that are as good as the titles on the checklist.

- Document delivery services carry no weight in the evaluation.

- Checklists approve titles; there is no penalty for having poor titles.

- Checklists fail to take into account special materials that may be important to a particular library.

Obviously, the time involved in effectively checking lists is a concern. Spotty or limited checking does little good, but most libraries are unable or unwilling to check an entire list. Checklist results show the percentage of books from the list that is in the collection. This may sound fine, but there is no standard proportion of a list a library should have. How would you interpret the fact that the library holds 53 percent of some list? Is it reasonable or necessary to have every item? Comparisons of one library's holdings with another's on the basis of percentage of titles listed are of little value, unless the two libraries have almost identical service populations and/or mission statements.

This lengthy discussion of the shortcomings of the checklist method should serve more as a warning than a prohibition. There *are* benefits from using this method in evaluation. Many librarians believe that checking lists helps to reveal gaps and weaknesses in a collection, that the lists provide handy selection guides if the library wishes to use them for this purpose. They think that the revelation of gaps and weaknesses may lead to reconsideration of selection methods and policies. Often, administrators outside the library respond more quickly and favorably to information about gaps in a collection when the evaluators identify the gaps by using standard lists than when they use other means of identifying the weaknesses. Also, as seen with the *GreenGlass®* product, list checking can allow groups of libraries to more effectively work together and plan for collective storage and retention. (More on collaborative collection development in chapter 10.)

Expert Opinion (Impressionistic Assessment)

Today, experts primarily play a role in collection assessment by helping CM staff formulate a sound assessment project using a variety of techniques. In the past, people such as Robert Downs (1941) conducted the collection assessments for libraries as experts. Such "experts" did employ best/recommended lists as part of their assessment, but also drew on their experience and opinions about strengths and weakness. There are still occasions when the outside expert is needed, most often when the library believes that such a person will have more credibility with funding authorities or other outside bodies. There are also rare occasions when the outside group hires an expert to do the assessment, if the group thinks an unbiased judgment is necessary.

Today it is rare that this is the sole technique used for assessment. The most common time this occurs is during accreditation visits when a visiting team member walks into the stacks, looks around, and comes out with a sense of the value of the collection. No consultant who regularly uses this technique limits it to shelf reading or reviewing library websites or lists of online resources and collections available. Rather, consultants prefer to collect impressions from the service community as well as from CM staff. Although each person's view is valid only for their own areas of interest, in combination, individuals' views should provide an overall sense of the service community's views. (This approach falls into the category of user satisfaction.) Users make judgments about the collection every time they look for something. They will have an opinion even after one brief visit. Thus, the approach is important, if for no other reason than that it provides the evaluator with a sense of what the users think about the collection.

The obvious weakness of the impressionistic technique is that it is overwhelmingly subjective. Certainly the opinions of those who use the collection regularly as well as the views of subject specialists are important. However, impressions are most useful as one element in a multifaceted evaluation project.

Comparative Use Statistics

Comparisons across a number of institutions can offer useful, if limited, data for assessing a collection. The limitations arise from institutional variations in objectives, programs, and service populations. For instance, a community college with a strong emphasis on transfer programs will have a library collection that reflects that emphasis, whereas a community college that focuses on vocational programs requires a rather different collection. Comparing the two would be like comparing apples to oranges.

Some useful comparative evaluation tools have been developed as a result of technology and growth of bibliographic utilities. A widely used product/service is OCLC's *WorldShare® Collection Evaluation* (http://www .oclc.org/en/collection-evaluation.html). The service draws upon the OCLC's huge bibliographic database. With it, a library can select a peer group—up to 10 peers—for comparison purposes. It is possible to compare your collection with the group as a whole or library by library. You can identify your unique holdings and strengths and weaknesses based on volume counts in a class number in your collection. Only OCLC members can use the service since it draws on OCLC's cataloging database. The data from doing such analysis is very useful, if somewhat expensive. Cheryl Bain and her colleagues at McGill University (2016) described their experience with *WorldShare® Collection Evaluation* as the basis of analyzing their science and engineering monographs. Results provided an overview of their collection by subject area, size, age, and format type, "quickly . . . and without requiring a great deal of technical expertise" (p. 149).

Another assessment tool that public and some academic libraries are using is the *Bowker Book Analysis System™ (BBAS™)*. The service combines material from *Choice* and the *H. W. Wilson Standard Catalogs* to form the assessment database. The system assists in identifying gaps and duplication in the collection. Bowker's website describes the service and states:

> BBAS is a powerful collection-analysis tool and an essential
> resource for academic librarians to electronically compare their
> library's collection against Resources for College Libraries
> (RCL). This customizable, self-service analysis tool eliminates
> tedious manual comparison via customized reports for data
> cleansing and management, and instant identification of the
> gaps and overlaps in your collection—so you can make better
> informed selection decisions. (http://www.bbanalysis.com/)

George Mason University coupled *BBAS™* with other tools such as OCLC's Collection Evaluation tool in a pilot assessment of its collection. As noted by Madeline Kelly (2014), there were some challenges that had to be

---

Check This Out

Not every institution can afford such resources as *BBAS™* or *WorldShare®*, and thus must develop their own method of assessing collections. Redwood Library in Newport, Rhode Island, did just this, utilizing *Excel* workbooks to contain their assessment data. The process used by Redwood is chronicled in Robert Kelly's 2016 article "Collection Assessment and Development at a U.S. Membership Library: A Case Study" (*Collection Management* 41, no. 2: 82–93).

From the Advisory Board

Advisory Board member Susan Koutsky notes that:

Montgomery County (Maryland) Public School libraries use a tool from Follett called *Titlewave®* (https://www.titlewave.com/) which is integrated into our library management system, Destiny. Libraries can upload MARC records of holdings and run a collection analysis, which provides detailed reports of numbers of holdings in call number ranges as well as date ranges, number of holdings per student, ratio of fiction to nonfiction and print to digital, and numbers of holdings within reading levels. The reports also analyze call number and date validity, which aids in catalog management. The call number/date range reports in particular can be quite revealing and are useful in purchasing and weeding decisions and in justifying those decisions to administrators.

---

worked around with *BBAS*™ data as "it could not account for Mason's eBook holdings, so all results had to be double-checked against the Mason catalog manually. There were also concerns among liaison librarians about the quality of the *Resources for College Libraries* list and the classification scheme used by RCL" (p. 588).

Using Standards as an Assessment Method

There are published standards for almost every type of library. The standards cover all aspects of library operations and services, including collections. Some standards have a section about print collections and sections dealing with other formats. The standards vary over time, and they sometimes shift from a quantitative to a qualitative approach and back again. These shifts make long-term comparisons problematic. Quantitative standards have proven useful, in some instances, especially for libraries that do not achieve the standard.

The *Standards for Libraries in Higher Education* developed by the Association of College & Research Libraries suggests using ratios such as "a ratio of volumes to combined total student FTE or headcounts" (2018, p. 8) as one means of assessing adequacy. The standards also list outcomes of the type accrediting agencies often ask. One such outcome is, "The library provides access to collections aligned with areas of research, curricular foci, or institutional strengths" (p. 18). The point of the outcomes is to emphasize why assessment is a vital part of a sound CM program. Patricia Iannuzzi and Jeanne M. Brown (2010) reported on the results of a 2010 survey of academic directors regarding what they thought should be revised in the earlier version of the document. Their article concluded by noting, "our colleagues have clearly indicated a need to align library standards with regional accreditation standards" (p. 487).

The American Association of School Libraries division of ALA issued the *National School Library Standards for Learners, School Librarians, and School Libraries* in 2017 (https://standards.aasl.org/). The standards are intended to be used in conjunction with state library standards and grade-level content standards and focus on the "qualities of well-prepared learners, effective school librarians, and dynamic school libraries" (https://standards.aasl.org/beliefs/). A school media center standard related to collections is *School Library Programs: Standards and Guidelines for Texas*

Check This Out

The following site provides links to many of the state standards for school libraries: https://www.cde.ca.gov/ci/cr/lb/schoollibstnds2017.asp.

(2017). The document notes, "The school library program includes a carefully curated collection of current materials in a variety of formats, including curation of open educational resources (OER) that are uniquely suited to support inquiry learning and the needs and interests of all users" (p. 5). The standards also provide guidance on how to think about how that statement translates into reality by outlining four levels: Exemplary, Recognized, Acceptable, and Below Standard. The levels identify quantitative and qualitative issues such as collection size and formats, age of materials, and evaluative tools.

As mentioned above, public library standards also appear in state documents. In the case of Wisconsin, for example, the Public Library Development Team of the Wisconsin Department of Public Instruction produces public library standards. The latest edition of the standards is designed around three levels or tiers of service. Libraries must meet all standards at the first tier before progressing to the second tier. A library in the third tier must meet all of the first and second tier standards as well as all but two third-tier standards (2018, p. 3). Two of the first tier collections and resource standards are: "24. The library's collection is regularly evaluated for retention, replacement, or withdrawal, as at a rate determined by the library's adopted collection management schedule" and "32. The library provides access to resources in formats appropriate to the needs of all population groups in the community" (p. 14). The second tier standard focuses on the library's ability to provide collections unique to the community (p. 21).

Use-Centered Methods

Circulation Studies

Studying collection use patterns is a very common method for evaluating collections. Two basic assumptions underlie usage studies: one, that the adequacy of the print collection is directly related to its use, and two, that circulation records provide a reasonably representative picture of collection use. Use data, normally viewed in terms of circulation figures, are objective, and the differences in the objectives of the institution that the library serves do not affect the data. They also serve as a useful check on one or more of the other evaluation methods. Usage data are essential in deselection projects (we cover deselection later in this chapter). The ILS in use can easily and quickly generate reams of data regarding item usage. While the system can output the data quickly, the staff time that goes into assessing the data and deciding what to do about the results is substantial.

What to do with all the data generated by an ILS can be a challenge, so thinking about what the purpose of the project is—withdrawal or storage—can help keep the data to a manageable size. There are problems in interpreting circulation data in terms of the value of a collection. Circulation data cannot reflect use generated within the library, such as reference collections and noncirculating journals. Even for circulating items, there is no way of knowing how the material was used; perhaps the book was used to prop

---

Check This Out

One institution developed a unique method of assessing its collection based upon the local environment and collection use. The Millsaps-Wilson Library staff at Millsaps College, in response to an accreditation review, worked to determine if recent acquisitions adequately matched academic programs at the college. Jamie Bounds Wilson detailed the process in her 2016 article "Assessing Collection Development and Acquisitions at the Millsaps-Wilson Library, Millsaps College" (*Mississippi Libraries* 79, no. 1: 4–7). The library used their own "Collection Development Policy Scope of Library Collections by Library of Congress Classification" document as a template that they combined with circulation and interlibrary loan statistics. College programs were assigned to call number ranges, and analysis pointed to areas where circulation was high, but the number of items added was low (p. 6). The method helped them determine what collection areas matched college programs.

As the authors noted in their conclusion, this method need not be restricted to analyzing academic programs alone: "Instead of comparing acquisitions to academic programs, libraries could evaluate purchases in specialized subject areas, genres, or any other collection that needs analysis" (p. 7).

Check This Out

In the early 1980s, Paul Metz (Virginia Tech Libraries) conducted what was then considered the first full-scale study analyzing circulation data in order to determine library collection use. Metz repeated the study and reported the results in his 2011 article "Revisiting the Landscape of Literatures: Replication and Change in the Use of Subject Collections" (*College & Research Libraries* 72, no. 4: 344–59). Metz found the results of the current examination strongly correlated with those of the original study, and noted: "Even the fairly significant shifts in the overall use of subject literatures appear to result, as was argued in *Landscape*, not from micro-level changes in library use within the disciplines, but rather from demographic changes in the population of active users" (p. 359). The original study was published as *The Landscape of Literatures: Use of Subject Collections in a University Library* (Chicago: American Library Association, 1983), and is worth reviewing.

---

open a window or press flowers. Nor can you determine the value derived by the person from a circulated item.

In the public library setting, circulation and in-house use data can be useful in determining the need for multiple copies as well as subject areas of high use in which the library has limited holdings. School libraries have very limited collection space and having "dead wood" (unused items) occupying valuable shelf/floor space is rarely acceptable.

Customer Perceptions

Users' opinions about collection adequacy, in terms of quantity, quality, or both, are significant factors in their overall view about library quality. On the positive side, users know, or think they know, if the material in the collection has met their needs; on the negative side, past experiences will affect users' assessments for good or bad. A person who has used material from only one collection may be more positive about the collection than it warrants because of lack of experience with any other collection. Likewise, a person who has experience with a large research collection may be overly critical of anything less. Knowing something about the individuals' past library experiences can help evaluators assess the responses more accurately. One must also be careful in interpreting self-selected samples; those volunteering information are often part of a small but vocal segment of the user population and may unduly influence the evaluation.

There are at least two commercial products for helping libraries gauge users' attitudes regarding service quality, including collections. One product is *LibQUAL+®*, which is a set of tools for soliciting, tracking, understanding, and acting "upon users' opinions of service quality" (http://www.libqual .org) of libraries. Although some have raised questions about the adequacy of *LibQUAL+®* as the sole assessment method (e.g., Edgar, 2006), it is a useful tool. Conducting such a study can provide data that is both local and comparative with other libraries. It is, in essence, a gap measurement process of the type Quinn (1997) mentioned. Individuals filling out a survey form are asked to indicate, using a nine-point scale, three responses to each question: the person's minimal expectation for a service, the person's desired expectation, and, last, the perceived level of service. A "gap" is present when there are differences between expectations and perceptions.

Some libraries are now using products from Counting Opinions. The organization's statement of purpose/service is to provide "comprehensive, cost-effective ways to capture, manage and measure performance data, including open-ended customer feedback, qualitative and quantitative data, trends, benchmarks, outcomes and peer comparisons" (http://www.countingopinions .com). Their list of customers includes both academic and public libraries. Two of the company's products are *LibSat*, designed to provide "continuous customer satisfaction and feedback management" (http://www.countingopinions .com/#libsat), and *LibPAS*, developed for library performance assessment (http://www.countingopinions.com/#libpas).

Focus groups are another commonly employed method for gathering user views regarding collections and other services. Fran Mentch, Barbara Strauss, and Carol Zsulya (2008) reported on a project that combined *LibQUAL+®* with the results of focus group input. As they noted, "surveys are good at gathering breadth of data; focus groups are good at gathering depth of data" (p. 118). In their conclusion, they observed that, "Pursuing an area of concern in *LibQUAL+®* surveys by conducting focus group sessions on the library's collections, access to it and its use was an appropriate and informative research activity, which yielded usable results" (p. 127).

One point to keep in mind is that normally focus groups pull from an active, interested population. If only actual users are sampled, the institution

---

Check This Out

An excellent resource for learning about using focus groups, which is a more complex process than just talking to people, is the six-volume *Focus Group Kit* by David Morgan and Richard Krueger (Thousand Oaks, CA: Sage Publications, 1998). Krueger also authored a one-volume work, *Focus Groups: A Practical Guide for Applied Research* (5th ed. Los Angeles: Sage, 2015), intended as a practical guidebook to the topic. It is also useful for work in this area.

Check This Out

In addition to providing an overview of the checklist method for assessment they developed for the University of Florida Libraries, Michelle Leonard and Steven Carrico provide suggestions for relaying survey results to stakeholders in their "Developing a Sustainable Collection Assessment Strategy" article referenced below. It is well worth the read.

---

may leave out a large number of people in the service population and fail to discover the answer to two basic questions: Why are nonusers non-users? Is it because of collection inadequacies?

No matter the method chosen, once customer perceptions are included as part of the collection assessment strategy, it is important to share the results of the data obtained from them. As noted by Michelle Leonard and Steven Carrico (2017): "Sharing results with users will encourage users to participate in future qualitative studies; and by reaching out to faculty, students, and researchers with information from assessment efforts, it can provide opportunities to discuss collection objectives, resource prioritization, and budgeting for a specific subject area" (p. 174).

Use of ILL Statistics

One factor that people occasionally overlook in the assessment process is the frequency of use of interlibrary loan (ILL) and/or document delivery services. Heavy use of such services may or may not signal a collection issue for the users. There are at least three aspects regarding the use of these "other library resources"—physical access to other facilities, traditional ILL, and document delivery services. People often use several libraries to meet their various information requirements: educational libraries for academic needs, special libraries for work-related information, and public libraries for recreational materials. They may also use such libraries for a single purpose, because no one type to which they have access can or does supply all the desired data. It is this latter group that has implications for collection development officers. Just knowing that some segment of the service population is using two or more libraries is not enough. The issue is why they are doing so. Again, the reasons may be something other than collection adequacy—closer proximity to where they live or work, different or more convenient service hours, more or better parking, and so forth. However, it is also possible that the problem *is* the collection, and learning from the users their reasons for securing information from other libraries will be of assistance in thinking about possible adjustments in collecting activities. One

---

From the Advisory Board

Advisory Board member Wendy Bartlett suggests:

Another great "gut check" is to simply look at hold shelves. If patrons are routinely having to "call in" from other branches . . . local ILL in a way . . . then you clearly need more copies. I always tour the hold shelves on branch visits to see if I see patterns.

Check These Out

There are a number of articles describing "on demand" purchasing as a result of ILL use. Three recent articles worth reviewing are:

Carol Kochan and Jennifer Duncan's 2016 article "Analysis of Print Purchase on Demand Titles Ordered via Interlibrary Loan: A Collection Development Perspective" (*Collection Management* 41, no. 2: 51–65), where data from five years' worth of purchase on demand ILL was examined at Utah State University.

Daniel L. Huang's 2015 article "Flipped Interlibrary Loan (F.I.L.L.): Putting Interlibrary Loan in the Driver's Seat of Acquisitions" (*Journal of Interlibrary Loan, Document Delivery & Electronic Reserves* 25, nos. 3–5: 61–74), describing the activities at Lehigh University to use ILL data to inform permanent acquisition of titles requested.

Gerrit van Dyk's 2011 article "Interlibrary Loan Purchase-on-Demand: A Misleading Literature" in *Library Collections, Acquisitions, & Technical Services* (35, nos. 2/3: 83–89), which discusses the overhead costs of accessioning materials in a "purchase on demand" environment, including acquisitions, cataloging, and maintenance costs.

Additional cases are reviewed in Laura Costello's 2017 book *Evaluating Demand-Driven Acquisitions* (Cambridge, MA: Chandos).

---

example of such a study is provided by Forrest Link, Yuji Tosaka and Cathy Weng, who analyzed the collections at the College of New Jersey Library. They developed a simple formula to determine the ratio of unmet needs in the collection. The formula combined both ILL and circulation data and was useful in determining which user groups depended more on ILL and which subject areas were most heavily requested (2015, p. 748).

CM staff should periodically review ILL data for journal articles, if for no other reason than copyright compliance. (Note: This has becomes less of a concern as libraries subscribe to so-called "Big Deals" for journal databases.) There should be a careful consideration of whether it is better to add a print or electronic subscription or depend upon a commercial service that pays a royalty fee for each item delivered. An overall review of ILL data may reveal areas of the collection that are too weak to meet all the demands or that may need greater depth of coverage.

Likewise, document delivery data may also provide useful clues for collection development officers, assuming one employs a broad definition that includes full-text materials in online databases. The library needs to review/assess the use of the databases. Who is using what and for what purpose? The key issue is long-term versus short-term needs and how the archiving of the electronic information is or is not handled by the vendor(s).

Bibliometric Studies

Bibliometric methods are particularly valuable for assessing serial collections. Two of the most common techniques are citation and content analysis. Of those two, citation analysis is what most CM personnel employ when working with their serial collections. Ben Wagner noted, "Librarians have long consulted journal impact factors (JIFs) in making journal acquisition and cancellation decisions. Given the misuse of these impact factors by many tenure/promotion committees and national governments as a surrogate evaluation of the quality of an individual's publications, it is also one of the few bibliometric tools well known to many within the scholarly community" (2009). The misuse Wagner mentions arises from the not uncommon use in tenure and promotion process for academics as well as to assess the "value" or importance of the research activities of a department or even an entire institution.

A JIF is a number derived by calculating the number of citations to articles in a journal over a two-year timeframe and dividing by the number of articles the journal publishes in one year. The underlying assumption of JIFs is the more influential or important an article is to a field, the more often it will be cited by others and, by extension, the more important articles a journal publishes, the more important the journal is. CM personnel use the impact factor when looking at what journals they ought to have in their collection; however, the most common time to use it is during the very painful and, in academic libraries, politically sensitive time when journal subscriptions must be reduced. As Wagner suggested, academic administrators and faculty are reasonably aware of the impact factor, thus, its use as a major consideration in the "keep or drop" decisions is generally accepted.

Knowledge of the concept does not assure there will be no complaints about decisions made that employ JIFs from faculty or departments impacted by the decisions. There are many complaints about the nature and use of JIFs. Two of the common complaints about the impact factor that do have some validity are that citation usages do vary from discipline to discipline and journals may and do make editorial decisions, unrelated to research quality, in order to enhance their impact number.

So, where do those JIFs come from? Although there are a few sources (such as Science Gateway, http://www.sciencegateway.org/rank/index.html), the primary resource is Clarivate Analytics' (formerly Thomson Reuters) *Journal Citation Reports®* (http://ipscience-help.thomsonreuters.com /incitesLiveJCR/JCRGroup/jcrOverview.html). The *Reports*, as of mid-2018, cover over 12,000 journals—including over 3,300 publishers. The service provides a variety of options to consider when making selection or cancellation decisions in addition to the impact number. There are subject groups that help address the issue of differentials in citation patterns between disciplines. There is also a feature entitled the "cited half-life" that provides some insight in how long the citation impact lasts. When used with careful thought regarding limitations, JIFs can be another useful tool for assessing a collection.

Citation analysis can also be employed when working on projects related to starting a new program that will require collection support. Compiling a

---

Something to Watch

J. Richard Gott III (2010) proposed an alternative to the standard citation ranking system, named the E-Index (*Physics Today* 63, no. 11:12). This system factors in the efforts of all contributors, something that is lacking in the current system of ranking. It will be interesting to see as time passes whether or not the E-Index becomes as popular as earlier citation ranking methods. As of mid-2018 we have not found any evidence that his approach has taken off. However, yet another alternative to JIF was proposed in 2017 by Lutz Bornmann. He suggested calculating a "confidence interval" for journal articles that would reflect the number of papers published and citations received by an article ("Confidence Intervals for Journal Impact Factors," *Scientometrics* 111, no. 3: 1869–71). It remains to be seen if this proposed method will become popular, but it does provide more evidence that alternatives to JIFs are being developed.

From the Authors' Experience

When the authors have engaged in a collection assessment project of their own collections or when serving as consultants, we employ the following steps after determining the library's goals and objectives:

1. Develop an individual set of criteria for quality and value.

2. Draw a random sample from the collection and examine the use of the items (database sample).

3. Collect data about titles wanted but not available (document delivery requests).

4. Check records of in-library use if available and compare with circulated use to determine if there is a variation by subject.

5. Find out how much obsolete material is in the collection (for example, science works more than 15 years old and not considered classics).

6. Use the database sample to determine the average age of items in a given subject area.

7. If checklists have some relevance to the library, check them, but also do some research concerning the usefulness of these checklists.

---

sample of appropriate reports or studies recently completed elsewhere and then checking the cited references against holdings records to determine which items already exist in the collection provides useful information. If the collection lacks a substantial percentage of the sample citations, the collection will not adequately support the new program without additional funding for acquisitions in the area of interest.

Deselection—Weeding

Deselection work is important, if often the last of many tasks, in a sound CM program. "Selection in reverse" is one way to think about the process. The older term for the process, and one still often used, is weeding. Without an ongoing deselection program in place, a collection can quickly age and become less and less attractive and more difficult to use. As Tim Held noted, "Without weeding, the latest information is difficult to find, as is the older material of enduring worth" (2018, p. 137). Different library types have different goals for the process. For example, public, school, and special libraries carry out the process primarily for replacement or withdrawal purposes. Academic libraries, on the other hand, engage in the process to perhaps withdraw some items, but most often to identify items that could be stored in less costly space.

All libraries ultimately face collection storage space problems. The need for collection space is almost as old as libraries themselves. One of the earliest references to the problem in the United States is in a letter from Thomas Hollis (Harvard's president at the time) to Harvard College's Board of Governors in 1725. He wrote, "If you want more room for modern books, it is easy to remove the less useful into a more remote place, but do not sell them as they are devoted" (Carpenter, 1986, p. 122). More than 100 years passed before Harvard followed Hollis' advice; today, like most major research libraries, Harvard uses remote storage as part of everyday collection development activities.

Selection and deselection are similar activities: first, they are both necessary parts of an effective collection development program; and second, both require the same type of decision making. The same factors that lead to the decision to add an item could lead to a later decision to remove the item. As suggested in chapter 4, the book selection policy in place should also govern deselection projects.

Years ago, Eugene Garfield (1975) noted that weeding a library is like examining an investment portfolio. Investment advisors know that people don't like to liquidate bad investments. Just like frustrated tycoons, many librarians can't face the fact that some of their guesses have gone wrong. They continue to throw good money after bad, hoping, like so many optimistic stockbrokers, that their bad decisions will somehow be undone. After paying for a journal for 10 years, they rationalize that maybe someone will finally use it in the 11th or 12th year. We explore some of the psychological issues related to deselection/weeding later in this chapter.

Before implementing a deselection program, the CM staff should decide on the goal/s of the project. This process should include an analysis of the present staffing situation (as such projects are time consuming and labor intensive), as well as user interest, concerns, and cooperation. Time should also be spent developing a clear picture of project costs and what to do with the materials identified as less useful for the active collection.

Frequently the withdrawal of less useful items becomes a matter of public concern. Withdrawal can take the form of placing the items in a gifts and exchange program or through a book sale, or working through such vendors

Check These Out

Just as all weeding projects do not need to involve the entire collection, the methods established for identifying titles to be removed from the collection need not be complex. Eve-Marie Miller (2016) relates the process used at Santa Rosa Junior College (CA) that involved the use of colored dots placed on the materials in the Reference Collection by the subject selectors. The dots indicated whether or not the title would be weeded, shifted in the stacks, or retained in their current location. The process and outcome are outlined in Miller's article "Making Room for a Learning Commons Space; Lessons in Weeding a Reference Collection Through Collaboration and Planning" (*The Serials Librarian*, 71, nos. 3–4: 197–201).

Likewise, Christopher McHale and his colleagues Francine Egger-Sider, Louise Fulk, and Steven Ovadia provide a deselection alternative to "walking the stacks" in their 2017 article "Weeding without Walking: A Mediated Approach to List-Based Deselection" (*Collection Management* 42, no. 2: 92–108).

Kiri L. Wagstaff and Geoffrey Z. Liu studied the prospects of automatically classifying weeding candidates through a machine learning system they developed and found initial results to be successful. They note such systems do "not replace human processing, but [it] can instead provide an initial assessment of the list of candidates, which allows librarians to focus their time and attention on those items most likely to be weeded" (p. 246). Their 2018 article "Automated Classification to Improve the Efficiency of Weeding Library Collections" (*The Journal of Academic Librarianship* 44, no. 2: 238–47) is an interesting read.

Check This Out

An article that compares the activities of six used-book vendors is Ladislava Khailova's 2014 piece "Trash or Cash? Partnering with Online Booksellers to Dispose of Deselected Academic Library Monographs" (*Behavioral & Social Sciences Librarian* 33, no. 2: 59–76). It is well worth the read if considering the use of such a vendor.

---

as Better World Books (https://www.betterworldbooks.com/) or Zubal Books (http://zubalbooks.com/) who sell deselected library books and return a portion of the proceeds to the library. Although putting the items in the dumpster can raise questions about the library's stewardship, in actuality, many school districts have deselection policies that prohibit selling items that have been weeded. In these cases, the only way to dispose of these materials is through recycling or by placing them in the dumpster. Occasionally, the material goes into a recycling program after it has gone through numerous sales or exchange efforts.

Storing, in contrast, retains the item at a second level of access. Second-level access normally is not open to users and is frequently some distance from the library. Most second-level access storage systems house the materials as compactly as possible to maximize storage capacity. Compact shelving for low-use material is coming into widespread use as libraries attempt to gain maximum storage from existing square footage. Generally, a staff member retrieves the desired item from the storage facility for the user. Depending on the storage unit's location and the library's policy, the time lapse between request and receipt ranges from a few minutes to 48 hours. Nevertheless, this arrangement is normally faster than interlibrary loan. An example of such a facility is the University of Maryland's Severn Library, which opened in 2016 (http://www.lib.umd.edu/severn).

Below is a more detailed discussion of how deselection/weeding varies by library type. We look at academic libraries last because of their focus on storage rather than withdrawal.

Public Libraries

Public libraries have an overarching goal of supplying materials that meet the current needs and interests of the service community. In the public library, user demand is an important factor influencing selection and deselection. Therefore, materials no longer of interest or use to the public are candidates for withdrawal. A public library rule of thumb is that collections should completely turn over once every 10 years.

Certainly there are differences due to size. Small and branch public libraries generally focus on high-demand materials, with little or no expectation that they will have preservation responsibilities. (An exception would be in the area of local history, where the library may be the only place one might expect to find such material.) Large public libraries have different responsibilities that often include housing and maintaining research collections. Thus they have to consider a wider range of issues, more like those confronting academic libraries, when undertaking a deselection program. Chris Jones (2007) made the point that public libraries must consider every factor in their deselection activities. He noted, "Yes,

From the Authors' Experience

A former colleague of the authors had the following to say about weeding in public libraries, which was seconded by a librarian in a school library setting:

Publication date is definitely a factor in much of the nonfiction where librarians must be sure that they no longer stock books identifying Pluto as a planet or Brontosaurus as a dinosaur. Good children's librarians will remove these as soon as the errors of fact are noted, rather than waiting for a burst of deselection activity.

Public librarians who still engage in hands-on collection development (rather than having it done centrally) tend to rely on their own knowledge of their customers and the books to assess the usefulness of their collections. They have their own set of questions they might use to assess the collection when they are assigned to a new branch:

- Do I have enough California mission books to satisfy the perennial fourth grade homework assignment need?
- How many copies of *Diary of a Wimpy Kid* are available?
- Do we have copies of the books that I use over and over again for family storytime and class visits?
- Does the number of books in other languages seem likely to meet the needs of this community?

Experienced children's librarians can also tell a lot by a quick perusal of the sorting shelves to see what has been checked out or cleared from the tables. For most, it really is more of an art than a science.

From the Advisory Board

Advisory Board member Wendy Bartlett notes that some automated systems like *Collection HQ* (from Bridgeall Libraries, https://www.collectionhq.com/) are being designed to make weeding lists a possibility at every branch and desk; this is a huge improvement over taking books off the shelf and looking up their use, or ordering centralized lists from the ILS from busy Help Desks.

size does matter—but freshness cannot be ignored. Weeding is as important to a library collection as it is to a healthy and attractive garden" (p. 172).

Sometimes a weeding project can have unexpected results; an example was the Free Library of Philadelphia. Auditors expect to find items purchased still available or a solid paper trail explaining their absence. When the Philadelphia City Controller's office conducted its review of the library, it concluded that the library was in violation of the city charter by "destroying hundreds of thousands of books." Although the report acknowledged that weeding was a generally accepted practice in libraries, it also stated that "this practice had gone awry" (St. Lifer and DiMattia, 1979, p. 12). At issue was the library's failure to try to find takers for the worn

---

Check These Out

Four resources are especially useful in planning public library weeding projects:
Stanley J. Slote's *Weeding Library Collections* (4th ed. Englewood, CO: Libraries Unlimited, 1999) remains a good starting point for planning and implementing
a deselection project in any type of library. Joseph P. Segal's Evaluating and *Weeding Collections in Small and Medium-Sized Public Libraries: The CREW Method*
(Chicago: American Library Association, 1980) provides a foundation for the use of
the CREW method, which stands for Continuous Review Evaluation and Weeding.
The CREW concept was revisited by Jeanette Larson for the Texas State Library
and Archives Commission in *CREW: A Weeding Manual for Modern Libraries* (2012,
https://www.tsl.texas.gov/ld/pubs/crew/index.html), as well as Rebecca Vnuk in her
2015 *Weeding Handbook: A Shelf-by-Shelf Guide* (Chicago: ALA).

Both Slote and Segal emphasize the use of circulation data, with Slote's system
relying on circulation data (shelf life) to identify candidates for weeding. Segal's system uses age of the publication, circulation data, and several subjective elements he
labels MUSTY (M = misleading, U = ugly [worn out], S = superseded, T = trivial, and
Y = your collection no longer needs the item). Larson's title updates the MUSTY criteria to MUSTIE (M = misleading, U = ugly, S = superseded, T = trivial, I = irrelevant
[to the clientele of the library], and E = may be obtained Elsewhere.

The ideas and methods described in these resources are useful in all types of small
libraries, especially school library media centers.

---

books it had withdrawn (admittedly the numbers involved were substantial—360,000 volumes).

School Library Media Centers

School library media centers employ highly structured collection development practices. In most schools and school districts, the media center
expends its funds with the advice of a committee consisting of teachers,
administrators, librarians, and, occasionally, parents. The need to coordinate collection development processes with curriculum needs is imperative.
Typically, media centers lack substantial floor space for collections. Thus,
when there is a major shift in the curriculum (new areas added and old ones
dropped), the library must remove most of the old material. To some degree,
the media center's deselection problems are fewer because there usually
are other community libraries or a school district central media center that
serve as backup resources.

In addition to the Slote, Segal, Larson, and Vnuk titles previously
mentioned, there are two older articles that provide sound advice about
weeding school media collections: Anitra Gordon's (1983) "Weeding: Keeping Up with the Information Explosion" and the Calgary Board of Education, Educational Media Team's (1984) "Weeding the School Library Media
Collection." Gordon's article, though short, provides a good illustration of
how one may use some standard bibliographies in a deselection program.
The Calgary article provides a detailed, step-by-step method for weeding
the school collection. Newer resources available on the topic include Donna
Baumbach and Linda L. Miller's *Less Is More: A Practical Guide to Weeding
School Library Collections* (Chicago: American Library Association, 2006)

From the Advisory Board

Advisory Board member Susan Koutsky relates a recent experience with deselection:

Two years ago, I began a multi-year weeding project in my school library. It was evident that the collection hadn't been weeded in many years, and the idea of weeding the entire collection was a bit daunting, especially given time constraints. I began with the biography and "everybody" (picture) book sections. Weeding criteria included number of copies needed, publication date, number of times circulated in past 5 years, ties to the curriculum and use in classes, outdated information, and overall appearance, including worn books and outdated illustrations. I did this at the end of the school year, and when students returned in the fall, they noted all the "new books" in the library. In reality, when I removed all the worn out, dated books, the remaining books looked fresh and inviting. I am sure many books were newly discovered because they were no longer hidden among the old books. My advice for school librarians is definitely weed the collection, and go a section at a time.

A great "nuts and bolts" article for school librarians on weeding is Ramona Kerby's "Weeding Your Collection" in *School Library Monthly* (February 2002, 18, no. 6: 22–31). She utilizes the CREW method and gives advice section by section.

---

and Melissa Allen's "Weed 'Em and Reap: The Art of Weeding to Avoid Criticism" (2010).

Special Libraries

The category "special libraries" is so heterogeneous that meaningful general statements are almost impossible to make. Special libraries have to exercise the most stringent deselection programs because of strict limits on collection size that are usually the result of fixed amounts of storage space. It is not surprising, given that the cost of corporate office space is so high, that libraries must make efficient use of each square foot they have allocated to their operations. Thus, the special library must operate with the businessperson's eye toward economy and efficiency. Also, the collections of such libraries usually consist of technical material, much of it serial in character and often with a rapid and regular rate of obsolescence, at least for the local users.

A major concern of special libraries is meeting the current needs of their clients. In such a situation, deselection is easier because of comparatively straightforward and predictable use patterns, the small size and homogeneous nature of the clientele, and the relatively narrow service goals for the library. Deselection takes place with little hesitation because costs and space are prime considerations. The bibliometric measures we covered earlier in the chapter are valuable in establishing deselection programs in special libraries.

Academic Libraries

The purpose of the academic research library has been to select, acquire, organize, preserve (this has had special emphasis), and make available the full record of human knowledge. CM officers in such institutions seldom view

---

Check This Out

Bruce White (2017) reflected on the value of citation and circulation data as factors for deselection in academic libraries in his article "Citations and Circulation Counts: Data Sources for Monograph Deselection in Research Library Collections" (*College & Research Libraries* 78, no. 1: 53–65), noting, "Neither circulation nor citation data can stand as full proxies of the value of a title, but, in reflecting the status of a title within the scholarly community, citedness should be considered at least equally with circulation" (p. 63). His article is worth reviewing.

---

current demand as a valid measure of an item's worth. Potential or long-term research value takes highest priority. That said, why are deselection programs part of research libraries' or other academic libraries' activities?

The role of the college and university library is evolving. Whenever librarians discuss the changing role, they cite the information explosion as one cause along with the ever-increasing availability of e-resources. Marvene Dearman and Elizabeth Dumas observed, "Many years ago libraries were simply judged by the number of volumes on the shelves, no matter what the condition or usefulness of the item" (2008, p. 133). This was especially true in the case of libraries who were members of the Association of Research Libraries (ARL), who at one point based their "rankings" on title and volume counts. The end result of using this benchmark was that few collections were weeded in fear of having their ranking diminished due to a drop in volume count. Most CM officers now understand that it is futile to expect any one institution to locate and acquire all of the relevant material that comes into existence; nor can they organize it, house it, or make it readily accessible to their users.

One challenge is the inevitable lack of collection space for academic libraries while needing to both retain existing items as well as add new material. Certainly the increasing availability of new e-resources (born digital) as well as ongoing digitization efforts does ease the space challenges. However, most academic libraries have substantial "legacy" collections of print material, and printed scholarly titles are continuing to appear and be acquired. Slowly but surely the collection space shrinks and eventually disappears. CM or Access Services/Circulation personnel can make fairly accurate estimates of when the shelving space will be gone. More often than not, expansion of on-campus collection space before the existing space is gone is not too likely, especially under tight economic conditions. Thus, it is imperative to plan on how to handle the situation before it actually happens. The usual plan is for a deselection project.

Barriers to Deselection

One piece of library folklore helps slow or stop many deselection programs: that is, no matter how strange an item may seem, at least one person in the world will find it valuable—and that person will request the item 10 minutes after the library discards it. We have never met anyone who has had it happen, but people believe that it does. There is the proverb: one person's trash is someone else's treasure, and CM staff faces this issue when undertaking a deselection project. It is almost guaranteed that someone, given the chance, will object to the withdrawal or storage of any item in the collection.

Deselection, especially for withdrawal purposes, is not something most librarians enjoy. There is the issue of a bad investment/judgment call that Garfield wrote about. When it is about withdrawing worn-out items or material that you know will become out of date at some point and need to be replaced, the process is easy; however, when it is the fact an item was not used or not used in many, many years, it is much more time consuming and difficult to do.

Most of us were taught by parents and teachers to treat books and magazines with respect. In fact, we learned to have great respect for anything printed. The idea of tearing pages or otherwise damaging a book or magazine goes against all we learned. The problem is that we are confusing the information contained in a package with the packaging. Some material becomes dated and must go, or people will act on incorrect information (prime examples are a loose-leaf service with superseding pages or dated medical or legal information). Travel directories and telephone books are other examples of materials that should go. Long-term value of other materials is less clear, and it is easy to find reasons to save them. In essence, our childhood training adds to the difficulties in removing items from a collection. If the library's goal is to purge rather than store the item, the problem is even bigger. Some of the more common reasons for not thinning a collection are:

- Lack of time
- Procrastination
- Fear of making a mistake
- Concern about being called a "book burner"
- Concern about dealing with opposition to such a project, especially common in academic library settings

These reasons are, to a greater or lesser extent, psychological.

The issue of time to conduct such work is very real and significant. Today all library staff members are asked to do more and additional tasks, especially when economic conditions force hiring freezes or loss of an FTE when a person resigns. There is no question that properly done deselection projects take a substantial amount of time. Where to find that time is difficult. However, as Brice Austin (2002) noted, "While selecting materials for storage is never easy, our experience confirms what Lee Ash (1963) suggested long ago: that the longer one delays the process, the more difficult it becomes" (p. 58). We would add to that thought that delays will also require more time.

Sometimes, librarians never suggest deselection because they assume that there will be opposition from faculty, staff, general users, board members, or others. Naturally, there will be opposition. However, if no one raises the issue, there is no chance of gaining user support. The possibility also exists that the assumed opposition will never materialize and that users from whom one least expects help turn out to be strong supporters. As suggested by Simona Tabacaru and Carmelita Pickett, "collaborating with

---

Check This Out

Megan Lowe surveys the literature on the effects of deselection on librarians in her 2017 annotated bibliography "The Emotional Dimensions of Deselection: An Annotated Bibliography" (*Codex* 5, no. 1: 38–50).

From the Authors' Experience

The last library where Evans worked full-time faced a serious collection space challenge. Although the university was committed to building a new library, everyone knew that five or more years of fundraising would be required before there would be a hope of starting construction. The library knew that at current annual rates of acquisitions the collection storage space would be exhausted in less than two years. A further complicating issue was 240,000 books that were in a cooperative storage facility would be returned to the library in less than 12 months due to the cooperative's regulations. The 240,000 books had been selected for storage over a four-year period in which librarians and faculty made book by book decisions. The university had decided to use a document storage firm (Iron Mountain) to store low-use items until such time as there was a new library.

The problem: how to select 600,000 volumes to store in less than 18 months. The solution: store the existing 240,000 remotely stored items and store all bound journals.

The solution was far from easy, nor was it all that fast to accomplish. Librarians heatedly debated the pros and cons, but finally decided to recommend the bound journal move to the faculty library committee. Two factors helped make the final choice. First, the library had electronic versions of almost all the print titles and students much prefer using those resources to having to find the bound volume and make photocopies. Second, and probably most important, the librarians realized there was not enough time for an item by item selection process of monographs and still carry out all their other duties. The faculty library committee and faculty Senate debated the matter for some time and eventually signed off on the project.

This is a small example of the challenges and time commitment required for a "simple" storage project.

subject librarians, technical services personnel, and faculty could improve acceptance and support needed for completing storage projects successfully" (2013, p. 114). Putting off deselection to avoid a conflict just increases the problem as well as the likelihood that when deselection does occur, the process will generate opposition. Fear of possible political consequences has kept libraries from proposing a deselection program. However, it is likely that a deselection process done in a routine manner will not be noticed or opposed by users. As Ginny Collier (2010) noted, "There will always be books that people ask for that your library won't have. You need to be strong, and do what's best for your collection. Books that languish, unused, on the shelf are of no use to anyone" (p. 51).

Occasionally, libraries encounter legal barriers. Although not common, they can arise and they are time-consuming. The problem arises in publicly supported libraries where regulations may govern the disposal of any material purchased with public funds. In some cases, the library must sell the material, even if only to a pulp dealer. Any disposal that gives even a hint of government book-burning will cause public relations problems; this stems from general attitudes toward printed materials. The library should do all it legally can to avoid any such appearance.

Deselection Criteria

Deselection is not an overnight process, and it is not a function that one performs in isolation from other collection development activities. Persons involved in deselection must consider all library purposes and activities.

Some of the most important issues are library goals, the availability of acquisition funds for new titles, the relationship of a particular book to others on that subject, the degree to which the library functions as an archive, and potential future usefulness of an item. Only when one considers all the factors can one develop a successful deselection program. After the staff recognizes the need for a deselection project, several lists of criteria can help in the deselection process. The following is a fairly comprehensive list:

- Duplicates
- Unsolicited and unwanted gifts
- Obsolete books, especially in the areas of science, medicine, and law
- Superseded editions
- Books that are infested, dirty, shabby, worn out, juvenile (which wear out quickly), and so forth
- Books with small print, brittle paper, and missing pages
- Unused, unneeded volumes of sets
- Periodicals with no indexes
- Low/non-used items

The mere fact that a book is a duplicate or worn out does not necessarily mean that one should discard it. Past use of the item should be the deciding factor. Also, consider whether it will be possible to find a replacement copy.

Three broad categories of deselection criteria exist, at least in the literature: physical condition, qualitative worth, and quantitative worth. Physical condition, for most researchers, is not an effective criterion. In most cases, poor physical condition results from overuse rather than nonuse. Thus, one replaces or repairs books in poor physical condition. (There is little indication in the literature on deselection that poor condition includes material with brittle paper. As discussed in chapter 14, brittle paper is a major problem.) Consequently, if the library employs physical condition as a criterion, it will identify only a few items, unless brittle paper is part of the assessment process.

Qualitative worth as a criterion for deselection is highly subjective. Because of variations in individual value judgments, researchers do not believe that this is an effective deselection method. Getting people to take the time to review the material is difficult. Any group assessment will be slow. Researchers have shown that a library can achieve almost the same outcome it would from specialists' reviewing the material by using an objective measure, such as past circulation or other usage data, if one wishes to predict future use. Also, the deselection process is faster and cheaper when past-use data are available.

The problems that arise in monograph weeding also apply to serials or microformats. A major difference, however, is that journals are not homogeneous in content. Another difference is that the amount of space required to house serial publications is greater than that required to house monographs. Thus, cost is often the determining factor in weeding (that is, although there may be some requests for a particular serial, the amount of space that a publication occupies may not be economical or may not warrant retaining the full set in the collection). Of course, one should not forget users. Considering the benefits and drawbacks, in terms of customer service, that result from an active deselection program is a step in the process. Based on personal

---

From the Authors' Experience

A colleague of the authors described how she has addressed reluctant weeders:

One of the challenges all libraries face is staff reluctance to "weed" items that have been part of the historical core collections. One approach I used was to move the "items" from the main floor to a temporary holding location in the back room. That way, if the librarian was right and the item was indeed needed it was easily available; but, if the item was not asked for . . . (and out of sight of the librarian) for a time—it was easier to migrate to the "weeded" pile.

---

research projects, the percentage of librarians who think that a user should be able to decide which materials to use out of all possible materials available (that is, no deselection) is much smaller than the percentage of librarians who strongly believe that a no-weeding policy is detrimental to the patron. Even academic faculty members lack complete familiarity with all the materials in their own subject fields; faced with a million volumes or more in a collection, how can we expect a student to choose the materials most helpful to his or her research without some assistance?

Storage

Large libraries, particularly research libraries, generally deselect for storage rather than withdrawal. These are two different processes. Often, criteria useful in making discard decisions do not apply to storage decisions. It is important to recognize that the primary objective of these two different forms of treatment is not necessarily to reduce the total amount of money spent for library purposes. Instead, the primary objective is to maximize, by employing economical storage facilities, the amount of research material available to the patron. The two main considerations for a storage program are: (1) What selection criteria are most cost-effective? and (2) How will the library store the items?

In the classic *Patterns in the Use of Books in Large Research Libraries*, Herbert Fussler and Julian Simon (1969) reported some interesting ideas and statistical findings concerning the use factor in selective weeding of books for storage. Although they recognized that frequency of circulation or use of books is not always an accurate measure of the importance of books in large research libraries, Fussler and Simon hoped to determine whether some statistical method could identify low-use books in research library collections. One of their goals was to sort the collection into high- and low-use materials. High-use items would remain in the local collection, and low-use items would go to a remote storage facility (p. 3). They found that use and circulation data was effective for the first cut, that is, to identify potential materials. The final judgment of what to send to storage or discard remained with the collection development staff and other interested persons. Blindly following use data can create more problems than it solves. The authors concluded that past use of an item was the best predictor of future use (p. 143). Given the nature of a large research library, they thought a 15- to 20-year study period provided the best results, but a 5-year period provided adequate data.

Fussler and Simon's findings indicate that their methods would produce similar percentages of use in libraries regardless of type, clientele, and collection size. They concluded that scholars at various institutions have similar reading interests. Finally, they identified three practical alternatives for selecting books for storage:

1. Judgment of one or a few expert selectors in a field.

2. An examination of past use of a book and/or its objective characteristics.

3. A combination of these two approaches. (p. 145)

Of these alternatives, they concluded that an objective system (that is, a statistical measure) ranks books more accurately in terms of probable value than does the subjective judgment of a single scholar in the field. They did recommend, however, that subject specialists and faculty review the candidate books identified using objective means before moving the books to remote storage.

Richard Trueswell (1965) quantitatively measured the relationship between the last circulation date of a book and user circulation requirements and their effect on weeding. He hoped to determine a quantitative method of maintaining a library's holdings at a reasonable level while providing satisfactory service to the user. (One can also use his method to determine the need for multiple copies, thus increasing the probability a user finds the needed books.)

Trueswell's basic assumption was that the last circulation date of a book is an indication of the book's value. He determined the cumulative distribution of the previous circulation data, which he assumed represented the typical circulation of a given library. Next, he determined the 99th percentile, which he used as the cutoff point for stack thinning. By multiplying the previous monthly circulation figures and the distribution for each month after establishing the 99th percentile, he was able to calculate the expected size of the main collection (p. 22).

In applying this method to a sample from the Deering Library at Northwestern University, Trueswell predicted that a library could satisfy 99 percent of its circulation requirements with just 40 percent of its present holdings (p. 24). That is, the library could move 60 percent of its collections to storage without significantly affecting the majority of users. Trueswell did admit that many of his basic assumptions were questionable and that future research would yield more reliable data. Additional research, including that by Trueswell, supported his initial results.

Many other deselection studies exist, and they all generally agree that deselection based on past-use data provide the most cost-effective results. Although most of the studies were from academic libraries, Stanley Slote (1997) found that the method also worked in public libraries.

Check This Out

While circulation data can provide important insights to a deselection decision, Alex McAllister and Allan Scherlen's 2017 article "Weeding with Wisdom: Tuning Deselection of Print Monographs in Book-Reliant Disciplines" (*Collection Management* 42, no. 2: 76–91) raises the issue of using quantitative criteria when deselecting books in the humanities, which tend to rely upon older, low-circulating titles. Their article advocates the development of disciplinary criteria when engaging in deselection activities, especially when dealing with materials in the humanities.

Check These Out

Three articles on selecting titles for storage that are worth a look are:

Amy Lucker's 2012 article "Deal with the Devil: A Participatory Model for Off-Site Storage Selection" (*Art Documentation: Bulletin of the Art Libraries Society of North America* 31, no. 2: 285–92), detailing how users were consulted in decisions for off-site storage made by librarians at the Stephen Chan Library at the Institute of Fine Arts, New York University.

Charlotte Priddle and Laura McCann's 2015 piece "Off-Site Storage and Special Collections: A Study in Use and Impact in ARL Libraries in the United States" (*College & Research Libraries* 76, no. 5: 652–70), describing how storage facilities are utilized for special collections.

Anastasia Guimaraes and Jared Collins chronicle the process used at the Hesburgh Libraries at the University of Notre Dame to prepare approximately one million volumes for transfer to off-site storage in their 2018 article "How to Move a Mountain: The Preparation and Transfer of One Million Volumes to an Off-Site Storage Facility" (*Serials Librarian* 74, nos. 1–4: 228–33).

Although circulation data is as sound a predictor of future use as you can find, it does rest upon several assumptions that staff must understand and accept. One assumption is that circulated use is proportional to in-house use. What that proportion is depends on local circumstances. A second assumption is that current use patterns are similar to past and future patterns. (Trueswell revisited the same library over a period of 10 years and found the same results each time. Of course, that does not mean that the patterns would be the same 50 or 100 years from now.) A third assumption is that statistically random samples provide an adequate base for determining use patterns. A known limitation of circulation data is that a few customers can have a major impact on circulation (otherwise known as the 80/20 rule). Failure to take in-house use into account in a deselection program dependent on use data as the main selection criterion will have skewed results. Additionally, criteria for storage must address the ability to reverse the decision if circulation of stored items is deemed necessary, as advocated by Dan Hazen (2000). He also acknowledged that some rare or vulnerable items may need to remain off-site, regardless of their use patterns (p. 6). The Severn Library policy, developed by the University of Maryland Libraries, includes such a statement (https://www.lib.umd.edu /collections/severn-collection-policy).

One factor to keep in mind is that the automated circulation systems now in use in many libraries will make it possible to collect valuable data for a project. With many systems, it is possible to collect data about in-house use by using a handheld reader and then downloading the data to the system. In the past, in-house use data was particularly time-consuming to collect. Slote's book has an excellent chapter on using computer data in a deselection project.

Points to Keep in Mind

- Assessment is a process that a library employs to look at its collections, services, and other activities to make judgments about quality and effectiveness.

- Accountability is when an outside body looks at library operations to make judgments regarding the library such as its quality, compliance with regulations, effectiveness, and overall value.

- Ongoing collection assessment is an indication of a healthy CM program.

- Assessment methods may be divided into two broad categories: collection-centered and use-centered.

- Each assessment method has its pros and cons; employing a number of methodologies that will balance out the cons is a sound assessment practice.

- Deselection is a necessary component of any sound CM program.

- There are two broad outcomes of a deselection project—withdrawal for the collection or storage in a low-cost facility, off-site in most instances.

- Past usage (circulated and in-house) data is the best predictor of future use.

References

Allen, Melissa. 2010. "Weed 'Em and Reap: The Art of Weeding to Avoid Criticism." *Library Media Connection* 28, no. 6: 32–33.

Association of College & Research Libraries. 2018. *Standards for Libraries in Higher Education*. Chicago: Association of College & Research Libraries, a division of the American Library Association. http://www.ala.org/acrl/sites/ala .org.acrl/files/content/standards/slhe.pdf.

Austin, Brice. 2002. "Establishing Materials Selection Goals for Remote Storage: A Methodology." *Collection Management* 27, nos. 3/4: 57–68.

Bain, Cheryl D., April L. Colosimo, Tara Mawhinney, and Louis Houle. 2016. "Using WorldShare Collection Evaluation to Analyze Physical Science and Engineering Monograph Holdings by Discipline." *Collection Management* 41, no. 3: 133–151.

Baumbach, Donna J., and Linda L. Miller. 2006. *Less Is More: A Practical Guide to Weeding School Library Collections*. Chicago: American Library Association.

Brannen, Michelle H., Sojourna J. Cunningham, and Regina Mays. 2016. "Assessment Committees: Good Practices from ARL Libraries." *Performance Measurement and Metrics* 17, no. 3: 224–40.

Calgary Board of Education, Educational Media Team. 1984. "Weeding the School Library Media Collection." *School Library Media Quarterly* 12, no. 5: 419–24.

Carpenter, Kenneth E. 1986. *The First 350 Years of the Harvard University Library*. Cambridge, MA: Harvard University Library.

Chant, Ian, and Matt Enis. 2014. "The Numbers Game." *Library Journal* 139, no. 8: 28.

Collier, Ginny. 2010. "The Reluctant Weeder." *Children and Libraries: The Journal of the Association of Library Service to Children* 8, no. 2: 51–53.

Dearman, Marvene, and Elizabeth Dumas. 2008. "Weeding and Collection Development Go Hand-in-Hand." *Louisiana Libraries* 71, no. 2: 11–14.

Downs, Robert. 1941. "Technique of the Library Resources Survey." *Special Libraries* 32 (April): 113–15.

Edgar, William B. 2006. "Questioning LibQUAL+: Expanding Its Assessment of Academic Library Effectiveness." *portal: Libraries and the Academy* 6, no. 4: 445–65.

Fussler, Herman H., and Julian L. Simon. 1969. *Patterns in the Use of Books in Large Research Libraries*, rev. ed. Chicago: University of Chicago Press.

Garfield, Eugene. 1975. "Weeding." *Current Contents* 15 (June 30): 26.

Gordon, Anitra. 1983. "Weeding: Keeping Up with the Information Explosion." *School Library Journal* 30 (September): 45–46.

Graf, Anne Johnsonville, and Benjamin R. Harris. 2016. "Reflective Assessment: Opportunities and Challenges." *References Services Review* 44, no. 1: 38–47.

Harer, John B., and Bryan R. Cole. 2005. "The Importance of the Stakeholder in Performance Measurement: Critical Processes and Performance Measures for Assessing and Improving Academic Library Services and Programs." *College & Research Libraries* 66, no. 2: 149–70.

Hazen, Dan C. 2000. "Selecting for Storage: Local Problems, Local Responses, and an Emerging Common Challenge." *Library Resources & Technical Services* 44, no. 4: 176–83.

Held, Tim. 2018. "Curating, Not Weeding." *Technical Services Quarterly* 35, no. 2: 133–43.

Iannuzzi, Patricia A., and Jeanne M. Brown. 2010. "ACRL's Standards for Libraries in Higher Education: Academic Library Directors Weigh In." *C&RL News* 17, no. 9: 486–87.

Jones, Chris. 2007. "Maintaining a Healthy Library Collection: The Need to Weed." *Aplis* 20, no. 4: 170–72.

Kelly, Madeline. 2014. "Applying the Tiers of Assessment: A Holistic and Systematic Approach to Assessing Library Collections." *Journal of Academic Librarianship* 40, no. 6: 585–91.

King, Douglas. 2009. "How Can Libraries Determine the Value in Collecting, Managing, Preserving, and/or Cataloging E-Resources?" *Journal of Electronic Resources Librarianship* 21, no. 2: 131–40.

Larson, Jeanette. 2012. *CREW: A Weeding Manual for Modern Libraries*. Rev. ed. Austin: Texas State Library and Archives Commission. https://www.tsl.texas .gov/ld/pubs/crew/index.html.

Leonard, Michelle, and Steven Carrico. 2017. "Developing a Sustainable Collection Assessment Strategy." In *Proceedings of the 2016 Library Assessment Conference: Building Effective, Sustainable, Practical Assessment*, ed. by Sue Baughman, Steve Hiller, Kate Monroe and Angela Pappaldaro, 172–80. Washington, DC: Association of Research Libraries. http://old .libraryassessment.org/bm~doc/32-leonard-2016.pdf.

Link, Forrest E., Yuji Tosaka, and Cathy Weng. 2015. "Mining and Analyzing Circulation and ILL Data for Informed Collection Development." *College & Research Libraries* 76, no. 6: 740–55.

Lockett, Barbara, ed. 1989. *Guide to the Evaluation of Library Collections*. Chicago: American Library Association.

Mentch, Fran, Barbara Strauss, and Carol Zsulya. 2008. "The Importance of 'Focusness': Focus Groups as a Means of Collection Management Assessment." *Collection Management* 33, nos. 1/2: 115–28.

Perrin, Joy M., Le Yang, Shelly Barba, and Heidi Winkler. 2017. "All That Glitters Isn't Gold: The Complexities of Use Studies as an Assessment Tool for Digital Libraries." *The Electronic Library* 35, no. 1: 185–97.

Public Library Development Team, Wisconsin Department of Public Instruction. 2018. *Wisconsin Public Library Standards*, 6th ed. Madison: Wisconsin Department of Public Instruction. https://dpi.wi.gov/pld/boards-directors /library-standards.

Quinn, Brian. 1997. "Adapting Service Quality Concepts to Academic Libraries." *Journal of Academic Librarianship* 23, no. 5: 359–69.

Segal, Joseph P. 1980. *Evaluating and Weeding Collections in Small and Medium-Sized Public Libraries: The CREW Method.* Chicago: American Library Association.

Slote, Stanley J. 1997. *Weeding Library Collections*, 4th ed. Englewood, CO: Libraries Unlimited.

St. Lifer, Evan, and Susan DiMattia. 1979. "City Rebukes Philadelphia Library on Weeding Practices." *Library Journal* 121, no. 9: 12.

Tabacaru, Simona, and Carmelita Pickett. 2013. "Damned If You Do, Damned If You Don't: Texas A&M University Libraries' Collection Assessment for Off-site Storage." *Collection Building* 32, no. 3: 111–15.

Texas State Library and Archives Commission and the Texas Education Agency. 2017. *School Library Programs: Standards and Guidelines for Texas.* Texas Administrative Code, Title 13. Cultural Resources, Part I. Texas State Library and Archives Commission, Chapter 4. School Library Programs, Subchapter A. Standards and Guidelines, Section 4.1. https://tinyurl.com/TX-SLP.

Trueswell, Richard. 1965. "Quantitative Measure of User Circulation Requirements and Its Effects on Possible Stack Thinning and Multiple Copy Determination." *American Documentation* 16, no. 1: 20–25.

Vnuk, Rebecca. 2015. *Weeding Handbook: A Shelf-by-Shelf Guide.* Chicago: American Library Association.

Wagner, A. Ben. 2009. "Percentile-Based Journal Impact Factors: A Neglected Collection Development Metric." *Issues in Science & Technology Librarianship* no. 57 (Spring). http://www.istl.org/09-spring/refereed1.html.

10
Cooperation, Collaboration, and Consortia Issues

We collaborate because it benefits us and our users, but sometimes we collaborate because we know it will benefit other
librarians and other users.
                    —Jill Emery and Michael Levine-Clark, 2017

Collaboration touches nearly every area of libraries. Academic
libraries collaborate to enhance and expand services beyond
what one institution can do physically or financially on its own.
                    —Sunshine Carter and Danielle Ostendorf, 2017

It is nearly impossible for any one library to hit the moving
target of comprehensive access to relevant content. Working
together, however, libraries can take advantage of a characteristic that may be the most important for collection access going
forward: flexibility.

                                        —Katie Birch, 2017

Academic libraries are adjusting with varying degrees of ur-
gency and with emphases that depend on their local circumstances and mission to new information and education environments, and they are doing so in many aspects of their work by
collaborating more closely than heretofore, deepening their
dependence on other libraries and indeed restructuring work
strategically through these partnerships.

                                        —Robert H. Kieft, 2014

It is difficult to imagine what state our libraries would be in today, regardless of type, if libraries did not collaborate. Working together, which is one
of the first definitions you find in a dictionary for the word collaboration,

has a long history in U.S. librarianship. The notion that libraries represent a "public good" may be widely held by society; however, how much support that "good" is worth is limited. Only through libraries working together are they able to offer the quality and range of services that exist today.

We have touched on the idea of working together in various chapters of this book. In particular, we discussed joint efforts in the chapter on technical services and collection management. Library collaboration is far broader than collection development, and as our opening quotations suggest, such activities are very important in providing users with the broadest possible range of information resources.

The library lexicon has a number of labels for working together—cooperative projects, shared projects, reciprocal projects, consortia, and resource sharing are the most common ones. The arrangement ranges from casual agreements (a verbal yes or a handshake) to highly structured legal frameworks. Some of today's major formal projects (for example, OCLC) started with a casual handshake approach and over time became more complex.

Activities undertaken with a handshake are usually very low risk and ceasing to be a partner is easy and carries no penalties or obligations. Cooperative projects tend to be narrow in focus and involve low resource costs (staff, time, and funding). One such low-cost cooperative activity is agreeing to let other library users have access to your collection in return for your users having borrowing rights in their libraries (reciprocal borrowing agreements). Two examples are reciprocal agreements at Northern Virginia Community College and George Mason University (http://library.gmu.edu /for/visitors/groups) and borrowing privileges for faculty, graduate students, and researchers at Chesapeake Information and Research Library Alliance (CIRLA) member institutions (http://www.cirla.org/reciprocal.html).

Benefits are likely to vary between partners (Library A may gain more than Libraries B, C, and D); however, the low resource costs make the varying benefits less important to the lower benefit libraries as they see obvious benefits from working together or just being helpful. Successful cooperative efforts can lead to greater collaboration and even the creation of a consortium.

Consortia are highly structured, often legally incorporated entities, with elected officers and boards of directors. Most have mission and goal statements that do not fully match any one of the member libraries' statements. There is very often an annual cost for being a member that helps pay the group's operating costs. Partners expect to realize substantial benefits from their membership. Resource requirements are high, especially for those groups that negotiate prices for databases, and there are substantial risks for all partners when one or more members fail to contribute their share of the funding.

Where to place OCLC in terms of working together is not easy. In a very real sense, it is unlike any other library effort. One very significant factor in its rather unique status is that it is both national and international in scope. This is a far cry from its Ohio origins when it was a local cooperative effort. It still describes itself as nonprofit cooperative; however, few other library cooperatives have paid board members or seek to generate revenues that are 2 to 4 percent higher than operating expenses (https://www.oclc.org /en/about/finance.html?cmpid=md_ab_financial). Whatever its status, it is without doubt a major factor in libraries' ability to provide quality service at the lowest possible cost. In many ways, OCLC today is more like other traditional library vendors than it is what most people think of as a library consortia.

From the Authors' Experience

Evans was heavily involved in a group that evolved from being a collaborative effort of a few private academic libraries into a state-wide consortium. Based on conversations with founding members, the original group met the definition of a cooperative during its first few years of existence. From the earliest days, the purpose was to help libraries get better prices for their acquisition of online databases. Initially, a large research library carried the leadership responsibilities with the other libraries playing little or no role in the operations.

When Evans' library joined the group (Southern California Electronic Libraries), there were eight members. By then there were some problems when it came to handling the funds to pay for purchases—some business offices raised questions about sending funds to another institution for the acquisition of something for their campus. As a result, the group became more formal, creating a set of bylaws, formally sharing the workload (group chairperson, secretary, and treasurer), and establishing a business checking account to handle payments to vendors. It also added the word Consortia to its name.

The new structure worked well for some years until the membership grew and the dollar amounts for purchases reached six and, occasionally, seven figures. Given the success of what was first a local (Los Angeles) and then expanding to a fully regional (southern California) collaborative group, private academic libraries across the state began asking to become members. The membership realized it was becoming ever more risky to operate as a voluntary group and the library directors were in effect committing their home institutions to being totally responsible for the full cost of any contract the group signed with a vendor.

Members recognized the need to incorporate in order to limit individual member financial liabilities. It was equally clear the workload was getting too great to be handled by library directors voluntarily committing hours of time to the group's activities (now called the Statewide California Electronic Libraries Consortium—SCELC; http://scelc.org). A membership dues structure was created to provide funding for hiring staff of a SCELC office. Today, SCELC has 112 members and 217 affiliate members, including institutions in Arizona, Hawaii, Texas, and Nevada. Special libraries are now included in the lists of SCELC members in addition to its original academic library base.

Background

Libraries have been engaging in joint ventures for a long time—well over 100 years in the U.S. Many of the joint venture projects, both successful and not so successful, relate in some manner to library collections. Thus, you would expect libraries would have mastered the process. Overall, they do know what is necessary for achieving a successful joint venture. They have also learned that each new effort will bring with it some new challenges and that the truly successful programs must change with the changing times. Robert Kieft and Bernard Reilly (2009) summarized CM joint ventures when they wrote:

> The arduous, variegated, and occasionally distinguished history of collections cooperation on scales large and small is as old as Melvil Dewey, with interest in the last ten years moving from the periphery of specialized materials to the heartland of electronic journals and reference works. This interest now seems

poised to move from that heartland to the back yard of librarians' everyday work on the development of circulating collections. (p. 106)

The efforts that Kieft and Reilly referred to range from something as simple as ILL activities to projects to preserve the ever-growing mountain of digital materials. Outside factors generally play a key role in motivating the start of joint venture activities as well as impact the way in which those activities change over time.

Most of the early efforts focused on internal library operations; certainly they led to service improvements, reduced library costs, and improved collection depth and breadth, but they were not very visible to the majority of users. Many of today's projects are often something users see and appreciate. Shirley Kennedy (2008) reflected the general public's growing awareness of collaborative efforts when she wrote: "What is cool is that we have the Pinellas Automated Library System, which lets you browse or search through the collections of all 15 member libraries, select or reserve materials, and have them sent to a library convenient to you" (pp. 18–19).

Sharing Collection Items

One of the oldest resource sharing activities was the loaning of books between libraries. Loans to libraries may have occurred in ancient Egypt and Greece, but the evidence is sketchy. There was a famous "loan" of the Athenian state copies of the works of Aeschylus, Sophocles, and Euripides to the library of the Egyptian pharaoh Ptolemaios III Euergetes (ruled 247–222 BCE). However, Ptolemaios kept the valuable originals and returned only copies to Athens. Cooperative loaning of materials from library to library in Western Europe goes back at least as far as early medieval times, if not the so-called "Dark Ages" (Jackson, 1974). Monasteries often loaned out books for copying to the scriptoria of other monasteries, sometimes hundreds of miles distant. These libraries sometimes never recovered the loaned materials, due to the exigencies of medieval travel, warfare, fire, barbarian raids, and the occasional thief.

U.S. libraries started an informal ILL program in the early 1900s and the operating rules were codified in 1917. Borrowing activity remained low until the 1950s when a standardized request form was adopted by the American Library Association. In the 1960s, "union catalogs" and serials lists containing the holdings of multiple libraries greatly aided the ability to locate wanted materials, and the introduction of the OCLC interlibrary loan subsystem in the 1970s allowed the electronic transmission of requests. ILL continues to evolve today through the medium of the Internet, resulting in speedier fulfillment of requests and more user control over the process as well as generating greater satisfaction. Without much doubt, ILL is a prime example of cooperation—no bylaws, no officers, and no membership fees—just a sharing of collections between libraries on a voluntary basis. ILL/document delivery activities are beyond the scope of this book; however, there is an obvious linkage between CM and those activities, as well as a linkage between those services and CM resource sharing.

While ILL remains an important component of library service and a form of resource sharing, a new type of service now probably generates the highest volume of items being shared between libraries. ILS products have allowed for the creation of fast, effective, and easy to use means for libraries to share items in their collections without significantly increasing staffing

---

Check This Out

Collaborative efforts can take many forms. One group that has emerged is the Rethinking Resource Sharing Initiative (RRSI), formed to "advocate for a revolution in the way libraries conduct resource sharing" (http://rethinkingresourcesharing.org). Such efforts are likely to become more in demand, as noted by Beth Posner (2007) in her article "Library Resource Sharing in the Early Age of Google" (*Library Philosophy and Practice* 9, no. 3: 1–10): "Because of an increased awareness of online information, people may request more obscure items from more ILL departments, which will encourage more libraries to get involved in resource sharing" (p. 6).

---

costs. Local and regional consortia have expanded the use of other libraries' collections by local users through several approaches.

Some consortia are single library types. Perhaps the most widely known is OhioLINK (http://www.ohiolink.edu/), which is comprised of 120 full members, including 93 academic libraries and the State Library in Ohio. Three examples of multi-type consortia are LINK+ (California), TexShare (Texas), and the Northern Lights Library Network (Minnesota). LINK+ (http://csul .iii.com/screens/linkplusinfo.html) is a group of academic (both public and private) and public libraries with a union catalog database of the members' holdings. The system allows local users to conduct a search of both the local OPAC and the union catalog. If the local library does not hold the item sought, a user (who is in good standing) may request the item from a member library that does have the item. Delivery time to the local library is, on average, less than three days.

TexShare (https://www.tsl.texas.gov/texshare/index.html) is "a consortium of Texas libraries joining together to share print and electronic materials, purchase online resources, and combine staff expertise. TexShare services are available to patrons of participating member libraries all across Texas, regardless of institution type, size, or location" (https://www.tsl.texas .gov/texshare/fact_sheet_faqs.html). One feature of the program is a TexShare library card that allows a person to borrow from any member library.

The Northern Lights Library Network is "a cooperative network of members in academic, public, school, and special libraries in 23 counties of North-central, North-west and West-central Minnesota" (http://www.nlln .org/about-nlln.html). It employs a courier service similar to the LINK+ program for getting items to its users. One special feature of Northern Lights is its 24/7 reference service.

There are hundreds of such consortia, far too many for us to cover in all their various forms and services. Consortia have become a mainstay in collection sharing activities. Users especially like the speedy delivery of documents that often took weeks or months to secure through a standard ILL service. In addition to sharing collections that are currently available in institutions, some groups of libraries are beginning to look to the future and consider retention decisions for resources for their users. The Eastern Academic Scholars' Trust (EAST, https://blc.org/east-project) was formed in 2012 to address the very issue of print retention. The project is managed by the Boston Library Consortium with funding from an Andrew W. Mellon grant, and takes advantage of services from OCLC's Sustainable Collection Services (SCS). Activities of SCS were discussed in chapter 9. As noted by Stearns (2016), "EAST is the first large-scale monograph program to explore the role of volume availability and condition in its retention decisions" (p. 13).

From the Authors' Experience

One organization that does not fit the traditional vendor mold but operates more as a consortia is LYRASIS. LYRASIS was formed in 2008 through the merger of existing member organizations in the Mid-Atlantic (PALINET), the Southeast (SOLINET), and New England (NELINET). Although on one level LYRASIS acts like a vendor representative or go-between for individual libraries, it also works for the good of the entire group through initiatives such as its professional development opportunities, Leaders Circle (https://www.lyrasis.org/Leadership/Pages/Leaders-Circle.aspx), and Catalyst fund grants (https://www.lyrasis.org/Leadership/Pages/Catalyst-Fund.aspx). LYRASIS members include public, academic, museum and government libraries. The University of Maryland Libraries joined the Leaders Circle in 2017.

We should note that not all such consortia succeed in difficult economic times. One example is Nylink New York, which told its 300+ members in mid-2010 that it was closing its operations due to financial shortfalls. It ceased operating in May 2011. Such announcements serve to remind people that while everyone loves resource sharing and the other benefits of collaborative/consortia programs, there is no "free lunch." It takes people, time, effort, and a good amount of money to make these projects work.

Shared Collection Building

An early example of a major national collection building/resource sharing project was the Farmington Plan. A very large percentage of today's research library collections are a direct result of that plan and other post–World War II cooperative acquisition programs. The Farmington Plan and several other joint ventures had grand hopes and scale. Essentially the hope was for U.S. research libraries to never again face the lack of information about other parts of the world that became painfully clear at the onset of World War II.

How did the Farmington Plan address the ambitious goal of having at least one copy of research or intelligence interest material in a U.S. research library? The basic structure used the model that the Library of Congress (LC) and research libraries created to distribute the books gathered from postwar Germany. If there was only one copy available, LC retained it; additional copies were allocated on the basis of having a wide regional distribution and existing collection strengths. Essentially, the Farmington Plan concept was to distribute collection/subject responsibility among libraries based on their institutional research interests and existing collection strength. The Farmington Plan operated until 1972, when it became too complex, costly, and operationally difficult for libraries to manage. The Farmington Plan was a collaborative venture with officers, assigned roles, bylaws, and other organizational structures.

Check This Out

For readers interested in gaining a better understanding of the true legacy of the Farmington Plan and later cooperative efforts, see Ralph D. Wagner's detailed monograph *A History of the Farmington Plan* (Lanham, MD: Scarecrow Press, 2002).

Check This Out

ConnectNY (http://connectny.org/) is a consortia of academic libraries in New York state. The ConnectNY Collection Development Working Group prepared an informative overview of collaborative collection development in *A ConnectNY White Paper: The Power of Cooperation: Consortial Collection Development and ConnectNY* (2016, http://connectny.org/wp-content/uploads/2016/08/CollectionDevelopmentWhitePaper_FInal_2016_05.pdf).

Of particular note is the "State of the Art CCD in Five Library Consortia: A Comparison" table appearing on pages 11–12. It is well worth the read.

Today, we have nothing as grand in scope or hope as the Farmington Plan. That does not mean there are no joint efforts in shared collection building underway. Some that actually preceded Farmington are very much alive and doing rather well. One such effort is the Triangle Research Libraries Network (TRLN, http://www.trln.org/), based in North Carolina. TRLN began in the 1930s when Duke and North Carolina Universities decided to combine some of their collection funding to expand collection depth for both institutions. TRLN currently has 10 members, and its purpose "is to marshal the financial, human, and information resources of their research libraries through cooperative efforts in order to create a rich and unparalleled knowledge environment that furthers the universities' teaching, research, and service missions" (http://www.trln.org/about/). The economic times of today are not quite as tough as they were during the Great Depression, but they are tough enough to warrant continued efforts to share building activities.

TRLN provides a solid example of the benefits of collaborative collection building. In 2006, the group undertook an overlap study—such studies indicate the percentages of titles held by multiple libraries. At the time of the study, there were four member libraries. The study indicated that 71 percent of the titles in the database were held by just one library; the number of records in the database was 5,158,309 and only 2 percent were held by all four members (http://archive.trln.org/coop.html). Similar studies in consortia such as OhioLINK and LINK+ have produced similar results. The notion that each library, large and small, has something unique to bring to the table for users when it comes to resource sharing is accurate.

On a smaller scale, there are cases where libraries in consortia with an online union catalog and courier services are entering into very informal handshake collection building arrangements. Most simply agree to check

---

Something to Watch

Although monographs, journals, and databases are frequently the focus of consortial purchasing activities, both eBook and streaming media programs have also been explored by consortia. Sheryl Knab, Tom Humphrey, and Caryl Ward describe the efforts of a group of libraries in New York to launch a patron-driven video pilot in their 2016 article "Now Streaming: A Consortial PDA Video Pilot Project" (*Collaborative Librarianship* 8, no. 1: 41–54), while Marmot Library Network established an eBook collection and circulation model, described in Jimmy Thomas and Mark Noble's 2016 article "The Douglas County Model in Western Colorado" (*Journal of Library Administration* 56, no. 3: 326–334).

From the Authors' Experience

One collaborative effort is the HathiTrust (http://www.hathitrust.org), which the University of Maryland (UMD) Libraries joined in fall 2010. HathiTrust was originally formed in 2008 by the 13 universities of the Committee on Institutional Cooperation (now the Big Ten Academic Alliance or BTAA), along with the University of California system and the Library of Virginia, primarily as a repository for digital collections. Since that time, membership in the HathiTrust has grown to over 130 individual institutions (universities and public libraries), including the Biblioteca de la Universidad Complutense de Madrid and the University of Queensland.

The HathiTrust provides preservation and access capabilities for both public domain and in-copyright works provided by member institutions as well as from Google, the Internet Archive, and Microsoft. Member institutions can take part in HathiTrust either by depositing their own digital content or by "participating in the long-term curation and management of the depository in return for enhanced services for accessing and using materials in the digital library" (http://www.hathitrust.org /partnership). The size of HathiTrust allows it to forge partnerships that one institution would be unable to do. A recent offshoot of the HathiTrust is the HathiTrust Research Center (HTRC), which provides research access to the public domain titles in HathiTrust for text and data mining applications (https://analytics.hathitrust.org/).

Daniel Mack, Associate Dean of Collection Strategies and Services at the UMD Libraries, describes HathiTrust as "an invaluable resource for collection development in the twenty-first century library. HathiTrust offers libraries the opportunity to work as proactive agents in creating a shared digital repository" (personal interview, February 2018). At the time this volume was written, UMD was continuing efforts to improve discovery and fulfillment of HathiTrust materials, and was also adding content to the database. Mack states that "HathiTrust lets us think beyond the local collection, without restriction of format or location. Library users can find and use material from around the world and across centuries to support their research and teaching. Librarians can make innovative and effective collection development decisions that let us better leverage our collections budget. HathiTrust really does offer us a portal into the twenty-first century virtual library."

A number of presentations and articles on the background and activities of the HathiTrust may be found on their website (http://www.hathitrust.org/news_publications). One publication that provides an overview of the development of HathiTrust as well as its operations is Jeremy York's 2010 IFLA conference presentation "Building a Future by Preserving Our Past: The Preservation Infrastructure of HathiTrust Digital Library" (http://www.hathitrust.org/documents/hathitrust-ifla-201008.pdf). Another article that reviews the impact of HathiTrust on local preservation and collection decisions is Heidi M. Winkler and Joy M. Perrin's 2017 piece "HathiTrust and Local Digital Stewardship: A Case Study in How Massive Digital Libraries Affect Local Digital Resources Decisions" (*International Journal of Librarianship* 2, no. 1: 32–41).

the union catalog prior to ordering an item. If the item is not in the database, the library moves ahead with the acquisition process. Should it already be in the system, the selector makes a judgment regarding the need for additional copies. Such arrangements do cut down on the number of lower-use items in the system, stretching limited funds for the collection building.

One area where the issue of duplication is a challenge is with e-resources. Many of these items are acquired through consortial purchases. The result is a growing homogeneity in e-resources, which may not be sustainable in the current economic climate. Some state libraries, such as Arizona, Minnesota, and Louisiana, have purchased access to selected journal databases that are made freely accessible to state residents, thus reducing the need for numerous libraries to pay for access. Others, such as North Carolina (NCLive, http://www.nclive.org/), have gone beyond purchasing access to journal databases to include other materials such as eBooks, videos, primary source materials, and reference tools. We will explore the issues related to cost, access, and duplication of e-resources in chapter 13.

Sharing Collection Storage

A long-standing collaborative program that addresses storage of low-use materials and collaborative collection building is the Center for Research Libraries (CRL, http://www.crl.edu). CRL started out as the Midwestern Inter-Library Center (MILC), founded in 1949 as a regional cooperative remote storage facility. (Research libraries have been remotely storing collections for many years and had discussed the concept for even longer.) From the outset, MILC/CRL acquired some low-use materials on behalf of its membership (for example, college catalogs and state government publications). Rather quickly, CRL became a national library asset, which continues to acquire and lends a variety of low-use materials. It often picked up Farmington Plan subject responsibilities when a library wished to drop the subject. Today, membership is open to any library willing to pay the annual membership fee.

Some individual campuses have created large storage facilities for their own collections; Harvard is a prime example. The University of California (UC) library system created two such facilities—the Northern and Southern Regional Library Facilities. The Southern facility was established in 1987 and now "provides space for University of California library materials, archives and manuscript collections. Utilizing high-density shelving, the collections are stored in a climate-controlled environment that is designed to preserve the collections" (http://www.srlf.ucla.edu/default.aspx). To gain an understanding of the scale of such units, it held 6,545,422 items at the time this volume was being prepared and accepted materials from all 10 UC campuses, particularly those in southern California. It also houses a digitization unit for rare or deteriorating items (http://www.srlf.ucla.edu/about/).

In addition to collections housed by individual libraries and library systems, individual consortia such as the Big Ten Academic Alliance (BTAA) have developed shared repositories for their materials. In addition to addressing shared storage of print materials, a working group was

---

Something to Watch

In addition to individual consortia creating shared print programs, the Rosemont Shared Print Alliance was formed in 2016 as a "collaboration of regional programs interested in coordinating their efforts on a larger scale to ensure the retention of and access to print journal backfiles" (https://rosemontsharedprintalliance.org/). As of mid-2018, alliance members included the BTAA, FLorida Academic REpository (FLARE), ScholarsTrust, and the Western Regional Storage Trust (WEST). Goals of the alliance included establishing standards for collection growth and retention of print journal titles, adopting a common metadata standard, and creating a common access guideline for individuals who wish to use the content held in the collections (https://rosemontsharedprintalliance.org/strategic-directions).

established in 2017 with representatives from Illinois, Maryland, Michigan, Michigan State, Northwestern, Penn State, and Wisconsin to explore the feasibility of a program to cooperatively manage widely held microformat sets in a distributed retention model.

Reasons for Engaging in Joint Ventures

You can identify several benefits that can arise from any library joint venture. One such benefit is the potential for improving both user and staff access to information as well as to the materials themselves. Earlier we noted that lack of information about holdings was a problem in the past for ILL resource sharing. Some networks that include a variety of library types, for example, Northern Lights and LINK+ in California, share their collections through maintaining an online union catalog and a courier service.

A second benefit of collection sharing is it vastly increases the breadth and depth of material available to users of member libraries. For example, when Loyola Marymount University (LMU) library joined LINK+, campus library users went from having access to a collection of just over 500,000 volumes to having online access to a collection of more than 4 million titles and 6 million copies. Although the LMU collection was the smallest added to the database up to the time it joined, more than 37 percent of the LMU items were unique to the system. As we noted earlier, almost every new member to such consortia, regardless of size, will add some unique titles to the database.

An obvious third benefit is that a joint project may assist in stretching limited financial resources. Too often, people view cooperative collection building ventures as a money-saving device. In truth, they do not save money for a library; rather they help broaden the range of materials available.

There are times when collaborative projects can lead to a benefit in terms of greater staff specialization. In such cases, a person can concentrate on one or two activities rather than on five or six. The resulting specialization should produce better overall performance. Naturally, better performance should lead to better service, and thus greater user satisfaction.

By actively promoting the existence of collaborative efforts and services, a joint project can enhance the visibility of the library in a positive manner. It may also be useful in demonstrating the library's stewardship of the funding it was given for collection building purposes as well as value for monies spent (more items, better, faster service, for example).

A final benefit, although one not frequently discussed, is the improvement in the working relationships among cooperating libraries. This is particularly true in a multi-type system. People can gain a better perspective about other libraries' problems as a result of working together on mutual

Check This Out

One title that provides examples of successful collaboration efforts is *Space and Organizational Considerations in Academic Library Partnerships and Collaborations*, edited by Brian Doherty (Hershey, PA: Information Science Reference, 2016). This work includes chapters addressing collaborative open access projects as well as collaborative collection development and management of both print and electronic resources. It is well worth a look.

Check This Out

Tony Horava provides an insightful overview of the strengths and challenges of consortial activities in his 2018 article "The Role of Consortia in Collection Management" (*Technicalities* 38, no. 2: 16–19). It is worth a look.

---

problems or goals. Also, learning about the special problems that another type of library encounters helps a person to know what its staff can or cannot do. Some systems have found this to be so valuable a benefit that they have set up exchange internships for staff members, both professional and nonprofessional. Mark and Allan Scheffer and Nancy Braun (2009), in writing about people working in groups and the challenges in doing so, effectively suggested that "the real issue, it seems, lies far more in the attitudes people bring to the process of working together toward a commonly-held goal. The major sticking point, in other words, is not so much what people do in groups, but who they are in groups" (p. 3). The more people get to know and trust one another, the more effective they become at working together.

Murray Shepard (2004) outlined four advantages that three Canadian academic libraries (one large, one medium, and one small sized) identified as arising from their collaboration:

- Remote storage of little used materials,
- Development of web-based, unified and integrated online "catalogue,"
- Joint purchases of online resources, and
- Rationalization of information resources. (p. 1)

His essay provides good information on what it takes to have a successful joint venture.

Collaboration on the Personal Level

Gayle Chan and Anthony W. Ferguson (2002) suggested that working together with other organizations is a challenge and, "Collaboration . . . is an unnatural act. It is natural for institutions to be concerned with protecting their own interests but unnatural for them to voluntarily compromise their interests. Even if consortia representatives agree to work together, because of differing needs and capabilities, getting them to all arrive at the same decision is difficult, thus making the purchase of a [resource] very time consuming (p. 16)." This is due to many factors. There are occasional issues between units. There are also the occasional differing personality concerns that may lead to problems in coordination, cooperation, and sharing that we touched on in chapter 7. When the effort involves other libraries, there is a limited at best understanding of the individuals involved or their library's situation and capabilities. In essence, there are as many organizational cultures in operation as there are libraries working together for a common end. Bottom line: it is not as easy as it might seem.

Collection management staff always has a need to work closely with users in order to create practical collections. Finding ways to get busy people to take time to work with you on such matters takes some ingenuity. School librarian Eleanor Howe (2008) wrote about a collaborative effort she participated in with a high school English teacher. The teacher was interested in expanding the library collection for doing research papers in the honors English classes he taught. Howe and teacher developed an exercise for the students in which they were given broad latitude in selecting a research topic. Once the students selected a topic, they were to prepare a written recommendation for the purchase of one item for that library that would be useful in writing a paper on the selected topic. Although the budget would not allow for the purchase of all the recommended items, it did average about 10 such purchases a year. At the time Howe submitted the article, the effort was successful enough that another teacher asked to have her students involved. According to Howe, one outcome was that the students "gained the most: they improved their search, resource evaluation, and writing skills; they developed ownership and pride in their library by contributing to its collection; and they created a more relevant collection available for all students" (p. 9).

Anthony Fonseca and Van Viator (2009), in writing about academic librarians and faculty collaboration as a means of enhancing librarians and the library's visibility, concluded, "These collaborative efforts lead to better recognition of librarians on the academic campus, especially in the realms of information literacy and collection development" (p. 87). While it is theoretically possible to build appropriate academic collections without the active input from faculty, the process is much more effective when there is a collaborative effort. Fonseca and Viator's article cited above provides some sound ideas for how to go about gaining such relationships. Melissa Campbell (2010) expanded on the subject of librarian-teacher collaboration by suggesting the following roles in the process: "Within the framework of faculty-librarian collaboration . . . faculty [are] responsible for providing the source material as well as the internal framework for interpretation. Librarians serve as the 'hyperlink,' i.e., the 'click through' in that they understand what the ideas are connected to as well as how they are connected" (p. 33).

Making Collaborative Projects Work

Several times in this chapter we have stated that successful collaborative-consortia activities require time, effort, and money from each participant. There is no doubt that these are three of the keys to success, but they are not the only ones.

In 1994, Rosabeth Kanter identified eight "I's" as the elements necessary for partnerships to succeed:

- Individual excellence
- Importance
- Interdependence
- Investment
- Information
- Integration
- Institutionalization
- Integrity (p. 100)

"Individual excellence" means each partner/member has something of value to contribute to the joint effort. This does not mean that all contributions must be equal, just that each does have something to add to the mix. We already noted that for consortia with online catalogs, even the smallest collection added to the database contributes at least a few unique items. Kanter also made the point that the motivation for the effort must be positive rather than negative, thus the "values" of the input must be for that positive purpose.

"Importance" relates to the positive motivation for the partnership. It also implies the purpose(s) of the program matches some or all of the participant's long-term goals and their organizational missions. When that is the case, you have in place something that will drive the group forward to achieve the program's goals. This is not as easy as it appears; it is especially challenging when it comes to multi-type library consortia. For example, all the participants may agree that acquiring online databases at a reasonable cost is a goal but may disagree on the products. The question of what to focus on first can be contentious.

"Interdependence" is almost self-explanatory: there needs to be a reorganization so that all the participants will gain something that they would not if they went it alone. What that something is will likely vary somewhat from library to library and consortia to consortia (lower costs, deeper collections, or faster document delivery, etc.).

"Investment" is something we have mentioned several times in this chapter in terms of time, effort, and money. As Kanter noted, such investments become tangible evidence of the participants' long-term commitment to the venture (1994, p. 100). Without such a commitment, the probability of the effort failing is very high.

"Information" is, as is true for any work situation, essential for success. The exchange of accurate, timely information/communications is essential for consortial activities. The reason is libraries do not have much latitude when it comes to shifting resources during a fiscal year and consortia have even less flexibility. Often those individuals who most actively look after consortial operations are part-time, or, if full-time, they are few in number. Keeping members informed about the bad and good news in terms of a library's contribution(s) as soon as possible helps the group make adjustments more effectively.

"Integration" is vitally important to a consortia's long-term success as well as a major factor in its demise (lack of integration). Collection sharing requires some adjustments in local practices, regardless of what form that "sharing" takes. The greater the changes required, the greater the challenges for achieving integration. Many consortia have started with small steps and have waited until all the members have integrated those steps before moving on to larger scale projects. For example, just instituting a courier service calls for local adjustments regarding who does what when or even who takes on new duties. Change, especially in the workplace, is not something some people accept willingly. Just one member having problems getting the service up and running can cause others to question the value of that member, the service, or both. Such doubts can erode the trust necessary for successful consortial operations.

"Institutionalization" refers to a point we made early in this chapter: the fact that collaboration and consortia ventures call for a formalization of roles. One factor that you see in long-lasting efforts is that the assigning of roles is done in a manner that reduces the risk that the departure of one person (not that person's home institution) from the group will cause the group to have serious operational problems. This can be a challenge to accomplish as individuals with strong leadership skills are naturally going to come to the forefront. If the group recognizes the need to truly share leadership, they have a good chance of staying successful in the long-term.

"Integrity" and trust are the foundations upon which strong collaborative and consortia ventures are built. Building trust takes time and often such ventures at least start with senior managers leading the effort. This also generally means there are some strong personalities involved, including individuals who may not be used to having to be too accommodating at their home institutions. During the initial stages there may be a fair amount of "I'm the big fish in this pond" with an implied threat of "I will take my marbles and go home if I don't get my way." It takes more than a meeting or two to work through such issues, and time together is the best way to reduce such problems. To have a successful partnership there must be trust and compromise as well as true teamwork. As noted by Pamela Jones, an executive director of a consortia, "By thinking 'we' before 'me' when working with the consortium, the individual member will be able to identify the services and programs they can contribute to and participate in for the greatest value not only at the local level, but also at the community level" (2017, p. 117). Generally the members of the controlling board are library directors. There is a practical reason for this; there must be the authority to commit a library to new or modifications of a program element. However, there must be thoughtful, meaningful, and ongoing consultation with all the partners for there to be success in any cooperative effort.

Group Decision Making

Collection management personnel have to think about several categories of decision making—their own, colleagues they work with on an individual basis, internal library groups (committees and teams), and external groups (collaborations, consortia, professional associations, etc.). If anything, group decision making is even more complex than those made by the individual.

As we noted in chapter 6, effective decision making is about making a choice from a number of possible options when several good possibilities often exist. As the number of options increases, it appears as if the choice is harder and harder to make. That is somewhat true; however, the more options you consider, the more likely the final selection will be the best, or one of the best. When you are part of a group the process is more complex and such group decisions are becoming increasingly more common in the workplace. As Alexander Chizhik, Robert Shelly, and Lisa Troyer (2009) wrote, "In the modern world, even endeavors that were considered individualistic a decade ago, like computer programming, are now collaborations among large and small groups" (p. 251).

In the past, making selection decisions was probably 75 to 80 percent an individual's choice to make. Yes, public and school librarians did and do employ selection committees where group decisions are the norm. However, more often than not they are composed of internal staff with, occasionally, user representation. Such groups are something of a "middle ground" between total individual decision making and total outside group decision making. They share many of the external group aspects; however, the composition of the internal selection committee is normally comprised of people with whom you have worked and interacted with over some time. That characteristic means that trust and shared cooperative efforts are much easier to achieve. The balance of this chapter focuses on the external group decision making issues.

You should not think of decision making as a singular event. The vast majority of decisions develop over time. Yes, there is the moment of choice, but generally there is an elapse of time between knowing a decision is necessary and the decision point. Even quick gut decisions usually draw upon some prior knowledge related to the circumstances calling for a decision. Research suggests that people who view decision making as a process rather than an event are more effective (Garvin and Roberto, 2001).

What the group views as the goal for the decision is important—a search for the best outcome or making a case for a position. In the case of collaborative/consortia ventures, many times there is a need for doing both, which adds another layer of complexity to the process. While this may exist for an individual's decision, it becomes critical in the group setting. When a group views its goal as advocacy or making the case there is often a sense of competition to see if one's personal view can prevail. When it comes to multitype consortia there are several "constituencies" to factor into the process as well. That type of atmosphere does not lend itself to optimal decisions (or at least not ones that are rapid). Strong personal views, values, biases, and hidden agendas get in the way of meaningful and open exchanges. It also has a tendency to limit the number of alternatives developed and evaluated.

Another issue is that advocacy or vigorous debate about positions or alternatives can generate some degree of conflict. Eden King, Michelle Hebl, and Daniel Beal (2009) noted, "The characteristics of interactions within teams, including the amount of conflict and cooperation that exists, are of utmost importance in determining team effectiveness, and thus are the focus of a great deal of scholarly research" (p. 265). Conflict is where the concept of fight, flight, and flow often comes into play. The concept is that some people will fight very hard for their position(s) on matters, while others, in the face of conflict, simply give up (flight) and refuse to discuss the issue further. Neither situation is likely to result in good decision making. What you need to be (or hope there are a few other such people in the group) is willing to keep things moving (flow) and actively seek the middle ground. In a group setting, it is likely there will be two, if not all three, of these three behaviors present and this will impact the group process and the quality of the decision reached.

Conflict, in and of itself, is not a problem. It can be beneficial when it is cognitive rather than emotional in character. The challenge is to achieve the highest possible cognitive level and the lowest level of emotional conflict. One way to help achieve this is to carefully frame the decision goals for the group. Another technique is to monitor the group and call for a timeout when emotions are running high.

Groups can easily fall into the trap of "groupthink." Two factors frequently play a role in groupthink. Perhaps the most common is the desire to get/keep things moving along. This often results in too quick of a decision, without much effort to develop (much less assess) multiple options. The second common factor is the desire to be a team player; this too can

---

Check This Out

A good source for guidance on group/team decision making is H. Frank Cervone's 2005 article "Managing Digital Libraries: The View from 30,000 Feet; Making Decisions, Methods for Digital Library Project Teams" in *OCLC Systems & Services* (21, no. 1: 30–35).

Check These Out

An outstanding article, if complex for those uncomfortable with quantitative methods, is Robert M. Hayes' 2003 piece entitled "Cooperative Game: Theoretic Models for Decision-Making in the Context of Library Cooperation," found in *Library Trends* (51, no. 3, Winter: 441–61).

An older but in-depth review of the management issues in consortial efforts is G. Edward Evans' 2002 "Management Issues of Co-operative Ventures and Consortia in the USA. Part One" and "Management Issues of Consortia. Part Two" (*Library Management* 23, nos. 4/5: 213–26 and nos. 6/7: 275–86).

Lisa German's 2008 "It's All About Teamwork: Working in a Consortial Environment" is a solid discussion of what is required in order to have successful collaborative projects (*Technicalities* 28, no. 3: 1, 12–15).

---

reduce options and very likely limit thoughtful critical assessment or idea generation.

Generally in consortia, and like groups, decisions become a situation where concessions and consensus are the keys to a resolution. Another "c" for such decision making is consideration—you should not always get what you would like, if the group is to succeed. A final "c," often the most significant, is the presence or absence of coalitions. In many ways, the existence of coalitions assist in moving matters forward as they normally reduce the number of variables in play with a large group.

A major challenge for such groups, as the authors can attest to from personal experience, is determining what is "best." The number of bests is substantially greater in a consortial environment than for a single library. There are the bests for each institution, the bests for coalitions, and, of course, the bests for the group as a whole.

Building trust is always a factor in group decision making, but it becomes more of a challenge for consortial members as they have less time together. Time is a key factor in creating trust and it is in limited supply in such situations. A related factor is that, more often than not, institutional representatives at such meetings are senior, if not *the* senior, manager. Generally such people are not used to having their ideas or views as openly challenged. Time together, trust, concessions, and consensus are the key elements for successful consortial decision making.

Points to Keep in Mind

- Cooperation involves the exchange of something (work, money, etc.) between the partners with each gaining something from the cooperative effort (but not necessarily equal) benefits.

- Collaboration calls for combining resources with others in order to produce a "new value" that equally benefits all the partners.

- A consortia is a formal structure that pools the resources of members to achieve benefits that are, or may be, too costly than any one member could realize independently.

- All of the above can provide benefits for users and libraries; however, to be effective, they require committed people, lots of time and effort, as well as significant financial resources.

- Joint ventures do not save money, they stretch existing resources. There is no "free lunch" for libraries.

- The benefits of joint ventures vary from library to library as well as by the nature of the project. Most librarians agree that the benefits gained far outweigh the resources required to make the venture a success.

- The elements that help ensure success are individual excellence, importance, interdependence, investment, information, integration, institutionalization, and integrity.

- Group decisions must be based on concessions, consideration, consensus, and trust.

References

Birch, Katie. 2017. "How Flexible Is Your Future Collection?" *OCLC Next* (blog). February 9, 2017. http://www.oclc.org/blog/main/how-flexible-is-your-future -collection/.

Campbell, Melissa. 2010. "Collaborations Between Librarians and Faculty in a Digital Age." *Education Digest* 75, no. 6: 30–33.

Carter, Sunshine, and Danielle Ostendorf. 2017. "Processes and Strategies for Collaboratively Purchasing Electronic Resources." *Collaborative Librarianship* 9, no. 1: 58–71.

Chan, Gayle, and Anthony W. Ferguson. 2002. "Digital Library Consortia in the 21st Century: The Hong Kong JULAC Case." *Collection Management* 27, no. 3/4: 13–27.

Chizhik, Alexander W., Robert K. Shelly, and Lisa Troyer. 2009. "Intragroup Conflict and Cooperation: An Introduction." *Journal of Social Issues* 65, no. 2: 251–59.

Emery, Jill, and Michael Levine-Clark. 2017. "Libraries and the Collaborative Imperative." *Collaborative Librarianship* 9, no. 1: 1–2.

Fonseca, Anthony J., and Van P. Viator. 2009. "Escaping the Island of Lost Faculty: Collaboration as a Means of Visibility." *Collaborative Librarianship* 1, no. 3: 81–90.

Garvin, David A. and Michael A. Roberto. 2001. "What You Don't Know About Making Decisions." *Harvard Business Review* 79, no. 8: 108–16.

Howe, Eleanor B. 2008. "Collaborating with Teachers to Empower Students @ Your Library®: Building a Relevant Collection with Student Recommendations." *Learning & Media* 36, no. 3: 8-9.

Jackson, Sidney L. 1974. *Libraries and Librarianship in the West: A Brief History.* New York: McGraw-Hill.

Jones, Pamela. 2017. "Why We Do That Thing We Do: What Consortia Executive Directors Want Library Directors to Know." *Journal of Library Administration* 57, no. 1: 114–22.

Kanter, Rosabeth Moss. 1994. "Collaborative Advantage: Successful Partnerships Manage the Relationship Not Just the Deal." *Harvard Business Review* 72, no. 4: 96–108.

Kennedy, Shirley Duglin. 2008. "True Confessions." *Information Today* 25, no. 9: 17–19.

Kieft, Robert H. 2014. "Beyond My People and Thy People, or the Shared Print Collections Imperative." In *Rethinking Collection Development and*

Management, edited by Becky Albitz, Christine Avey, and Diane Zabel, 297–319. Santa Barbara, CA: Libraries Unlimited.

Kieft, Robert H., and Bernard F. Reilly. 2009. "Regional and National Cooperation on Legacy Print Collections." *Collaborative Librarianship* 1, no. 3: 106–8.

King, Eden B., Michelle R. Hebl, and Daniel J. Beal. 2009. "Conflict and Cooperation in Diverse Workgroups." *Journal of Social Issues* 65, no. 2: 261–85.

Scheffer, Mark, Allan Scheffer, and Nancy Braun. 2009. "Collaborative Consultation: A Principled Foundation for Collective Excellence." *Supervision* 70, no. 9: 3–5.

Shepard, Murray. 2004. "Library Collaboration: What Makes It Work?" *IATUL Annual Conference Proceedings* 14: 1–11.

Stearns, Susan. 2016. "EAST by Northeast." *Collaborative Librarianship* 8, no. 1: 7–15.

11
Print and Media

Comic books and graphic novels have become a part of library culture, and video games are on their way to doing the same.
—Edward Francis Schneider, 2014

Traditional attitudes toward self-published books are changing. While long decried as the worst-written dregs at the bottom of the publishing barrel, self-publishing has started to attract reputable titles to its ranks thanks to new technologies and business models.
—Greg Landgraf, 2015

We librarians think we know what it means to build print collections because for a long time print was the only game in town, but in order to build the print libraries of the future, we need to give more thought to what print means in a digital age.
—Amy Brunvand, 2015

Like all partnerships, the one between librarians and publishers requires work and has benefits for both sides.
—Elsa Anderson, 2016

Undoubtedly, the digital age is changing and will continue to change the composition of library collections, how libraries budget for collections, and how libraries go about their business. However, as seen in the Brunvand quote above, that does not mean libraries have abandoned traditional print and media materials in lieu of their digital counterparts. Quite the contrary. In 2015, Two Sides, an organization dedicated to the production and sustainability of print publications, reported results of a survey conducted in the U.S. and U.K. on issues related to print and digital media. The survey indicated that 88 percent of respondents said they "understood, retained or used information better when they read print on paper compared to lower percentages (64 percent and less) when reading on electronic devices." Over-all results showed an 81 percent preference for print resources (2015).

In chapter 1, we included an extended discussion about libraries, read-ing, and their futures. It is our belief that libraries, with materials in both print and electronic formats, and reading do in fact have long-term futures. Further, we believe that the so-called "legacy" or "traditional" formats will remain a vital part of library collections for a long time. The focus of this chapter is on those materials selected in a tangible, physical format such as print, images, games, etc. Each of those broad format types encompasses a wide range of materials. Books range from the most popular to the most scholarly titles, and appear in hardback, paperback, large print, and elec-tronic format. Each subtype has slightly different factors to consider when deciding whether to add it to the collection. We cover digital resources in chapters 12 and 13.

Producers of Library Collection Resources

Organizations that produce the informational/recreational materials that libraries collect, whether they be in print or electronic format, face challenges in today's digital world. All producers, whether for-profit or not-for-profit, must generate at least enough income to continue to operate. Just as libraries struggle with technology's rapidly changing character, so do the producers. Their work is further challenged by the range of formats they must address. Which development will last? How soon should a "hot new" development be adopted? Adopting too soon may result in financial losses, while waiting until it is too late may result in the market being saturated by the early adopters. Even with ideal timing, determining the best pricing model is difficult. As noted by Alastair Horne (2017), "publishing is increasingly fragmented, [so] far as formats are concerned. Instead of just a hardback followed, a year or so later, by a paperback, we now have an increasing range of formats, each con-tributing a smaller amount to the overall publishing economy" (p. 6).

When it comes to products to offer, everyone (producers, librarians, and users) would like to have top-quality, low-cost items, covering almost all subjects and user interests. However, cost and income are the driving forces in what producers decide to issue. Ann Steiner (2018) observed that "large-scale publishers . . . keep an extensive frontlist each year . . . [how-ever] they aim to publish fewer books and focus on the most promising titles. The problem is that no one knows what will sell well until it is well on the path to success. No one had heard of Harry Potter or James Grey before they became runaway successes" (p. 121). Even the not-for-profit produc-ers, such as university presses, have to attempt to break even each year. Such presses know that very few of the new titles they produce will sell well enough to recover production costs. Thus, a few titles must do well enough to generate the income that allows for a break-even year. In good economic times, the university may be willing to cover any losses in a year as part of its obligation to scholarship; however, in difficult times it may not be able to underwrite a series of losing years. For-profit presses have even less leeway since their shareholders and owners expect positive annual returns. This is difficult in a challenging market. Jim Milliot (2017) analyzed the publish-ing field and found that "although total revenue of the world's 50 largest book publishers topped $50 billion in 2016, last year was not an easy one

---

Check This Out

The *Publishers Weekly* website issues an annual overview of top publishing companies that reappears in their journal publication. The most recent online entry was Jim Milliot's article "The World's 54 Largest Publishers, 2017" (August 25, 2017; https://tinyurl.com/Milliot-PW) that appeared in the journal publication as "Pearson Rises Above" (*Publishers Weekly* 264, no. 35: 56–59). These annual overviews are well worth a look.

---

for global publishing giants. Less than half of the top 50 publishers posted revenue gains in 2016, with the balance reporting sales declines" (p. 56).

It would be difficult for most producers to stay operational, if all they could depend upon were sales to libraries. This is not to say library purchasing is insignificant; it is significant—U.S. public libraries spent well over $528 million on print books alone in 2016/2017, representing 34.27 percent of acquisition expenditures as reported in the *Library and Book Trade Almanac* (Barr, 2017, pp. 243–245). The percentage of book purchases compared to overall spending in academic and special libraries during that same period were lower than public libraries (7.6 percent and 10.7 percent, respectively), but still represented a significant amount (Barr, 2017, pp. 246–249). Even ALA's publication program is not solely dependent on library sales—there is an expectation that there will be at least some sales to individuals and perhaps even some sales as textbooks. Commercial publishers that have "lines" that focus on librarianship spread their focus between several markets, especially on textbooks. Editors must make their decisions, at least in part, on what the sales potential may be for a title and not just the content—schlock may sell well.

What is a "typical" return for a 250-page trade book selling for US$25.00? The following are the costs for a hypothetical first press run:

Suggested retail price	$25.00
Printing/binding	−2.00
	23.00
Warehouse/distribution	−2.00
	21.00
Discount to retailer	−12.50
	8.50
Overhead (including editorial)	−2.00
	6.50
Marketing	−1.50
	5.00
Author royalty (10–15%)	−1.25[*]
Profit	3.75

---

[*] Most royalties are based on the net sales income, not the list price. Also, neither publishers nor authors receive any income from resales.

Types of Producers

Some years ago, the publication *Book Industry Trends* (Book Industry Study Group) developed a 10-category system for grouping the book publishing industry in the United States. Despite recent changes in the publishing industry, these categories continue to be useful today:

Trade	Mass market
Book clubs	Mail order (including email)
Religious	Professional/Specialty presses
University presses	El-Hi (elementary and high school textbooks)
College textbook	Publisher/distributor

Four of the above are firms that CM personnel interact with, to some degree, on a regular basis—Trade, Mass Market, University Presses, and Professional. We include the Religious category in the Professional/Specialty category. School library media centers may have occasional dealings with an El-Hi press; however, since the main focus of these publishers is on textbook series, it is more likely that the school district will deal with such firms. We will also touch on self-publishers and small and government presses. Serial producers are covered in chapter 12.

It is important to note that publishers today often issue more than books. Most of the major publishers have a number of lines—trade, textbook, and paperback (mass market), for example. Some publishers, like Sage, have rather extensive lists of serial titles. Presses with a trade line often have an audiobook division to capitalize on new book titles, while a few also issue DVDs.

Trade publishers produce a wide range of titles, both fiction and nonfiction, that have wide sales potential. HarperCollins (News Corp.); Macmillan; Little, Brown (Hatchette); Thames & Hudson; Penguin Random House; and Simon & Schuster are some well-known trade publishers. Many trade publishers have divisions that produce specialty titles, such as children's, college textbooks, paperback, and reference titles. Trade publishers have three markets: bookstores (online and brick and mortar), libraries, and wholesalers.

Professional/Specialty publishers restrict output to a few areas or subjects. Infobase publishing (Facts on File, Cambridge Educational, Chelsea House) and Grey House are examples of specialty publishers in the field of reference titles. These publishers' audiences are relatively smaller and more critical of the material than are trade publishers' audiences. Some of the specialties include reference, paperback, children's, religious, music, cartographic, and subject areas such as librarianship. Some examples are art (e.g., Abrams Books), music (e.g., Schirmer), science (e.g., Academic Press/Elsevier), technical (e.g., American Technical Publishers), law (e.g., West Publishing/Thomson Reuters), and medical (e.g., W. B. Saunders/Elsevier). Many professional/specialty books require expensive graphic preparation or presswork. Such presswork increases production costs, which is one of the reasons art, music, science, medical, and technology titles are so costly. Discounts tend to be low for titles in this category.

Mass-market/paperback publishers produce two types of work: quality trade paperbacks and mass-market paperbacks. A trade publisher may have a quality paperback division or may issue the paperbound version of a book through the same division that issued the hardcover edition. The publisher may also publish original paperbacks, that is, a first edition in paperback.

The majority of mass-market paperbacks are reprints of titles that first appeared in hardcover. Some of the genre fiction series are original in paper such as Harlequin titles and are low cost because of their mass-market appeal. Their distribution differs from that of other books. Therefore, they sell anywhere the publisher can get someone to handle them. The paperback books on sale in airline terminals, corner stores, and kiosks are mass-market paperbacks. These books have a short shelf life compared to hard covers.

El-Hi publishers, such as Cengage Learning, Pearson, and McGraw-Hill Education, occupy one of the highest risk areas of publishing. Most publishers in this area develop a line of textbooks for several grades, for example, a social studies series. Preparation of such texts requires large amounts of expertise, time, energy, and money. Printing costs are high because most school texts feature expensive color and other specialized presswork. Such projects require large, up-front investments that must be recouped before realizing a profit. If enough school districts adopt a text, profits can be substantial, but failure to secure adoption can mean tremendous loss.

University/Scholarly presses, because they are part of a not-for-profit organization, receive subsidies that help underwrite their costs. Most are part of an academic institution such as the University of California Press, a museum such as the Museum of Northern Arizona, a research institution such as the Peterson Institute for International Economics, or a learned society like the American Philosophical Society. The subsidies come through two main sources—institutional and authors.

The role of the scholarly press in the economical and open dissemination of knowledge is critical. Without scholarly presses, important works with limited appeal do not get published. Certainly there are times when a commercial house is willing to publish a book that will not show a profit because the publisher thinks the book is so important, but relying on that type of willingness will, in the long run, mean that too many important works would never appear.

Institutional subsidies take a variety of forms such as free space and/or utilities for the press's operation, underwriting some or all of the cost of salaries and benefits, and covering marketing expenses. Today there is a growing use of "page charges" as a means of underwriting publication costs. This is very common in the field of scientific and technical journal publishing. The author must pay a fee for each published page. In some cases, the author built that cost into a research project; in other cases, the author's home institution pays the fee for the person. Unlike "self-publishing" efforts, the reason for the charges is to help recoup what can be very costly press work such as complex charts and graphs or color requirements. Discounts for scholarly press titles are normally modest at best.

Check This Out

Each year since 1976, Pushcart Press has issued a volume in the "Pushcart Prize: The Best of the Small Presses" (http://www.pushcartprize.com/index.html) series. It also issues an Editor's Book Award as a way to "identify and publish manuscripts that are rejected by today's bottom line, profit driven commercial presses" (http://www.pushcartprize.com/pushcartpress.html).

Although they were not included in the original categories listed by the Book Industry Study Group, *small presses* are important for academic, public, and school libraries. Small presses are often thought of as literary presses by some people, including librarians. Anyone reading the annual "Small Press Round-Up" in *Library Journal* could reasonably reach the same conclusion. The reality is that small presses are as diverse as the international publishing conglomerates. Size is the only real difference. Many address regional interests and topics that are not of interest to their bigger brothers.

In addition to Gale's *Publisher's Directory* mentioned in chapter 6, a good guide to the output of small presses is *Small Press Record of Books in Print* (*SPRBIP*) published by Dust books. The *SPRBIP* is the definitive record of books in print by the small press industry, listing more than 44,000 titles from more than 5,100 small, independent, educational, and self-publishers worldwide and is available on CD-ROM or online (http://www.dustbooks .com/sr.htm). Many of these presses are one-person operations, a sideline from the individual's home. Such presses seldom publish more than 10 titles per year. The listings in *SPRBIP* show the broad range of subject interests of small presses and that there are both book and periodical presses that fall in this category.

Some people assume that the content of small-press publications is poor. This is incorrect, for small presses do not produce, proportionally, any more poor quality titles than do the large publishers. Often, it is only through the small press that one can find information on less popular topics. Small presses are also critical in developing collections for school and public libraries that have large minority populations. One listing of small presses that publish books by and about "people of color" is produced by the Cooperative Children's Book Center at University of Wisconsin at Madison (http://www .education.wisc.edu/ccbc/books/pclist.asp).

Government presses are the world's largest publishers. The combined annual output of government publications—international (United Nations); national (U.S. Government Publishing Office); and state, provincial, regional, and local jurisdictions—dwarfs commercial output, although most output is now in a digital format. In the past, many people thought of government publications as being characterized by poor physical quality or as uninteresting items that governments gave away. Today, some government publications rival the best offerings of commercial publishers and those publications issued in print tend to cost much less. (The government price does not fully recover production costs, so the price can be lower.) Most government publishing activity goes well beyond the printing of legislative hearings or actions and occasional executive materials. We further explore government documents in chapter 12.

Before we move on from producers of books, we should identify two other types of publication venues—self-publishing and private presses, and further discuss the "on demand" concept. In the past, *self-publishing firms* earned themselves a negative reputation. Self-publish presses differ from other publishing houses in that they receive almost all of their income from the authors whose works they publish. An example of such a press is America Star Books (http://www.publishamerica.com/), while another example is CreateSpace™ (https://www.createspace.com/), an Amazon.com company that facilitates independent book, music, and film production. Today, self-publishing is becoming more accepted, as noted by Robin Bradford (2016): "While some librarians feel that buying a self-published book is a revolutionary act, there has been a lot of progress made toward readers accepting them as just books, the same as any other in the marketplace" (p. 53).

From the Authors' Experience

While preparing this edition, Saponaro received an unsolicited email from a self-publishing firm that promised her, among other things:

- Free of charge publication
- Simplified and fast publishing process
- Worldwide sales of your work
- No commitments/fees
- You remain the only copyright holder of your work
- Access to eco-friendly Print-on-Demand technology

Obviously, offers from firms such as these should be investigated fully before proceeding, but this provides an example of their outreach techniques.

Another newer entry into the self-publishing press arena is Unbound (https://unbound.com/), a UK-based publishing house that has successfully taken advantage of the climate for crowdfunding. Unbound's business model is such that readers pledge their financial support for a book before it comes out, and are rewarded not only with a copy of the book but also—if they pledge enough money—with additional benefits such as signed copies, having their names printed in the book, or meeting the author. As of mid-2018, over 177,000 people from 191 countries had pledged over £6.2 million (US$7.9 million) to fund 380 projects (https://unbound.com/how-it-works). As observed by Alastair Horne, "Not only does this model enable a publisher to be absolutely sure that a book will earn back its costs before deciding to publish it, it also creates an army of advocates who will talk about the book on social media, boosting its profile and so increasing later sales" (2017, p. 7).

Closely related to self-publishers are *hybrid publishers*. These presses charge a fee, similar to traditional self-publishers, but are selective in their publications and authors often benefit from editorial support. As noted by

---

Check These Out

Resources that explore self-published titles in library settings include:

Heather Moulaison Sandy (2016) explores how public libraries can support author services in "The Role of Public Libraries in Self-Publishing: Investigating Author and Librarian Perspectives" (*Journal of Library Administration* 56, no. 8: 893–912).

Robert J. Grover, Kelly Visnak, Carmaine Ternes, Miranda Ericsson, and Lissa Staley prepared a guidebook entitled *Libraries Partnering with Self-Publishing: A Winning Combination* (Santa Barbara, CA: Libraries Unlimited, 2016). Their work includes a section on how school and public libraries can support authors, as well as trends in writer support services.

Essays in Self-Publishing and Collection Development: Opportunities and Challenges for Libraries, edited by Robert Holley (West Lafayette, IN: Purdue University Press, 2015), likewise touches upon library support of writers, as well as the overall impact of self-publishing on library collections.

the Independent Book Publishers Association (IBPA): "Although hybrid publishing companies are author-subsidized, they are different from other author-subsidized models in that hybrid publishers adhere to professional publishing standards. Regardless of who pays for editorial, design, and production fees, it is always the publisher that bears responsibility for producing, distributing, and ultimately selling professional-quality books" (http://www.ibpa-online.org/page/hybridpublisher). In February 2018, the IBPA Advocacy Committee published nine criteria for professional hybrid publishers. These include vetted submissions; a commitment to editorial, design, and production quality; and a strategic approach to distribution (http://www.ibpa-online.org/resource/resmgr/docs/IBPA-Hybrid-Publisher-Criter.pdf).

Self-publishing enterprises always show a profit and never lack material to produce. They offer editing assistance for a fee, and they arrange to print as many copies as the author can afford. Distribution is the author's chore, although some firms, for a fee, will handle this work as well. Many authors who use such presses donate copies of their books to local libraries, but such items frequently arrive with no indication that they are gifts. Note: Although these publishers do not vet the titles they print in the same manner as traditional publishers do, not all of their output is lacking in merit. Thus, when unsolicited titles do arrive at the library, a selector is well advised to examine the item.

As for *publish-on-demand* (POD) initiatives, such activities can conceivably allow publishers to produce single copies of a wider variety of titles at an affordable cost. Advances in digital publishing certainly make it much easier, faster, and more economical for titles to be printed in smaller batches—or even one title at a time. As noted by Brooke Warner (2017), "From the vantage point of a traditional publisher, POD is a seamless process. If a book starts its life cycle by having been printed offset, with plenty of inventory during those early months immediately following publication, its eventual move to POD will go unnoticed by bookstores. For these publishers, the act of flipping a book to POD is akin to turning down the tap on a faucet" (p. 82).

One technology that was intended to facilitate POD in settings such as libraries was the Espresso Book Machine® (EBM) from On Demand Books (http://www.ondemandbooks.com/). Some of the features of the EBM include its ability to "print, bind, and trim on demand at point of sale perfect-bound library-quality paperback books with full-color covers . . . in minutes for a production cost of a penny a page" (http://www.ondemandbooks.com/images/EBM_Brochure.pdf, p. 1). Institutions that could not afford the high purchase price could look at leasing options available from On Demand.

POD installations in libraries appear not to have become as widespread as anticipated by its developers, likely because of the cost of an EBM and because the technology is still relatively new—items produced in such a manner may not be the same quality as those generated by a "traditional" publisher. Further, once produced, EBM titles still require some technical processing on the part of libraries (Arlitsch, 2011, p. 65). At the time we were preparing this text, the EBM had limited installations in library settings, including Michigan State University (https://lib.msu.edu/ebm/), the University of Utah (http://www.lib.utah.edu/services/espresso-book-machine.php), and Sacramento (CA) Public Libraries (http://www.saclibrary.org/Services/I-Street-Press/). Given budgetary limitations faced by many libraries, it is doubtful the EBM will expand its foothold much further into the library market, although we anticipate the concept of print on demand will continue to evolve with developments in technology.

Check This Out

David Cody provides an overview of the history of the Kelmscott Press, one of the most celebrated private presses in the 1890s, in "Morris and the Kelmscott Press" (*Victorian Web*, November 6, 2014: http://www.victorianweb.org/authors/morris/kelmscott .html).

Private presses are not business operations in the sense that the owners do not always expect to make money. Most private presses are an avocation rather than a vocation for the owners. Examples are Kelmscott, Bird and Bull, and Poull Press. In many instances, the owners do not sell their products but give them away. Some of the most beautiful examples of typographic and book design originated at private presses. Large research libraries often attempt to secure copies of items produced by private presses.

Media Formats

Thomas Wall once suggested the following definition of nonprint materials:

1. The item must appeal to the sight and/or hearing of the library user.

2. Under normal conditions, the item must require additional equipment for usage.

3. The printed word must not represent the essence of the medium. (1985, p. 131)

For a time, the profession had strong differences of opinion regarding the role, if any, of nonprint materials in a library's collection. Some librarians held the belief that nonprint/media formats distracted libraries from their primary mission—the promotion of lifelong reading, especially the reading of quality literary titles. Further, they believed such collections drained essential resources from print material. Essentially, such people viewed libraries as being in the "book" rather than the "information" business. However, this mindset has shifted, with the recognition that media can and does play an important role in virtually all library collections. Sally Mason noted that "visual media will only become more important to library service in the future. . . . It is not enough for librarians to 'capitulate' on the issue of visual media. We must become leaders and advocates . . . helping the public to learn what is available, to sort through multiple possibilities, and offering guidance in the use of media to obtain needed information" (1994, p. 12). The Association of College & Research Libraries division of ALA (ACRL) developed *Guidelines for Media Resources in Academic Libraries* to address issues surrounding the inclusion of media in academic libraries. First published in 1999, the *Guidelines* were later revised in both 2006 and 2012, and most recently in 2018. One of the key assertions of the *Guidelines* are that media "materials are as vital and diverse as any print or text-based collection in an academic library" (ACRL, 2018), showing the key role media play in collections.

Regardless of differences in philosophy, various nonprint formats have been present in libraries for over 100 years. (Music recordings were one of the first nonprint items added to library collections.) Media resources have been an interesting, varied, and challenging component of collections. In today's digital environment, they remain interesting and challenging, if perhaps not as varied as in the past.

Further, there is a general recognition that media play an important role in having an informed society. Anyone reading *Publishers Weekly* (*PW*) or shopping on Amazon.com knows that publishers and booksellers no longer limit themselves to just books and magazines. They see themselves as being in the information business. Regular columns in *PW* on audio and video releases indicate that producers and vendors view this field as an important market. Although the ACRL *Guidelines* referenced above focus on media in academic libraries, much of what they advocate applies to public and school library settings as well. In particular, "media librarians must assess rapidly evolving new formats and be ready to adopt them when they stabilize and when it has been determined that they meet content and programmatic needs within the institution" (ACRL, 2018).

In this chapter, we provide an overview of basic forms of media, following Hall's basic definition, including audio and video, as well as other nonprint/nonmonograph materials (such as graphic novels) and the issues surrounding their inclusion in library collections. Digital representations of audio and video are further explored in chapter 13.

Media Issues

Media formats present several challenges for the library and its acquisitions budget. As noted in Hall's defining characteristics of media, these formats almost always require some type of equipment in order to access their content. Thus, there is both the cost of buying the equipment and maintaining it on an ongoing basis. Failure to maintain the equipment will damage the medium used with it, which is much more fragile than paper-based content. There is also, at times, an issue of equipment compatibility when ordering new titles (such as DVD or Blu-ray).

Because media items are generally used with equipment, they wear out or are damaged more quickly than print materials, especially when the public may check them out for home use. Fred Byers once noted, "Temperature and humidity conditions can markedly affect the useful life of a disc; extreme environmental factors can render discs useless in as little as a few days" (2003, p. 2). Although his example was somewhat extreme (and a scenario that neither authors have experienced), Byers did report that both deterioration and technological obsolescence are two key challenges when working with CD and DVD media. Also, unlike print, some media, such as video, often have restrictions on how they may be used. A concept called "performance rights" affects library usage. Performance rights are addressed later in this chapter.

As identified by Byers, an ongoing media issue for libraries is the speed of technological change. Those working with end-users have to keep pondering the question, "How many times must we purchase a copy of Beethoven's Fifth Symphony or the movie *Gone With the Wind*?" Since the 1960s, the music recording collections have moved from vinyl disks (in several different sizes and speeds) to cassettes (in several variations) to CDs. A similar series of changes took place in terms of motion pictures—from film (16 mm and 8 mm) to cassette (VHS and Beta) to DVD and now Blu-ray. Changes in technology leave libraries with legacy collections of items many users view as dinosaurs. Moving too quickly into a format that does not last is a waste of funds, yet waiting too long can also be costly, if for no other reason than losing users' goodwill and support.

Long-term preservation of media can become an issue for some libraries—the material wears out quickly and the equipment changes very fast as well—but there are also short-term issues related to wear, damage, and security to consider as well. Given media's changing formats, your work life in this area will be interesting, to say the least.

Audio Formats

Audio and video formats are frequently held in school, public, and academic library settings. In terms of audio recordings in libraries—both spoken word and music—there is great diversity and incompatibility concerns, at least in terms of the legacy collections. In public libraries, the music recordings were/are usually part of the circulating collection. For educational libraries the purpose is usually instructional, with limited, if any, use outside the library. This is the media category that most clearly reflects the long-term influence of a changing technology on library collections, ranging from vinyl records of various speeds, to tapes of various speeds, to cassettes—various tracks, CDs, and now downloading.

Although we cover streaming music in chapter 13, we note here that the widespread use of Internet audio streaming, iPods, and other electronic gear has made music recordings a low-use item in most libraries. Many libraries retain their older recordings because often the performance has not yet migrated to a digital form. A few libraries are purchasing relatively low-cost equipment and software that allows earlier recording formats to be converted to an MP3 format; however, the library must be careful to do this in compliance with copyright laws. For libraries that continue to purchase music in CD format, one review source is the *CD Hotlist* produced monthly by Rick Anderson. Unlike other review sources, CD Hotlist is "primarily a recommendation service. You will find very few negative reviews here; in virtually every case, an album is [included] precisely because it is recommended" (https://cdhotlist.com/about/).

For public libraries, audiobooks have become almost as important as the video collection. As noted by Maria Cahill and Jennifer Moore (2017), "Although audiobooks could theoretically serve as the sole format of a text, in almost all cases they are an alternate presentation of a book available in a text-based format" (p. 23). Audiobooks are easily accessible in automobile CD players or via other portable digital media players, resulting in a significant demand. While reading a small paperback on a crowded subway or bus can be difficult, listening to a pocket-sized player with a headset allows the listener to close out the noise, to some degree, and enjoy a favorite piece of music or listen to a bestseller. The same is true for those commuting in their cars or just out for a power walk. Audiobooks are also popular with individuals learning English as a second language, and are frequently purchased by community colleges and public libraries for these purposes. Another value of audiobooks is providing those with vision impairments additional opportunities to enjoy print material that goes beyond those available through the National Library Service for the Blind and Physically Handicapped (https://www.loc.gov/nls/) service provided by the Library of Congress. In school libraries, audiobooks not only help English as a second language (ESL) kids, they can help with overall reading skills. Students can listen to an

---

Check These Out

Annette Lamb, in her 2018 article "Listeners' Advisory Part 2: Connecting Audiobooks with Today's Readers" (*Teacher Librarian* 45, no. 3: 62–65), outlines several strategies for marketing audiobooks in the school library in order to connect students, parents, and teachers with audiobook materials.

Sharon Grover and Lizette Hannegan's *Listening to Learn: Audiobooks Supporting Literacy* (Chicago: ALA, 2012) provides an overview of suggested audiobooks from kindergarten through grade 12, as well as a discussion of audiobooks and learning standards and criteria for evaluating audiobooks for selection.

Both are worth the read.

---

audiobook and read the print book at the same time to reinforce such skills as decoding and fluency.

Reviews for audiobooks are contained in some of the same review sources for print titles we mentioned in chapter 6. Additional sources include a listing of links to award-winning audio works (both music and spoken word) maintained by ALA (http://www.ala.org/aboutala/offices/library/alarecommends/recommendedlistening), and review sources for audiobooks including:

- The "Audio Media" section of the *School Library Journal* website (https://www.slj.com/?subpage=Reviews%2B,Media,Audio),

- The "Audio Media" section of the *Library Journal* website (https://www.libraryjournal.com/?subpage=Reviews%2B,Media,Audio),

- The "Booklist Reader Audiobooks" section of the *Booklist* website (https://www.booklistreader.com/category/audiobooks/),

- *AudioFile*'s "Best Of" listing (https://www.audiofilemagazine.com/bestof/) recap of top audiobooks reviewed in that source the prior year, and

- *AudioFile*'s online blog (https://www.audiofilemagazine.com/blog/) with news and reviews of current audiobook titles.

Video

In terms of video, most libraries that have them have been or are weeding their film collections in terms of 16mm and 8mm formats. About the only environments in which such films are found are academic libraries, special collections, and archives. Like many of the other formats, film content has migrated to a digital form (DVDs and increasingly to streaming video). Videocassettes (VHS) are still found in collections, primarily because much of the content is not yet available in a digital form, and because of the cost to duplicate formats.

Format battles in the video field have been ongoing for some years now. One well-known battle was between Beta and VHS, with VHS being declared the winner. A more recent struggle was between DVD, Blu-ray, and HD-DVD. By 2008, the HD-DVD format had fallen out of the contest, leaving DVD and Blu-ray to continue the competition (see Brian Cozzarin et al., 2012, for a discussion of the format battles and their outcome). Today, libraries are once again caught in the middle of a commercial battle where they must bet on a winning side or spend limited funds duplicating the same content in competing formats. One issue is that a DVD player cannot play a Blu-ray disc; however, most Blu-ray players can play the older DVD format. Although prices for Blu-ray players have fallen, only 44 percent of U.S. households had a Blu-ray player as of early 2016, instead preferring streaming video (Morris, 2016). Because of this, the future user base for the DVD/Blu-ray format is unclear. Notwithstanding the Blu-ray issue, most libraries still have substantial collections of VHS material and DVDs, although their circulation rates may be experiencing a slight decline. As noted by Ian Reid (2017), "Spending on CD/DVDs . . . is relatively unchanged over the last five years but mean circulation of these items has decreased at -6.5 percent per year . . . likely a result of increases in use of music and video downloading services" (pp. 23–24).

Given the quick release of DVDs after a film is in theaters, DVD collections generate some of the same issues as bestseller books. Everyone wants it now, not next month after all the talk has faded. Brodart offers the DVD equivalent of the McNaughton book-rental plan where a library may lease multiple copies of a popular DVD title for a short time and return all or some of the copies after the demand has died down (http://www.brodartbooks .com/subscription-services/dvd-purchase-plus-plan/page.aspx?id=100224), while Baker and Taylor's "Scene and Heard" service offers CD, DVD, and Blu-ray titles (http://www.btol.com/ps_details.cfm?id=35) in a similar fashion. *Educational Media Reviews Online* (http://emro.lib.buffalo.edu/emro/) is a database of video, DVD, and audio CD reviews written by librarians and teaching faculty that can be useful in selection activities. Additionally, the Video Round Table of ALA compiles an annual list of notable videos for adults (http://www.ala.org/rt/vrt/notablevideos), while ALA's Association for Library Service to Children likewise produces a list of notable children's videos (http://www.ala.org/alsc/awardsgrants/notalists/ncv/ncvpastlists). Both resources can also provide valuable insight when selecting titles.

One concern, especially for public libraries, is the potential for complaints about its video collection. Public libraries usually address movie and other ratings (such as graphic/manga novels and video games) in their collection development policy. School library media centers have somewhat less exposure to challenges because of the instructional nature of the collections; however, even in these libraries it is possible to have a parent complain about a video, such as one dealing with evolution. Very often the complaint will raise the question about the suitability of certain titles for young viewers and the need for "protecting the children." This was the major factor in the creation of the movie rating system.

The Motion Picture Association of America (MPAA; https://www.mpaa .org/film-ratings/) has a rating system for its releases—the familiar G, PG, PG-13, R, and NC-17 one sees in the entertainment section of the newspaper or on IMDB (http://imdb.com). The Classification and Rating Administration (CARA) within MPAA establishes each film's rating. While these ratings have no legal force and, in fact, are based on the somewhat subjective opinion of

---

Check This Out

Mary S. Laskowski covers all aspects of video collection development, including a discussion of vendors and suppliers and licensing and copyright, in her work *Guide to Video Acquisitions in Libraries: Issues and Best Practices* (Chicago: ALCTS Publishing, 2011).

A Word About Anime

Libraries that do select films often do so in both live-action and animation. The anime form or style of animation originated in Japan, and the term anime has now come to refer to both the animation style as well as films created in that style. Anime is popular among all age groups, and is different from Western animation in its use of visual effects and more adult story lines. Anime first came to the U.S. in the 1980s via the imported Japanese television series *Astro Boy*, and has remained popular, and a part of library collections, ever since. Thomas Disher, Jacob Jett, and Jin Ha Lee reported on the results of a study of anime in public libraries in their article "Investigating the Status of Anime Collections in Public Libraries" (*iConference 2017 Proceedings*, Wuhan, China. pp. 561–567, http://hdl.handle.net/2142/96767), while Laura Pope Robbins (2014) explored "Bringing Anime to Academic Libraries: A Recommended Core Collection" (*Collection Building* 33, no. 2: 46–52).

Check These Out

Two good examples outlining the concept of performance rights to patrons are Williams Libraries' "Public Performance Rights" page (https://libguides.williams.edu /copyright/PPR-video) and "How Do I Find Out If a Movie Has Public Performance Rights" from the Enoch Pratt Free Library (http://www.prattlibrary.org/locations/sights andsounds/index.aspx?id=11096).

the CARA rating board, the general public accepts them as appropriate. The key is the content of each film in terms of its suitability for children.

The unfortunate fact is that even a collection of G- and PG-rated titles does not ensure that there will be no complaints. One possible way to handle the situation, although it is not always easy to accomplish, is to create two sections for video, one in the children's/young adult area and another in the adult area. This will not forestall all complaints, but it could help. In addition, some public libraries have restricted minors from checking out "R" materials. These libraries still have to deal with the issue of adults watching these materials on public machines, so such issues need to be considered and, if possible, addressed in the collection development policy. You might want to check the video policies of some other libraries such as those for the West Orange Public Library (http://www.wopl.org/video-borrowing-policy) or Lincoln Public Library (https://lincolnlibrary.com/dvd-blu-ray-loan-policy) for examples of how these libraries addressed the issue.

Videos are an important source of programming for public libraries, although such programming can be something of a problem because of performance rights, which are a component of the copyright law. For libraries in educational settings, performance rights can be an even greater issue. Purchasing performance rights for video content normally adds an additional cost element to the selection. We discuss the legal aspects of performance rights in chapter 15.

Other Material Formats

Many libraries, because of space, maintenance, and low user interest, are disposing of their collections of reel film, filmstrips, slides, and flat pictures. (We hope they do so with care and don't discard items of long-term

---

Check This Out

Libraries are also beginning to experiment with creating a "library of things" or nontraditional collection, as detailed in *Audio Recorders to Zucchini Seeds: Building a Library of Things*, edited by Mark Robison and Lindley Shedd (Santa Barbara, CA: Libraries Unlimited, 2017). It is well worth the read.

---

societal value solely because of storage space concerns.) Most filmstrips were designed as instructional material and required special projectors, but many of the items are now digitized and available online. The same is true of many slide sets. Flat pictures have always presented challenges in organization and access. Scanning images is an approach to keeping pictorial materials in order and increasing access, especially if available via the library website, assuming there are no outstanding copyright issues.

Maps and Globes

Maps are a form of pictorial material, and most libraries have traditionally held at least a small collection, in addition to atlases in the reference collection, and perhaps an occasional globe. Internet map sites, such as Map-Quest or Google Maps, have significantly reduced the demand for road maps in libraries. Information found on such sites provides what most people were seeking when they came to the library "looking for a map," that is, street and highway information.

Maps actually come in a variety of forms and content. Large public libraries, academic libraries, and many business and industrial libraries have extensive collections. Maps take the form of graphic representations of such things as geological structures, physical features, economic data, and population distributions. They may be in a variety of forms: folded, sheets, raised relief, globes, and even aerial or satellite images, although print maps are currently seeing a decline in popularity as users are showing a preference for computerized maps. Selectors must have clear guidance as to a map collection's scope and purpose. Although a collection might incorporate aerial photographs, including satellite photographs, should it also house remote sensing data from satellites? Are raised relief maps worth including, or are they a commercial product of no real informational value? Clearly the users' requirements will determine the answers to these and many other questions about the collection. The University of Oregon Library has a listing of publishers and distributors for maps that can be useful for selection purposes (https://library.uoregon.edu/map/mappublink), while the Map and Geospatial

---

Check This Out

Some libraries, such as the Osher Map Library and Smith Center for Cartographic Education at the University of Southern Maine (http://www.oshermaps.org/), are digitizing some of their more fragile globes in order to make them more accessible to users. Alison McCarty reviews the work done to make this collection available in her *Public Libraries Online* article "Osher Map Library Brings its Globes to the Public" (February 23, 2016; http://publiclibrariesonline.org/2016/02/osher-map-library-brings-its-globes-to-the-public/).

Information Round Table of ALA has a number of resources (http://www.ala
.org/rt/magirt/publications) for those interested in map collections, as well
as an online newsletter, *base line* (http://www.ala.org/rt/magirt/publications
/baseline).

Games, Toys, and Puzzles

Should libraries acquire games, toys, and puzzles? While some may
question their utility in collections, the reality is that public and school
libraries have ever-growing collections of games, both educational and recreational in character, while toys have been a part of libraries since at
least the Great Depression (Nicholson, 2013, p. 345). Christopher Harris
advocated considering games and toys as one of many curriculum-aligned
instructional resources, thus easily justifying them as part of collections
(2013, p. 10). Carly Bastiansen and Jennifer Wharton (2015) further underscored the importance of such collections today, noting: "even on a small
scale, library toy collections offer crucial and significant early literacy support to the public" (p. 14). Examples of such efforts include the circulating
toy and kit collection at Cuyahoga County (OH) Public Library (https://
www.cuyahogalibrary.org/Borrow/Toys-and-Bookable-Kits.aspx) and the
circulating board game collection at Bucks County (PA) Library System
(http://www.programminglibrarian.org/programs/circulating-board-game
-collection). Further evidence of the growing importance of games in
library collections was that the eleventh academic Games, Learning, and
Society conference was held in 2016, while the American Library Association–sponsored Games and Gaming Round Table (http://www.ala.org/rt
/gamert) was formed in 2011. An additional resource supporting librarians
and other educators is the USA Toy Library Association (http://www.usatla
.org/USA_Toy_Library_Association/Welcome_to_the_USA_Toy_Library
_Association.html) that issues a newsletter and maintains a directory of
toy libraries.

While we agree with the opening quotation from Edward Schneider on
the importance of video games, nonboard games are among the most complex items to select, acquire, and support of all the media formats in a collection. Two of the major reasons for the complexity are the fact that there
are multiple platforms (each widely owned by users) for playing games and
that there are often multiple releases for a title. Certainly both issues exist,
to some extent, for video titles. However, as of 2018 there are at least nine
platforms for electronic games. Although the platforms compete for market
share, the competition has not focused on whose standards or technology
will win; rather, it is whose games attract and hold players' attention longest
and money spent on products for a given platform. The following are the
game platforms available in 2018:

- New Nintendo 2DS XL™
- Nintendo Switch™
- Playstation 4 Slim™
- Playstation 4 Pro™
- PC/MAC based games
- Xbox 360 E®
- Xbox One X/S®
- PlayStation® Vita
- Wii™

When such a variety of platforms is combined with cross-platform
releases of a title, you can see where there would be serious collection budget

---

Check These Out

Jennifer Burek Pierce looks at the history of games and toys in public libraries in her 2016 article "The Reign of Children: The Role of Games and Toys in American Public Libraries, 1876–1925" (*Information & Culture* 51, no. 5: 373–98), while Amy J. Catalano explores how "Games, Toys and Other Play Things" can meet current curricular needs in her title *Collecting for the Curriculum: The Common Core and Beyond* (Santa Barbara, CA: ABC-CLIO, 2015, pp. 37–46).

Check These Out

Video Game Librarian (http://www.videogamelibrarian.com/) is a site for librarians with resources, reviews, and suggestions for incorporating games into libraries, while *Games in Schools and Libraries* is a "podcast and blog dedicated to exploring how games are used in a wide variety of school and library related activities" (http://www.inversegenius.com/games-in-schools-and-libraries).

---

concerns for selectors. Few traditional library vendors handle games, and at the time of this writing there was no source for placing a standing order.

Like motion pictures, games have a rating system. Most video games released in North America carry a rating from the Entertainment Software Rating Board (ESRB, http://www.esrb.org/), a nonprofit, self-regulatory, third-party entity formed in 1994 by what is now the Entertainment Software Association. ESRB ratings consist of three parts: a rating category addressing age appropriateness, content descriptors, and more recently, a description of interactive elements. The ESRB rating appears on the front of the box and there are seven categories: EC, early childhood; E, everyone 6 and up; E10, everyone 10 and up; T, teen 13 and up; M, mature 17 and up; AO, adults only 18 and up; and RP, rating pending. In addition to the rating for the title, 1 of more than 30 different content descriptors (e.g., alcohol reference, blood and gore, etc.) appears on the back of the box elaborating on elements that may be of interest or concern to users and/or their guardians, while interactive elements for online games clarify the amount of online purchases, user interactivity, or location sharing associated with the game. The rating system complexity and the need to provide information about system requirements exemplify the types of challenges that face libraries that are collecting games. Games also raise some serious policy issues, in particular how to monitor who uses what rating.

Graphic Novels

While many of us may recall reading the comic strips included with the Sunday paper and equate them with graphic novels, William Boerman-Cornell, Jung Kim, and Michael Manderino (2017) define graphic novels as "any book length narrative that uses the conventions (or symbolic language) of a comic book to tell a story" (p. 18). Their length differentiates them from comic books, and they can cover virtually any field or topic. Manga, a visual art form first popularized in Japan, is considered one form of graphic novel. Characteristics of this art form include "characters with disproportionately big eyes . . . backgrounds that are often more suggested, blurred, or impressionistic than photorealistic, and some distinctive symbolic elements (e.g., drawing an adult character as a little kid when depicting childish emotions)" (Boerman-Cornell et al., 2017, p. 19). As a result of the large influence of television, advertising, and the Internet, today's adolescents are an extremely visual generation of multimedia learners, and graphic novels have been recognized for their ability to support literacy efforts (see Eileen M. Richardson, 2017; Dawn K. Wing, 2015; Carrye Kay Syma and Robert G. Weiner, 2013; and Michele Gorman, 2003, to name a few), which is why we include a discussion of them among other visual media such as video and games. As noted by Karen Gavigan (2014), "Providing non-traditional texts through visual literacy formats, such as graphic novels, can engage students' interest in a subject" (p. 98). Given their tie to literacy, it should not be surprising to find graphic novels in school library media centers, public libraries, as well as some academic libraries.

The range of subject matter covered in graphic novels is virtually limitless. Joy Fleishhacker (2017) acknowledges the ability of graphic novels to present scientific concepts in a more accessible manner for students. Emilia Packard (2017) further observes that "it is entirely possible to create a microcosm of your library within the graphic novel collection that reflects your patronage, emphasizes diverse experiences, and provides popular works alongside titles ripe for discovery" (p. 48). For their benefits, a decision to include such titles may not come without conflict. Even what may seem like a fairly straightforward selection (due to the item's popularity) may still have complicating factors surrounding it. Challenges to the material are one factor to recognize. As reported by Heidi MacDonald (2017), "As demand

---

Check These Out

Studies that explored incorporating graphic novels into the collection include Aimee Slater's 2017 article "Graphic Novels: Collecting, Cataloging and Outreach in an Academic Library" (*Journal of Academic Librarianship* 43, no. 2: 116–20) and Joel Crowley's 2015 article "Graphic Novels in the School Library" (*School Librarian* 63, no. 3: pp. 140–42).

Sources for more information on selecting graphic novels include:

- Francisca Goldsmith's *Reader's Advisory Guide to Graphic Novels* (2nd ed. Chicago: ALA, 2017).

- Kat Kan's list of resources for locating and evaluating graphic novels for collections: http://www.brodart.com/pdfs/Graphic_Novels/GraphicNovelHelpful Resources.pdf.

- The "Graphic Novels" page (http://www.education.wisc.edu/ccbc/books/graphic novels.asp) maintained by the Cooperative Children's Book Center at the University of Wisconsin–Madison. This site includes review sources, awards and recommended lists of readings on the genre.

- "Great Graphic Novels for Teens" (http://www.ala.org/yalsa/great-graphic -novels), a set of recommended lists produced annually by the Young Adult Library Services Association of ALA.

- The Comic Book Legal Defense Fund has a number of resources for libraries, including suggestions for placement of graphic novels in the collection and sample responses to challenges (http://cbldf.org/graphic-novels-suggestions -for-librarians/).

for graphic novels and comics grows—especially among younger patrons—attempts to censor and remove certain titles from library shelves are also increasing" (p. 19). The impact of adding such materials, in terms of demand for them, is another factor. Mary Simmons and Beth O'Briant (2009) experienced such an unexpected increase in demand and noted, "You begin to feel claustrophobic as the hordes of high school students encircle you like buzzards on a road kill. Could this scenario be real—and happen in your media center? It happened to us, and it can happen in your media center, if you begin to add graphic novels and manga" (p. 16). While locating sources of graphic novels to include in the collection may seem to be a daunting task, Brodart offers a selection service for these materials, similar to its plans for bestselling books and DVDs (http://www.brodartbooks.com/library-collection-development/graphic-novels/page.aspx?id=370), while Baker & Taylor publishes a quarterly online catalog for graphic novels (http://www.baker-taylor.com/pub_details.cfm?id=320) with sections on core lists, award-winning titles, and best sellers.

Prints and Photographs

Methods of capturing images via photography have existed since the 1830s, and photographic images can appear in such physical formats as slides, glass plate negatives, and polyester and acetate film. Unlike books or other media that are acquired through traditional acquisitions methods, photographs and image collections are more likely to be acquired as a result of a donation (such as from a faculty member or instructor). Given the special storage and preservation issues associated with photos, slides, and other images, such items are more likely to be found in museum, academic library, or special collections. However, some larger public libraries, such as New York Public Library   (https://www.nypl.org/about/divisions/wallach-division/photography-collection) or Los Angeles Public Library (LAPL; http://tessa.lapl.org/photocol.html), also maintain photography collections that include images taken by notable photographers (such as Ansel Adams at LAPL, http://photofriends.org/tag/ansel-adams-fortune-magazine-collection/) or that otherwise capture local history. In addition, some libraries' collections have absorbed the holdings of newspaper photo morgues (such as the *Baltimore News American* photos held by the University of Maryland Libraries, https://archives.lib.umd.edu/repositories/2/archival_objects/480658).

As noted by Joanna Norman (2002), "many institutions struggle with decisions in effectively managing their collection and minimizing risks associated with handling original photographic media" (p. 362). As such, preservation concerns for these materials must be taken into account by libraries that have existing collections or seek to bring photographic materials into their collection. Traditional slide and image collections such as those at the SUNY Buffalo Library are being transformed into digital collections (http://digital.lib.buffalo.edu/collection/VS001/), while

---

Check This Out

For a detailed overview of the history of images and their use in collections, including collection management, digitization, and intellectual property rights, see Margot Note's *Managing Image Collections: A Practical Guide* (Oxford: Chandos Publishing, 2011).

other institutions such as the Getty Library (Schuster, 2012) have opted to close their slide libraries. Professional organizations such as the Visual Resources Division of the Art Libraries Society of North America (https://www.arlisna.org/) and its Collection Development Special Interest Group (https://www.arlisna.org/organization/divisions/94-visual-resources-division) can provide support and advice to libraries with existing collections or those considering adding image formats to their collections. In addition, the Association of College & Research Libraries division of ALA sponsors the Image Resources Interest Group (https://sites.google.com/site/acrlirig/) as an additional resource point.

Format Selection Considerations

We noted in chapter 6 that the primary goal of selection is to create a cost-effective collection that meets the needs of the service population, and three of the key factors to consider regardless of format are content, purpose, and cost. However, when dealing with formats other than the traditional print monograph, additional considerations often need to come into play in the selection decision. As noted by Steven Knowlton (2014), three questions may be raised when determining which format to select:

1. Who will use the title?
2. How will the title be used?
3. What are the objectives of the library's collection management program? (p. 1)

While Knowlton's questions were in reference to selecting between a print and online version of a book, his questions are useful starting points for any format-based selection decision. First and foremost, consideration must be made for who will be using a title—is a DVD of a documentary to be used by one patron suitable, or does the library need to consider making films available via a streaming service (covered in the next chapter) to reach a large group of students? Next on Knowlton's list is how the title will be used. In school and academic library settings, this question may be easier to discern—as requests for a specific format may be made by a teacher,

---

Check These Out

Policy examples for selection of audiovisual materials in libraries can be readily found via a Web search. Several worth reviewing include:

- The Audio-Visual Materials Policy from the University of Northern Iowa—https://library.uni.edu/divisions/content-discovery-division/resource-management-unit/audio-visual-materials-policy,

- The Clark County (OH) Public Library Audiovisual Collection Development Policy—https://ccplohio.org/wp-content/uploads/2017/03/AV-Collection-Policy.pdf, and

- The Baltimore County Public Schools Selection Criteria for School Library Media Center Collections—http://lsteml1.pbworks.com/f/BCPS+collection+policy.pdf.

Check These Out

The Arizona State Library has a detailed overview of selection criteria for audiovisual materials (https://azlibrary.gov/libdev/continuing-education/cdt/selection-audiovisual) that is worth reviewing. It includes guidelines for phasing out obsolete formats and equipment.

Marcia Mardis devotes a chapter (chapter 8, "Criteria by Format") of her book *The Collection Program in Schools: Concepts and Practices* (6th ed. Library and Information Science Text Series. Santa Barbara, CA: Libraries Unlimited, 2014) to traditional and legacy formats found in school library collections. Her discussion of each format includes a comparison of advantages and disadvantages as well as special selection considerations (such as storage, subscriptions, etc.), implications for collection development, and copyright considerations. Her chapter is well worth the read as many of the formats covered (such as CDs, graphic materials, and DVDs) are likely to be found in academic and public library settings as well as school library settings.

faculty member, or graduate student and intended for classroom use. Public libraries may not know the ultimate use of a resource—regardless of format. However, a format decision should also be made in relationship to the rest of the collection, its strengths, and its core focus as outlined in the collection development policy.

Other considerations include physical characteristics of the item itself—which can bring with it a host of additional factors such as storage issues, accessibility, durability, ease of use and the prospect of obsolescence of both the material and technology needed to access it. (Recall the Beta vs. VHS discussion from earlier in this chapter.) The Carnegie Library of Pittsburgh addressed the issue of obsolescence in its collection policy—indicating "Older formats are discontinued when customer needs and technological advances result in obsolescence" (2013, https://www.carnegielibrary.org/about/policies/collection-development-and-management/). Obviously, there are a number of important considerations to keep in mind when selecting nonprint materials, but these resources can be well worth the time and effort in terms of their usefulness and use.

Points to Keep in Mind

- Print books will continue to be published for the foreseeable future.

- Producers of materials collected by libraries face challenges of generating enough income to survive and successfully adapting to changes in technology.

- Print titles are not the only format contained in library collections. Media formats have been and will be an important element in a library collection, especially as we go deeper into what some label the "postliterate age."

- Audiobooks are not only popular for their recreational value but also for their use in literacy efforts.

- Nonbook materials, such as maps, globes, toys, puzzles, and games, are popular in libraries, and resources in these formats have been used in combination with literacy programming.

- Media selection must not only consider content and potential usage, but also technology issues, which are in a state of rapid change, as well as the selection constant of cost considerations.

References

ACRL Guidelines for Media Resources in Academic Libraries Task Force. 2018. *Guidelines for Media Resources in Academic Libraries.* American Library Association: Association of College and Research Libraries. http://www.ala.org /acrl/standards/mediaresources.

Anderson, Elsa. 2016. "Print to Electronic: The Library Perspective." *Publishing Research Quarterly* 32, no. 1: 1–8.

Arlitsch, Kenning. 2011. "The Espresso Book Machine: A Change Agent for Libraries." *Library Hi Tech* 29, no. 1: 62–72.

Barr, Catherine, ed. 2017. "Library Acquisition Expenditures, 2016–2017: U.S. Public, Academic, Special and Government Libraries." In *Library and Book Trade Almanac,* 62nd ed., 243–51. New York: Information Today.

Bastiansen, Carly, and Jennifer Wharton. 2015. "Getting Ready for Play!" *Children & Libraries: The Journal of the Association for Library Service to Children* 13, no. 4: 13–29.

Boerman-Cornell, William, Jung Kim, and Michael Manderino. 2017. *Graphic Novels in High School and Middle School Classrooms.* Lanham, MD: Rowman & Littlefield.

Bradford, Robin. 2016. "What's in a Publisher?" *Library Journal* 141, no. 6: 53.

Brunvand, Amy. 2015. "Taking Paper Seriously." *College & Research Libraries News* 76, no. 7: 392–93.

Byers, Fred R. 2003. *Care and Handling of CDs and DVDs—A Guide for Librarians and Archivists.* NIST Special Publication 500-252. Gaithersburg, MD: National Institute of Standards and Technology.

Cahill, Maria, and Jennifer Moore. 2017. "A Sound History." *Children & Libraries: The Journal of the Association for Library Service to Children* 15, no. 1: 22–29.

Cozzarin, Brian Paul, William Lee, and Bonwoo Koo. 2012. "Sony's Redemption: The Blu-ray vs. HD-DVD Standards War." *Prometheus* 30, no. 4: 377–94.

Fleishhacker, Joy. 2017. "Collection Development." *Knowledge Quest* 45, no. 4: 24–31.

Gavigan, Karen W. 2014. "Shedding New Light on Graphic Novel Collections: A Circulation and Collection Analysis Study in Six Middle School Libraries." *School Libraries Worldwide* 20, no. 1: 97–115.

Gorman, Michele. 2003. *Getting Graphic! Using Graphic Novels to Promote Literacy with Preteens and Teens.* Worthington, OH: Linworth Pub.

Harris, Christopher. 2013. "Gaming the Common Core." *School Library Journal* 59, no. 10: 1.

Horne, Alastair. 2017. "Publishing: The Last (and Next?) Five Years." *Indexer* 35, no. 1: 2–9.

Knowlton, Steven A. 2014. "Print, Electronic or Both? How Libraries Choose a Format When Purchasing Books." *Tennessee Libraries* 64, no. 2: 1.

Landgraf, Greg. 2015. "Solving the Self-Published Puzzle." *American Libraries* 46, no. 11/12: 44–47.

MacDonald, Heidi. 2017. "Library Demand for Graphic Novels Keeps Growing." *Publishers Weekly* 264, no. 20: 19–28.

Mason, Sally. 1994. "Libraries, Literacy and the Visual Media." In *Video Collection Development in Multitype Libraries,* edited by G. P. Handman, 9–13. Westport, CT: Greenwood.

Milliot, Jim. 2017. "Pearson Rises Above." *Publishers Weekly* 264, no. 35: 56–59.

Morris, Chris. 2016. "Blu-Ray Struggles in the Streaming Age." *Fortune.Com.* January 8, 2016. http://fortune.com/2016/01/08/blu-ray-struggles-in-the -streaming-age/.

Nicholson, Scott. 2013. "Playing in the Past: A History of Games, Toys, and Puzzles in North American Libraries." *Library Quarterly* 83, no. 4: 341–61.

Norman, Joanna. 2002. "Photographic Collections Management." *Journal of Educational Media & Library Sciences* 39, no. 4: 362–73.

Packard, Emilia. 2017. "A Course in Comics." *Library Journal* 142, no. 20: 48–50.

Reid, Ian. 2017. "The 2017 Public Library Data Service Report: Characteristics and Trends." *Public Libraries* 56, no. 5: 20–30.

Richardson, Eileen M. 2017. "'Graphic Novels Are Real Books': Comparing Graphic Novels to Traditional Text Novels." *Delta Kappa Gamma Bulletin* 83, no. 5: 24–31.

Schneider, Edward Francis. 2014. "A Survey of Graphic Novel Collection and Use in American Public Libraries." *Evidence Based Library and Information Practice* 9, no. 3: 68–79.

Schuster, Tracey. 2012. "Thinking Outside the Drawers: Closing the J. Paul Getty Museum's Slide Library." *Visual Resources Association Bulletin* 39, no. 3: 1–3.

Simmons, Mary, and Beth O'Briant. 2009. "Journey into the World of Manga and Graphic Novels." *Library Media Connection* 27, no. 4: 16–17.

Steiner, Ann. 2018. "The Global Book: Micropublishing, Conglomerate Production, and Digital Market Structures." *Publishing Research Quarterly* 34, no. 1: 118–132.

Syma, Carrye Kay, and Robert G. Weiner, eds. 2013. *Graphic Novels and Comics in the Classroom: Essays on the Educational Power of Sequential Art.* Jefferson, NC: McFarland.

Two Sides. 2015. *Reading from Paper or Reading from Screens. What do Consumers Prefer? A Survey of U.S. Consumers Undertaken by Two Sides, May 2015.* June 23, 2015. https://twosidesna.org/US/Reading-from-Paper-or-Reading-from -Screens—What-do-Consumers-Prefer/.

Wall, Thomas B. 1985. "Nonprint Materials: A Definition and Some Practical Considerations on Their Maintenance." *Library Trends* 34, Summer: 129–40.

Warner, Brooke. 2017. "The Hidden Stigma of POD." *Publishers Weekly* 264, no. 52: 81–82.

Wing, Dawn K. 2015. "Graphic History." *School Library Journal* 61, no. 11: 25.

12
Serials

The prominence of electronic resources in many libraries' collections does not render obsolete traditional print management tasks like receiving, claiming, and binding, contrary [to] common perception.

—NASIG, 2016

Most readers are familiar with (and indeed weary of) the long-running serials crisis: budgets have stagnated as the cost of serials for STEM disciplines continue to rise.

—M. Brooke Robertshaw, Michaela Willi Hooper, and Kerri Georgen-Doll, 2017

And nothing tells us more about changes in libraries than does the Big Deal, a publisher's strategy for delivering packages of electronic journal content to libraries that would not have been possible without both the WWW and ejournals.

—Matthew Ismail, 2017

Serials, regardless of format and especially magazines and journals, serve a basic function in accessing information. That is, they disseminate small amounts of information about the most recent efforts of individuals to inform others about some new development. Because of their timeliness and readability, serials are frequently the "go to" source for authoritative information for many people. Although both analog and digital versions have some limitations as well as advantages, serials are an essential component in the information cycle. They are a major element in almost any type of library collection. Paper-based serials are what you might call the "version of record" in terms of permanence, while e-serials are much more searchable than their print cousins and are generally always available.

Paper-based serials do have a permanence issue, at least those published more than 50 years ago—their paper is acidic and becomes brittle with age. With repeated handling, acidic paper can crumble into dust. Paper serials are also costly to maintain in terms of shelf space and binding. They are also susceptible to theft—articles and issues can and do go missing as some individuals try to reduce their own personal photocopying costs. Additionally, there is rarely a record of who uses what, unlike their digital versions. Microformats (microfilm and fiche), aside from being disliked due to needing special machines to access, have their own issues in terms of space and housing requirements, as well as preservation issues such as vinegar syndrome. (More on vinegar syndrome in chapter 14.)

E-serials, while considered to be a preferred format for acquiring and preserving serials, have more long-term permanence issues than do the paper versions. Most users have a belief that print and e-journals are identical. That is not always the case, especially when you consider some resources omit photographs, charts, tables, graphs, and advertisements from the online "equivalent" of the print title. Some users also believe that e-journals are superior to print titles. For many years, funding authorities did, and some still do, believe e-journals will save money in comparison to print subscriptions. Funding authorities also had, and may still harbor, the hope that e-resources will render the library obsolete, thus saving significant amounts of money. Both users and funding agencies probably rarely, if ever, think about long-term access; they believe the information will always be there. CM personnel understand e-serial shortcomings and do their best to address the issues whenever they can.

There are some commonalities in how the two formats are selected and managed. We start our coverage by looking at the commonalities.

What Is a Serial?

Users and librarians employ words such as *journal, magazine,* and *periodical* interchangeably. Such usage masks some significant differences and fails to denote the many variations that exist. Thomas Nisonger (1998) devoted more than six pages in his book to how different groups attempted to define serials. The electronic world is changing the nature of serials and the way libraries process them. The Internet has even changed what a library should consider a serial. T. Scott Plutchak (2007) suggested that "The serial as defined by librarians is an anachronism in the digital age, and will not survive for long. . . . This matter of definitions bedevils us all, and I'm sure you've had the same kinds of discussions in your institutions that we've had in mine as we try to figure out how to shoehorn these new information resources that we're dealing with into the same old categories" (p. 81). The Library of Congress defines serials as "Print or non-print publications issued in parts, usually bearing issue numbers and/or dates. A serial is expected to continue indefinitely" (https://www.loc.gov/issn/issnbro.html).

Plutchak's point is well taken; that is, the library focus has been, and still is to a large extent, on the physical format rather than content. However, at present the old definitions still exist and are widely used in libraries. We draw upon the early work of Fritz Machlup and Kenneth Leeson (1978) for our discussion of serial types. They developed an 18-part classification system for serials. Their system covered all types of serials, including serials "not elsewhere classified."

The first category is *institutional reports*. Institutional reports are annual, semiannual, quarterly, or occasional publications of corporations, financial institutions, and organizations serving business and finance as well as most other organizations. Academic and public libraries serving business programs and interests frequently need to acquire this type of serial. Corporate libraries actively collect this category. Most of the reports available to libraries and information centers are free for the asking. Collecting in this area is labor intensive, because it requires maintaining address and correspondence files, especially if a library collects much beyond the large national corporations. Thanks to online resources, such as EDGAR Online from the Securities and Exchange Commission (http://www.sec.gov/edgar .shtml), filings are now available from a number of sources.

Yearbooks and *proceedings* are annuals, biennials, and occasional publications, bound or stapled, including yearbooks, almanacs, proceedings, transactions, memoirs, directories, and reports of societies and associations. Many libraries collect these serials, especially academic, special, and large public libraries. The more libraries that collect a particular society's or association's publications, the more likely it is that a commercial vendor will handle a standing order for the material. Unfortunately, a significant number must be obtained directly from the society or association. Again, this category normally requires setting up and maintaining address and correspondence files, which is only slightly less labor intensive than doing the same for annual reports of organizations.

Superseding serials fall into one of two categories, both of which are labor intensive in their paper-based format. One group consists of the superseding serial services (each new issue superseding previous ones). These include publications such as telephone directories and product catalogs. The second group consists of the nonsuperseding serial services, many of which were print-based loose-leaf publications that provided information such as changes in accounting rules or government regulations. In the past, both groups often required careful filing of new material and the removal of other (older or superseded) material. Most of the services are now available online, reducing most of the staffing and training issues, and are only available from the publisher. Examples of such services are the *Daily Labor Report* from the Bloomberg BNA (formerly the Bureau of National Affairs, https://www.bna.com/labor-relations -week-p5933/) and the *Standard Federal Tax Reporter* from Wolters Kluwer/ CCH (http://www.wolterskluwerlb.com/pdfs/tax/FED.pdf).

Nonsuperseding serials are less of a problem, and some are available from serial jobbers. However, the materials in this class tend to be expensive, and many must be ordered directly from the publisher. Indexing and abstracting services fall into one of these two classes. All types of libraries need a few of these reference serials. Certainly, online journal databases have reduced the need for such services. However, services such as *Biological Abstracts* and *Chemical Abstracts Service* are still an essential component of most academic library collections.

Newspapers are one of the obvious serials that libraries acquire in both print and electronic formats. Serial jobbers such as W. T. Cox (http://www .wtcox.com/) or EBSCO (https://journals.ebsco.com/) handle a majority of subscriptions for major domestic and international newspapers for libraries, while the local daily is often managed directly between the library and the subscription office of the paper. Selectors must decide how soon users want/ need access to nonlocal newspapers. The greater the need for speedy access, the greater the cost for the library, and delivery options are at the discretion of the newspaper. For example, *The Times'* (London) print edition used to be available at several different speeds, each with a different cost, ranging from daily airmail to weekly packets. More recently, because international papers can be printed in a destination country and no longer need to be mailed from their originating country, the *Times* is only available in print via surface mail within the U.S., while also being available online and in microfilm. Of note is that the *Times* itself is a Monday–Saturday publication, so subscribing libraries must also have a separate subscription to the *Sunday Times* in order to have seven-day coverage. Unlike its U.K. counterpart, *The New York Times* continues to offer several print editions, including late edition, national, and northeast edition, New York metro edition, large-type weekly, braille weekly, weekly packets, and others. Something to keep in mind is that the digital version often does not include everything that was in the print edition, such as classified ads and "inserts."

Almost all major newspapers are somewhat available online; we say somewhat because at the time this was written, newspapers were struggling with the issue of staying in business. They are trying to develop a workable model for generating income to replace revenue lost due to rapidly declining paper subscriptions and advertising. As a result, they often allow free access to a limited version of a story and provide access to the full story when a reader pays a fee (per-story fee, monthly fee, and annual fee are some of the models in use). Libraries can also provide online access to current and historical newspapers through several database vendors such as NewsBank (http://www.newsbank .com/) or ProQuest (http://www.proquest.com); some of the serials aggregators include some newspaper coverage as well, for example EBSCO*host*® (http:// www.ebscohost.com/). NewsBank and ProQuest offer historical products that are full-page searchable images of the print—meaning viewers will see the paper as it appeared originally in print, including advertisements. However, even these versions will still exclude photographs from printed search results from time to time, due to copyright and licensing restrictions.

Newsletters, leaflets, news releases, and similar materials are a form of serial that some libraries actively acquire. Corporate libraries are the most active in gathering material in this category, especially those supporting marketing, lobbying, and public relations activities. Many of the items in this class are free; all a library needs to do is ask to be placed on the distribution list. Other items, especially newsletters containing economic or trade data, can be exceedingly expensive. A number of U.S. services cost in excess of $20,000 for quarterly newsletters of only a few pages. It is at that point that one can begin to fully appreciate the difference between the cost of the information and the cost of the package in which it comes.

Magazines are the most common and the category that most often comes to mind when thinking about serials. Magazines are mass-market or popular serials; Machlup and Leeson divided them into five subgroups. These are the titles that almost any serial jobber will handle for a library. Following are the five subgroups:

- Mass-market serials and weekly or monthly news magazines (such as *Newsweek* and *Economist*)

- Popular magazines dealing with fiction, pictures, sports, travel, fashion, sex, humor, and comics (such as *Sports Illustrated* and *Harper's Bazaar*)

- Magazines that popularize science and social, political, and cultural affairs (*Smithsonian* and *National Geographic*)

- Magazines focusing on opinion and criticism—social, political, literary, artistic, aesthetic, or religious (examples are *Foreign Affairs* and *New Yorker*)

- Other magazines not elsewhere classified. An example of such a title is an organization publication (governmental or private) that is really a public relations vehicle, sometimes called a "house organ." These publications often contain general-interest material, but there is usually some clearly stated or implied relationship between the subject covered and the issuing organization (e.g., *Plain Truth*). Another type of publication in the "other" category is the magazine found in the pocket of airline seats.

Libraries may receive a substantial number of house organs because their publishers give them away. Vendors seldom handle this type of magazine.

Public and school libraries still subscribe to a number of paper-based serials. From the public library perspective, the fact remains that some people still do enjoy reading magazines and newspapers—"leafing" through the pages looking for items of interest. Also, readers often have wide-ranging interests that go beyond their ability to personally subscribe to everything of interest. There is also the practical issue of how many public access computers are available and how long it is reasonable for a person to use the machine. Reading a newspaper or magazine takes a fair amount of time when using a computer screen as the reading source.

Academic libraries also retain such subscriptions for both user needs and legal reasons. As we have noted, digital and paper-based editions can be somewhat different. Most digital versions do not include advertisements and some do not include letters to the editor or photographs. Any institution with a marketing program wants access to ads, while those with journalism programs will likely want access to photographs. There can be legal reason for the retention of paper versions as well. In some cases, digital "Big Deal" agreements contain a clause that limits the number of paper-based subscriptions that may be canceled while still retaining access to the digital package of titles. ("Big Deals" are discussed later in this chapter.)

Journals are titles that are of interest to a narrower segment of the population, sometimes referred to as "informed laypeople," researchers, and scholars. This category has four subcategories:

- Nonspecialized journals for the intelligentsia who are well informed on literature, art, social affairs, politics, and so on (*Science* and *American Indian Art Magazine* are examples)

- Learned journals for specialists—primary research journals and secondary research journals (*American Indian Culture and Research Journal* and *Applied Physics Research,* for example)

- Practical professional journals in applied fields, including technology, medicine, law, agriculture, management, library and information science, business, and trades (*RQ* or *School Library Journal,* for example)

- Parochial journals of any type but addressed chiefly to a parochial audience—local or regional—(*Kiva* or *Arizona Highways*).

Most titles in these categories are available from library vendors, although the library must place direct orders for some of the more specialized journals.

From the Authors' Experience

Saponaro worked at an institution that maintained duplicate print, microfilm, and online subscriptions to major papers such as the *New York Times* and the *Washington Post*. This was due to the fact that even the online historical (page image) version did not always include photographs, which were needed often enough by researchers to warrant maintaining subscriptions to multiple formats, even in challenging budgetary times.

Most parochial journals must be purchased directly from the publisher; local history and regional archaeological publications are examples of this class of serial. Sometimes a library must join an association to obtain its publications.

The final serial category consists of "government publications, reports, bulletins, statistical series, releases, etc. by public agencies, executive, legislative and judiciary, local, state, national, foreign and international." With these variations in serials in mind, it is clear why there is confusion about terms and why there are challenges in collecting and preserving them. Each type fills a niche in the information dissemination system. Although they do create special handling procedures and problems, they are a necessary part of any library's collection. The one constant with serials at this point is that they will change moving forward. Stephen Bosch and Kittie Henderson (2014) opened their article with the following:

> The birth of the World Wide Web 25 years ago was the big bang event that spurred more change in the serials and scholarly publishing world than seen in the century that preceded it. . . . But in the serials ecosystem, as in nature, not all things evolve at the same rate, and the cumulative impact of subtle steps can bring about profound change over time. (p. 32)

Government Information

Government documents have been and remain a component of library collections. Like almost all other collection resources there has been a steady shift away from paper-based publication of government information. Such information arises from all levels of government, although most people first think of the federal government when they hear the term. A great deal of government information falls into the serials category—as many titles are ongoing and numbered and/or dated.

At the federal level, there is a library depository program through which publications are distributed to member libraries to ensure public access to government information. The Government Publishing Office (GPO; https://www.gpo.gov/) oversees the Federal Depository Library Program (FDLP; https://www.fdlp.gov/) in addition to serving as the official publishing arm of the federal government. Although GPO continues to distribute tangible materials to libraries, the majority of their publications are produced electronically and made available to the public via GovInfo (https://www.govinfo.gov/). While GPO produces a majority of the documents libraries acquire in print or access electronically, other government units such as the U.S. Census Bureau (https://census.gov/library/publications.html) and the Library of Congress (https://www.loc.gov/loc/pub/) also distribute publications in print and electronically.

Check This Out

The Library of Congress maintains an extensive list of U.S. executive branch websites (https://www.loc.gov/rr/news/fedgov.html) that also includes links to independent agencies such as the Central Intelligence Agency and the General Services Administration. It also maintains similar lists for state government agencies (https://www.loc.gov/rr/news/stategov/index.html) and international organizations (https://www.loc.gov/rr/news/io.html).

In some ways, state and local government information is of even higher interest to patrons than is federal material. It is also less easy to locate (at least for end users) and the most challenging to identify. Perhaps the most difficult category to locate are cross-jurisdictional bodies. It will take an extra effort to identify the party that is responsible for making the group's actions/decisions available to the public. The bottom line for state and local governments is there are no aggregators. Some states, for example South Carolina, California, and Colorado, have depository programs for their state publications material.

Essentially, making direct contact with state or local government agencies is the best method of acquiring these materials. You can gain some insight into what is available at the local governmental level by subscribing to *Index to Current Urban Documents* (ICUD; http://www.urbdocs.com/), which covers materials from 500 U.S. and Canadian cities. Another resource for finding state and local government information is USA.gov (http://www.usa.gov), a product administered by USAGov, a division of the U.S. General Services Administration's Technology Transformation Service. In terms of local government, it is best for county information as finding city material is a challenge.

There is, of course, some research interest in government information from other countries and NGOs (Non-Governmental Organizations). Probably the two NGOs of most interest to libraries are the United Nations (https://shop.un.org/) and UNESCO (United Nations Educational, Scientific and Cultural Organization; http://www.unesco.org/new/en/unesco/resources/publications). The Library of Congress also has a cooperative acquisitions program through its Overseas Operations Division (https://www.loc.gov/acq/ovop/) to assist libraries in obtaining publications from countries where their field offices are located. Other countries have their own equivalent of the GPO and offer publications online. These include:

Something to Ponder

Managing a federal government documents collection can be more involved than simply acquiring publications as they are issued. There are legal requirements that must be followed by libraries participating in the FDLP program. Two FDLP resources worth reviewing are the Requirements & Guidance page (https://www.fdlp.gov/requirements-guidance/legal-requirements) and the Depository Collection and Development guidelines (https://www.fdlp.gov/requirements-guidance/guidance/14-depository-collection-and-development). It is important to note that these FDLP requirements only govern materials received through the federal depository library program. Materials a library purchases or acquires outside of the FDLP are not subject to any legal requirements and can be handled like all other library materials.

- Canada—http://www.publications.gc.ca/site/eng/home.html
- The Federal Republic of Germany—https://www.deutschland.de/en
- India—https://www.india.gov.in/my-government/documents
- Mexico—https://www.gob.mx/publicaciones
- The Republic of South Africa—https://www.gov.za/document/latest
- The United Kingdom—https://www.gov.uk/government/publications

It is likely only the larger academic libraries need to spend much effort on locating and maintaining links to government information sites from other countries.

Serial Producers

Serial publishers are different from other information publishers/producers. One major difference is that most mass-market serials have in-house staff generating the publication content. They also frequently make use of freelance writers with modest subject expertise for material. Another difference is many serial producers depend upon advertising rather than subscription/sales as their major source of income. For many types of serial producers the institutional market is their financial foundation. Library users' interest in serials is an important element of the serial producers' long-term success.

For some library users, serials are the most frequently consulted library resource. In the not-too-distant past, it was print-based serials, and today it is a combination of print and digital that many people expect and want. People still subscribe to some paper-based newspapers and magazines, but turn to libraries for many titles that they had subscribed to in the past. Professional associations still issue information on paper, but are increasing their use of digital publications. Some, such as ALA divisions, now only publish an electronic version of their journals.

Currency is very important for those who use serials on a regular basis. Serial update intervals can be very short, even daily as in the case of many newspapers. Articles in a serial are also short (compared to book-length treatments of the same topic) and focus on a fairly narrow subject. Readers with very specific information needs frequently find that serials provide the desired data more quickly than books. Finally, serials are often the first printed source of information about a new subject or development. People use serials as a source for learning about new things. Also, the sheer volume of new information appearing in serials far exceeds that of books.

Selection Models

There are a few generalizations regarding serial selection that can help reduce the scope of your decision making. One is that different academic subjects/disciplines tend to have varying levels of interest in serials. The fields of science, technology, engineering, mathematics, and medicine (commonly abbreviated as STEM in the literature) are very dependent on serial publications. Such journals are, on average, the costliest and have a habit of splitting into ever narrower topics. (The notion of scholars adding new knowledge results in what some skeptics say is fewer and fewer people knowing more and more about less and less. The end result is generally more and more titles about ever narrower topics.) At the opposite end of the spectrum are the humanities, which depend more on books than on serials. Between these two are the social sciences, some of which are more similar to the science disciplines (e.g., psychology, linguistics, physical anthropology), and others of which are more similar to the humanities (e.g., political science, education, and social anthropology).

Another generalization is serials change over time as new editors, editorial boards, or publishers make major and minor shifts in the content and/or purpose. From a selector's point of view, a change in a title is a signal to rethink the title's appropriateness for the collection. For some journals and magazines, there is a long history of title changes, which can be confusing for end-users who may not know of the changes over time and may think the library has fewer holdings than it actually does. Steve Black (2009) succinctly summed up the library view regarding the changing character and titles of serials by noting, "Since changes in title create work for librarians and confusion for patrons, librarians want title changes to occur only for compelling reasons" (p. 200). Although his comment focused on titles, other changes also create the issues he mentioned—such as frequency of publication, scope of coverage, and, in the case of scholarly journals, even splitting into two titles with slightly different coverage.

Essentially the potential changing nature of a serial title means the decision-making process never completely ends. Another unfortunate aspect of today's library economic environment is the need, from time to time, to cancel some serial subscriptions. This results in a whole new decision process.

Yet another generalization is that a decision to subscribe to a serial is a more significant decision than monographic purchase decisions. Several factors account for the difference. Because serials are ongoing, they often become a standing financial commitment for the library and thus become a fixed element in the materials budget. Because print serials arrive in parts/issues, there must be an ongoing process for receiving the material and maintaining records about what did or did not arrive. Unfortunately, few print serials arrive in a form that allows for easy long-term storage or heavy use; therefore, libraries must develop a means to preserve them such as binding—an additional cost factor. In addition, print serials occupy large amounts of storage space, which over time becomes scarce. When adding a title that has been published for some time, one must also consider the question of back files—prior volumes. E-serials are not immune to the cost of immediate and long-term storage/access issues and in some ways those issues are more difficult to overcome. We explore these issues later in this chapter as well as in chapter 14.

A print serials collection that does not provide for quick, easy, and inexpensive scanning or photocopy service will quickly become a collection of covers and advertisements as the articles will disappear. Certainly e-serials have reduced the need for high-capacity photocopy; however, there is a replacement cost—printing capability.

There are five serial selection models: cost, citation analysis, worth or use, polling, and core lists. There are many variations, but the five listed form the basic models for selecting serials. Much of the work done in this area is relatively recent and more the result of having to cancel rather than to start subscriptions.

Cost models of selection are the oldest and have the greatest number of variations. One of the most complex models deals with the real annual cost of a serial. The annual cost consists of six elements: acquisition cost, processing cost, maintenance cost, storage cost, utility or use cost, and subscription price. *Acquisition costs* include such things as selection, order placement, and time spent in working with the subscription agent or publisher. *Processing costs* cover check-in, claiming, routing, cataloging or other labeling, adding security strips, and shelving in public service for the first time. *Maintenance costs* involve binding, microfilming or acquiring microform, selecting for remote storage, and possibly discarding. *Storage costs* entail calculating the linear feet of storage space (either or both shelf and cabinet space) used by the title and the cost of the space. *Utility* or *use costs* are the most complex to calculate. They incorporate costs of time for such things as retrieval from a storage location (library staff only), pick-up and reselling, answering questions about the title ("Do you have . . . ?," "I can't find . . . ," and "What is the latest issue you have?"), and all other required assistance (assistance with microform readers, for example). The last, and often the lowest, cost is the subscription price. The sum of these costs represents the real annual cost of the title for the library. Looking over the list of costs makes it clear that it will take some time to calculate the individual cost centers. However, once one determines the unit costs (for example, the average time to shelve an issue), it is fairly easy to calculate the cost for a given number of issues of a title. With an annual cost for each title, selectors can determine which titles to continue or discontinue.

Obviously, the cost model does not work well for e-serials that are part of an aggregated database or "Big Deal" package. You rarely get to pick which titles in the database you wish to make available, and many packages have titles added to the package, some of which you would never subscribe to in the first place. However, the cost model can still be effective for standalone titles, which do still exist.

Like cost models, citation analysis paradigms take several forms. The main objective, from a selection point of view, is to identify frequently cited titles. Citation analysis can help identify a core collection for a field and provide a listing of titles ranked by the frequency with which they are cited. Another collection development use of citation analysis is in evaluating a collection. (Could a set of papers/reports have been done using this collection?) Citation analysis information is most useful in large or specialized research collections, although core collection information is valuable to smaller and nonspecialized collections as well.

Using the Bradford Distribution, one can rank titles to develop information for collection policy use as well to make decisions regarding current subscriptions. The goal of this ranking is to identify all journals containing articles relevant to a given subject and to rank them in order based on the number of relevant articles they publish in a year. The pattern, according to Bradford's Law of Scattering, will show that a few journals publish the majority of articles and a large number of journals publish only one or two cited articles. If one equates a basic collection with holding journals that contain 20 percent of the relevant material, one might subscribe to only 3 or 4 titles. For libraries with a comprehensive collecting goal, the subscription list may contain several hundred titles. For example, Tozzer Library (Harvard), at one point, had a current subscription list of more than 1,200 titles just for coverage of anthropology and archaeology. Even that total did not cover the global output of anthropology and archaeology titles.

Journal worth models usually involve some information about title usage along with other data. The model involves cost, use, impact factor, and information about the nature of the publication (core subject, for example) to calculate a cost-benefit ratio.

Check This Out

To learn more about Bradford's Law of Scattering and its applications, see Jeppe Nicolaisen and Birger Hjørland's 2007 article "Practical Potentials of Bradford's Law: a Critical Examination of the Received View" in the *Journal of Documentation* (63, no. 3: 359–77).

As one might assume, most of the models require a substantial amount of data collection. If their only utility lay in making selection decisions, few libraries would use them. Their major value comes into play when the library must cut subscriptions. Having collected data that is similar for all the titles makes the unpleasant task a little easier. What librarians hoped would be a rare occurrence has, for some libraries, become an almost annual task. Each time the task becomes more difficult, and the models demonstrate their value.

Polling experts and using lists of recommended journals are other methods for identifying what to buy or keep. Both suffer from being less directly linked to the local situation, unless the experts are local users. One can find lists of journals in relatively narrow subjects, often listed with recommendations, or at least comments, in journals like *Serials Librarian* (Routledge) and *Serials Review* (Taylor & Francis).

Identifying Serials

You might think that in today's e-environment there would be no need to "identify" a serial title, much less place a subscription for a paper-based edition. There is no question that the serial aggregators and publishers have, more or less, covered the major journal and popular magazine titles. There are, however, a host of "small magazines" (literary in character primarily), specialty publications (hobbies, recreational titles, for example), and regional publications (titles such as *Arizona Highways* and *Kiva*) that exist outside the publisher/aggregator packages. Local user interests often require seeking out such titles. Three useful general guides are *ULRICHSWeb*™ (ProQuest, http://www.proquest.com/products-services/Ulrichsweb.html), *Serials Directory* (EBSCO, https://www.ebsco.com/products/research-databases/serials-directory), and *Standard Periodical Directory* (Oxbridge Communications, http://www.oxbridge.com/SPDCluster/theSPD.asp). Another source that is particularly strong for newspapers and newsletters is the *Gale Directory of Publications and Broadcast Media* (Gale Research, https://tinyurl.com/GaleDPBM). For literary publications, a good source is *International Directory of Little Magazines and Small Presses* (Dustbooks, http://www.dustbooks.com/d.htm).

E-Serials

E-serials are no different from other collection resources in the sense they have legal issues (see chapter 13 for a discussion of licensing issues) and preservation concerns (chapter 14). Selection decisions can be complicated and if anything, they require greater scrutiny/assessment efforts than other materials (see chapter 8).

Despite these challenges and depending on the type of library and its holdings, e-serials can be among the library's most heavily used resources.

Something to Watch

Recent offerings such as *Flipster* from EBSCO (https://flipster.ebsco.com/) and *Zinio* (https://www.zinio.com/) are capable of recreating an entire journal print edition digitally. One benefit of such services is that they make popular magazines accessible to individuals with limited vision as they can access material simply by enlarging the text. Further, unlike individual articles from databases, such services also allow patrons to download entire issues for offline reading.

Also depending on the situation, they can also represent an ever-growing percentage of collection development funds. Users hold several beliefs about e-serials; some are accurate and a number are only partially accurate. Of all the beliefs the one that is 100 percent true is that e-journals are much more searchable than their paper-based versions. Database search engines generate more useful information in a shorter time than was ever possible for a single user in a print-only environment.

The notion that e-resources are available 24/7 is not completely accurate. Certainly their availability is far superior to print journals given few libraries were or are open at all hours every day. However, anyone who engages in almost daily searching of journal databases has occasionally seen the "server not found" error message. Such messages are generally the result of overloaded server demands somewhere in the system. Another service disruption is that all servers eventually require some maintenance, which means eventually there must be some down time on the vendor's end. A few vendors do their maintenance on a regular schedule, which allows the library to post that information for users. Lack of availability is a minor problem for most users; however, CM officers ought to monitor the lack of access situation, especially when the library pays for access on the basis of number of simultaneous users. Increasing that number is usually a modest cost consideration, which in return generates greater user satisfaction.

There is also the common belief that e-journals are "full-text." In most cases this is a rather mixed bag. Most are full-text in terms of articles, but perhaps only as an html file. (Anyone required to provide page citations is not too happy when only an html version of an article is accessible.) Different e-vendors have varying definitions of what they mean and provide as "full-text." Regular users of an e-journals database may be aware, on some level, that it may be necessary to download the text portion of an article in one particular database and do another download(s) for any graphic material (or locate them via another means, such as a print/microform copy). *Nexis Uni*™ is such an example. Users interested in letters to the editor, editorials, advertising, photographs, or tables often find that the e-version lacks one or more of those features. They begin to realize there are differences between the print and e-version of a journal, newspaper, or magazine issue.

The notion that e-journals are superior to the paper format also has another wart—that they are the most current. The reality is sometimes they are and sometimes they are not. E-journals are not always more, or even as, current as the hard copy publication. Today it is less of a problem than when almost all of the hard copies had to be scanned before becoming available for database access. The major issue with currency today is the "embargoes" that some publishers place on digital access to their material. An embargo means that a predetermined time must pass after a paper issue appears and when that material will be made available digitally. Embargoes range in length from a few weeks to a number of months. Why the embargo? The answer is some publishers see it as a means of maintaining paper subscriptions as well as benefiting from online access.

Do E-Serials Save Libraries Money?

Serial costs have been a long-standing issue for libraries, both in print and digital form. For most libraries 60 percent or more of the total collection development funds go toward acquiring serials of various types. For many large libraries that percentage is well above 75 percent. Double-digit annual rate hikes for serials have been something of the norm over the past 50 years, at least for the larger academic and public libraries. There was a hope the shift from paper to digital editions would help control the annual price increases. That hope was in vain. If anything, the costs have escalated more as libraries often cannot cancel the paper subscription when they acquire digital access to the material. In terms of e-serials costs, the picture is murky. Some libraries had/have a hope that going solely electronic would cut costs. The December 2010 issue of *College & Research Library News* carried an article related to such hopes. Michael Hanson and Terese Heidenwolf wrote about a small college library's experience with employing a pay-for-view service for some journal articles. The authors indicated the library goals for the project were twofold. They had hoped "not only to [increase] users' access to journals and [reduce] costs, but also to [get] a better picture of what our faculty and students would use if they had access to all of a publisher's titles" (p. 586). After a year of use, the library found there was little match between what was used and what it had subscribed to in the past. Previous subscriptions were used, but not as much as "new titles." Hanson and Heidenwolf concluded their article by noting, "we expect that when we have a year's worth of use data from other publishers' packages they will similarly reveal that our selections were not as on-target as we had presumed" (p. 588). Although the article did not explore the cost side of the project, you might expect, given the usage data for both old and new titles, the prospect of cutting costs were dim at best.

How do vendors set their prices for e-serials? Some of the factors that complicate the situation are:

- Pricing that links paper and digital versions of a title (dropping a paper subscription may raise the price of the e-version),

- Pricing based on the concept of "site" (frequently, branches of a library each count as an independent unit rather than as part of a single system),

- Pricing based on the number of simultaneous users (maximum number of readers allowed at one time),

- Pricing based on a license for a single library versus one obtained through a consortium, and

- Pricing based on only receiving current issues of a title or having access to both the current issues and back files.

Publishers frequently employ a dual pricing model for some time for print titles—offering one price for individual subscribers and another, higher cost, for institutions and libraries. The rationale behind the model was that the institutional subscription provided access for many readers, some of

---

Check These Out

In 2013 Ava Seave wrote an article for the Forbes.com website with the title "You'll Need a PhD to Make Sense of the Pricing Schemes Publishers Impose on Libraries" (https://tinyurl.com/ASeave-2013). Although the article is primarily about eBooks, much of the material also relates to e-serials.

Another worthwhile article is Pula Sullenger's 2016 piece "The Promise of the Future: A Review of the Serials Literature, 2012–13" (*Library Resources & Technical Services* 60, no. 1: 12–22). The essay covers a variety of topics in addition to serials pricing. There are similar reviews in *Library Resources & Technical Services* from time to time that are excellent for gaining an overview of current serial trends.

An article focusing specifically on the pricing of journals in the STEM fields is Lewis G. Liu and Harold Gee's 2017 work "Determining Whether Commercial Publishers Overcharge Libraries for Scholarly Journals in the Fields of Science, Technology, and Medicine, with a Semilogarithmic Econometric Model" (*Library Quarterly* 87, no. 2: 150–172). Their results are likely not surprising to any library with serial subscriptions in these disciplines. Their article is worth a look.

---

whom might be individual subscribers, if it were not for the institutional subscription. For electronic serials, some publishers and vendors employ a somewhat similar tiered model. This model is based on a range of factors, such as the size of the library's acquisition budget or the number of potential readers/users. Most of the tiered schedules have multiple tiers available, using such factors as an acquisitions budget (under $100,000, $100,001 to $250,000, and so forth) as price points. Tiered pricing is rather common for consortia purchases, and the final cost for a library becomes a function of how many libraries decide to participate in the deal.

Some publishers allow free online access when a library or individual places an order for a print subscription. An example is *The Economist,* which allows for online access to back issues, additional material for a story in the print issue, and access to additional news stories. (One reason for providing the access for libraries is that it appears to maintain a subscriber base, which is a factor in how the publication is able to charge advertisers—more subscribers equals a higher advertising fee. The extra material available online becomes a bonus for the library users.)

For years, libraries believed that the "Big Deal," a collection of serial titles from a publisher (Emerald or Taylor and Francis) or aggregator (EBSCO for example), might be a solution to the serial cost access concerns. That has also proven to a false hope. Cost considerations aside, the Big Deal may be less than ideal. Sven Fund (2017) noted, "The concept of the Big Deal and its practical implications have become an intense battle ground between publishers and librarians" (p. 16). Susan deVries (2017) expanded on Fund's comment, noting, "Big Deal packages were supposed to be a help to libraries, but in the long run it seems to be an unsustainable model lacking budget flexibility" (p. 20).

Big Deals were and are a more significant issue for academic libraries than they are for other types of libraries. The reason is while there is some growth in popular magazines and elementary–high school (el-hi) serial titles, they are modest at best and have little impact on a public or school library package put together by an aggregator beyond the expected annual price increase. Many of the publisher packages include all their journal titles (almost always academic in character and reflecting the constant growth in

---

Check These Out

Lindsay McKenzie (2018) explores how "'Big Deal' Cancellations Gain Momentum" in her *Inside Higher Ed* piece (May 8, 2018; https://tinyurl.com/McKenzie-2018).

In her article, McKenzie describes the SPARC Big Deal Cancellation Tracking website (https://sparcopen.org/our-work/big-deal-cancellation-tracking/). Both the article and tracking site are worth the look.

Something to Watch

The "pay-per-view" model has been successfully piloted at some institutions. Rick Fought wrote of a pilot undertaken at the Health Sciences Library (HSL) at the University of Tennessee Health Science Center in his 2014 article "Breaking Inertia: Increasing Access to Journals During a Period of Declining Budgets: A Case Study" (*Journal of the Medical Library Association* 102, no. 3: 192–196). The pilot involved cancelling 24 journals in order to provide access to over 700 titles. It remains to be seen how this model would work in a larger-scale situation, or its long-term effects; however, it may be a viable option to explore.

---

new titles of narrower and narrower focus) as well as adding new titles from professional societies and small specialty publishers. New content added to the annual price increase creates significant budgetary issues for libraries. Also unlike popular serials, academic researchers and students often do need to go back in time to learn what has gone on before "today." The vendors of Big Deal packages quickly saw the opportunity to offer such back file collections, and of course, they did so for more money.

Library Big Deals are rather like cable and satellite television packages; there is no picking and choosing the titles you need: you get what you get, whether you like it or want it or not. The notion of "cord cutting" has not been extensively utilized, primarily due to the lack of reasonable options for doing so. In the future, there is the possibility the "pay for view" model that newspapers employ will grow in popularity. It has already been explored by some, such as Jonathan Harwell and James Bunnelle—who described some of the challenges of such a model, such as how charges would work and who would pay the cost. However, the challenges do not mean the concept should be abandoned. As Harwell and Bunnelle (2017) noted, "We need functionality for building library collections with an option to buy articles seamlessly, on the fly, as we do with books and films" (p. 38).

Managing Serials

As is true of all collection formats, serials require some degree of managing, some of which are specific to serials, such as ongoing checking in and claiming missing issues. Other management concerns are binding and preservation. (Chapter 7 addressed binding while preservation is covered in chapter 14). Another special aspect is libraries rarely "own" e-serials. Instead, they lease access to serial content through licensing agreements/contracts. When it is time to renew the agreement, there may be changes in the terms and conditions, so a review of renewals may be as involved as the initial agreement and necessitate negotiations almost as involved over the new terms. When it comes to e-resources, and especially e-serials, there are a variety of terms to master. This discussion could have been placed in the next chapter (e-resources); however, given the major role e-serials play in the management process, we decided to place it here.

E-resources are wonderful, especially from the end-user's perspective. However, they create a number of challenges for CM personnel, their libraries, as well as consortia. For the individual, there is a virtual alphabet soup of technical concepts with implications for e-materials to understand—some of which are DC®/DCMI, DLF, DMCA, DOI®, DRM, EAD, ERMI, OAI, PURL, SFX®, and XML. All of these, and more, relate to managing library e-resources in one way or another. Because you are likely to run across these concepts in your CM work, we briefly review them below.

Dublin Core® (DC®, http://dublincore.org/) is outside the scope of this text, but will likely be encountered elsewhere in your degree program. The Dublin Core Metadata Initiative (DCMI) currently administers the Dublin Core® and focuses on providing standards to assist in finding, sharing, and managing digital information. Many of the standards underlay a majority of the e-products a library provides access to and the manner in which the library provides that access.

The Digital Library Federation (DLF, https://www.diglib.org) is a program managed under the umbrella of the Council on Library and Information Resources (CLIR). Although DLF membership is composed primarily of research libraries, its initiatives benefit any library engaged in creating and maintaining e-resources. One such effort was the ERMI (Electronic Resource Management Initiative), which became the framework for the developing electronic resource management systems (Anderson, 2014, p. 6) for licensed products.

DMCA (Digital Millennium Copyright Act of 1998, P.L. 105-304, http://www.copyright.gov/legislation/dmca.pdf) is a law whose scope is broad and has implications for how all e-resources are handled. We cover this law and other copyright issues in chapter 15.

A Digital Object Identifier (DOI®; https://www.doi.org/) is somewhat like an ISBN or ISSN. A DOI® is designed to be a permanent indicator of an item's location on the Web, thus making the management of "intellectual property in a networked environment much easier and more convenient, and [allowing for] the construction of automated services and transactions" (http://www.doi.org). Some libraries use the DOI®, when available, rather than a URL as it provides a more stable link to the material. A listing of publications on the DOI® concept is available at http://www.doi.org/publications.html.

DRM (Digital Rights Management) is a set of "technologies" that e-producers (books, games, music, serials, and video) may employ to control access to and use of their copyrighted material, especially copying, by third parties. From a library resource point of view, the use of DRM technologies can and may prevent legal fair use activities by end-users. Knowing what, if any, DRM technologies are embedded in a product or service is important during the selection process. The ALA Digital Rights Management page (http://www.ala.org/advocacy/copyright/digitalrights) provides a glossary of terms as well as links to DRM resources and legislation. This is a legal issue that we will explore in more depth in chapter 15.

EAD (Encoded Archival Description, http://www.loc.gov/ead/index.html) began at the University of California, Berkeley, and is now part of the Library of Congress' service program, in partnership with the Society of American Archivists. It is a standard for machine-readable finding aids for e-materials created by archives, libraries, museums, and repositories. The standard employs SGML (Standard Generalized Markup Language) and XML (see below) as the base for encoding information.

The OAI (Open Archives Initiative) is a group that

> develops and promotes interoperability standards that aim to facilitate the efficient dissemination of content. OAI has its roots in the open access and institutional repository movements. . . . Over time, however, the work of OAI has expanded to promote broad access to digital resources for eScholarship, eLearning, and eScience. (http://www.openarchives.org/)

One of the accomplishments of this group was the development of a metadata harvesting program we mentioned in the repository section of chapter 13—OAI-PMH.

OpenURL is the standardized (and very familiar) "Web address." It was developed by the National Information Standards Organization (NISO), a component of the American National Standards Institute (ANSI), as standard Z39.88. OCLC (http://www.oclc.org/research/activities/openurl/default .htm) is the body currently responsible for maintaining the standard. A Persistent Uniform Resource Locator (PURL) helps address the problem of disappearing URLS. PURLs, also developed at OCLC but managed by the Internet Archive since 2016 (http://archive.org/services/purl/), enable individuals to locate items even if the original Web address has changed. In this way, PURLs provide a "continuity of references to network resources that may migrate from machine to machine for business, social or technical reasons" (http://www.oclc.org/research/themes/data-science/purl.html).

SFX® (http://www.exlibrisgroup.com/category/SFXOverview) is an Open URL link resolver. SFX® is a proprietary program developed by Ex Libris. SFX® is a component in many institutional repository (IR) programs, as we will discuss in chapter 13. Many libraries use SFX® as it provides extra benefits such as e-usage data. Having sound e-usage data is critical when it comes to evaluating collection resources.

XML (eXtensible Markup Language, http://www.xml.com/) is one of many document markup languages in existence. With any full-text material, whether book or serial, one issue to consider is the way the text was digitized: ASCII, Adobe, HTML, or SGML. ASCII is the oldest and in many ways the easiest approach to digitization. However, with ASCII, one loses most of the formatting of the original document, as well as any images. Adobe Acrobat PDF (Portable Document Format) is an approach that retains formatting and images and is frequently encountered on the Internet. HTML (Hypertext Markup Language) is probably the most common method used on the World Wide Web. It is in fact a sublanguage of SGML (Standard Generalized Markup Language). Many organizations used SGML to digitize their internal documents; however, currently the favored standard is XML. There are several advantages to using XML; it is an international standard, and it is device and system independent. Having documents in a standard markup language makes it easier to change systems without incurring significant document conversion costs.

The above is just a sample of the variety of terms encountered by CM personnel and their libraries when they become involved with e-resources. End users don't really care about the technology side of e-resources, they just want them available 24/7; how that takes place is the library's concern. By the time you read this chapter, it is highly likely the soup will be even thicker. One source that can be helpful in deciphering other terms encountered is Joan M. Reitz's *ODLIS: Online Dictionary for Library and Information Science* (http://www.abc-clio.com/ODLIS/odlis_A.aspx).

Cancelling Serials and Other E-Resources

One unique aspect of e-resource management, at least in many academic libraries, is the need to cancel titles/packages. Although primarily an academic library concern, it is not unheard of for public libraries to face the same situation. Unfortunately, cancelling serials is not something new for libraries; such projects existed in the paper-only world, and going digital has done nothing to change the picture.

Library users have little interest in understanding serial vendors and library issues so long as "their" titles are available. Their interest peaks sharply when there is the prospect of having to cancel titles, with the potential for their titles disappearing. After the better part of four decades of having to engage in at least one cancellation project, librarians have a good idea of what some of the most common user questions are. Preparing answers to the expected questions can help reduce the stress that will arise from having to undertake such a project.

The obvious first question will be, in some form, "why?" In an academic library context, the question may be, "Why now? Didn't we do this a few years ago?" (In all likelihood, the "few years ago" will be three or four years in the past; it just seems more recent.) How the library responds depends on the local circumstances; however, the typical answer will relate to the lack of funds due to institutional issues. The most common causes are a "steady state" budget, an actual reduction in funding, and/or a shortfall in enrollment. The latter is more often than not a factor in academic institutions, but could also occur in school districts. A "steady state" provides no more than last year's funding allocation, which in a few years of such funding means the annual inflation rate will essentially be a form of budget cutting.

Another question from users will be some variation of, "Why do serials increase so much more than the CPI?" Most libraries will have some type of response already in place as budget authorities ask a similar question rather frequently during budget request cycles. Libraries can draw upon five cost driving factors when formulating a response. These factors apply to any type of library setting.

First and foremost is the "profit" factor for all the producers of serial resources. The quotations concerning profit are because some publishers are nonprofit organizations. Such organizations (professional associations, for example) may not have an obligation to generate shareholder income, but they do need to generate enough income to remain operational (break-even). The hope is all of their publications will break-even, and perhaps do a little better in some years to offset down years. A second force is for most serials there is a slight monopolistic situation. That is, for many titles, there is

---

Check This Out

EBSCO regularly produces a serials price projection as a way of informing librarians of the landscape of serials looking forward. The reports generally come out in the fall and are available via the EBSCO website. Although produced as a promotional item, the reports are informative and are worth a look. A recent report is available at: https://www.ebscohost.com/promoMaterials/EBSCO_2018_Serials_Price_Projections.pdf.

almost no competition from another title; certainly there is some competition in the popular magazine market but for the vast majority of titles there is little or no pressure to keep prices down.

A third factor is the loss of advertising income. Many nonprofit journals carry some advertising, if more limited in number than you see in popular magazines. More and more advertising dollars go to Web platforms and less and less to paper-based formats. If you doubt there has been a major reduction in ads placed in serials, compare a current issue of a popular magazine with one published 20 years ago. The lost advertising income is made up by increasing the subscription cost.

The rising price of subscription costs often results in a drop in the number of subscribers (the fourth factor). Fewer subscribers can have an impact on the amount the publisher can charge an advertiser, thus starting a nasty cycle in terms of revenue

Fifth, larger publishers are acquiring smaller firms or gaining access to their content and distribution rights, which in turn limits price competition. If nothing more, that practice means "Big Deals" offer more titles and content, which the vendor believes justifies a further price increase. Will providing this information satisfy users? Probably not completely; however, they will begin to grasp there is little they or the library can do to limit the price escalation beyond dropping some titles/packages.

Beyond money matters an almost guaranteed question will be, "Who will decide, and on what basis will the cancellation decision(s) be made?" A related question often is, "Will I have a voice in the matter?" Although such questions are most likely to arise in an academic library environment, they can come up in any setting. Providing some level of input from users can help maintain/improve community relationships as long as it is understood that cuts must occur and will take place. In the case where departments have assigned titles, allowing the department to identify titles to cancel (however reluctantly) is one possibility. In a public library setting, a list of titles to potentially drop could be posted for users. Users could then vote for two or three titles to keep while knowing X number of titles must go (those with the fewest retain votes). Letting users have input in the decision-making process may reduce the number of complaints received later.

The knotty issue of usage is likely to come up—what counts as true use will generate debate. Even in the print-only days, some users would say (when a title was up for cancellation and usage was the driving decision factor) that they used this title on a regular basis and always returned it to its proper

---

Check These Out

Anthony Raymond wrote an article (2017) about serial cancellations that is well worth a read: "Canceling Serials Based on Their Availability in Aggregated Full-Text Databases" (*Against the Grain* 29, no. 2: 30–33). That same issue of *Against the Grain* also includes an article by Hilary M. Davis and Gregory K. Raschke, who describe the process of creating data-informed and community-driven feedback loops to manage a journal review and cancellation project ("Data Informed and Community Driven: Using Data and Feedback Loops to Manage a Journal Review and Cancellation Project," *Against the Grain* 29, no. 2: 12–20).

An older article about a cancellation project, but one that is worth consulting, is Jeanie M. Welch's "Is There Life After Serials Cancellation?" (*Bottom Line* 1996, vol. 9, no. 2: 18–20), as it outlines the stages of such a project.

location, which would lead to an underreporting of actual usage. (We look at e-usage in the following section.) The reality is no measure of usage will satisfy everyone, yet it is a valid metric for looking at value for money spent.

Cancellation projects are painful for everyone. However, such projects are a fact of life for most libraries and appear to be with the profession for some time to come. Developing a plan for handling the process before having to implement one is one way to get user 'buy-in" in advance and perhaps make it somewhat less painful.

Usage Data

Several assessment initiatives have been undertaken in response to the need for gathering solid, informative usage data for e-resources. Two such efforts are Project COUNTER (Counting Online Usage of NeTworked Electronic Resources, http://www.projectcounter.org/) and the *Revised Guidelines for Statistical Measures of Usage of Web-Based Information Resources* produced by the International Coalition of Library Consortia (ICOLC, 2006, http://icolc.net/statement/guidelines-statistical-measures-usage-web -based-information-resources-1998-revised-2001-0). Project COUNTER was launched in 2002 as a means of setting standards to consistently report usage statistics and operates through the publication of a series of Codes of Practice, which are guidelines for the production of vendor reports (https:// www.projectcounter.org/code-of-practice-sections/general-information/). ICOLC's *Guidelines*, on the other hand, establish consistent "boundaries" for what should be included in vendor statistical reports, without compromising user privacy or confidentiality.

COUNTER and ICOLC address usage data from the vendor side of the equation. Additionally, the implementation of a local electronic resource management system (ERMS, discussed below) allows individual libraries to track acquisitions, usage data, and licensing efforts. ERMSs are largely credited to the work of Tim Jewell (2001, 2004) at the University of Washington and the Digital Library Federation. Unfortunately, such systems can be cost prohibitive for some libraries. However, low-cost alternatives are available, ranging from open-source products (Doering and Chilton, 2009) to Web 2.0 applications (England and Diffin, 2014) and link resolver analysis (Smith and Arneson, 2017) or the use of simple spreadsheet software.

Serial Management Tools

We discussed the paper-based serials control process in chapter 7. Here we explore the tools that assist in managing e-resources known as electronic resource management systems (ERMS). We placed the coverage of such systems here because e-serials are the most complicated of most libraries' e-resources.

There are three basic approaches to serials management—homegrown, vendor packages, and open source packages. As of this writing, the homegrown approach is still the typical system. Such systems draw on the capabilities of the ILS, and some degree of customization, to more effectively represent the e-holdings. As the number of such holdings has grown, the staff effort required is becoming too much for some libraries and they move to one of the other approaches.

Vendor ERMS exist as packages from aggregators, such as EBSCO, and firms that just focus solely on ERMS such as Serials Solutions®. Some ILS firms, such as Innovative Interfaces and Ex Libris, also offer an ERMS module that is fully linked to their overall package. It seems likely there will be more such offerings available by the time you read this as e-resources become an ever greater part of a library's collection.

Open access systems may become the ultimate choice for libraries as budgets become tighter and tighter. The main challenge of an open access system, as is true of a homegrown system, is the need for technical expertise within the library to effectively employ the open access systems. A secondary issue is the time commitment required to keep the system functional, again often not readily available. A clear plus is that it is free.

The most widely used open access system, at the time of this writing, is *CORAL* (Centralized Online Resources Acquisitions and Licensing, http://coral-erm.org/) developed by the University of Notre Dame Library. Two other systems that existed for a time as options to *CORAL*, but were decommissioned or otherwise no longer used by the originating institution were *CUFTS* (Simon Fraser University Library, https://www.lib.sfu.ca/about/initiatives/researcher) and *ERMes* (University of Wisconsin, La Cross library, http://murphylibrary.uwlax.edu/erm/).

So what does an ERMS do for a library? There are two basic aspects of such systems—assisting users in identifying and accessing desired information from e-resources and second, assisting staff in managing such resources. While it is true all collection materials are acquired in some manner, e-materials have some special features such as the library not owning the material or restrictions on how the material may be used. They are also frequently acquired through consortia. Such information does not easily fit into the ILS acquisition module that was originally based on a paper-based system.

In an earlier section, we mentioned the knotty problem of usage. ERMs help standardize usage data. One problem was that database suppliers often employed a usage tracking system that was unique to the firm, making it almost impossible to compare usage across packages. Today there is the aforementioned code of practice (COUNTER) that vendors are expected to implement that provides comparable usage data. In addition, there is an ANSI/NISO standard (Z39.93-2014, SUSHI—standardized usage statistic harvesting initiative) standing committee that functions as a maintenance body for COUNTER's code of practice. ERMS automatically incorporate COUNTER into the system.

From the end-user's perspective, the most valuable feature of ERMS lies in their ability to locate e-resources beyond the library's OPAC, especially full-text material. Another feature of highly functional systems is

---

Check These Out

Two titles on the topic worth consulting are:

Reengineering the Library: Issues in Electronic Resources Management edited by George Stachokas on behalf of the Association for Library Collections & Technical Services (Chicago: ALA Publications, 2018), which explores advances and challenges electronic resources management (ERM) in academic libraries.

The ABCs of ERM Demystifying Electronic Resource Management for Public and Academic Librarians by Jessica Zellers, Tina M. Adams, and Katherine Hill (Santa Barbara, CA: Libraries Unlimited, 2018), which includes discussions of such topics as vendor relations and troubleshooting access issues.

multiple database searching using a single query (common names for this functionality are federated searching, discovery, cross searching, and meta searching).

Points to Keep in Mind

- Serials represent a major part of a library's collection.
- Serials exist in a variety of forms and most libraries collect two or more of those forms.
- Serials consume at least 60 percent or more of a library's collection development funds.
- Serials normally represent an ongoing financial commitment.
- Serial prices almost always increase annually and thus take more of the available funding each year.
- Serials shifting from paper to digital formats has not changed the cost picture for libraries.
- E-serials have some important advantages over paper editions, but do generate special management challenges.
- Electronic resource management is complex technically and requires ongoing staff support.
- Electronic resource management has several elements; two of the more significant components are how the library provides access to its e-resources and how it handles the maintenance of such materials.
- Electronic resource management systems are essential to effectively handle all library e-collection materials, especially serials.

References

Anderson, Elsa K. 2014. "Introduction." *Library Technology Reports* 50, no. 3: 5–10.

Black, Steve. 2009. "Editors' Perspectives on Current Topics in Serials." *Serials Librarian* 57, no. 3: 199–222.

Bosch, Stephen, and Kittie Henderson. 2014. "Steps Down the Evolutionary Road." *Library Journal* 139, no. 7: 32–37.

deVries, Susan. 2017. "The 4 Economics of the Big Deal: The Bulls, the Bears and the Farm." *Against the Grain* 29, no. 1: 18, 20, 22.

Doering, William, and Galadriel Chilton. 2009. "ERMes: Open Source Simplicity for Your E-Resource Management." *Computers in Libraries* 29, no. 8: 20–24.

England, Lenore, and Jennifer Diffin. 2014. "Erm Ideas and Innovations." *Journal of Electronic Resources Librarianship* 26, no. 3: 193–202.

Fund, Sven. 2017. "Choosing Independence or Feeding the Beast? The Big Deal and Small or Society Publishers." *Against the Grain* 29, no. 1: 16, 18.

Hanson, Michael, and Terese Heidenwolf. 2010. "Making the Right Choices: Pay-Per-View Use Data and Selection Decisions." *College & Research Library News* 71, no. 11: 586–88.

Harwell, Jonathan, and James Bunnelle. 2017. "ATG Special Report—Purchasing Articles by Demand-Driven Acquisition: An Alternative Serial Distribution Model for Libraries." *Against the Grain* 29, no. 1: 35–39, 43.

Ismail, Matthew. 2017. "State of the 'Big Deal.'" *Against the Grain* 29, no. 1: 1, 10.

Jewell, Timothy D. 2001. *Selection and Presentation of Commercially Available Electronic Resources*. Washington, DC: Digital Library Federation and Council on Library and Information Resources. http://www.clir.org/pubs /reports/pub99/pub99.pdf.

Jewell, Timothy D., Ivy Anderson, Adam Chandler, Sharon E. Farb, Kimberly Parker, Angela Riggio, and Nathan D. M. Robertson. 2004. *Electronic Resource Management: Report of the DLF ERM Initiative*. Washington, DC: Digital Library Foundation. http://old.diglib.org/pubs/dlf102/.

Machlup, Fritz, Kenneth Leeson, and Associates. 1978. *Information Through the Printed Word*. New York: Praeger.

NASIG. 2016. *Core Competencies for Print Serials Management*. Approved and adopted by the NASIG Executive Board, May 30, 2015. Revised April 25, 2016. http://www.nasig.org/site_page.cfm?pk_association_webpage_menu=310 &pk_association_webpage=8576.

Nisonger, Thomas. 1998. *Management of Serials in Libraries*. Englewood, CO: Libraries Unlimited.

Plutchak, T. Scott. 2007. "What's a Serial When You're Running in Internet Time?" *Serials Librarian* 52, nos. 1/2: 79–90.

Robertshaw, M. Brooke, Michaela Willi Hooper, and Kerri Georgen-Doll. 2017. "Finding the Silver Lining . . . in the Serials Budget Crisis." *Against the Grain* 29, no. 2: 16–18.

Smith, Kelly, and Jens Arneson. 2017. "Determining Usage When Vendors Do Not Provide Data." *Serials Review* 43, no. 1: 46–50.

13
E-Resources and Technology Issues

Over the past ten years, a central topic at the forefront of conversation in the library community has been the dichotomy between patron use of print and electronic resources. This problem has affected both public and academic libraries, with serious implications for where and how libraries will allocate (and lobby for) their future financial resources.

—Terrance Luther Cottrell
and Brigitte Bell, 2014

In the ensuing decade-plus, streaming video moved from being a novelty to becoming essential for libraries, providing video contentment to their constituency.

—Deg Farrelly, 2016

License agreements between libraries and vendors/publishers then become the primary means of communicating agreed-on perpetual access rights and procedures.

—Andrew R. Grissom, Steven A. Knowlton,
and Rachel Elizabeth Scott, 2017

But despite double-digit growth in OA [open access], scientific societies and commercial publishers alike agree that the vast bulk of their publications will remain wedded to the traditional subscription model for the foreseeable future.

—David Kramer, 2017

Each new edition of this title has had greater and greater emphasis on e-resources. To remain viable, libraries must adjust to their changing operating environments, especially those occurring in their service populations. Two key change drivers are technology and the people who employ such technology in their daily lives. People have very different approaches to how, when, and where they use technology to seek information as well as how they use that information.

If libraries did not reflect the ever growing dependence on e-resources, they would rapidly become more and more marginalized. Marginalization would, in all likelihood, translate into a steep decrease in the support given the library. That would create a downward spiral as less and less funding would make it increasingly hard to transform collections and services. Thus, today's libraries devote more and more of their funds to some technologically related efforts, including e-collections.

One reflection of technology's impact on librarianship is in ALA's *Core Competencies of Librarianship* adopted in 2009. The statement outlines eight core areas, one of which focuses upon technology. Section 4 (Technological Knowledge and Skills) consists of four subtopics that relate in one way or another to collections. For example, competency 4A relates to "Information, communication, assistive, and related technologies as they affect the resources, service delivery, and uses of libraries and other information agencies" (http://www.ala.org/educationcareers/sites/ala.org.educationcareers/files /content/careers/corecomp/corecompetences/finalcorecompstat09.pdf). Section 2 of the document relates to information resources competencies. The concept of electronic resource management, which we explored in chapter 12, was addressed in section 8 of the statement.

Sarah Pritchard made a point that still remains valid today, noting: "in the digital environment, we still have resources, staff, and facilities that combine in various ways to acquire and provide information. These recombinations challenge traditional definitions of library organization. . . . All parts of a library are involved, not just some pieces that we can conveniently segregate as a special type of content or a special service" (2008, pp. 219– 220). Her article explores what these recombinations are and how they will possibly change in the near future.

Jesse Holden (2010) expanded on the impact of technology and libraries when he noted: "Navigating the information universe is complex in that it requires maximizing resources in a way that simultaneously *expands* and *narrows* the available content that is required by an end user by distilling the most useful content from the broadest number of sources" (p. 11). Accomplishing such tasks calls for many skills and, more often than not, several people.

What do we mean by e-resources? We believe materials either converted to or "born" digital fall under the e-resources umbrella. In today's digital world, almost all new materials might well be thought of as "born digital" as few people are using typewriters to prepare reports, articles, or book manuscripts, at least in developed countries. However, current usage of "born digital" relates to material first appearing in a digital form. Some such items may later be issued in a paper format, but the initial release was electronic. We address the following in this chapter:

Books	Serials
Digital video	Digital music
Web links	Institutional repositories

Differences Between Traditional and E-Resources

There are at least seven major differences between print and digital collection management. Perhaps the most important difference is that a library rarely owns its electronic materials. With e-resources, what a library often pays for is access; with a physical product, a library has full control. As long as the library pays appropriate fees and its usage complies with the legal agreement (license or contract), the access to an electronic resource will remain in place. However, should there be a failure on the library's part, the vendor can, and occasionally does, "pull the plug" on availability for the library's users (unless perpetual rights were purchased for the item or resource in question). Even in the days when libraries did receive a physical product (CD-ROMs, for example) containing digital content such as an indexing service, the library agreed to either return or destroy the CD-ROM upon receipt of an updated version. Today's e-environment makes it much easier for the vendor to control library compliance by simply cutting the connection to the database.

A related difference is e-resources come with a license or contract that governs what the library may do with the resource. Many of these legal agreements contain clauses outlining to whom and how to provide access to the e-material. Often these limitations—a third difference—go against the library philosophy of service, such as being open and available to all or sharing resources with others. What the limitations are varies from vendor to vendor. Some of the more common are restrictions that limit or forbid the use of the content for interlibrary lending, limits on the number of individuals who may access the material at the same time (simultaneous users), restrictions on the use of the material by non–library cardholders (any user group not identified in the license), remote access availability (proxy server issues and in-library usage), and even restrictions making the library liable for how an individual makes use of the information gathered after leaving the building.

Another difference is the final decision to purchase access to most e-resources comes after a trial period. That is, the vendor allows access to the product for a period of time. How long that period is varies, but it almost always is 30 days or more. There are several reasons for wanting/demanding a trial:

Something to Ponder

Publishers and database vendors use a variety of pricing models, so it is important to understand those models. Daniel Liston (2013), a legislative analyst, prepared a document for the Connecticut legislature on eBook pricing (https://www.cga.ct.gov /2013/rpt/2013-R-0153.htm). The overview includes a useful chart detailing the eBook license "cycle" as well as a listing of the "Big Six" publishers' policies at that time and their pricing models.

Since the time of Liston's work, the American Library Association (2016) prepared a chart detailing policies of the "Big Five" (formerly six) publishers (http://www.ala.org /tools/sites/ala.org.tools/files/content/Big-Five-Ebook-Terms-011816.pdf). The spectrum of use ranged from HarperCollins, which requires licenses to be renewed after 26 uses, and Simon and Schuster, which institutes a one-year expiration date on books licensed, to Hachette, which releases eBooks with unlimited single-use circulations.

Clearly the publisher pricing model can become a major consideration during the selection process for eBooks.

- The relatively high cost of e-products
- The variety of search platforms available from vendor to vendor
- The actual content of the database or product
- The ease of use in terms of staff and users
- The technical requirements that need to be met to make the product available given a library's infrastructure.

To be effective, from a decision-making perspective, the trial ought to allow full end-user access. Few vendors have trouble allowing such access as they expect/hope that the end users will add pressure to the library to provide ongoing availability to the product.

A complicating factor in making a final acquisition decision is often based on a consortial membership (a fifth difference). As mentioned in earlier chapters, such purchases are based on group decision making that tends to be complex (many voices, many opinions) and drawn out. More often than not, the library's costs to take part in "the deal" are unknown until almost the last minute—needless to say, cost is a critical decision factor. The final cost is generally governed by the number of libraries taking part as well as their full time equivalent enrollment (FTE), where a last minute dropout or joiner may impact the price, which in turn may influence another library's decision to participate or not.

When it comes time to assess an e-service, the library may find that it is highly dependent upon data supplied by the vendor—a sixth difference. Such data may not really address the evaluation issues that are important to the library. Assessment was addressed in chapter 8.

The final difference is permanence. There are three aspects to this in terms of e-resources. First and foremost, as we noted above, the library does not own the product/service. When it becomes necessary to cancel a service, it may be possible to retain access to the material that was available during the time the library paid for access. That, however, is something the library must address at the time of purchase. A second issue is that what is there today may not be there tomorrow even though the library is fully paid up. Vendors can and do pull material from their product without notifying the library. This is especially true of aggregator databases. Naturally, there is the long-term preservation of electronic resources in general—they are actually less permanent than traditional formats. We will cover all these issues in more detail in chapter 14.

From the Authors' Experience

Vendor trials can be a useful way to determine whether or not a product would be worthwhile to pursue, although Saponaro has found that in addition to managing the technical aspects of trials (IP addresses, etc.), trials may also require the extra step of managing expectations of users participating in the trial. Any publicity for a trial should clearly indicate that a trial in and of itself does *not* guarantee that the resource will be added to the library collection. This is particularly true in cases where the ability to license one e-resource that is offered via trial can only occur if another e-resource is canceled. Saponaro has encountered cases where the latter was not made clear, and the result was unhappy end users who expected an existing resource to remain available as well as the resource that had been offered via a trial and later acquired.

Check This Out

Rebecca Donlan published an interesting essay, "Decision Points for Going E-Only: Beware the Fallacy of the Single Solution," that looked at issues related to what you get in the print or e-version of an item (*Reference Librarian* 2007, 47, no. 1: 121–24).

Selection Issues

Almost all of the factors that you consider for traditional formats apply, to some degree, to e-resources. However, e-selection decisions are also different. Broadly speaking, there are seven categories in e-selection—content, limitations, costs, people factors, technical, cancellations/archival issues, and assessment.

One major difference that needs to be considered is whether the e-product would or could replace something that already exists in the collection. The most common place for this issue to arise is with e-serial packages. In the early days of such packages, libraries thought about and sometimes did cancel their print subscriptions for titles in the package with the idea the monies freed up by the cancellation would help pay for the package. This rarely worked as intended as often the e-version was not identical to the paper version. Another factor that arose was that some publishers place an "embargo" on the e-version—not allowing it to appear for some time period after the paper copy appeared. Essentially the notion of saving money by canceling a paper subscription to help cover the cost of an e-package does not always work, as was noted in chapter 12. When you have paper-based copies of a high percentage of the package titles, a reasonable question is, will the electronic versions provide a true enhancement of service?

Content

Depending on what the e-product is—book, serial, music, video—one of the first questions to ask is does this product fill a real need or gap in the collection or is it just a means of showing others that the library is active in the digital world? The latter reason is not good stewardship of limited funding. You should rather identify some e-products that users actually need, thus demonstrating forward-looking collection building and good stewardship. An obvious related question is what is the quality of the content and reputation of those who put the package together? When it comes to packages, there are two aspects of content quality to think about. First is the traditional quality of each title in the package, followed by the package's total quality.

Yet another question that is rather important is, what does a vendor or producer mean by the phrase "full-text"? Does it mean everything that appears in the print version(s) of the titles, including advertisements? As was seen in chapter 12, often all that is meant is the text of the article in the case of serials. Some vendors do not include article graphics in their context but rather create separate files of figures, photographs, and charts, making it highly inconvenient for readers. What about color graphics? If the product does not handle color, images using color may be very difficult to interpret in various shades of grey. What about letters to the editor, or corrections of errors from prior issues? All are questions worth some consideration.

A second quality issue is illustrated in Table 13.1. There is a significant amount of duplication between aggregator packages. The data in the table

Table 13.1   Title Overlap and Coverage Timeframes

Library Journal
from 05/01/1976 to present in *Academic Search Premier*
from 05/01/1976 to present in *Business Source Premier*
from 05/01/1976 to present in *Education Source*
from 05/01/1976 to present in *Health Source: Nursing / Academic Edition*
from 05/01/1976 to present in *MasterFILE Premier*
from 01/01/1984 to present in *OmniFile Full Text Mega Edition*
from 01/01/1996 to present in *ABI / INFORM*
from 01/01/1996 to present in *ProQuest Research Library*
from 09/01/1996 to present in *Education Full Text*

Journal of Academic Librarianship
from 03/01/1975 to 05/31/2004 in *Academic Search Premier*
from 03/01/1975 to 05/31/2004 in *Business Source Premier*
from 01/01/1984 to 05/31/2004 in *MasterFILE Premier*
from 01/01/1993 to 1994 in *ScienceDirect Freedom Collection*
from 01/01/1993 to present in *ScienceDirect Journals*

Teacher Librarian (Vancouver)
from 09/01/1998 to present in *ProQuest Research Library*
from 09/01/1998 to present in *Academic Search Premier*
from 09/01/1998 to 2/29/2016 in *Education Full Text*
from 09/01/1998 to present in *MasterFILE Premier*
from 09/01/1998 to 2/29/2016 in *Wilson OmniFile Full Text Mega Edition*

The Economist (London)
from 1843 to 2013 in *The Economist Historical Archive*
from 07/07/1990 to present in *MasterFILE Premier*
from 01/01/1992 to present in *ABI / INFORM Global*
from 01/04/1992 to present in *ProQuest Research Library*
from 07/19/1997 to present in *Economist Newspaper*

Harvard Business Review
from 10/01/1922 to present in *Business Source Premier*

People (New York, NY: 2002)
from 1890 to 1982 in *Reader's Guide Retrospective*
from 01/10/1994 to present in *Academic Search Premier*
from 1/1/1984 to present in *MasterFILE Premier*

---

was collected from an academic library that has made a major commitment to providing e-resources. The first three titles in the table are in all of the major aggregator packages.

As Table 13.1 illustrates, not only is there duplication of titles, but there are also differences in time periods covered by the packages.

Although not all that common, a few publishers have chosen to allow only selected aggregators to include a title in their package, *Harvard Business Review (HBR),* for example. That means if you need access to an electronic version of *HBR* you must subscribe to one of a select number of EBSCO databases (such as *Business Source Premier*) and all the other titles in that package, or subscribe directly from Harvard Business School publishing. An individual or a library can subscribe to the journal in print that comes with the online title. In many cases, libraries may not wish to bind the print issues due to space limitations, and are left with issues arriving they do not want.

All of the above makes for complex decision making; it is especially hard when the package under consideration is through a consortia arrangement. There are time pressures as well as information questions to handle, and this is just the start of the selection process.

Limitations

Limitations related to e-resources fall into two broad categories—access and rights. Access issues can be numerous in some contracts. Some of the most common are who may have access to the material—some examples are "authorized" (only registered borrowers), "walk in" users, in-library access only, and authenticated access for remote users. Sometimes there are restrictions on the number of simultaneous users. Almost always there is a sliding scale of fees for increasing the base number of users beyond the number in the standard agreement. The good news about this fee is that you can always start with the base number and increase it, if usage indicates there is a need. Almost all the access limitations may be dealt with by paying more for the service. However, there are almost always issues beyond the cost that complicate the decision process—the library having to address its technological infrastructure, for example.

What rights or obligations are tied to the package/service varies, but they are often more difficult to resolve than those of access. Limiting or forbidding the use of the material for resource sharing activities such as ILL are fairly common practices and hard to impossible to modify. One limit to which a library ought not to agree to is one that holds the library liable for the usage a person makes of the material accessed after leaving the library or online. Even the copyright laws do not try to impose such an obligation on libraries.

Cost

In many ways, purchasing a new automobile is the closest activity that we all do that mirrors the process of a library acquiring an e-service. There is a starting price and after going through a series of possible additions or subtractions, a final price. Getting to the final cost always seems to take longer than expected. Cost considerations are significant, and often cost is the determining factor in the decision to acquire an e-product or service. However, you often have to wait until after all the issues are known before the cost is finalized. That final figure may turn an otherwise positive decision process into a negative one.

What are some of the cost factors that you must resolve before getting to the final cost figure? One of them is the discount that may be available. Like a new automobile, there is a suggested retail price; however, everyone knows that price is rarely the final cost. If the vendor is a firm with which the library has done substantial business over a number of years, there is likely to be some discount for the library "going it alone." When the library is part of a consortia, the final price is often not settled until well after the trial period ends as the number of participants is finally settled.

Also, like a new car, products may offer optional extras or upgrades; this is especially true of journal full-text databases. Usually the base product offers access to articles from the current issue to some point back in time. For example, base coverage may be for the previous 10 years; however, the journals in the database probably have a history much longer than that. The vendor usually offers back-issue coverage at an additional cost. Some vendors break down back files into increments of 10 to 15 years, each at an added charge. It might seem obvious that a library with an interest in certain titles might well have the back issues in paper form and there would be no need to purchase access to a digital format as well. That is often the case; however, more and more users are becoming accustomed to having 24/7 remote access to journals, and they pressure the library to have key titles available in digital format as far back as possible. Additionally, space considerations also can force libraries to invest in an electronic back file in order to withdraw print titles to reclaim needed shelf space.

People Issues

With traditional print materials, you do not have many "people issues" to think about. Perhaps the only real concern might be whether a title selected will cause complaints about its inclusion in the collection. Such is not the case with e-resources. There are both end user and staff factors to take into account.

Ease of use is a major consideration regarding almost all e-resources. Questions to consider include: Will the product require staff training? How easy will it be for the public to use, or will users require staff assistance? Each e-vendor's product(s) that have a search capability try to differentiate its product(s) from other vendors by employing a proprietary search engine and features. Each new vendor, for the library, is likely to have something different regarding access methods for their material. How easy or complex that process is should be part of the selection thought process. Clearly, more intuitive search processes are better for both the user and staff.

Products or services that involve downloading, such as eBooks, music, or videos, often call for staff involvement. First-time users of the product or service are likely to require some assistance even when the person has experience with downloading materials, as the vendor is likely to have some special requirements. There are some services that require creation of a user account or individualized password by the library staff. All of these activities add to the staff workload, which seems to grow exponentially with little prospect of hiring new staff. Thus, what may seem like a very small increase for one or more staff members from the addition of one new e-service can grow into a sizable workload issue. Another related matter is, given extended library service hours and the fact that most users assume anyone working in a library is a "librarian," more public service staff will need detailed training for the new product. It is no longer just the reference librarians who must know more than a little about each e-product or service. Work roles are blending more and more in most libraries.

Technical Issues

In some ways, technical issues along with fiscal concerns are the driving forces in the final selection decision for e-resources. One technical issue is where the content will reside. Factors to consider include whether or not it will exist on the library's server or the vendor's server, or is it otherwise Web-based? Servers have maximum limits on simultaneous access, after which point response time begins to decline and, in extreme cases, shuts down. Thus, having a sense of how great the load would be, if the product is housed on the library's server, may be critical to reaching a decision

> ## From the Authors' Experience
>
> Saponaro has first-hand experience as to how a service that appears seamless on the end-user side, demand-driven acquisitions (DDA), can require back-end attention and staff time. A subset of the DDA program in use at an institution Saponaro worked at included a patron-mediated component, meaning title requests for specific items that could not be automatically purchased via DDA were forwarded to the "back office" to be reviewed and approved by staff. Saponaro and a colleague were responsible for monitoring the queue, which had its ebbs and flows in terms of volume, but needed constant monitoring nonetheless. Saponaro and her colleague worked together to ensure each request received a response in a timely manner (two business days was the goal)—but it did require communication, schedule coordination, and cross-training, and represented a "hidden" cost of the program.

regarding whether or not to acquire a product. If the load is too great, the library may be able to have the database hosted elsewhere, for an extra fee. Another technical consideration is the robustness of the library's information communication technology infrastructure. Certainly, the library could upgrade both server and infrastructure, but it will increase overall costs.

Another question to answer is how much technology support is needed and/or available from library staff. For most libraries today, staffing can be a challenge, and committing any significant amount of time to maintaining or sustaining a new product, beyond user support, is problematic. Knowing what is required beforehand is essential for making an informed purchase decision.

Similarly, clarifying what, if any, special equipment or software will be needed is another important issue. For example, what accommodation is possible for the visually impaired and at what cost? In addition, the question of accessing the content must be fully understood. Access options range from password access to Internet protocol–secured access, barcode access (such as the code on a person's borrower card), or proxy-server access, all of which may require ongoing staff attention. Another concern is whether or not the resource allows for remote access, or is only accessible within the library. Either option has staffing implications.

Assessment Options

While circulation and processing statistics have long been kept for print library materials, e-materials can present special challenges when it comes to quantifying and evaluating their use. Such challenges were succinctly described by Martha Whittaker (2008), who observed:

> On the face of it, keeping track of usage in the digital environment should be much easier than in the print environment. . . . Computers are good at counting things. It is not easy, however, because there are so many variables in the way people access and use digital materials. We cannot just look at circulation statistics or scan the unshelved books and journals on tables at the end of the day for accurate usage information. (p. 443)

Assessment challenges or not, given that more and more libraries commit a majority of their materials budget to electronic resources means

---

Check These Out

Rachel A. Fleming-May and Jill E. Grogg discussed the basic concepts surrounding use and usage studies for e-resources in their 2010 article "Chapter 1: Assessing Use and Usage" (*Library Technology Reports* 46, no. 6: 5–10). In addition, Lanette Garza provides an overview for developing a playbook or road map for ongoing assessment in her 2017 article "The E-Resources Playbook: A Guide for Establishing Routine Assessment of E-Resources" (*Technical Services Quarterly* 34, no. 3: 243–256). Both are well worth a look.

---

serious assessments must occur as these expenditures are usually long-term commitments. John Bertot, Charles McClure, and Joe Ryan (2001) noted; "Without the development, collection, analysis, and reporting of electronic resource and service measures . . . libraries are misrepresenting their overall service usage and potentially damaging their ability to compete for scarce funding resources in their communities" (pp. 1–2). Although almost every vendor *claims* to provide usage data, few provide what a library actually needs in order to determine the actual value to end users. Thus, libraries have been taking on the job. One big question is what constitutes "usage"— is any search, including mistakes in spelling, considered a search? Do gross numbers really provide much useful information?

John Bertot, Charles McClure, and Joe Ryan (2001) provided a very comprehensive approach for evaluating e-resources. They suggest a matrix approach that incorporates many of the elements one uses in the electronic selection process: technical infrastructure, information content, support issues, and management issues. To that, they suggest adding in those elements in terms of their extensiveness, efficiency, effectiveness, service quality, impact, usefulness, and adoption (pp. 62–73). (One should read their publication, as we only very briefly outline their major ideas.)

Efficiency and effectiveness elements are what they sound like. *Extensiveness* is how much of the electronic service users access; this can be a major factor with aggregator packages. *Service quality* is how well the activity is accomplished; one suggested measure would be the percentage of users who find what they need. *Impact* is a measure of what, if any, difference the service makes to other activities. *Usefulness* is a measure of how appropriate the service is for a class of users or an individual. *Adoption* is a measure of how much, if at all, users incorporate the service into individual or organizational activities.

Check These Out

Two fairly comprehensive books on e-resource assessment are Richard Bleiler and Jill Livingston's *Evaluating E-Resources* (Washington, DC: Association of Research Libraries, 2010) and Andrew C. White's *E-Metrics for Library and Information Professionals: How to Use Data for Managing and Evaluating Electronic Resource Collections* (New York: Neal-Schuman, 2006).

A recent article on the topic that explores how e-resources are assessed at Trinity University is Lanette Garza's 2017 piece "The E-Resources Playbook: A Guide for Establishing Routine Assessment of E-Resources" (*Technical Services Quarterly* 34, no. 3: 243–56).

Many electronic products provide, as part of the package or as an optional addition, report software that allows one to easily monitor who is using what when. You can and should load management report software onto the servers that provide access to electronic resources. Management reports will provide some of the data needed to evaluate electronic resources and the "value" of different products and services to local as well as remote users.

Cancellation or Loss of Service

E-resource purchases have some special considerations regarding product cancellation and/or loss of service. Some issues to consider include: What happens if a library must drop an e-product or service? What happens if the e-vendor goes out of business? What happens if the e-vendor merges with another firm? The first "what if" unfortunately is just as common an occurrence today as it was when there were no e-products or services. The latter two, while not that common, do take place from time to time. In the past, when the library possessed and owned a book, journal, recording, etc., it retained something for the monies spent when one of the above scenarios occurred. With e-products, unless you are careful during the selection process, the likely outcome of any of the above situations is that suddenly you are left with nothing. The money is gone, and with it, so is the information. There are three broad aspects to the above "what if" situations—legal, technical, and long-term preservation. In this chapter we look at technical issues, chapter 14 covers long-term preservation, and chapter 15 will address the legal side of the picture.

The "what ifs" apply to almost all e-products and services; however, e-serials, given their popularity with users, are the format most often addressed in the literature. The technical issues are the same for eBooks, music, serials, and video. Libraries have three common methods for gaining access to e-materials—through aggregator packages such as EBSCO's *Primary Search* (https://www.ebsco.com/products/research-databases/primary-search) and Gale's *Biography In Context* (http://www.gale.com/c/biography-in-context); via publishers' packages, for example Sage's *Sage Reference Online* (http://sk .sagepub.com/reference) and offerings from Alexander Street Press including *Ethnographic Video Online* and *Music Online* (https://alexanderstreet.com /products/ethnographic-video-online-series and http://search.alexanderstreet .com/musp); and title-by-title from publishers.

Early in the new e-product/service consideration process it is wise to request a copy of the vendor's standard contract or license. Not all e-vendors include perpetual access in their service agreements. Those who do generally offer it as an added cost feature. Those that do not have such a clause may be willing to add it. Such access rights may be included in agreements in rather ambiguous terms. Jim Stemper and Susan Barribeau (2006) quoted one such vague statement: "Licensor and Licensee shall discuss a mechanism satisfactory to the Licensor and Licensee to enable the Licensee to have access . . . and the terms of such access" (p. 102). Their article reports on an analysis they conducted of 50 e-agreements for journals from both aggregators and publishers. Knowing the content of an agreement, and not just in reference to long-term access, is very useful during your deliberations regarding an e-acquisition.

So, what if you and the vendor do reach a satisfactory agreement regarding perpetual access? What is it that the library will have should it become necessary to cancel a subscription/service? Actually, the library will be better off in the case of a vendor/publisher having problems than when the library has budget problems. At best, the library will receive one or more html or XML text files, or receive the material in some other format—such as PDFs, for example. However, what should be remembered is that you will end up with lots of data, but not the search interface. The only access to the data will be when a person knows the full citation for the desired item. Essentially, the library would/will have to pay someone to create some type of search capability—not something many libraries could afford. There would also be some potential copyright issues as there are only a finite number of ways to search databases.

Although they may be seen as an alternative in such a situation, archival services such as LOCKSS (https://www.lockss.org/) and Portico (http://www.portico.org/) are of limited value in the above circumstances. In the case of LOCKSS, the library must have an active subscription for the title or service. That does not help in cancellation times, which are likely to continue well into the future. Portico services are also not useful for cancellation access. We discuss these services as well as others in more detail in chapter 14.

At the time this volume was being prepared, few good options existed to protect the library's investment in e-resources when the library falls on hard economic times and must start canceling titles and services. There are better protections, if far from ideal, available to cover circumstances that are vendor/publisher related. Giving serious thought to the "what if the library has to cancel" question during the selection phase is rather important.

E-Formats

Electronic collections go beyond those purchased from vendors and publishers. Diane Kovacs (2007) noted that "Some digital collections are preservation projects designed to ensure that fragile historical materials are available for future generations. Libraries participate in many local history projects and preservation projects" (p. 73). Two examples of such collections include the American Memory project, sponsored by the Library of Congress (https://memory.loc.gov/ammem/browse/updatedList.html), and the University of Maryland Libraries Digital Collections (http://digital.lib.umd.edu/). However, there is one digitization project that has gained far more press and attention than any other: the Google Books Project (http://books.google.com, discussed later in this chapter). In addition, many libraries provide links to websites through their discovery systems or library web pages. EBooks, serials, music, video, data sets, and institutional repositories are also covered in the following sections.

eBooks

Today, publishers find the Web something of a challenge and many are still struggling to find a satisfactory method to employ it and generate an adequate income stream to remain profitable. Some have tried issuing "born digital" titles with less than great success. Most can offer other firms, such as Amazon and Barnes & Noble, e-versions of titles they released in paper. Finding the proper pricing structure for this approach is still very much up in the air. Perhaps the type of eReaders on the market in 2018 and beyond (such as Kindle, Sony Reader, and Nook) will overcome the proprietary issues that caused earlier eReaders to fail.

eBook readers present something of a conundrum for both publishers and libraries. As Emilie Algenio and Alexia Thompson-Young (2005) noted, "Publishers want to sell books to customers and libraries want to lend books

From the Advisory Board

Advisory Board member Susan Koutsky suggests several online resources that are used for student research and contain authored articles as well as articles written by the producer:

Some examples are ProQuest's *CultureGrams®* (https://www.proquest.com /products-services/culturegrams.html; containing articles and information on over 200 countries), Capstone's *PebbleGo™* (https://www.pebblego.com/, for early elementary, containing information on animals, biographies, science, and social studies topics), *Britannica School* (https://school.eb.com/, online encyclopedia and dictionary), ProQuest's *SIRS® Knowledge Source®* (https:// www.proquest.com/products-services/sirs_knowledge_source.html, information on current topics including pro/con coverage), and *Teachingbooks.net* (https:// www.teachingbooks.net/, multimedia resources on books and authors). These resources not only contain the articles and information, they may allow readers to listen to the articles, play educational games, link to other age appropriate websites, and enjoy other features of enhanced content. These online resources allow students to conduct research on a topic in a safe environment, instead of simply "Googling" a topic, which can lead to a daunting overabundance of hits, many of which may be inappropriate. As with other E-resources, trial periods are offered and the selection issues are similar.

She notes that some of these resources are purchased by the local school system, and some are purchased by the State of Maryland's SAILOR research database budget, which buys online resources for use in public and school libraries (http://www .sailor.lib.md.us/services/databases/).

to users. eBooks challenge both of these goals, since one eBook could be accessed by multiple library users at a time or could be protected by software that requires payment per view" (p. 114). Just how eReaders and library service will play out is impossible to accurately predict; however, libraries have effectively dealt with a variety of information delivery systems in the past and we expect they will do so again.

eReaders

Personal eReaders are extremely popular, even among individuals who are not technologically inclined. It appears likely that the current generation of eReaders will have greater staying power than their predecessors. This is in part because there will continue to be a steady and varied supply of titles available to download. There is also a strong probability that the current single function units will morph in some manner with the existing multifunction cell phones, iPods, MP3 players, and other handheld devices.

For libraries, the readers present challenges for creating new service models as well as acquisition budgets. First, there is a question of just how many individuals will be willing to pay the cost for an electronic device that is a single-function proprietary device. Which eReader to start with? Although the situation is somewhat different today, there is still the memory of both the cassette and DVD video format battles as well as what happened to libraries that jumped on the eReader bandwagon after the first readers appeared on the market.

Once a library starts providing services for eReaders, there are still questions regarding which platforms to support, how much money to commit to the service, and whether users should pay some or all of the costs. And, perhaps most importantly, how to handle the increased workload that current readers would create for the staff. It should be kept in mind that there are digitized eBooks that libraries can provide access to online and there are titles intended for downloading onto a reader. There are some remaining eBook barriers to consider:

- Lack of standards for software and hardware;
- Usage rights (single user) tend to go against the operating philosophy of libraries (open access);
- Pricing models that are rather unrealistic for library budgets, especially during lean economic times; and
- Lack of a library-based "discovery" system (titles are currently available only through OPACs, which do not match the ease of use of Google and Yahoo when searching for titles).

Efforts to get eReaders into the education market have been more or less a research and development activity rather than for market penetration. Anne Behler and Binky Lush (2011) reported on a joint project between Sony and the Penn State University Libraries to test 100 of Sony's EBook Readers for general-use lending and in classroom settings. One issue the libraries had to contend with during the pilot was that the Sony reader is designed for a single user, or at best a family (the usage terms are for no more than five readers for a single download)—which represents serious costs as well as workload considerations. The project's major finding, in terms of library usage, was that "overall, the students were glad to have tried a Sony Reader but indicated that the devices would need to show significant improvement in functionality before they would be feasible in an academic setting" (p. 83). One of the significant factors in reaching that conclusion, and one that seems applicable to any size library, was the considerable staff time that was required in order to create numerous separate logins, passwords, alias email accounts, and load books onto readers. The readers did not fare much better in the classroom setting.

Google Books Project

We are reasonably certain that anyone with more than passing interest in the Web and reading has some knowledge of the Google Books Project (GBP). To say GBP has mixed reviews from many people and diverse groups is an understatement. Probably the only people completely happy with the concept are the attorneys that represented the various parties involved in the litigation over Google's idea. Challenges to the concept were not limited to those from the United States. Other countries put forward strong objections as well. At a September 2009 hearing convened by the European Commission, Google attempted to answer some of the European concerns. They were not all that successful, and in May 2011, three French publishers filed a lawsuit against Google for what they termed illegal scanning of thousands of their titles without permission (*CILIP Update*, 2011, p. 10). Despite this action, in July 2011, Google announced a partnership with the British Library to digitize their materials (Kelley and Warburton, 2011, p. 14).

The goal of the GBP, in a nutshell, was to digitize all the books in major U.S. and foreign libraries and make them available to anyone, with some advertisements associated with what a person views. At some point, only limited access would be provided unless a subscription fee is paid. Google originally envisioned that end users who searched the system would "see basic bibliographic information about the book, and in many cases, a few snippets—a few sentences showing your search term in context. If the book is out of copyright, you'll be able to view and download the entire book. In all cases, you'll see links directing you to online bookstores where you can buy the book and libraries where you can borrow it" (https://books.google.com/googlebooks/library/).

The notion that some company would be allowed to make digital copies of copyrighted works got the attention of many rights holders who sued Google in 2005. The case was complex and took until October 28, 2008, before an initial settlement was reached. The settlement was revised and submitted to the federal judge hearing the case in 2010; in March 2011, the judge rejected the proposed settlement, indicating that it would give Google "a significant advantage over competitors, rewarding it for engaging in wholesale copying of copyrighted works without permission" (*Authors Guild et al. v. Google Inc.,* 2011, p. 2).

There were several components to the service side in the 2010 proposal (all users—free service, all users—fee-based service, free "Public Access Service" [PAS] for public libraries and not-for-profit academic institutions, and institutional subscriptions). One aspect of the revised proposal was particularly noteworthy as clearly Google expected to generate a revenue stream from, if nothing more, than just posting advertisements on the displayed pages. Although not implemented, the proposed PAS component was intended to be available for public and nonprofit academic libraries/institutions upon request on a one "terminal" basis. A public library system would be allowed one such terminal in each building in its system. Academic libraries would be eligible for terminals based on institutional FTEs.

It is unclear what the drafters of the agreement had in mind by the phrase "not commercially available." Are books for sale by out-of-print dealers "commercially available"? It seems likely that the dealers would say so as much of their stock are titles not yet in the public domain and available for purchase. There is no indication there was anyone from that field at the table when the proposed settlement was reached in 2005. Lawsuits continued for years over various aspects of the project, with a primary focus on the copyright and the fair use aspects the project raised. In April 2016, the U.S. Supreme Court declined to hear an appeal by the authors, ultimately ending the court battles for the project (Opderbeck, 2016, p. 194).

As court cases increased and different parties received at least some partial positive outcome, the rate of scanning for the project slowed. As noted by Somers (2017), "Despite eventually winning *Authors Guild v. Google*, and having the courts declare that displaying snippets of copyrighted books was fair use, the company all but shut down its scanning operation." Another factor contributing to the slowdown related to quality control. Rapid scanning is not always the best way to achieve good quality. Problems with metadata are reported as high and include works being attributed to an author years before that person was born. Other problems include pages not being readable, only part of the page actually scanned, and even hands and fingers occupying most of the scanned image.

Elisabeth Jones (2017) observed, "Though it is admittedly unlikely that Google will start taking public votes on how to run its Google Books site

---

Check These Out

An article that discusses the impact of the Google Books project in the U.S. and abroad is David W. Opderbeck's 2016 article "Implications of the Google Books Project Settlement for the Global Library Community" (*International Information & Library Review*, 48, no. 3: 190–95).

For a concise outline of the history of the Google Books project and litigation surrounding it, check out the *Google Books Litigation Family Tree* from the Library Copyright Alliance: http://www.librarycopyrightalliance.org/storage/documents/google -books-litigation-tree-18apr2016.pdf.

---

anytime soon, it has demonstrated some willingness to act on feedback from users and has also been responsive to critiques leveled at it by the media" (p. 256). Beyond the fact that Google may be more responsive to users moving forward, as noted by Howard (2017), "many librarians and scholars see the legacy of the project differently. In fact, academics now regularly tap into the reservoir of digitized material that Google helped create, using it as a data set they can query, even if they can't consume full texts. It's a pillar of the humanities' growing engagement with Big Data."

Alternatives to Google Books

Alternatives to the Google Books Project include Project Gutenberg (http://www.gutenberg.org/) and HathiTrust. Project Gutenberg was founded in 1971 with a mission "to encourage the creation and distribution of eBooks" (http://www.gutenberg.org/wiki/Gutenberg:Project_Gutenberg _Mission_Statement_by_Michael_Hart). Since its inception, Project Gutenberg has grown to include over 57,000 titles as of mid-2018—a majority of which are in the public domain. Project Gutenberg is unique in that it is based upon the premise of User-Generated Content (UGC), where individuals are free to contribute content to the project.

HathiTrust (http://www.hathitrust.org/), on the other hand, is a membership-based organization. Titles in the project come from member libraries who also participated in the Google Books project, but it also includes content scanned by participating libraries themselves. The level of access granted to view individual titles is based upon the copyright of the work itself (http://www.hathitrust.org/access_use). HathiTrust currently includes digitized books, although in the future, the Trust may evolve to include other archival material. Although speaking on the concept of Institutional Repositories (IR, discussed later in this chapter), Furlough (2009) made the following observation that can be applied to the Hathi model: "Commercial agents, such as Google, can outperform existing library systems on speed and breadth of basic searches, but the preservation and scholarly use of digital assets are still fertile ground for libraries, technologists, and library users" (p. 20).

Check This Out

For a step-by-step discussion of how titles are added to Project Gutenberg, see Nicholasa Tomaiuolo's 2009 article "U-Content Project Gutenberg, Me, and You" in *Searcher* (17, no. 1: 26–34).

Online Music/Audio

Selecting music resources, whether print scores, CD recordings, or digital files, calls for an understanding of the subject in more depth than most other format and subject areas. Daniel Zager (2007) identified 11 elements in the selection decision:

- Composer
- Instrumentation
- Editor and reputation
- Series
- Score type (full, study, vocal/piano)
- Competing versions by other editors/publishers (p. 568)

- Genre and work
- Edition/Arrangement
- Publisher and reputation
- Date (new or reprint)
- Cost

Although the focus in the above is slanted toward classical music, these elements are applicable to almost all other music genres. They are also not all that different from the general selection elements we covered in chapter 6.

Music was one of the first nonprint formats that libraries added to their collections more than 100 years ago. It remained a mainstay in many academic and public libraries until the start of the 21st century. Libraries with such collections today find them aging and not the most current, as issues within the recording industry and the digital world have made developing an e-music collection a challenge. As is true of so many e-information resources, music has been entangled with legal issues. D. J. Hoek (2009) wrote:

> I am not an expert on current or future technologies, and I certainly am no authority on copyright or licensing, but I do have a particular interest in building, preserving, and providing access to music collections. It appears that recent changes in the distribution of sound recordings are challenging our ability to continue this most foundational aspect of our profession. (p. 55)

The change Hoek referred to was, and remains, the growing use of download-only music files, especially from major record labels. One of his examples of the challenges for libraries trying to acquire such recordings was Deutsche Grammophone's decision to release a 2008 prize-winning recording of Berlioz's *Symphonie Fantastique* by the Los Angeles Philharmonic Orchestra only as a digital download file. Why is this problematic? The issue is that such files are only legally available from the company or from iTunes, both of which have a license agreement stating the file is only for sale to end users. The sticking point is that libraries are, and always have been, distributors of information, not the end users.

So, what are the options for libraries wishing to provide access to digital music files for their users? There are a few choices available beyond securing downloads from recording companies that do not have end-user only licenses. The only option is through aggregator services, something that some music librarians believe does away with one of CM's basic functions— selecting individual items. One of the firms offering such packages is Alexander Street Press (https://alexanderstreet.com/products/open-music-library), which started online music access in 2010. One of their products, *Music Online: Smithsonian Global Sound for Libraries,* "is the largest and most comprehensive streaming audio collection of world music. It currently provides streaming access to over 44,000 tracks from the Smithsonian archives and world music archives in Asia and Africa" (https://alexanderstreet.com /products/music-online-smithsonian-global-sound-libraries). The files are fully accessible on mobile devices, and users can create personal playlists. The vendor eventually hopes to have over 1 million recordings available. Libraries subscribing to all of the collections will also get access to a collection of 140,000 popular music files.

Another music aggregator is Naxos Music Library (http://www.naxos musiclibrary.com). It is a service specifically designed for music education and libraries. Naxos provides access to liner notes, original cover artwork, and other production data. Other features include a pronunciation guide for composer and artist names; a glossary and guide to musical terms and work analyses; interactive music courses for Australia, Canada, South Korea, the U.K., and the U.S.; graded music-exam playlists; and a "junior" section. Subscriber fees are based on the number of simultaneous users the library requires.

A not-for-profit "aggregator" is DRAM, which focuses on the educational community's interest in streaming music (http://www.dramonline.org/). Its focus is on U.S. music. The service is available to member libraries (academic and public) and allows in-library and remote access to its files through an authorized institution. The maximum fee, in 2018, was less than $2,000 for the largest academic libraries and $800 for the largest public libraries. Another service is Freegal® Music, an offering from Library Ideas LLC (http://www.libraryideas.com/freegal.html), with over 15 million songs available as of mid-2018. Their catalog includes offerings from Sony Music, as well as music videos. Notably, their audio files come DRM-free, and do not require special software or devices to use.

A major online resource for reference material about music is *Oxford Music Online* (http://www.oxfordmusiconline.com/). Included in the package is *Grove Music Online,* which itself contains *The New Grove Dictionary of Music and Musicians* (2nd ed.), *The New Grove Dictionary of Opera*, and *The New Grove Dictionary of Jazz* (2nd ed.), and updates to these titles. *Oxford Music Online* also includes access to *Norton Grove Dictionary of Women Composers* and the *Grove Dictionary of Musical Instruments* (2nd ed.).

We end this section about online audio with a brief note regarding audiobooks. EBSCO offers audiobooks and Apple- and Android-compatible eBooks for libraries to make available to users either through direct purchase,

---

Check These Out

A good article on using an "aggregator" for library music collection building is Stephanie Krueger and Philip Ponella's 2008 essay "DRAM/Variations3: A Music Resource Case Study" in *Library Hi Tech* (26, no. 1: 68–79).

A sound summary of the history of joint efforts in creating music collections in libraries is Karl Madden's 2010 article "Cooperative Collection Management in Music: Past and Present" found in *New Library World* (111, no. 7/8: 333–46).

An interesting article by a nonlibrarian that deals with collecting musical recordings is Carlos R. Abril's 2006 piece "Music That Represents Culture: Selecting Music with Integrity" in *Music Educators Journal* (93, no. 1: 38–45).

Kate Pritchard's 2010 article "Let's Get This Party Started" provides insight into how a library might use streaming music with teenagers (*School Library Journal* 56, no. 3: 34–37), and is also worth a look.

short-term lease, or as part of a subscription package on its EBSCO*host*® platform (https://www.ebscohost.com/ebooks/user-experience/audiobooks). Two other resources are OverDrive (http://www.overdrive.com/) and Recorded Books (http://www.recordedbooks.com/). OverDrive is a relatively recent supplier to libraries and focuses on digital material, while Recorded Books has a K–12 focus.

Video

You may have seen, and perhaps read, an article or two regarding possible changes to the concept of *net neutrality*. If so, you, like many others of us, probably gave only a passing thought, if any, to what implementations there might be for libraries if such changes took place. In the past, any data packet on the Internet was, and as of the time we prepared this section still is, treated the same (net neutrality). That is, no packet had a higher or lower priority for transmission. What some bandwidth service providers (telephone and cable companies, for example) propose is a system of preferential service for those who pay a fee. What that would mean, if it happens, is any organization paying a fee could deliver faster, better quality material (especially image-rich files such as video) than those not paying the fee. Those proposing the change argue that packets taking up more bandwidth should pay higher fees and the current system penalizes everyone with, if nothing more, having slower service. Opponents suggest such a system would allow those with "deep pockets" to dominate service. In late 2010, the Federal Communications Commission (FCC) voted in favor of the net neutrality order (Terry, 2011, p. 108). However, in 2011, "two bills seeking to prohibit the FCC from regulating the Internet have already been introduced, H.R. 96 and H.R. 166" (Terry, 2011, p. 112). As of August 2018, the issue was still a matter of debate. The end result will probably be something in between the opposing views, with some type of prioritization of data with an associated cost, but at a much lower level than bandwidth companies want.

Our point in discussing the above is that libraries must carefully consider how capable their technological infrastructure is before moving into online video activities. Available bandwidth matters for both the sending and receiving parties.

There are two aspects to online video and libraries—access to content produced by others and access to library-generated content. Both are likely to increase in importance over time as it is obvious people like visual materials. Just looking at the growth of YouTube makes it clear how attractive video material is for many people.

Library-generated content is a topic beyond the scope of this book, but something CM officers should keep in mind. This area is likely to grow quickly and become enmeshed with collection management activities. While commercial video production quality may be desirable, it is clear that anything slightly above the average YouTube quality is acceptable to most people. Thus, with even modest equipment with some planning, time, and effort

---

Something to Watch

As the concept of net neutrality is in flux at the time of this writing, one source to monitor is ALA's Network Neutrality site (http://www.ala.org/advocacy/telecom/netneutrality) that contains updates to the topic as they occur.

on the library's part, a library can produce acceptable online video content. What are some of the possibilities?

- On-demand "how-to-use" instruction for library services/databases
- On-demand information literacy sessions
- On-demand library tours
- On-demand reviews of collection resources by staff and/or users
- On-demand staff training sessions
- On-demand "how-to-do" pieces on some activity (not necessarily library related—fixing a leaky faucet—with perhaps a connection to existing library resources)
- Public relations material, coverage of library events, storytelling, and so on.

The list is only limited by your imagination and, of course, the time to do it.

On the academic library side, the University of Maryland (UMD) Libraries conducted a pilot program for streaming video via the Kanopy service in summer 2017 (http://umd.kanopystreaming.com/), where the entire Kanopy catalog was de-duplicated against existing holdings of the discovery system and remaining titles were made available. Through this program, UMD students, faculty, and staff could access titles from on or off-campus, and titles triggered for purchase were retained by the UMD Libraries in their collection. The program, although only a pilot, clearly demonstrated the popularity of such services. The UMD experience echoes an earlier program spearheaded by members of the Arizona University Libraries Consortium (AULC)—including the University of Arizona, Arizona State University, and Northern Arizona University libraries—who partnered with Films Media Group (FMG) to access titles from within the FMG catalog; when any title was accessed three times AULC purchased the perpetual streaming rights for that title. The AULC hosted the files on its server (Farrelly, 2008, p. 67). As noted by Farrelly (2008), "the AULC/FMG On Demand agreement is believed to be the first and a unique attempt at a patron-driven acquisition model for streaming video" (p. 68).

We have already mentioned four sources of online video—Alexander Street Press, Kanopy, Films Media Group, and OverDrive. OverDrive offers popular movies, television series, and children's programs. We also mentioned Naxos in the section on online music; that firm also provides online video of musical performances and is strong in the area of ballet. Other firms that are beginning to take hold in the library market are Swank® (https://www.swank.com/digital-campus/), which offers content from television and major motion picture studios, and Hoopla (https://www.hoopladigital.com/), concentrating on the public library market, which offers music and eBooks in addition to its video content. In addition, another relatively new source of video content is IndieFlix (http://www.indieflix.com/), developed to showcase independent films. The library subscription version is branded InstantFlix: Powered by IndieFlix, and is popular in public libraries. For more information on digital collections available, consult ALA's *Digital Video Collections Guide* (http://connect.ala.org/node/183711), which covers both licensed and open video collections.

Check These Out

An article on streaming video worth reviewing is Kathy Fredrick's 2008 piece "Streaming Consciousness: Online Video Sharing" in *School Library Media Activities Monthly* (24, no. 10: 44–46).

Sara E. Morris and Lea H. Currie explore whether or not streaming services are worth the investment in their 2016 article "To Stream or Not to Stream?" (*New Library World*, 11, nos. 7/8: 485–498), while Mary Wahl discusses the "decision tree" created to facilitate streaming video acquisitions in her 2017 article "Full Stream Ahead: Designing a Collection Development Workflow for Streaming Video Content" (*Library Resources & Technical Services* 61, no. 4: 226–36).

Jason Paul Michel, Susan Hurst, and Andrew Revelle (2009) wrote about "Vodcasting, iTunes U, and Faculty Collaboration" in the *Electronic Journal of Academic and Special Librarianship* (10, no. 1, http://southernlibrarianship.icaap.org/content /v10n01/michel_j01.html).

Web Resources

As information professionals know all too well, there is "stuff" and then there is "good stuff" on the Internet. Libraries engage in serious efforts to help the public learn how to assess websites and other e-resources through programs such as information literacy sessions/courses. Another approach is to post links to the "good stuff" on library websites or online guides that are believed to be accurate, informative, and useful.

Is posting such links part of CM activities? We believe so. Selecting appropriate sites is not that different from selecting other library resources, although it is a little more time consuming. Unlike other resources, websites have a habit of changing over time. One great advantage of web pages is they are relatively easy to update and even take down. They also have a habit of changing URLs with no notice. Thus, unlike other resources that once in the collection do not change in character and content, websites are a moving target. That in turn means someone should monitor the sites on a regular schedule.

Surfing the Internet can be enjoyable, but is not all that efficient for identifying potential/appropriate sites for linking from the library's web pages. Seeking out online Webliographies is a quicker approach. Another method is to look at links other libraries have in place. Most libraries have a formal or informal list of libraries they consider peers and which they employ from time to time for comparative purposes. Starting with those libraries' websites is a good way to monitor what may be appropriate for your users. Discussion lists are yet another source for identifying possible additions for your links.

One concern with online material is there is no vetting of the type you come to depend on with other collection formats. Anyone can post anything, claim credentials not held, and so on, as no one is responsible for verifying any of the sites' content. Certainly the 2016/2017 "fake news" concerns reinforce the importance of having such assessment skills. Thus, when surfing for potential sites, you are on your own. Some of the more obvious issues are out-of-date information, opinions stated as facts, biases, and more and more often just plain old-fashioned fraud. None of us are experts on all the topics we may be responsible for when wearing our CM hats. Having some input from other information professionals is useful, if not essential.

One long-standing online, at least in Internet terms, resource for learning about websites that have been "reviewed" by information professionals is the Internet Scout Project (https://scout.wisc.edu/). The service has been operational since 1994 with the goal to develop "better tools and services for finding, filtering, and presenting online information and metadata. . . . Our turnkey portal software, for example, allows digital collection developers to share their unique online materials with colleagues and students throughout the world" (https://scout.wisc.edu/about). The *Scout Report* (https://scout.wisc.edu/report) appears online each Friday providing a current awareness service regarding Web resources. Another resource that can be particularly useful in school and public library settings is "Great Websites for Kids," maintained by ALA's Association for Library Service to Children (http://gws.ala.org/).

Needless to say, there are books listing websites; however, they are of limited value except in the first year or two after publication as addresses and content change quickly. Professional journals that review library materials generally also review potential online resources—for example *Booklist's* "Reference on the Web" section. *College & Research Library News* has an "Internet Resources" section in most of its issues that are topical in character. Although many of the topics are oriented toward higher education, many others are not. A very few examples of subjects that could be of interest to any type of library are:

- Keeping Workplace Burnout at Bay (July/August 2016)
- Haitian History and Culture (April 2017)
- Preparing for Retirement (December 2010)
- Research Data Management and Services (May 2017)
- Project-Based Learning Resources (July/August 2017)
- Presidential Research Resources (February 2018)
- Health Care Management Resources (September 2009)

College & Research Library News is an open-access publication, and its full-issue archives, including "Internet Resources" articles contained within issues, are available online at http://crln.acrl.org/index.php/crlnews/index.

Keeping links current and reevaluating online content takes time. Someone should have the responsibility to check all the links on a regular basis. When there is a change, the person(s) who selected the sites should review the pages to check on the changes. Broken links and poor-quality changes are not minor matters. Too many such problems will quickly lead to doubts about the quality of other library services, especially among younger users who spend large amounts of time online.

Institutional Repositories

There is no doubt that scholars and researchers, regardless of their discipline, have added new approaches to their collaborative activities over the past 10 to 15 years as the Internet became ever more available. It took a long time, more than 100 years, for librarians to begin to get a handle on what has been called the "invisible college" and associated "grey literature." New methods of communication and the ease of collaborating with scholars around the world have made the challenge for information professionals greater than ever.

What are the invisible college and grey literature? As you may guess, the "college" is a label for what is more popularly known as social networking. One desired outcome of scholarly work is to "advance humankind's knowledge" and perhaps improve life. One result of that objective is fewer and fewer individuals knowing more and more about less and less. In some fields of research/scholarship, there may only be a dozen or so people in the world with identical research interests. Getting to know and interact with those individuals is important for a researcher. They share ideas, data, and insights in order to advance all their work. In the days of snail mail, landline telephones, and travel grants, it was difficult to know all those in the world who shared one's research interests. International conferences were very important to the networking process. Today, email, social media, collaborative software, etc., have changed the picture dramatically.

"Grey literature" was and is the material, text, and data that results from the sharing between scholars. Only a small proportion of a researcher's work ever appears in the "open" or published literature (books and journals). Close colleagues often share drafts of potential open literature material. Feedback often leads to changes and often deletions, with the published version being very different from the early drafts. It was and is a vetting process prior to that of the traditional prepublication vetting. Some of the material that does not make "the final cut" can be useful clues to further work for others, if they learn about the material. Conference papers/presentations were and still are of value to people long after the program is concluded. Only a small percentage of such papers ever appear in the open literature. In the past, exchanging copies of such presentations was common. Today such exchanges still take place, but in electronic form. For a library serving researchers, tracking down hard copies of such presentations was difficult at best. That difficulty is compounded today.

Institutional repositories (IR) are an effort to capture and make available as much of the grey literature as possible. The IR concept itself is relatively new, with the term first being introduced post-2000. Clifford Lynch (2003), a proponent of information technology and of expanding its scope in libraries, defined institutional repositories as:

> a set of services that a university offers to the members of its community for the management and dissemination of digital materials created by the institution and its community members. It is most essentially an organizational commitment to the stewardship of these digital materials, including long-term preservation where appropriate, as well as organization and access or distribution. (p. 328)

Like the concept of the information commons, the idea of such repositories has a variety of meanings and functions depending upon the institution. To some degree, the term repository suggests one of the less positive views about academic libraries—as a storehouse of little-used, dusty materials. This is unfortunate as such programs are active in nature rather than static like a storehouse. Most scholars know little about IR services at present, and for a majority of those who do, the word repository is less than positive. Perhaps as they become aware of and use services such as OAIster® they will have a different view of the concept. We discuss OAIster® below.

The purpose of a repository program is to encourage the campus community (students and faculty especially) to deposit or contribute material they create as part of their teaching, learning, and scholarly activities that may have broader interest than the original purpose that led to its creation. Further, the program makes this material available, normally through open access, to anyone worldwide who has an interest in the topic.

A major open source repository software program is DSpace (http://www.dspace.org), first created in 1991 through a partnership by MIT and Hewlett Packard. Government, research, commercial, and academic institutions throughout the world currently use DSpace technology to manage their repository activities (http://registry.duraspace.org/registry/dspace). Other IR options include the *Digital Commons* from bepress™ (formerly Berkeley Electronic Press™; https://www.bepress.com/products/digital-commons/), Eprints' (http://www.eprints.org) Open Access and IR services, and ExLibris' (http://www.exlibrisgroup.com/) SFX® OpenURL link resolver and MetaLib® products. A library must decide which option will work best for its planned application.

What is included in many of the existing IRs? The most common elements are data sets, draft documents, other grey literature, theses and dissertations, grant proposals, conference presentations, and a variety of institutional digital material. In many ways, the IR concept is a variation of what the profit sector calls *knowledge management*. That is, IRs are an effort to gain some control over and provide structure and access to the many varieties of digital material every organization produces every day.

Access to the content of IRs is the key to success for library IR programs/services. Open access material is searchable through a Google search; however, those materials are lumped together with hundreds, if not millions, of other hits. Users, if they read or use some IR items, are unlikely to realize that fact. To employ a marketing term, the material is not "branded." Thus the material will do little to improve the scholars' perception of IR programs. Earlier we mentioned OAIster®, which is a free search tool designed just for IR materials. The program is accessible through its own URL (http://oaister.worldcat.org/). The program was developed by the University of Michigan Library's Digital Library Production Service and is now a joint program with OCLC. It employs what is called the Open Archives Initiative Protocol for Metadata Harvesting (OAI-PMH) program.

Gaining the support from the campus community to contribute material to the IR can be challenging. As noted by Tschera Connell (2011): "All institutional repositories face the issue of content recruitment" (p. 253). One

---

From the Authors' Experience

Often, individuals who place items in their local IR are keenly interested in the download or usage statistics. Saponaro recalls a time when one faculty member was working on a dossier for full professor and was extremely agitated when the statistics program used at the time for the IR reset the statistics count temporarily, thus drastically altering the perceived use of materials the individual had deposited. Wording was placed on the IR site indicating the temporary change in reporting—but it served as a good reminder of how important use is to those who submit materials to an IR.

In 2017, Montana State University, together with OCLC Research, the Association of Research Libraries, and the University of New Mexico joined forces to create a prototype service called RAMP (Repository Analytics & Metrics Portal) designed to improve institutional repository analytics. The project page (http://ramp.montana.edu/) includes links to research papers on the system. It is worth watching how RAMP continues to be developed and implemented.

method employed at some institutions in order to ensure materials are contributed is to require that all theses and dissertations be submitted in a digital format that is compatible with the IR software. A few institutions have expanded this concept to include undergraduate capstone or honors papers. Eleta Exline (2016) notes that when the IR was expanded at the University of New Hampshire, "unexpectedly, we found stronger campus support and fewer barriers to collecting undergraduate research than for faculty and graduate student scholarship" (p. 16).

With regard to establishing IRs, Mike Furlough (2009) cautioned that "No library should implement a digital repository program without examining the role it will play in its broader strategy for collection development, stewardship, and providing access to its primary constituencies. The strategy should be based on a clear understanding of the community's needs and the requirement for long-term stewardship of the data collected" (p. 22).

Creating an IR is not easy. There are three big issues involved: technology, staff time, and getting people to provide e-materials. Soo Young Rieh and Kevin Smith argued against widespread use of IRs, indicating the "(OAI-PMH) provides a structure for creating repositories searchable through Google and made interpretable with other repositories and search tools, but its application requires a degree of sophistication that may not be available at every university" (Rieh and Smith, 2009, pp. 12–13).

One final thought on IRs. Currently they are more likely to be found in a research university environment. However, as seen with DSpace, IRs can be created for virtually any organizational type. Given this, we think they will become even more widespread as the technology becomes less complex to use. Perhaps the label for the concept will change as well. School district libraries/programs might consider using an IR approach for teaching materials created by their faculty. Exemplary student work might also be included in such a program. Public libraries are beginning to engage in similar projects dealing with local special/unique items. Kendra Morgan and Merrilee Proffitt (2017) wrote in an OCLC research report:

> In an era when online discovery and access to information and knowledge is not only desirable but often an expectation, access to the materials stewarded by libraries and other cultural heritage organizations is of critical importance. These institutions hold a wealth of materials—not only those that are ubiquitously

---

Check These Out

The fall 2008 (vol. 57, no. 2) issue of *Library Trends* has the theme "Introduction: Institutional Repositories: Current State and Future," with several interesting articles, including "Perceptions and Experiences of Staff in the Planning and Implementation of Institutional Repositories" by Soo Young Rieh, Beth St. Jean, Elizabeth Yakel, Karen Markey, and Kim Jihyun (pp. 168–190) and Dorothea Salo's "Innkeeper at the Roach Motel" (pp. 98–123), which provides an argument for providing adequate resources for repository activities.

Larry Sheret and his colleagues Thomas Walker, Gretchen Beach, and Jingping Zhang offer "A Primer on How to Launch an Institutional Repository Successfully" in their 2015 *Charleston Advisor* article (16, no. 3: 48–55).

In addition, Jessie Daniel provides an in-depth overview of the scholarly communication landscape in *Being a Scholar in the Digital Era* (Bristol: Policy Press, 2016).

available, such as books and journals, but also unique materials collected on behalf of the communities they serve. (p. 6)

Their research found that 92 percent of the public libraries housed "unique physical items." That is not too surprising as resource sharing programs have found that even the smallest library has something special to add to the sum total. What was surprising was the authors found that 37.6 percent of those libraries had some type of digitization project underway. Thus, public libraries might become key components in local government's efforts to make better use of staff's digitally generated materials. When will these changes happen in the IR landscape? Perhaps not in the short-term, as the technology is presently too complex for most libraries. In time, however, that is very likely to change.

Open Access

What is open access (OA) and does it matter in terms of collection management? Open access material is freely available on the Internet, at least in theory (there can be some conditions on that availability). Essentially it is an approach that loosens the subscription model for access to scholarly information. It is similar to but different from the IR concept. Academic libraries and many scholars have been upset/frustrated for years by the constant, often double-digit, annual price increases for subscriptions for scholarly journals. Open access provides a means to circumvent such costs.

This is not the book to explore the complex details of the scholarly communication process, but a short summary goes something like this: scholars draw upon the work of other scholars to ultimately provide society with useful knowledge. To accomplish the sharing of information, scholars depend on a means of communicating their work outcomes, hence the scholarly journal. Research efforts are not inexpensive and more often than not the funds are from the public in the form of grants. Publishing/distributing the results is rather costly as the readership is small. (Remember the notion of fewer and fewer individuals knowing more and more about less and less.) The solution was to have a charge for publishing the results—a "page charge"—also usually covered with public funds and going to the publisher. The publisher in turn offered access to the material for a fee that includes a profit. Once again the source of monies to pay for a subscription was more often than not public. The result is a cycle of process that is underwritten by public funds and growing questions about publishers' ever growing profits. Open access (OA) has become an alternative approach to the dissemination of scholarly information.

As our opening quotation from David Kramer notes, OA is growing but the subscription model seems likely to remain the dominant feature in scholarly communication for some time as the "peer reviewed" article in a published journal is often considered the "gold standard" by which academic faculty promotion and tenure decisions are made. That means that libraries are not likely to see much relief from high journal subscription costs any time soon, as some faculty are not eager to give up the traditional model. The costs will continue to escalate whether the journal is print or digital in character.

OA comes in two "colors"—gold and green. Gold titles provide immediate and free access to material upon publication. The publishers depend on page charges for their income. (There is no "free lunch"; no matter what is done there are costs associated with distributing information of all types,

---

Something to Watch

The University of Maryland (UMD) Libraries created an Open Access Publishing Fund to improve access to research produced at UMD. The fund allows for up to 50 percent of article processing charges (ACPs) to be covered for a publication submitted by a UMD researcher (https://www.lib.umd.edu/oa/openaccessfund). UMD is one of several institutions such as Johns Hopkins and Berkeley that have such programs available to encourage publication in OA sources. For more on the Johns Hopkins and Berkeley experiences, see:

Robin Sinn, Sue M. Woodson, and Mark Cyzyk's January 2017 article "The Johns Hopkins Libraries Open Access Promotion Fund" (*College & Research Libraries News* 78, no. 1: 32–35).

Samantha Teplitzky and Margaret Phillips' 2016 piece "Evaluating the Impact of Open Access at Berkeley: Results from the 2015 Survey of Berkeley Research Impact Initiative (BRII) Funding Recipients" *College & Research Libraries* 77, no. 5 (2016): 568–581.

---

not just scholarly information.) Green titles become available in one of two ways. There is the "preprint approach" in which an article, upon acceptance by a publisher, is made available in a digital format to the author(s). They are allowed to post that version on their web pages and/or their institution's archive/IR site. The preprint may or may not be identical to what is published as it has not gone through the editing process. However, most such changes rarely impact the information contained in the paper. The second green option is free access to the "version of record" (publication) material after an embargo period that is determined by the publisher. The *Directory of Open Access Journals* (DOAJ) allows one way to locate OA titles. The *Directory* was launched in 2003 in Sweden, and is part of a nonprofit organization of the same name (https://doaj.org/about). Together with the Committee on Publication Ethics, the Open Access Scholarly Publishers Association, and the World Association of Medical Editors, DOAJ co-authored a set of

---

Check These Out

Mikael Laskso, Patrik Welling, and their colleagues provide a good overview as to the origins of the Open Access movement in their 2011 *PLoS One* article "The Development of Open Access Journal Publishing from 1993 to 2009" (6, no. 6, https://doi.org/10.1371/journal.pone.0020961). Notably, *PLoS One* is an open access journal.

OA funding models are reviewed by Christine Fruin and Fred Rascoe in their 2014 piece "Funding Open Access Journal Publishing" (*College and Research Libraries News* 75, no. 5: 240–243), while Kate Lara explores "The Library's Role in the Management and Funding of Open Access Publishing" in her 2015 *Learned Publishing* article (28, no. 1: 4–8).

Lillian Rigling, Emily Carlisle, and Courtney Waugh explore the process followed at the University of Western Ontario Libraries to create an OA values statement in "In Pursuit of Equity: Applying Design Thinking to Develop a Values-Based Open Access Statement" (*In the Library with the Lead Pipe*, July 25, 2018, http://www.inthelibrarywiththeleadpipe.org/2018/oa-statement/).

Principles of Transparency and Best Practice in Scholarly Publishing (https://doaj.org/bestpractice, 2014, rev. 2015) to aid in the development and maintenance of OA journals.

Kramer believes that most "scientific" articles will be available in some form of green access in the foreseeable future. (Note: most of his focus was on so-called hard sciences, not all scholarly publishing.) He reported that only 3,500 journals out of 21,500 titles tracked in one citation database fell into the gold category (2017, p. 24). Those figures suggest it may be some time, and hope, before libraries have budgetary relief in the cost of providing access to scholarly journals.

Data Sets

Data sets are a relatively new entry into the field of resources that libraries can and do acquire on behalf of their users. Researchers in the sciences have been using and producing research data for years, and the trend is migrating to the social sciences and humanities. A number of options exist for locating data sets from the subscription-based OECD *iLibrary* (http://www.oecd-ilibrary.org/statistics) to the membership-based Inter-University Consortium for Political and Social Research (ICPSR, https://www.icpsr.umich.edu/icpsrweb/). In addition to subscription and membership-based options, commercial vendors are starting to venture into offering subsets of their databases to be used for text or data mining (such as the service offered by Elsevier, https://www.elsevier.com/about/our-business/policies/text-and-data-mining), normally at a price. As noted by Beth Sheehan and Karen Hogenboom (2017), in many cases, "researchers must either fund the purchase themselves or seek additional help, and academic libraries are receiving these requests and beginning to recognize data as a fundamental collection development need" (p. 49). Once the source of the data set is identified, the data itself can be made available in any number of ways—from a site download to a hard drive shipped to the purchasing library.

As is the case for other library resources, key to the management of data sets is having a well-thought-out and visible policy or process outlining how and when data sets will be considered for purchase and how those data sets will be accessible after purchase.

Policy examples include those from the Library of Congress (https://www.loc.gov/acq/devpol/datasets.pdf) and the University of California at Berkeley (http://guides.lib.berkeley.edu/data). The University of Illinois (http://www.library.illinois.edu/sc/purchase/) and the University of Maryland Libraries are two institutions that have developed formal processes to solicit suggestions for text or data sets (https://www.lib.umd.edu/rc/data-and-text-mining). Sheehan and Hogenboom (2017) give a detailed review of the process followed at the University of Illinois Urbana–Champaign to establish their Data Purchase Program (http://www.library.illinois.edu/sc/purchase/). At least in the case of UMD, placing a request for a data set (much like placing a request for any type of library material) does not guarantee it will be acquired. Technical and licensing requirements for data sets are often far more complex than for more traditional resources such as databases or journals and impact the ability of libraries to purchase data sets. Concerns range from how the data is to be made available to the user, to how the data can be used, and how it is to be stored in the long term. At least at this point, there is little commonality in how data sets are marketed and acquired, but it is likely this form of resource will increase in popularity in the future.

Points to Keep in Mind

- Both traditional and e-formats will likely coexist for some time to come. Each has something to offer to libraries and their users.

- Selecting e-resources, although employing many of the same criteria as traditional formats, is a more complex process. There are more factors to take into account, especially technological factors, and it is often a group process with participants inside and outside your library.

- Technological considerations are central to making the final decision with the library's technological infrastructure and the vendor's technological requirements carrying equal weight in the final decision.

- eBooks are likely to increase in their popularity. For libraries, cost considerations and licensing issues create substantial challenges.

- E-music has become a challenge for libraries due to producer concerns regarding who may have access to what and on what terms.

- Streaming video is likely to become a major source of video content for libraries.

- Institutional repositories, while currently used to increase access to and use of scholarly information, have long-term potential for all libraries as technologies become easier to implement and maintain.

- Open access may help reduce serial budget increases in time but not in the near term.

- Data sets, while useful to researchers, can bring with them a host of technical considerations before purchase.

References

Algenio, Emilie, and Alexia Thompson-Young. 2005. "Licensing E-Books: The Good, the Bad, and the Ugly." *Journal of Library Administration* 42, nos. 3/4: 113–28.

Authors Guild et al. v. Google, 05 Civ. 8136 (DC 2011). http://www.nysd.uscourts.gov/cases/show.php?db=special&id=115.

Behler, Anne, and Binky Lush. 2011. "Are You Ready for E-readers?" *Reference Librarian* 52, no. 1/2: 75–87.

Bertot, John Carlo, Charles McClure, and Joe Ryan. 2001. *Statistics and Performance Measures for Public Library Networked Services*. Chicago: American Library Association.

CILIP Update. 2011. "French Publishers Sue Google for $14 Billion." 10, no. 6: 10.

Connell, Tschera Harkness. 2011. "The Use of Institutional Repositories: The Ohio State University Experience." *College & Research Libraries* 72, no. 3: 253–74.

Cottrell, Terrance Luther, and Brigitte Bell. 2014. "Expensing E-Books: How Much Should Patron Habit Influence Collection Development?" *Bottom Line* 27, no. 4: 142–46.

Exline, Eleta. 2016. "Extending the Institutional Repository to Include Undergraduate Research." *College & Undergraduate Libraries* 23, no. 1: 16–27.

Farrelly, Deg. 2008. "Use-Determined Streaming Video Acquisition: The Arizona Model for FMG on Demand." *College & University Media Review* 14, no. 1: 65–78.

Farrelly, Deg. 2016. "Digital Video—Merrily, Merrily, Merrily, Merrily Wading into the Stream." *Computers in Libraries* 38, no. 9: 4–8.

Furlough, Mike. 2009. "What We Talk About When We Talk About Repositories." *Reference & User Services Quarterly* 49, no. 1: 18–32.

Grissom, Andrew R., Steven A. Knowlton, and Rachel Elizabeth Scott. 2017. "Notes on Operations: Perpetual Access Information in Serials Holding Records." *Library Resources & Technical Services* 61, no. 1: 57–62.

Hoek, D. J. 2009. "The Download Dilemma." *American Libraries* 40, no. 8/9: 54–57.

Holden, Jesse. 2010. *Acquisitions in the New Information Universe*. New York: Neal-Schuman.

Howard, Jennifer. 2017. "What Happened to Google's Effort to Scan Millions of University Library Books?" *EdSurge*. August 10, 2017. https://www.edsurge .com/news/2017-08-10-what-happened-to-google-s-effort-to-scan-millions-of -university-library-books.

Jones, Elisabeth. 2017. "The Public Library Movement, the Digital Library Movement, and the Large-Scale Digitization Initiative: Assumptions, Intentions, and the Role of the Public." *Information & Culture* 52, no. 2: 229–63.

Kelley, Michael, and Bob Warburton. 2011. "British Library, Google Plan Digitization Project." *Library Journal* 136, no. 12: 14.

Kovacs, Diane K. 2007. *The Kovacs Guide to Electronic Library Collection Development*. 2nd ed. New York: Neal-Schumann.

Kramer, David. 2017. "Steady, Strong Growth is Expected for Open Access Journals." *Physics Today* 70, no. 5: 24–28.

Lynch, Clifford. 2003. "Institutional Repositories: Essential Information for Scholarship in the Digital Age." *ARL Monthly Report*. No. 226. Washington, D.C. Association of Research Libraries.

Morgan, Kendra, and Merrilee Proffitt. 2017. *Advancing the National Digital Platform: The State of Digitization in US Public and State Libraries*. Dublin, OH: OCLC. http://www.oclc.org/research/publications/2017/oclcresearch -advancing-national-digital-platform.html.

Opderbeck, David W. 2016. "Implications of the Google Books Project Settlement for the Global Library Community." *International Information & Library Review* 48, no. 3: 190–95.

Pritchard, Sarah. 2008. "Deconstructing the Library: Reconceptualizing Collections, Space, and Services." *Journal of Library Administration* 48, no. 2: 219–33.

Rieh, Soo Young, and Kevin Smith. 2009. "Institutional Repositories: The Great Debate." *Bulletin of the American Society for Information Science and Technology* 35, no. 4: 12–16.

Sheehan, Beth, and Karen Hogenboom. 2017. "Assessing a Patron-Driven, Library-Funded Data Purchase Program." *Journal of Academic Librarianship* 43, no. 1: 49–56.

Somers, James. 2017. "Torching the Modern-Day Library of Alexandria." *The Atlantic*. April 20, 2017. https://www.theatlantic.com/technology/archive/2017 /04/the-tragedy-of-google-books/523320/.

Stemper, Jim, and Susan Barribeau. 2006. "Perpetual Access to Electronic Journals: A Survey of One Academic Library's Licenses." *Library Resources & Technical Services* 50, no. 2: 91–109.

Terry, Jenni. 2011. "Net Neutrality." *College & Research Libraries News* 72, no. 2: 108, 112.

Whittaker, Martha. 2008. "The Challenge of Acquisitions in the Digital Age." *portal: Libraries and the Academy* 8, no. 4: 439–45.

Zager, Daniel. 2007. "Essential Partners in Collection Development: Vendors and Music Librarians." *Notes* 63, no. 3: 565–75.

14
Preservation Issues

Libraries are in an unprecedented period of change. The predominant publishing model is moving from print to digital. Libraries seek to strike the right balance between providing information that today's researcher needs just in time and preserving materials in print for tomorrow's researcher just in case.
—Margaret K. Maes and
Tracy L. Thompson-Przylucki, 2012

To put the idea as fair and clearly as we can, we do not want any living beings in our collections (objects).
—Bogdan Filip Zerek, 2014

We function in a physical world, and all library collections rely, to some degree and in a variety of specific manners, on physical properties interacting with and reacting to the environment.
—Francisca Goldsmith, 2015

Preservation in the 21st century must be proactive, visionary, and cooperative. If it is not, vast amounts of cultural heritage are in danger of vanishing.
—Brian J. Baird, 2017

One of the most unnerving things about digital preservation is the requirement on the part of the information professional to see into the future, not only in terms of the technologies needed to maintain and provide access to a resource but also in terms of the actual institution holding the digital objects, its mission, and primary stakeholders, such as users.
—Edward M. Corrado and
Heather Moulaison Sandy, 2017

As we have seen throughout this text, developing and maintaining library collections takes a great deal of time and effort, as well as money. Most individuals forget that the cost of an item in a library collection does not only include the price tag of the item itself, but also includes any recurring licensing or subscription fees, equipment required for use, shelving, processing, and a host of other "hidden" costs. Those costs generally equal or exceed the item's initial purchase price. Achieving the maximum return on those investments over time is an essential part of the library's stewardship responsibility. This long-term stewardship is the focus of this chapter.

Preserving and conserving resources is an essential element in achieving long-term usage and value for monies spent. Some of the components of preservation and conservation are active, while others are passive. Many of the passive (prospective) elements are a matter of thinking and planning for possible eventualities. With luck, those plans never require implementation.

Successfully accomplishing long-term use and value of collections requires total staff involvement, not just by CM personnel. Certainly the CM officers will play a lead role in the process as well as carrying out some of the requisite activities. However, some of the activities that allow for the long-term success in this area are the responsibility of others. Preservation is an area where success is dependent upon true teamwork on the part of the entire staff. Depending on the size of the library, conservation is usually handled by one or two of the staff and/or by outside specialists.

People often use the terms preservation and conservation interchangeably. Doing so causes no great misunderstanding; however, the terms do have very different meanings in the world of archives, libraries, and museums. We follow the definitions of the terms developed by the Society of American Archivists (SAA). SAA's first two definitions of *preservation* are:

> 1. The professional discipline of protecting materials by minimizing chemical and physical deterioration and damage to minimize the loss of information and to extend the life of cultural property.
> 2. The act of keeping from harm, injury, decay, or destruction, especially through noninvasive treatment. (https://www2.archivists.org/glossary/terms/p/preservation)

The Society's definition of *conservation* is:

> The repair or stabilization of materials through chemical or physical treatment to ensure that they survive in their original form as long as possible. (https://www2.archivists.org/glossary/terms/c/conservation)

Michèle Cloonan offers an explanation to further differentiate between the two concepts, noting: "Although preservation and conservation have considerable overlap, if we were to distinguish between them. . . . Preservation is global; conservation is individual" (2011, p. 221). This chapter primarily focuses on preservation rather than conservation. That is, the maintaining of collections for as long as possible in their original state.

Libraries and Cultural Patrimony

Every culture creates its own artifacts. Throughout time, archives, libraries, and museums have come to be the primary guardians of society's heritage. Each institution has a role to play in attempting to ensure that knowledge, beliefs, values, etc. are preserved. Given the importance of the cultural record, efforts to secure the longevity of artifacts of cultural history are wide-ranging. To complement the United Nations' *2030 Agenda for Sustainable Development* (2015, https://sustainabledevelopment.un.org /post2015/transformingourworld), the International Federation of Library Associations and Institutions issued a statement in 2017 entitled *Libraries Safeguarding Cultural Heritage* (https://www.ifla.org/node/11387). The statement notes in part that "libraries are key partners for any effort to ensure preservation and access to our cultural heritage for future generations" (p. 1), and promotes preservation of all forms of cultural heritage, including those in a digital format, in public, special, and academic libraries. The American Library Association (ALA) also supports the concept of preservation by including it among its *Core Values of Librarianship* (ALA, 2004) and through its *Preservation Policy* (ALA, 2008). However, as advocated by Rebecka Sheffield, the concept of preservation may be broadened:

> By extending the ALA's *Core Value of Preservation* to include a duty to steward unexplored history, information professionals can leverage the collaborative zeitgeist surrounding digital preservation. We can begin to think about how to support other Core Values, including Social Responsibility and Diversity, with our collections and through the stewardship of unexplored history that remains outside of our custody. (2016, p. 582)

Most individuals, if they ever think about the matter, assume that once a library, archive, or museum acquires an item that it will be there forever. However, given the sheer volume of cultural artifacts created year upon year, professionals in these fields know that this is not the case for all items. In chapter 9, we covered the concept of deselection (withdrawing items from the collection). Museums use the term deaccession for their withdrawal or transfer process. Some archives have as part of their responsibilities housing the operational documents/records of its parent organization. Many of those records are only retained for a specified time (retention schedule is the term archivists/record managers use for the process), after which the material is usually destroyed. Clearly not every item has long-term value for cultural heritage purposes.

It is also reasonably clear to those in the information field (if not the general public) that some person or group of persons makes decisions regarding

---

Check This Out

While it is true not all things can be preserved, some items in cultural history are so unique to their times that calls are made precisely for their preservation. Modern-day "fake news" is one such construct. Although the present iteration of fake news has its roots back in yellow journalism of the early 1900s, its ephemeral nature via the Internet brings with it significant preservation challenges and opportunities. The October 2017 issue of *Preservation, Digital Technology & Culture* (46, no. 3) is devoted to a series of essays on the topic, including "Born-Digital News Preservation in Perspective" by Clifford Lynch (pp. 94–98) and "A Preservationist's Guide to #100hardtruths-#fakenews: One Fake News Preserve" by Alexandra Juhasz (pp. 103–108). The issue is well worth the read.

Check This Out

In *Preserving Our Heritage: Perspectives from Antiquity to the Digital Age* (Chicago: Neal-Schuman, 2015), editor Michèle Cloonan provides the context of preservation activities in libraries, museums, and archives through reprints of over 80 essays. Topics covered include time-based media, ethics, preservation policy, and sustainability. The work also includes a preservation timeline of activities from 750 BCE to late 2013. It is well worth a look.

---

what or what not to preserve. Preserving an item is no small decision as there is a daily cost, if very small in size, associated with its retention. It is a little like the story of the foolish businessman who agrees to hire a person for a penny for the first day's work and then to double that amount each succeeding work day. The first week's cost is still only a few cents; however, the amount becomes overwhelming a few weeks later. The cost of preserving some items may far outweigh any cultural heritage benefit or value. Many items retained are not actually assessed, but simply occupy space until a space problem or other issues force a thoughtful consideration. Information professionals play a significant role in transmitting cultural heritage, a role many do not think about as they carry on their daily work duties. Michèle Cloonan once noted (2007), "It is clear that preservation decisions may be multifaceted. In selecting items to preserve, the curator must be cognizant of the sensitivities that may ensue and the other issues they may face" (p. 141). She went on to pragmatically observe, "We can preserve some things some of the time, but not everything all of the time" (2007, p. 145).

Preserving the Investment in the Collection

Large research libraries, archives, or museums are not the only parties involved when it comes to preserving the collection investment. Even the smallest school library media center must get the "maximum mileage" out of the items it acquires. Thus, the first few sections of what follows has relevance for all libraries, regardless of their size or type.

There is a small percentage of materials that have a short useful (shelf) life, such as current magazines or newspapers. However, the vast majority of library acquisitions have a substantial, if not indefinite, expected shelf life. To realize a long-term shelf life, the staff must take steps to preserve the material.

There are several aspects to preserving a collection. Some are relatively simple to carry out such as proper handling and storage of materials, environmental control (temperature and humidity), security (to protect against theft and mutilation), disaster preparedness planning, basic conservation (binding and repair), and insurance. Most of these issues are broad concerns, and detailed discussion of them is beyond the scope of this book; however, we do briefly touch on each topic. All these factors work together to prolong the useful life of the materials in the collection. Even insurance fulfills this function, because claims payments will help the library replace damaged items.

Part of preserving the investment is taking the time to create an organized plan to do so. The Northeast Document Conservation Center (NEDCC) outlined a five-step method for doing so:

Check This Out

The Association for Library Collections and Technical Services (ALCTS) division of ALA promotes "Preservation Week" (http://www.ala.org/alcts/preservationweek) annually in order to bring attention to the needs for collection preservation. The Preservation Week site includes links to free preservation webinars, and resources for both libraries (including quick preservation tips) and patrons. Preservation specialist Donia Conn also has a monthly column on the site called "Dear Donia" that is also worth consulting (http://www.ala.org/alcts/preservationweek/advice).

---

1. Assessing Needs
2. Setting Preservation Priorities
3. The Preservation Planning Team
4. Writing a Preservation Plan
5. Maintaining the Preservation Plan (https://www.nedcc.org/preser vation101/session-1/1preparing-a-preservation-plan)

Some of these steps should seem familiar if you recall our discussion of collection development policies in chapter 4, particularly assessing needs and setting priorities. Also noteworthy is the concept of maintaining a plan once it is developed. Just as we noted a collection policy should not be written and set aside unmonitored, a preservation plan must also be periodically revised and updated. Admittedly, many libraries do not have a conservator or preservation expert on staff to consult when developing a preservation plan. However, there are resources available to consult such as the online Preservation Self-Assessment Program or PSAP (https://psap.library.illinois .edu/about) maintained by the University of Illinois at Urbana–Champaign. In addition, the NEDCC website includes step-by-step guidance for creating such a plan.

It should not be surprising to note that most media requires special preservation attention. This is normally done through a reformatting process, which we will discuss in the digital preservation section of this chapter.

Check This Out

The NEDCC is a nonprofit organization founded in 1973 as an independent conservation laboratory focusing on the conservation and preservation of paper- and film-based collections. Some of the many resources available from NEDCC include:

- *dPlan™*—an online tool for creating and maintaining disaster plans: https:// www.nedcc.org/free-resources/dplan-the-online-disaster-planning-tool

- *COSTEP*—a blueprint for preparing for area-wide disasters in coordination with local first responders: https://www.nedcc.org/free-resources/costep

- *Preservation 101*—a free online course on preservation basics: https://www .nedcc.org/free-resources/preservation-101.

Proper Handling

Some people may think that a library's obsession with keeping materials upright on shelves is simply an extension of the stereotypical image some hold of librarians, along with their ubiquitous use of sensible shoes and reading glasses. However, if people understood that some of these so-called "fussy" or "unnecessary" practices, such as keeping volumes upright on the shelf, are part of an effort to maximize usage of materials acquired with their money, the image might change a little. Storage and handling are the two fundamental steps in preserving a collection. Neither step requires extra expenditures on the part of the library, but do require the participation of all staff. Libraries purchase storage units from time to time; some thought is necessary regarding what the most appropriate type of storage unit is available for the particular format. (This does not necessarily translate into the most expensive unit.)

Too narrow and/or shallow a shelf (particularly for oversized/folio items) will result in items being knocked off and damaged, or worse—falling off and injuring someone. Filling shelves or drawers too tightly is a poor practice. Equally harmful is allowing the material to fall over on the shelf (because proper supports are lacking) or slide around in a drawer, because either practice will lead to damage in time. Buying adjustable shelving units provides the library a measure of flexibility.

Anyone with some experience in shelving books (except a conservation specialist) probably has found a way to squeeze "just one more book" onto a shelf when good practice calls for shifting the material to provide proper space. This often happens when shelvers are under pressure to finish shelving a book truck within a certain time period. Having sound performance standards is proper management; however, libraries must be certain that the reshelving standard includes time for shifting materials. Failure to do so leads to cracked book spines, as well as torn headbands resulting from users/staff attempting to pull an item from a tightly packed shelf. One study conducted at the University of Illinois at Urbana–Champaign (Teper and Atkins, 2003) found that 16 percent of the collection was damaged due to "mishanding, poor stewardship and overcrowding" (p. 220), showing that such poor housekeeping practices can and do have real results. Books should be vertical or horizontal on the shelf, not leaning this way and that. Fore-edge shelving should be avoided because it places undue strain on the binding (bindings are designed for horizontal or vertical storage). Proper supports and bookends help to keep materials in good order.

Check This Out

Not all institutions have opted to shelve materials by Dewey or LC call numbers. The New York Public Library (NYPL), for example, has opted to shelve materials in its flagship Manhattan branch by size, relying on a barcode affixed to each shelved item that contains coordinates as to its location, including its room, aisle, shelf, and tray. Anne Quito describes this system in her Weblog entry "The New York Public Library Has Adopted a Very Unusual Sorting System" (October 13, 2016; https://qz.com/802744 /the-legendary-new-york-public-library-shelves-books-in-its-underground-stacks-by -size-not-subject/).

The system works for NYPL because the stacks are not open to the public, and is not an option for most libraries. However, the article is still worth the read.

Part of CM's responsibility is to assure the staff understands the reason for housekeeping practices that appear arcane. Efforts to train the users in public and academic libraries are not likely to have much payoff when considering the time and effort required. However, such efforts are effective in a school library setting.

Environmental Control

Any discussion of environmental control in libraries must include not only the obvious factors (temperature and humidity), but other equally important factors such as light (both visible and ultraviolet radiation), mold, and insects. Each of these factors are important considerations in the health and well-being of library collections. Of these elements, climate control (temperature and humidity) is likely the most obvious, but can be a challenge for most libraries to realize. Few libraries are able to follow the example of the Newberry Library in Chicago, where 10 stories of stacks are double-shelled, windowless, and monitored by a computerized environmental system. Something much less complex will still help extend the useful life of most materials. The major concerns for environmental control are humidity, temperature, and light. Architects and librarians attempt to take these issues into account when planning a new library building. This is often easier said than done, because the ideal environmental conditions for humans and those for preserving materials don't match. For example, requirements for the book stacks for the Newberry Library storage facility calls for a temperature range of 60°F–67°F (https://www.newberry.org/conservation-resources).

Few people are happy engaging in sedentary work all day in a room with a 60-degree temperature. Most library designs place human comfort ahead of material preservation. The only time designers can effectively meet both sets of requirements is in situations like the Newberry, where the stacks are closed to the public and even employees are in the stacks for only short periods. Still, this arrangement does not answer all concerns about the environment for preserving materials. There also are differences in the ideal conditions for preserving various types of materials. Thus, building design characteristics are almost always a compromise with the people factor carrying the most weight.

Parent institutional energy conservation requirements also lead to cooler winter temperatures and warmer summer temperatures. Cooler winter temperatures are better for materials, but normally the temperature is still well above 65 degrees. The greatest damage occurs in summer, when reducing air conditioning costs becomes an institutional priority. (A related problem is that changes in air temperature affect relative humidity.) One way to reduce air conditioning costs is to turn off the system when the library is closed, but overnight shutdowns are damaging to materials. When the system is off for some time, such as the weekend, the temperature can rise dramatically. When the air conditioning is turned back on, the temperature falls fairly quickly. This roller coaster of temperature and humidity swings

---

Check This Out

For a detailed history of the construction of the Newberry storage facility and its environmental controls, see "The Ideal Preservation Building" by Bonnie Jo Cullison (*American Libraries,* 1984, 15, no. 10: 703).

is more damaging to materials than storing them at a steady, somewhat higher temperature. Temperature cycling is damaging (it ages paper prematurely), but so are high temperatures. For every rise of 10°C, book paper deteriorates twice as fast, with damage occurring for some at-risk materials at a rise of only 5°C (Henderson, 2013, p. 4). With rapid fluctuations in temperature, the primary problem is the humidity level, which causes damage to the materials.

Why is a swing in temperature and humidity damaging to collections? Almost every item in the collection is a composite of materials. Hard-bound volumes are the most complex in their composition. Certainly the bulk of material is paper of more or less standard weight; however, even that is inconsistent across a collection. For example, art books with high-quality color illustrations will have a coated paper for the illustrations while the text, more often than not, is on an uncoated paper. The different papers will expand and contract at different rates as the temperature and humidity varies, which stresses the volume. The reality is there is more than a difference in paper quality involved in a typical volume. Volumes also contain one or more types of cardboard in the binding, a cloth backing for the binding, thread used to sew the binding, and various adhesives. Each of these materials reacts to temperature and humidity at different rates. Media formats also consist of several types of material with different expansion and contraction rates. The amount of stress from one cycle of temperature and humidity fluctuation is very small. However, this issue is similar to the low daily cost of an item's long-term retention; over time the small increments add up to very real problems. For this reason, consistently monitoring the environment is an important step in a preservation program. Henderson (2013) suggested the following steps be followed in establishing an environmental monitoring program:

1. Establish targets for environmental conditions

2. Purchase and install equipment

3. Collect data

4. Analyze, present and act on results

5. Review (p. 6)

Henderson advises that more data is not necessarily better, but instead data should be collected in such a way that staff will know how to use it and be able to interpret it. Once the review is complete, the cycle begins again. A number of services and resources exist for such monitoring, including the eClimateNotebook® web-tool developed by the Image Permanence Institute (https://www.eclimatenotebook.com/). In some cases, environmental monitoring is provided as part of a state initiative, such as that provided by the Massachusetts Libraries Board of Library Commissioners (https://mblc.state.ma.us/programs-and-support/preservation/index.php); however, LYRASIS also has a loan service for environmental monitoring equipment for libraries that may not be able to afford their own equipment (https://www.lyrasis.org/services/Pages/Preservation-Loan-Services.aspx).

The NEDCC recommends a temperature of 70°F in collections with a 50 percent relative humidity (RH), which matches the ideal range for storage of microforms (NEDCC, 2017). In the past, different set points for temperature and RH for different types of media (such as photographs, video, etc.) were advocated. However, over time, these set points were reevaluated given the relative impossibility of achieving different set points in one system. As such, a compromise of a 45 percent RH for a mixed collection is considered acceptable (Canadian Council of Archives, 2003, pp. 13–15).

Recalling basic chemistry, we know that increasing the temperature also increases chemical activity. Roughly, chemical reactions double with each 10°C increase in temperature. Freezing books would be the best way to preserve them; however, it is not likely that readers would be willing to sit about in earmuffs, overcoats, and mittens. Libraries are fortunate to achieve a controlled temperature below 70°F in areas where people work for extended periods. One reason for wanting the lower temperatures is to slow down the chemical decomposition of wood pulp paper, which many books and journals contain. However, lower temperatures only slow the process; they do not stop it.

Wood pulp paper is not the only material that can benefit from a climate-controlled environment. A chemical process called vinegar syndrome can be slowed but not stopped at lower temperatures. Vinegar syndrome is a form of decay that occurs in film collections (including microformats) when acetate based film degrades. Acetate film was used extensively throughout the 1920s to the 1970s, and is likely to be found in the microform collections of academic and larger public and libraries. Thankfully, not all film is a candidate for vinegar syndrome, as film produced since the 1970s uses a polyester base, which is not susceptible (Mills, 2016, p. 40). A sign that the reaction is occurring is the presence of a tell-tale vinegar odor emitting from the affected film canister or microfilm drawer. Once the reaction process begins in one roll of film, the syndrome can spread from an affected film to adjacent film. Testing for vinegar syndrome is possible through the use of specially treated paper that changes color to reflect the amount of damage; however, once vinegar syndrome takes hold, it cannot be reversed. Cold storage, digitization, or withdrawal of the affected film reels are options for materials with vinegar syndrome.

Light, both natural and artificial, negatively influences preservation in two ways. First, it contributes to the heat buildup in a building. Naturally, designers take this into account when specifying the building's heating, ventilating, and air conditioning system. Fluorescent lighting is not a major heat contributor, but in older libraries where incandescent fixtures may still

Check These Out

Sources of additional information on film preservation and vinegar syndrome include:

Preservation Basics: Vinegar Syndrome—National Film Preservation Foundation—https://www.filmpreservation.org/preservation-basics/vinegar-syndrome.

Acetate Film Base Deterioration: The Vinegar Syndrome—Image Permanence Institute—https://www.imagepermanenceinstitute.org/resources/newsletter-archive/v12/vinegar-syndrome.

In addition, John Louis Bigourdan of the Image Permanence Institute has written extensively on the topic of film stability and storage issues. A bibliography of his work is available on the IPI website: https://www.imagepermanenceinstitute.org/resources/bibliography.

exist, the heat generated by the fixtures can be a problem. If the light fixtures are close to materials (i.e., in exhibit cases), there can be significant temperature differentials from the bottom to the top shelf in a storage unit. Sunlight can generate mini-climates, hotter near windows than the rest of the space. Ideally, a windowless library would eliminate the sunlight problem. However, most libraries have designs featuring numerous windows to provide natural lighting (thus reducing electric costs) and to satisfy users' desire to see outside. The cost of these designs has been high in terms of money spent after a few years to reduce the sunlight problem and to repair damaged materials. One low-cost solution to the sunlight problem is installation of blinds in collection areas near windows—however, to be effective, the blinds must be used.

A second concern with light is ultraviolet radiation, a result of sunlight, fluorescent, and tungsten lights. Ultraviolet light is the most damaging form of light because it quickly causes materials to fade, turn yellow, and become brittle. Windows and fluorescent light fixtures should have ultraviolet screens or filters built in or installed. Tungsten lighting has the lowest levels of ultraviolet radiation, but even these lights should have filters. The longer one exposes materials to unfiltered light, the more quickly damage occurs. As noted by Donia Conn (2012), all of these factors contribute to reduced readability and impact access to information, with the cumulative effects being irreversible. Thus, "even if you take a faded photograph down and store it in the dark, it will not return to its original appearance and will continue to fade when taken out again" (Conn, 2012, p. 1). Nonprint materials are even more sensitive and they require greater protective measures than do print materials.

Air filters that reduce the gases in the air inside the library are useful, if expensive. Urban activities pump a variety of harmful gases into the air every day. Some enter the building as people come and go, while others are generated by the furnishings, materials, chemicals, and even photocopiers used within buildings. Few buildings have airlocks and ventilating systems that remove all harmful gases. Whenever it is economical, the ventilation system should remove the most harmful substances. Sulfur dioxide is a major air pollutant and a concern for preservation programs, because it combines with water vapor to form sulfuric acid. Hydrogen sulfide, another common pollutant, also forms an acid that is harmful to both organic and inorganic materials. In addition to gases, air filters can also reduce the amount of solid particles in the building's air. Solid particles act as abrasives, contributing to materials wearing out. Dusty, gritty shelves wear away the edges of bindings—and, all too often, dusting books and their shelves is not in anyone's job description (or included as part of the regular custodial/maintenance contract).

An additional disadvantage of dust and dirt is that these particles include mold spores, which can cause problems if the air conditioning fails in warm, humid weather. It is important to note that different types of materials react differently to their environment, and some materials will be more susceptible to mold than others. It is next to impossible to avoid mold on collections, as Preston Livingston (2015) observed: "Mold spores are always present. When conditions become favorable, mold will grow" (p. 60). Mold is classified as either active (still growing) if the temperature and RH conditions are not stable, or inactive if the environment is more stable. However, inactive mold can and will become active should the temperature or RH conditions change, with mold growth starting to occur within 48–72 hours of such a change in conditions. Mold can be a serious problem for paper-based

From the Authors' Experience

Saponaro worked at a library that had such a large outbreak of mold one year triggered by high temperature variations and HVAC (heating, ventilating, air conditioning) system inefficiencies that an entire floor had to be closed to the public for an entire semester to address the situation (https://www.lib.umd.edu/news/2013/08/mck -5-floor-closed). Materials were paged for patrons during the time the floor was closed for repairs to the system and maintenance. Titles on the affected floor were individually inspected and those with excessive damage were withdrawn from the collection. Due to the vigilance and monitoring of the Preservation Department, such large-scale outbreaks have not occurred since that time.

collections and people as many molds can cause serious (even debilitating) allergy or respiratory problems for some people. However, as Livingston also relates, three main factors for reducing the impact of mold on collections are monitoring of humidity and temperature; maintaining the heating, ventilation, and air-conditioning (HVAC) system; and good housekeeping by cleaning. Cleaning methods can include dusting or vacuuming titles, although vacuuming with a HEPA filter is generally the preferred method.

Last but certainly not least, insects contribute to the destruction of books and other items in the collection. Silverfish enjoy nothing more than a feast of wood pulp paper, flour paste, and glue. Cockroaches seem to eat anything, but have a particular taste for book glue. Termites prefer wood, but wood pulp paper is a good second choice. Larder beetle larvae (bookworms), though lacking intellectual curiosity, can devour *War and Peace* in a short time. Bedbugs, although not always associated with libraries, have also become an issue to contend with of late, given the prevalence of travel by library patrons. As noted by Marta Murvosh (2013), "Although libraries are at lower risk of bed bug infestation compared with hotels, hospitals, and other public buildings where people sleep . . . if bed bugs get established, they can be difficult to eradicate" (p. 430). Finally, book lice enjoy the starch and gelatin sizing on paper. Other, less destructive insects can infest collections in the temperate zones; in a tropical setting, the numbers and varieties increase dramatically.

Control of insects presents a few challenges, because pesticides create pollution problems. Naturally, the best control is to keep the insects out. One way to control insects, especially cockroaches, is to keep food and drink out of the library. A second step is to keep the temperature and humidity as low as possible, because insects multiply faster and are more active at higher temperature and humidity levels. If the library faces a significant insect infestation, it is better to call on a commercial service rather than attempt to handle the problem with library staff.

What are the signs of insect infestation? Most of the insects that cause damage prefer the dark and to stay out of sight. When one sees them, it is

Check This Out

Bogdan Filip Zerek, author of one of the opening quotes for this chapter, devotes a chapter of his work *Protection of Library Collections: A Practical Guide to Microbiological Controls* (Oxford, UK: Chandos Publishing, 2014) to "Methods of Disinfection" (pp. 185–204).

> ## Check These Out
>
> Sarah Kittrell from Witchita Public Library (whose central branch closed for several days in 2012 due to an infestation; see http://www.kansas.com/news/article1096620 .html) provided a detailed overview of quarantine procedures and other suggested techniques for dealing with bedbugs in her Public Library Association (PLA) webinar "Don't Let the Bed Bugs Bite: Prevention and Treatment of Bed Bugs in Public Libraries" that is available for a small fee on demand (http://www.ala.org/pla/education/onlinelearning /webinars/ondemand/bedbugs). Resources from the webinar are also available on the PLA website: http://www.ala.org/pla/sites/ala.org.pla/files/content/onlinelearning /webinars/archive/PLA_Kittrell_Dont-let-the-bed-bugs-bite_Final.pdf.
>
> A thorough article on identifying, treating, and preventing infestations of bedbugs is "Beating Bed Bugs" by Nancy Richey, Sue Lynn McDaniel, and Elisabeth Knight (*Kentucky Libraries*, 2015, 79, no. 4: 11–14). As bedbug infestations have been found in public, special, and academic libraries, it is worth the read regardless of the library setting.

a signal that the population may be so large that there is nowhere to hide. Obviously, if one finds remains of insects on shelves, windowsills, or the floor, it is a sign of potential trouble. Unusual dust, "sawdust," or colored powder on bookshelves is likely to be "frass" (insect droppings), and is a clear indication of a problem. Other ways pests can enter the collection are through items returned by patrons. In some cases, libraries are trying to prevent such unwanted "returns" with their materials through public relations campaigns (for example, see: https://www.denverlibrary.org/returning-materials -have-come-contact-bed-bugs-or-other-pests). One resource to assist in identifying potential insect infestations is MuseumPests (http://museumpests .net/). This site is maintained by the Integrated Pest Management Working Group—a group of collection managers, conservators, entomologists, and others with an interest in pest management in museums and other collections. The site provides a number of resources (including fact sheets and an image library) as well as suggestions for addressing an active infestation.

Security

In addition to the amount spent on digital or other online resources, libraries spend millions each year on their physical collections. Given the investment, we include a discussion of the physical security of the collection in our discussion of preservation because some of the issues are conservation issues—for example, those arising from mutilation.

A full-scale library security program involves several elements. Broadly, the program's goals are to ensure the well-being of people and to protect the collections and equipment from damage or theft. What follows emphasizes the collections, with only passing mention of the people and equipment issues; topics covered include theft, mutilation, and disaster preparedness. For a fuller discussion of security programs, see chapter 16 of Evans, Saponaro, Christie, and Sinwell's *Library Programs and Services: The Fundamentals* (8th ed., 2015).

We tell people, only half in jest, that if a library wishes to identify its true core collection, all it has to do is prepare a list of all the lost and missing books and mutilated journal titles. Normally, these are the items that, for one reason or another, are (or were) under pressure from users, including high-use materials.

Every library loses books and other materials each year to individuals who, if caught by the security system, say they forgot to check the material out. Journals and other noncirculating materials are subject to some degree of mutilation. Each incident of theft and mutilation means some small financial loss for the library, if nothing more than the cost of the material and the labor expended making the item ready to circulate. Other costs include staff time in searching for the item, deciding how or whether to replace it, and acquisitions processing. Though a single incident seldom represents a significant cost, the total annual cost may be surprising, even if one calculates only the amount paid for replacement materials. Many academic libraries spend more than $20,000 per year on replacement materials, and few of those replacements are for items too worn to remain in circulation. This rate of loss occurs despite a high-quality electronic security exit system and targeting every book and every issue of every journal that goes into the collection. Needless to say, time and money expended to prevent theft or replace materials is time and money not spent on expanding user resources. The problem of theft is not unique to academic libraries. Public and school libraries also experience theft. As noted by Odin Jurkowski (2017), "The open nature of the school library with classes streaming in and out all day long, students individually visiting, and the limited number of staff for assistance let alone supervision only makes the task of securing books more difficult" (p. 159).

There are several givens for an exit control/security program. First, there will be some level of loss no matter what the library does. Second, the systems help basically honest people stay honest. Various methods of circumventing library security systems exist (see Allen, 1991; Tolppanen, 2000; and Charles, 2017 for examples). In other cases, security systems have been disabled or removed entirely by libraries due to their perceived ineffectiveness (Harwell, 2014). Therefore, the library must decide how important the problem is and how much loss it can tolerate. The goal is to balance the cost of the security program against the losses. The less loss the library will accept, the higher the security costs, so finding the proper balance is important.

Most libraries employ some mix of people-based elements and electronic systems for security. Door guards or monitors who check every item taken from the library are the most effective and most costly option. This method works well only when the person doing the checking is not a peer of the people being checked. That is, using students to check fellow students, much less their teachers, does not work well. Retired individuals are very effective. They interact well with users but also do the job without favoring anyone. The major drawback to exit monitors, after the cost, is, when there are peaks and valleys in the exit flow, there can be long queues during the peaks.

Electronic exit control systems are common and often give a false sense of security. Every system has a weakness that the person who regularly "forgets" to check out books eventually discovers, and the professional thief knows. Also, some materials (for example, magnetic tape and videotape) cannot have the "target" deactivated without damaging the content, and some materials simply do not have a place for a target. Some systems are susceptible to electronic interference, such as frequencies generated by computers or even fluorescent light ballasts. Finally, the inventive thief can jam the operating frequency and no one on the staff will know the difference.

Check These Out

Travis McDade, Associate Professor and Curator of Rare Law Books at the University of Illinois Law Library, is an expert on theft of rare books. He has authored several interesting titles on the topic, including:

- *Torn from Their Bindings: A Story of Art, Science, and the Pillaging of American University Libraries* (Lawrence: University Press of Kansas, 2018)—recounts the story of Robert Kindred's theft of antique illustrations and maps from academic libraries in the 1980s and how he was caught.

- *Disappearing Ink: The Insider, the FBI, and the Looting of the Kenyon College Library* (New York: Diversion Books, 2015)—tells the story of how David Breithaupt was brought to justice after the theft of materials such as letters from Flannery O'Connor from the Kenyon College Library.

- *Thieves of Book Row: New York's Most Notorious Rare Book Ring and the Man Who Stopped It* (Oxford: Oxford University Press, 2013)—tells the story of materials stolen from the New York Public Library in the 1920s.

Mutilation or vandalism is another ongoing problem, which, during a year, can generate a surprisingly large loss for the library. There are few cost-effective options for handling this problem, although having copy or scanning services available will help. Monitors walking through the building will reduce many security problems, but will not stop mutilation. One study found that 61 percent of users who saw someone mutilating library materials would not report the activity (Pedersen-Summey, 1990, p. 123). One option that customers do not like, but that does stop the mutilation of journals, is to supply only microform back files of journals that are subject to high mutilation. This option does not safeguard the current issues, and it requires providing microform reader-printers, which are more expensive than microform readers. Another option is to keep current issues of titles prone to theft or mutilation in a staff-only area and make them available for in-house use only. This option requires staff time and effort in terms of retrieving and refiling the titles, but can be an alternative to theft or mutilation concerns. Web-based services are a partial answer to some of the problems, assuming the library can afford the digital back files. Some libraries, such as the University of Oregon Libraries, have made public statements regarding mutilation of library materials and what patrons can do to stop it (https://library.uoregon .edu/catdept/presbind/mutilation). While theft and mutilation are a part of doing business, how much they ultimately cost the library depends on the local situation. Those costs come at the expense of adding greater variety to the collections and, in the long run, they hurt the user.

Disaster Preparedness

While it is not always easy to plan for a worst-case scenario, devoting time and effort to disaster preparedness planning before the event occurs is vital for the protection of people, collections, and equipment. Planners must think in terms of both natural and man-made disasters. Earthquakes, hurricanes, tornadoes, heavy rains, and floods are the most common natural disasters for which one should plan. Plans should not exclude natural disasters that are not native to the region. For example, while the West Coast of the U.S. is more likely, given its seismic activity, to experience an earthquake, that did not stop a 5.9 magnitude earthquake centered in Mineral, Virginia, from rattling over 27,000 books off the shelves at the University of Maryland Libraries 100 miles away in August 2011 (https://www.lib.umd .edu/news/2011/earthquake). While terrorism and social unrest are extreme forms of man-made disasters impacting libraries, the most common man-made disaster is water damage. Something as simple as a clogged gutter, faulty air conditioning system, broken pipe, or blocked bathroom drain can cause a great deal of water damage to collections, if left unchecked. In the case of a fire, water may cause more damage than the flames.

The following are the basic steps to take in preparing a disaster plan:

1. Study the library for potential problems. Often, the institution's risk management officer (insurance) is more than willing to help in that assessment.

2. Meet with local fire and safety officers for the same purpose.

3. Establish a planning team to develop a plan. This team may become the disaster response team.

4. Establish procedures for handling each type of disaster and, if appropriate, form different teams to handle each situation.

5. Establish a telephone calling or texting tree, or other fast notification system, for each disaster. A *telephone tree* is a plan for who calls whom in what order. Individuals to be notified include the library director, head of collection management, directors of information technology services and public services, and individuals who are responsible for business services and communications efforts.

6. Develop a salvage priority recovery list for the collections. Most plans do not have more than three levels of priority: first priority is irreplaceable, historical collections or costly materials; second priority is materials that are expensive or difficult to replace or that may be highly used after the disaster (reference materials or core serials titles); and third priority is the rest of the collection. Some plans include a category of "hand-carry" one or two items from the immediate work area, if the disaster strikes during normal working hours. Establishing priorities can be a challenge for planners, because everyone has some vested interest in the subject areas with which they work. A set of floor plans can be annotated with these priority levels and included in the disaster planning and response manual.

7. Create a communications plan for notifying the public and the methods to be used for doing so (website, social media, conventional media, etc.).

8. Develop a list of recovery supplies the library will maintain onsite (for example, plastic sheeting and butcher paper).

9. Include a list of resources—people and companies—who may assist in the recovery work.

After the planners finish a disaster response plan, the library should make it available to all staff onsite, as well as off-site so that disaster team

---

Check This Out

In the midst of an emergency, there may not be time to locate and read through a multipage disaster recovery plan. In *Library as Safe Haven: Disaster Planning, Response, and Recovery* (Chicago: Neal-Schuman, 2014) Deborah D. Halsted, Shari Clifton, and Daniel T. Wilson advocate for development of a one-page Service Continuity Pocket Response Plan or SCPReP (pp. 49–58) as a complement to the existing plan. Elements of communication, service continuity, and rescue and recovery of collections are captured in the response plan, intended to be readily available at all times to key library staff.

---

members may access it easily via a staff website or intranet. Others who may want copies are the group within the parent organization that plans for disaster response efforts and the local fire station. Practicing some of the response efforts is critical to achieving a successful outcome when a problem does strike. Once a disaster has occurred and the situation has returned to normal, it is important to review the existing plan in light of the current experience for any needed revisions or enhancements, the goal of which is to consider "additional activities to make recovery faster and more efficient" (Kahn, 2016).

Locating water, gas, and electrical system shut-offs is a good starting point for training the disaster team. Next, the team should check fire extinguisher locations to determine whether the units are operational and are inspected regularly. Additionally, the fire marshal or fire department may be consulted to offer staff training on how to use an extinguisher. Floor plans should clearly identify locations of shut-offs and extinguishers.

Salvage operations require careful planning and adequate personnel and materials. It is a good idea to develop a list of potential volunteers, if the situation is too large for the staff to handle within a reasonable time. Keep in mind that the library can count on only about 72 hours of assistance from volunteers—that is, 72 hours from the time the first request for assistance goes out. Thus, there should be planning for what to do after 72 hours, if the disaster is major. As Anne Prestamo (2018) observed, "Asking staff to return to work . . . knowing that they have their own home situations to cope with, is a big ask. I can attest to the fact that this can create significant stress on the homefront" (p. 107). Prestamo speaks from experience, as she encountered the impact of Hurricane Irma on Florida International University and its library in September 2017. The building remained intact and sustained only minimal damage, with no loss of collections. Other Florida libraries

---

Check This Out

While most disaster plans consider large events (earthquakes, floods), smaller events can have just as large an effect and should not be ignored in the planning process. In "Prepared for Anything and Everything: Libraries, Archives and Unexpected Small Scale Disasters," Dana Ray Chandler discusses how to plan for smaller events ranging from nesting birds to noxious odors. It is chapter 11 in the 2016 *Handbook of Research on Disaster Management and Contingency Planning in Modern Libraries,* edited by Emy Nelson Decker and Jennifer A. Townes (Hershey, PA: IGI Global, 240–256), which is also worth a look overall.

were not so lucky, with the Daytona Beach Regional Library facility being closed for extensive repairs until May 2018 (Castro, 2018).

Water damage is a potentially destructive problem, as is the development of mold and mildew that can occur as a result. Mold can develop in as little as 48 hours, depending on the temperature. The threat of mold is not limited to print materials, as it will also occur on film-based materials such as microfilm, photographs, and motion picture film. What basic steps should one follow in a water emergency? The best way to handle large quantities of water-soaked paper is to freeze it and process the material as time and money allow. Planners should identify companies with large freezer facilities and discuss with them the possibility of using or renting their freezers in case of emergency. Getting wet materials to the freezing units is a problem: milk crates, open plastic boxes, or clothes baskets work well, because they allow water to drain. Plastic interlocking milk crates are ideal, because they are about the right size for a person to handle when three-fourths full of wet material.

Freezer or butcher paper is best for separating the materials. Never use newsprint, because it tends to stick to wet paper and the ink comes off. Finally, find some drying facilities. There are three primary methods of drying wet books: (1) freezing/freeze-drying, (2) vacuum drying, and (3) vacuum freeze-drying. Vacuum freeze-drying is the best way to handle wet items. Often, vacuum drying facilities are difficult to locate and can handle only a small volume of material at a time, so materials may be in the freezer for a long time while a small quantity is done whenever the source and funding permit. While methods of treating print-based materials are fairly well established, media materials present special challenges. Joe Iraci (2017) studied the effects of water on electronic storage media such as magnetic tapes (audio and video), optical disks (CDs, Blu-rays), and flash media. While he found that media immersed in clean tap water resisted damage well, not all media are well made and not all water damage occurs from tap water. He recommended recovery within a 48-hour period, with air-drying being the preferred method for media recovery (p. 71).

Two other steps are important when designing a disaster preparedness plan. One is to identify the nearest preservation specialist(s), if there is not one on-site. Most are willing to serve as a telephone resource, and often they will come to the scene. A second important step is to arrange for special purchasing power. Although some groups, organizations, and companies may be willing to assist free of charge, many will not, and the library may need to commit quickly to a specific expense. Having to wait even a few hours for approval may cause irreversible damage.

Although most disasters are minor—a few hundred water-damaged items—a large disaster is always possible. One of the largest fires in a library setting occurred at the Los Angeles Public Library (LAPL) in April 1986. For more than 10 years, there had been concern about the fire danger, but the hope that a new building would be constructed forestalled major

---

Something to Note

University of Maryland Libraries Preservation Head Carla Q. Montori notes that there are document and media recovery services that come to your loading dock with a tractor-trailer-sized mobile freeze-drying unit, such as Belfor (a national company)—https://www.belfor.com/en/us/recovery-services/document-restoration.

Check These Out

A variety of disaster-related online information is available at the Conservation OnLine (CoOL) "Disaster Preparedness and Response" web page: http://cool .conservation-us.org/bytopic/disasters/.

The Disaster Mitigation Planning Assistance website (http://resources.conser vation-us.org/disaster/) provides sample disaster plans as well as a search tool for sources of services and supplies. The site is a joint program of the Library of Congress, Center for Great Lakes Culture, and the California Preservation Program.

Another source of information is ALA's Library Disaster Preparedness & Response LibGuide that includes links to resources from ALA groups and divisions, as well as other relevant organizations (http://libguides.ala.org/disaster).

modifications in the existing building. Although 400,000 volumes or 20 percent of the collection was destroyed in the fire, none of the over 400 patrons and employees in the building at the time the fire broke out were injured. Thirty years later, LAPL holdings exceeded 2.5 million items (LAPL Blog, 2016). One can only speculate what the costs and problems might have been with no disaster preparedness plan.

Another water-related disaster occurred at the Burton Barr Central Library in Phoenix, Arizona, where a July 2017 storm caused an estimated $10 million in damage to the facility. Although only a portion of the collection (approximately 7,000 items from the 500,000-item collection) was destroyed, the incident forced the facility to close for 11 months (http://www .phoenixpubliclibrary.org/AboutUs/Press-Room/Pages/Burton-Barr-Central -Library-Restoration-Updates-Archive.aspx). The actual storm only damaged the roof of the building; however, the true impact of the storm occurred when a cloud of dust particles disturbed by the storm and roof damage triggered the fire sprinkler system. A later investigation revealed issues with the sprinkler system had existed as early as 2008, but had not been acted upon. A total of 11 library employees were disciplined in the incident, with actions ranging from demotions and suspensions to firings. Several city employees also received personnel actions as a result of their failure to report the issues with the sprinkler system. Insurance and library-reserve funds covered the cost of the repairs and remediation (White, 2018).

Library insurance may assist in the recovery after a major disaster such as the ones described above; however, as noted by Miriam Kahn, "very few if any institutions have the insurance to cover the cost of purchasing an entire collection" (2016). Like personal home fire or renters' insurance, there is almost always a deductible as well as issues of what the insurance actually will cover. Most standard policies do not include flood damage except at an extra cost, and other water damage (such as a break in a sprinkler system pipe) may be a topic of debate with the insurance company. Plus, the process takes time.

It is essential to have-to-face discussions, prior to purchasing insurance coverage, in order to have a clear understanding of what is and is not covered and on what basis payments are made. Discussions regarding the collection valuation can be interesting, especially when it comes to what to do about coverage for special collections and archives materials. If a Shakespeare folio is stolen or destroyed by fire, it is highly unlikely that the library could ever replace it, even if the library insured the folio for several million dollars. Risk managers and insurance agents rarely see the point of covering something that is irreplaceable.

Anyone who has dealt with homeowners' or renters' insurance representatives and policies can understand the complexities involved. The usual payment is based on replacement value, based on depreciated value from time of purchase to time of claim, which often is much less than the actual replacement cost. An interesting CM question is, "Does the collection valuation increase or decrease over time?" What does *replacement* mean? Will there be funds to process the material, or merely to acquire it? What damage is covered? For example, in 1989, 12 ranges of shelving containing 20,000 volumes collapsed at the Columbia University library annex. Many, if not most, of the volumes were brittle, so the fall was very damaging. However, the embrittlement was a preexisting condition. After some long negotiations, the insurer agreed to pay for volumes with damage to the cover or text block attachments, but not for volumes with broken pages. There were questions about serial runs as well; this was finally resolved with the insurer paying for the entire run of back files, if more than one-third of the run was damaged (Gertz, 1992, p. 2). A more recent example occurred as we were preparing this volume, when a leak caused by a hailstorm in February 2018 damaged over 250 rare books at the California State Library in Sacramento. The oldest title damaged dated from 1860 and had a "puddle of water flowing out" as it was recovered (Moffitt, 2018). Some items were being sent to the Statewide Museum Center's freezer as part of remediation efforts. The total cost of the restoration effort had yet to be determined, but can be expected to be a sizable amount.

For a good discussion about basic insurance topics in relation to libraries, see Capron Hannay Levine and Bryan M. Carson's (2012) "Legally

---

Check These Out

The following books are excellent resources for thinking about disaster management in general as well as in terms of collections:

Heritage Preservation. 2017. *Field Guide to Emergency Response: A Vital Tool for Cultural Institutions*. Washington, DC: Heritage Preservation.

A short, informative guide to disaster response, including working with responders and documenting damage. Online supplementary resources, including a quick assessment guide and video tutorials, are available at http://www.conservation-us.org/fieldguide.

Kahn, Miriam. 2012. *Disaster Response and Planning for Libraries,* 3rd ed. (Chicago: American Library Association).

Includes a useful series of checklists and sample forms addressing building surveys, software and data recovery, microforms recovery, and vital and permanent records.

Mallery, Mary, ed. 2015. *Technology Disaster Response and Recovery Planning: A LITA Guide* (Chicago: ALA TechSource).

Includes risk management and disaster recovery for digital collections.

Matthews, Graham, Gemma Knowles, and Yvonne Smith. 2016. *Disaster Management in Archives, Libraries and Museums* (London: Routledge).

Provides an overview of disaster management efforts in cultural heritage institutions in the UK and worldwide.

Speaking—Loss Prevention and Insurance." Having insurance is a sound practice, because almost every library at some time will have a disaster of some type and size, but do not expect it to make the collection "whole" again (to return it to its before-claim status), to use an insurance term. Having insurance is one more step in protecting the library's and institution's investment.

All of the above applies to all library types to a greater or lesser degree. Preservation starts with the purchase decision (which ought to include consideration of how well the material will stand up to the expected use) and should end with the question of what to do about worn or damaged materials and items identified in the weeding process.

Digital Preservation

While disaster preparedness and preservation are in and of themselves major concerns for libraries, digital preservation is becoming more and more of an issue. The Association for Library Collections and Technical Services (ALCTS) division of ALA prepared a series of definitions for digital preservation, with their simplest being that these activities "combine policies, strategies and actions that ensure access to digital content over time" (2009). Despite the brevity of that definition, digital preservation as a concept remains complicated due to a host of factors. Brian Baird, author of one of our opening quotations, noted:

> The challenge of digital preservation is immense and grows larger every year as more and more information is made available in various electronic forms. But it is not just a matter of volume; it is also a matter of ever-changing formats, improved delivery and storage systems, and the complexity of the information being presented. (2018, p. 1)

The factors Baird identified are challenging in and of themselves, without adding in additional considerations such as determining what materials should be selected for treatment, whether the chosen materials can be digitized given copyright or provenance issues, what method is chosen to digitize the materials, and how to ensure access to the digitized materials in the future. (We cover copyright issues in the next chapter.) Digital preservation also requires a shift in mindset for individuals responsible for collection development. Instead of evaluating what is available and making purchase recommendations, the decision point now becomes which materials should be preserved long-term in an electronic format.

Technology factors, standards, and collaborative efforts all play a role in digital preservation activities. The technology aspects of digital preservation can be divided into two categories—storage and access. How and where digital material is stored is a major factor. For example, information once stored on zip drives, tape drives, and floppy discs, once considered standard forms of storage, is now difficult if not impossible to access. Some readers may not know much, or even know of, some of these examples. That is our point. Digital storage devices change rapidly, as does the rest of technology. How long the stored data will last and remain error free long-term is unknown. Amanda Rinehart and her colleagues warn that "the act of digitally transforming analogs still remains confusing with the array of standards and formats for digital surrogates, while poor quality digitization prevents adequate long-term digital preservation" (2014, p. 29). They point to the accidental erasure of high-quality recordings of the Apollo 11 moon landing as an example of unintentional data loss. Although digitized recordings remain of this key scientific accomplishment, they are of low quality that prevents additional analysis. For this reason we concur with Elizabeth Leggett, who urged libraries to retain the original copies of materials digitized wherever possible. She observed, "Tangible items have a much greater life span than digital ones. Not only is their predicted life span longer, but it's been proven to be longer through trial and error over thousands of years" (2014, p. 223).

Access is the second technological issue. This relates to hardware, operating systems, and software capable of retrieving the stored information/data. All of these elements change over time and not an insignificant number disappear from the marketplace. As Sneha Tripathi (2018) observed, "Advanced technologies for storage of digital information are abundant; however, technologies ensuring long-term preservation lag far behind" (p. 8). We would add to this statement "ensuring long-term preservation and access," because even if the storage device has uncorrupted data, if the hardware, operating system, and/or application are no longer available as functional entities, the information stored is worthless. Just as with hardware that was considered state-of-the-art at the time, software programs used to create the materials (for example, *WordStar* or *Lotus 1-2-3*) may no longer be available. Where do you find, in 2018 and beyond, *Lotus* or *WordStar* applications? You can, for a fee, get *WordStar* or other files converted by companies such as Advanced Computer Innovation, Inc., whose mission is to create "Accurate, easy-to-use and cost-effective file conversion" of applications such as *WordStar* (http://www.file-convert.com). Migration of content to a different and currently supported file type thus becomes a key digital preservation process, along with emulation—which "involves replicating a digital environment in which the digital object can be accessed in its original format" (Hart and de Vries, 2017, p. 24).

For good reason, libraries have serious concerns around technology issues as they relate to digital preservation. Many academic libraries house a special collections department and perhaps also the archives for their institution. The future of three different classes of objects—born-digital special collections materials, born-digital institutional records, and digitized special collections—are common concerns for such institutions. In addition, libraries have to wonder about the long-term commitment of commercial vendors of databases after the older materials cease to provide an adequate income stream. Who will indefinitely archive such material and at what cost? As more academic libraries create institutional repositories, thoughtful consideration needs to be given to long-term preservation and how to maintain document integrity.

Check These Out

Marc Kosciejew addresses options for long-term digital preservation and the threat of "bit rot" in his 2015 article "Digital Vellum and Other Cures for Bit Rot" (*Information Management Journal* 49, no. 3: 20–25). Robin M. Hastings explores the concept of recovery planning and cloud-based storage of digital assets in her work *Planning Cloud-Based Disaster Recovery for Digital Assets: The Innovative Librarian's Guide* (Santa Barbara, CA: Libraries Unlimited, 2017). Both are worth a look.

Check These Out

Digital preservation programs are not limited to large research institutions. Two resources that provide options for smaller-scale programs are:

Caro, Susanne. 2016. *Digitizing Your Collection: Public Library Success Stories*. Chicago: ALA Editions.

Caro covers considerations in launching a program, digitizing copyrighted material, overcoming staffing, getting the community involved, finding funding opportunities, long-term preservation, and marketing the collection.

Monson, Jane D. 2017. *Getting Started with Digital Collections: Scaling to Fit Your Organization*. Chicago: ALA Editions.

Monson addresses issues such as selecting a digital asset management system, developing workflows, options for metadata models, and strategies to preserve digital assets.

Answering the question about who should be responsible for digital preservation is not easy. Four main players have an interest in doing so as well as some responsibility. The originators (authors) of the content have a vested interest, but few of them have resources to do much beyond making backup copies of their work and rarely have time to migrate the material from platform to platform.

Publishers and the vendors who package and sell access to the information have the greatest resources, both technologically and financially, to address the preservation issue. However, given that most of them are for-profit entities, their focus is on revenue generation. Even nonprofit ventures, such as *Reveal Digital* (http://revealdigital.com/), generally have to break even financially, and they have little incentive to retain material that fails to produce income. The reality is that long-term storage of very low-use material will do almost nothing positive for the bottom line of such organizations.

Individual libraries and cooperative library efforts are the other two groups with a strong interest in long-term preservation. In the past, these two groups handled preservation activities and neither originators nor sellers took much notice, but today, information and intellectual property have taken on a significant financial value. As a result, publishers and vendors generally no longer sell the material, but rather lease it to libraries and place limits on what a library can and cannot do with material—including long-term preservation.

Just as with other CM activities, recommendations standards and guidelines have been developed over time to facilitate digital preservation efforts. Chief among these standards is the Open Archival Information Systems (OAIS) model. The model was first established by the Consultative Committee for Space Data Systems division of the National Aeronautics and Space Administration (https://public.ccsds.org/Pubs/650x0m2.pdf) in the early 2000s, and became an ISO standard in 2003 (ISO 14721). The ISO standard was revised and updated in 2012 (https://www.iso.org/standard/57284.html). Although originally developed as a mechanism for organizing data from space missions, OAIS has been adopted by libraries, archives, and similar organizations. As Brian Lavoie (2014) noted, the two primary functions of an OAIS repository are "to preserve information—i.e., to secure its long-term persistence—and second, to provide access to the archived information, in a manner consistent with the needs of the archive's primary users, or Designated Community" (p. 7). Elements within an OAIS environment are the information producers, consumers, management (dealing with what is to be archived), and the archive itself. More recently, OAIS has been supplemented by the PREFORMA project (PREservation FORMAts for culture information and e-archives; http://www.preforma-project.eu/), tasked with developing a suite of open source software programs for use within an OAIS environment. (See Mita, 2017, for a fuller description of PREFORMA and its work.)

Other support for digital preservation efforts comes from the National Information Standards Organization (NISO), the National Digital Stewardship Alliance (NDSA), and from ALA's ALCTS. NISO is responsible for maintaining the *Framework of Guidance for Building Good Digital Collections* (2007, http://framework.niso.org/). The framework was first developed by the Institute of Museum and Library Services (IMLS) in 2000, with NISO assuming responsibility for its maintenance and administration in 2003. The framework was intended to fulfill three purposes: provide an overview of activities involved in creating digital collections, identify resources to support development of such collections, and encourage community participation in development of best practices (2008, http://framework.niso.org/7.html).

Beyond the NISO framework, the NDSA *Levels of Preservation* is a four-tiered set of recommendations issued in 2013 for use by institutions either beginning or enhancing their digital preservation programs. The four levels address protecting, knowing, monitoring, and repairing data along five factors: storage and geographic location, file fixity and data integrity, information security, metadata, and file formats (https://ndsa.org/activities/levels-of-digital-preservation/). The levels progress in complexity as first-tier activities must occur before second-tier issues can be addressed, and so on. The guidelines are a resource, not a mandate, and the level that an item or collection is preserved at is the choice of the institution. In 2018, NDSA developed a working group to further adapt the levels (https://ndsa.org/working-groups/levels-of-preservation/).

ALCTS created a series of "Minimum Digitization Capture Recommendations" for libraries (2013, http://www.ala.org/alcts/resources/preserv/minimum-digitization-capture-recommendations). The goal of the recommendations were so that libraries do not need to redigitize materials at a later date. The recommendations cover both static (print) and time-based (audio/video) materials, as well as providing a list of best practices for storage. The recommendations advocate for having more than one copy of the items

---

Check These Out

While a comprehensive discussion of preservation metadata is beyond the scope of this book, two resources worth consulting on the topic are:

Seeing Standards: A Visualization of the Metadata Universe by Jenn Riley (2009–2010; http://jennriley.com/metadatamap/) evaluates 105 metadata standards based on such factors as function and purpose.

"A Survey of the Coverage and Methodologies of Schemas and Vocabularies Used to Describe Information Resources" by Philip Hider (*Knowledge Organization*, 2015, 42, no. 3: 154–63). Hider takes Riley's work and expands it into other areas beyond the cultural heritage sector.

digitized with these copies ideally made on different media and stored in different locations. The guidelines also cover the importance of standardized metadata to enhance access. Taken together, OAIS and the work of ALCTS, NISO, and NDC provide valuable guidance for digital preservation efforts.

Given the volume of materials eligible for digital preservation and the availability of resources, collaboration is the best hope for achieving long-term preservation goals. In writing about large-scale library preservation efforts, Paula De Stefano and Tyler Walters (2007) observed, "Collaboration and partnerships have allowed [research libraries] to pool resources, collect cooperatively, manage collections efficiently, achieve long-term preservation goals more effectively, and adapt to new technology" (p. 230). The following are some of the more established cooperative efforts:

JSTOR (http://www.jstor.org/)

JSTOR was founded in 1995 and archives scholarly high-quality academic journals in the humanities, social sciences, and sciences, as well as monographs and other materials valuable for academic work. The archives are expanded continuously to add international publications, and as of mid-2018, JSTOR provided access to more than 12 million academic journal articles, books, and primary sources in 75 disciplines. In 2009, JSTOR merged with and became a service of ITHAKA (http://www.ithaka.org/), a not-for-profit organization helping the academic community use digital technologies to preserve the scholarly record and to advance scholarship and teaching in sustainable ways. Libraries pay a rather substantial annual fee—tens of thousands of dollars—to participate in the program. See https://about.jstor.org /mission-history/for more details.

LOCKSS (Lots of Copies Keep Stuff Safe; https://www.lockss.org/)

Based at Stanford University Libraries, LOCKSS is an international community initiative that provides libraries with digital preservation tools and support so that they can easily and inexpensively collect and preserve their own copies of authorized e-content (https://www.lockss.org/about/what-is-lockss/). In addition to numerous libraries participating in the program, as of mid-2018, over 530 publishers had elected to use LOCKKS as their digital preservation and postcancellation partner.

Portico (https://www.portico.org/)

Portico has license agreements with over 550 publishers to "preserve their content for the long-term (including migrating or transforming the content as necessary) and deliver the content should specific trigger events occur" (https://www.portico.org/why -portico/). These events include a publisher ceasing to operate, failure of a publisher's platform for over 90 days, or back issues no longer being offered by a publisher.

CLOCKSS, or Controlled Lots of Copies Keeps Stuff Safe (https://www.clockss.org/clockss/Home)

Uses LOCKSS technology, but unlike LOCKSS (an open network), CLOCKSS is a closed system providing access to archived

material once a trigger event occurs (https://www.clockss.org
/clockss/Triggered_Content). Publishers allow access to specific
materials to CLOCKSS. CLOCKSS is different from other
initiatives (like Portico) because it makes all content triggered
from the archive freely available (https://www.clockss.org/clockss
/How_CLOCKSS_Works).

HathiTrust (https://www.hathitrust.org/about)

Created through a collaboration of the University of California
system and members of the Big Ten Academic Alliance in part to
"build a reliable and increasingly comprehensive co-owned and
co-managed digital archive of library materials converted from
the print collections of the member institutions" (https://www
.hathitrust.org/mission_goals), the archive included over 739
terabytes of data and over 16.4 million total volumes as of
mid-2018.

Project MUSE (https://muse.jhu.edu/)

Project MUSE is a nonprofit collaborative digital publishing
venture started in 1995 between libraries and publishers. Its
focus is on content from humanities and social sciences journals
from over 200 scholarly publishers, with electronic book content
added in 2012. Most recently, Project MUSE created MUSE
Open in 2016 for open access monographs (https://about.muse
.jhu.edu/about/story/).

PubMed Central (http://www.ncbi.nlm.nih.gov/pmc/)

The National Library of Medicine/National Institutes of Health
provides a free digital archive of biomedical and life science
journal literature through PubMed.

Beyond these initiatives, several organizations support digital preservation efforts in unique ways. These include the Center for Research Libraries (CRL; https://www.crl.edu/archiving-preservation/digital-archives), the
Digital Library Federation (DLF; https://www.diglib.org/), and the Digital
Preservation Coalition (DPC; https://www.dpconline.org/). First of these is
CRL, who began auditing and certifying digital repositories in 2006 in order
to provide additional assurance to the library community. HathiTrust, Portico, and CLOCKSS are among the six repositories certified by CRL to date.
(See https://www.crl.edu/archiving-preservation/digital-archives/certification
-assessment for report data and information on the additional repositories
certified.) DLF is a program of the Council on Library and Information
Resources (CLIR). Its work includes administering the CLIR shared post-
doctoral fellowship in data curation as well as managing grants for digitization of hidden special collections and archives. More recently, DLF has begun
curating a digital library of the Middle East (https://dlme.clir.org/). One of the
tools DLF has developed is the Digitization Cost Calculator (http://dashboard
.diglib.org/). Unlike using a standard calculator, participating institutions
use the Digitization Cost Calculator to enter data on the amount of time
and resources used to perform various tasks involved in the digitization
process. This data is then reported back in aggregate in order to generate
benchmarks for other organizations as they plan their digitization projects.

A Word About Data Curation

In addition to preserving traditional library materials (monographs, journals, media) in all formats, research libraries are beginning to enter into the realm of preserving research data output through data curation activities. The International Federation of Library Associations and Institutions (IFLA) sponsored a study to identify the tasks and responsibilities of data curators. Initial results were reported in Anna Maria Tammaro, Krystyna K. Matusiak, Frank Andreas Sposito, Ana Pervan, and Vittore Casarosa's 2016 article "Understanding Roles and Responsibilities of Data Curators: An International Perspective" (*Libellarium: Journal for the Research of Writing, Books & Cultural Heritage Institutions* 9, no. 2: 39–47). Updates to the project are available on the IFLA Projects website (https://www.ifla.org/library-theory-and -research/projects).

In addition to the IFLA activities, the Council of Library and Information Resources (CLIR) is also involved in several initiatives surrounding data curation, including sponsoring fellowships and performing environmental scans (https://www.clir.org/initiatives -partnerships/data-curation/). The Digital Library Federation (DLF) branch of CLIR also sponsors the eResearch Network community of practice to support data services and digital curation (https://www.diglib.org/opportunities/e-research-network/), as well as an annual international "Endangered Data Week" (https://endangereddataweek .org/) created in order to raise awareness for data curation issues.

Lisa R. Johnston provides an excellent overview of the concept of data curation in "Introduction to Data Curation," the first chapter in her 2017 edited work *Curating Research Data: Volume One: Practical Strategies for Your Digital Repository* (Chicago: Association of College and Research Libraries, 1–32).

The third supporting organization, DPC, was established in 2002 to address digital preservation issues in the UK and Ireland. In addition to serving as a community of practice, DPC has developed a "Bit List" of "Digitally Endangered Species." This list is a crowd-sourced exercise in identifying priorities for preservation, ranging from low risk to "practically extinct" (https://www .dpconline.org/our-work/bit-list). While digital preservation will continue to be a large issue for libraries to contend with, the existence and work of such organizations mentioned above gives reason to think that the profession will resolve the digital preservation problems in time to save many valuable materials.

Conservation

As we noted at the opening of the chapter, conservation efforts involve repair or stabilization of materials. Most of these are likely circulating materials. A recent comprehensive collection evaluation conducted at the University of Alaska Fairbanks Library included pH, paper condition, binding style, and condition as well as last circulation and shelving condition. The study revealed, perhaps not surprisingly, that approximately 68 percent of titles that circulated had damage due to one or more of the aforementioned factors (Rinio, 2016, p. 207). As such, the need for conservation treatment can and does come from a variety of sources, and elements in a library's conservation program include basic binding and repair programs. In-house repairs are fine as long as they employ good conservation methods and use materials that will not cause more harm. Ideally, repairs should be

---

Check These Out

Sharon McQueen and James Twomey provide a comprehensive overview of binding programs in their 2015 work *In-House Bookbinding and Repair* (2nd ed., Lanham, MD: Rowman & Littlefield). In it, they cover how to set up a program, as well as providing extensive examples of how to conduct repairs.

Syracuse University Library's Department of Preservation and Conservation has a YouTube channel with a series of step-by-step videos demonstrating various book repair techniques, as well as a video on "wet book rescue" (https://www.youtube.com/user/SULPreservation).

---

conducted by staff trained in conservation activities. However, all staff need to be aware that they should do nothing that cannot be undone later, if necessary. For example, one should avoid using any adhesive tape other than a reversible, nonacidic tape to repair a torn page. As noted by Tyson Rinio (2016), "In many cases, books are damaged more by the tape than the original damage the tape was intended to correct" (p. 202).

Most commercial binderies follow sound practices and employ materials that will not add to an already serious problem of decomposing books. Selecting a commercial binder should involve both the preservation/conservation staff and the chief collection officer, if the bindery operation is not under the supervision of either unit. Most libraries spend thousands of dollars on bindery and repair work each year, and having a reliable and efficient binder, who uses the proper materials and methods, benefits the library and its customers. Knowing something about bindery operations and the process the materials undergo can help the library staff responsible for selecting materials for binding to make better judgments about the type of binding to order, given the probable use of the material. Most commercial binders are pleased to explain their operations and give customers and new library employees tours of their plant.

One long-standing conservation issue for many libraries with large collections is acidic wood pulp paper. William J. Barrow is the person most often associated with identifying acid as the cause of the deterioration of wood pulp paper. (See John Church's 2005 article for an extensive review of Barrow's research and contributions to the field.) For school and all but the largest public libraries acidic paper is not a problem; collection items wear out or are deselected long before the paper quality is a concern. However, for libraries with long-term obligations this was and remains a significant worry.

Estimates vary as to just how big the problem is. One study that had significant impact in the 1980s and beyond was conducted by Gay Walker,

---

Check These Out

For further information on binding methods and materials see the American National Standards Institute (ANSI) ANSI/NISO/LBI Library Binding standard developed by the National Information Standards Organization (NISO) and the Library Binding Institute (LBI) (https://groups.niso.org/apps/group_public/download.php/18990/Z39.78-2000_R2018.pdf) and an informative guide prepared by ALA's ALCTS division for applying the standard (https://bomi.memberclicks.net/assets/lbc-documents/0838984840_lbiguide.pdf).

Check This Out

The Deterioration and Preservation of Paper: Some Essential Facts (http://www.loc
.gov/preservation/care/deterioratebrochure.html) from the Library of Congress Preservation Directorate is a simple but informative explanation of why and how paper degrades over time.

Jane Greenfield, John Fox, and Jeffrey Simonoff and involved the collections from the Yale library. Results of this study reported over 37.1 percent of the sampled titles had reportedly brittle titles, while 82.6 percent of the collection contained titles printed on acidic paper (1985, pp. 109–110). A *brittle book* is one in which a corner of a page breaks off when folded back and forth two or fewer times. Later studies of collections at Syracuse (Bond et al., 1987) and Brigham Young University (Silverman, 2016) reported different percentages and drew into question the levels identified by the Yale study, but the problem of acidic paper and its impact still exists and grows with each passing day if nothing is done to stop the process. Unfortunately, few libraries have sufficient funding to do more than address a small percentage of the items needing attention as the cost of doing conservation work with these items is very high.

Chemical residues and short fibers are factors in embrittlement. The longer the fibers in the paper, the stronger it is. When ground wood pulp replaced cloth/rags as the standard base for paper manufacturing, the long-term strength of paper dropped sharply. A weak paper combined with the acidic residue from sizing and bleaching, as well as lignin (a component of the wood used for paper), creates self-destructing material. At one end of the scale is newsprint, which is very acidic (the rapid darkening of a newspaper left in the sun occurs because of the acid/lingin in the newsprint); at the other end is the nonacidic (or alkaline) paper that more and more publishers are using in books.

Each year, the number of brittle items (titles published after about 1850 and until the early 1990s) already in the collection increases. What can be done about materials that are self-destructing in the stacks? Maintaining environmental factors (temperature, humidity, and light) at the recommended levels slows the chemical processes and is a first step to take. For the already-brittle materials in the collection, the two concerns are permanence

---

From the Advisory Board

Advisory Board member Susan Koutsky suggests the following resources for more information on the composition of paper and the effect of the environment on it:

Dugal, H. S. (Doug), and Salman Aziz. 1994. "Various Causes for the Darkening of Paper." *Alkaline Paper Advocate* 1, no. 1; http://cool.conservation-us.org/byorg /abbey/ap/ap07/ap07-1/ap07-104.html.

"Paper." PSAP—Preservation Self Assessment Program. University of Illinois at Urbana–Champaign. https://psap.library.illinois.edu/collection-id-guide/paper#wood pulpandnewsprint.

Check This Out

Spiros Zervos and Irene Alexopoulou provide an extensive review of the history of deacidification methods in their 2015 article "Paper Conservation Methods: A Literature Review" (*Cellulose* 22, no. 5: 2859–97). It is well worth the read.

(shelf life) and durability (use). Permanence is the first issue, and there are several ways to stop the acidic activity. After the acidic action is under control, several options exist to enhance durability. Several mass deacidification systems are designed to process large numbers of books at one time.

Given the magnitude of the acid paper problem, almost every large library faces decisions on what to do and how to approach the challenge. CM personnel play a key role in those decisions. When an item in the collection deteriorates to the point that it cannot be rebound, what should one do? A range of options exist, each with an increase in institutional costs:

- Ignore the problem and return the item to storage (lowest cost).

- Withdraw the item from the collection and do not replace it.

- Place the item in an alkaline protective enclosure made for the item and return it to the collection.

- Seek a replacement copy through the out-of-print trade (although likely the same issues of degradation will occur at some point due to the nature of the paper).

- Seek a reprint edition on alkaline paper.

- Convert the material to microfilm and decide what to do with the original.

- Convert the material to an electronic format and decide what to do with the original.

- Withdraw the item from the main collection and place it in a controlled access storage facility.

- Deacidify and strengthen the item and return it to use (very, very expensive). Given its expense and potential to destroy already brittle paper, only special collections items should be considered for this process. Reformatting (digitization) should be considered instead.

Check This Out

CoOL (Conservation OnLine; http://cool.conservation-us.org/) is a site developed and maintained by the Foundation of the American Institute for Conservation. It includes a directory of conservation specialists as well as access resources on a variety of conservation-related topics (http://cool.conservation-us.org/topics.html) such as library binding, mold, and pest management. CoOL also maintains the *Conservation DistList* (http://cool.conservation-us.org/byform/mailing-lists/cdl/) online discussion list with twice weekly posts on topics related to education and research on the issue of conservation.

Ignoring the problem is the most reasonable alternative for materials about which you are confident that long-term retention is unnecessary or undesirable and only a limited amount of use is probable. If there is little or no probability of use in the near future, withdrawing the item is probably the most effective option.

Points to Keep in Mind

- The total cost of an item in the collection goes beyond its purchase price and includes processing, long-term maintenance, and any preservation efforts or conservation treatment applied to it.

- Preservation and conservation of cultural heritage is essential for a society's ongoing success.

- Archives, libraries, and museums are three key players in the preservation of cultural heritage.

- Every type of library has, or should have, some interest in achieving the longest possible value and use of the items in its collection whether or not there is a cultural heritage value associated with these items.

- Basic library "housekeeping" practices are the foundation of preservation efforts.

- Activities such as proper shelving/storage methods, not packing storage units too tight, and the like all extend the useful life of collection items.

- Temperature and humidity control is a balancing act between people and collection needs. The closer you come to collection needs, the longer the items will last.

- Light, both natural and artificial, can cause irreversible damage to collection materials unless preventive measures are taken.

- Mold and insects are two additional threats to collections.

- Theft and mutilation affect libraries not only through the loss or damage of the original material, but through repair or replacement costs that redirect funds that otherwise could have been used to add other materials to the collection.

- Risk management is an element in a good preservation program, as is disaster preparedness.

- A disaster response plan should be created well before the onset of any incident. Once created, the plan should be widely shared and revisited regularly for needed updates. Staff must also be trained to aid in the response effort.

- Collection insurance will assist in rebuilding a damaged collection but is unlikely to cover the full cost of recovery.

- Long-term digital preservation has several components.

- How data/information are stored and the availability of the requisite hardware and software to access the material are two underlying factors for future use of the material.

- A series of guidelines and recommendations for digital preservation activities exist as a way of facilitating long-term preservation.

- Libraries, archives, and museums are collaborating in large-scale joint efforts in order to succeed in long-term preservation efforts.

- Speed of technological change is a contributing factor for libraries and others hoping to keep digital material accessible and understandable.

- During the last half of the 20th century, acidic wood pulp paper was the biggest preservation and conservation concern. While this still remains an issue, it has been far surpassed by 21st-century worries about the longevity of digital resources.

References

Allen, Susan. 1991. "The Blumberg Case: A Costly Lesson for Librarians." *AB Bookman's Weekly* 88, September 2: 769–73.

American Library Association. 2004. *Core Values of Librarianship*. June 29, 2004. Chicago: ALA. http://www.ala.org/advocacy/intfreedom/corevalues.

American Library Association. 2008. *ALA Preservation Policy 2008*. Chicago: ALA. http://www.ala.org/alcts/resources/preserv/08alaprespolicy.

Association for Library Collections and Technical Services, Preservation and Reformatting Section, Working Group on Defining Digital Preservation. 2009. *Definitions of Digital Preservation*. Association for Library Collections and Technical Services. June 18, 2009. http://www.ala.org/alcts/resources/preserv/2009def.

Baird, Brian J. 2017. "21st-Century Preservation Basics." *American Libraries* 48, no. 3/4: 56.

Baird, Brian J. 2018. *Practical Preservation and Conservation Strategies for Libraries*. Lanham, MD: Rowman & Littlefield.

Bond, Randall, Mary DeCarlo, Elizabeth Henes, and Eileen Snyder. 1987. "Preservation Study at the Syracuse University Libraries." *College & Research Libraries* 48, no. 2: 132–47.

Canadian Council of Archives. 2003. *Basic Conservation of Archival Materials: Revised Edition, 2003; Chapter 3: Environment*. Canadian Council of Archives. http://www.cdncouncilarchives.ca/rbch3_en.pdf.

Castro, Amanda. 2018. "Daytona Beach Library to Reopen After Hurricane Irma." *ClickOrlando.Com*. May 4, 2018. https://www.clickorlando.com/news/daytona-beach-library-to-reopen-after-hurricane-irma.

Charles, Patrick. 2017. "Book Thief." *AALL Spectrum* 21, no. 4: 47–50.

Church, John. 2005. "William J. Barrow: A Remembrance and Appreciation." *American Archivist* 68, no. 1: 152–60.

Cloonan, Michèle V. 2007. "The Paradox of Preservation." *Library Trends* 56, no. 1: 133–47.

Cloonan, Michèle V. 2011. "The Boundaries of Preservation and Conservation Research." *Libraries & the Cultural Record* 46, no. 2: 220–29.

Conn, Donia. 2012. *Protection from Light Damage*. Andover, MA: Northeast Document Conservation Center. https://www.nedcc.org/assets/media/documents/Preservation%20Leaflets/2_4_Light.pdf.

Corrado, Edward M., and Heather Moulaison Sandy. 2017. *Digital Preservation for Libraries, Archives and Museums*. 2nd ed. Lanham, MD: Rowman & Littlefield.

De Stefano, Paula, and Tyler Walters. 2007. "A Natural Collaboration: Preservation for Archival Collections in ARL Libraries." *Library Trends* 56, no. 1: 230–58.

Evans, G. Edward, Margaret Zarnosky Saponaro, Holland Christie, and Carol Sinwell. 2015. *Library Programs and Services: The Fundamentals*. 8th ed. Santa Barbara, CA: Libraries Unlimited.

Gertz, Janet. 1992. "Columbia Libraries Annex Disaster." *Archival Products News* 1, no. 2: 2.

Goldsmith, Francisca. 2015. *Crash Course in Weeding Library Collections* Santa Barbara, CA: ABC-CLIO.

Hart, Timothy Robert, and Denise de Vries. 2017. "Metadata Provenance and Vulnerability." *Information Technology & Libraries* 36, no. 4: 24–33.

Harwell, Jonathan H. 2014. "Library Security Gates: Effectiveness and Current Practice." *Journal of Access Services* 11, no. 2: 53–65.

Henderson, Jane. 2013. *Environment*. [London]: British Library Preservation Advisory Centre. https://www.bl.uk/aboutus/stratpolprog/collectioncare/publications/booklets/managing_library_archive_environment.pdf.

Iraci, Joe. 2017. "The Soaking Resistance of Electronic Storage Media." *Restaurator* 38, no. 1: 33–75.

Jurkowski, Odin L. 2017. *Technology and the School Library*. 3rd ed. Lanham, MD: Rowman & Littlefield.

Kahn, Miriam. 2016. "Plan for the Worst and Hope for the Best: Basic Disaster Response Plan Guidelines for Libraries." *Natural Hazards Observer*, XL, no. 6. https://hazards.colorado.edu/article/plan-for-the-worst-and-hope-for-the-best-basic-disaster-response-plan-guidelines-for-libraries.

LAPL Blog. 2016. "April 29 Marks 30th Anniversary of 1986 Fire." *Los Angeles Public Library*. April 29, 2016. https://www.lapl.org/collections-resources/blogs/lapl/april-29-marks-30th-anniversary-1986-fire.

Lavoie, Brian. 2014. *The Open Archival Information System (OAIS) Reference Model Introductory Guide*. 2nd ed. Digital Preservation Coalition. https://www.dpconline.org/docs/technology-watch-reports/1359-dpctw14-02/file.

Leggett, Elizabeth R. 2014. *Digitization and Digital Archiving: A Practical Guide for Librarians*. Practical Guides for Librarians, No. 7. Lanham: Rowman & Littlefield.

Levine, Capron Hannay, and Bryan M. Carson. 2012. "Legally Speaking—Loss Prevention and Insurance." *Against the Grain* 24, no. 4: 63, 65.

Livingston, Preston. 2015. "Mold Prevention and Remediation in a Library Environment." *Texas Library Journal* 91, no. 2: 60–61.

Maes, Margaret K., and Tracy L. Thompson-Przylucki. 2012. "Collaborative Stewardship: Building a Shared, Central Collection of Print Legal Materials." *Collection Management* 37, no. 3/4: 294–306.

Mills, Joe. 2016. "Op Ed: Our History Is Disappearing Under Our Noses—Literally! A Proactive Approach to Circumvent a Failing Preservation Technology." *Against the Grain* 28, no. 3: 40.

Mita, Amanda. 2017. "PREFORMA—Preservation Formats for Culture Information and E-Archives." *Technical Services Quarterly* 34, no. 3: 329–30.

Moffitt, Bob. 2018. "Sacramento Hail Storm Damaged 250 Very Old Books at California State Library." *Capital Public Radio*. February 28, 2018. http://www.capradio.org/110715.

Murvosh, Marta. 2013. "Don't Let the Book Bugs Bite." *Library Journal* 138, no. 12: 430.

NEDCC. 2017. *Microfilm and Microfiche*. Andover, MA: Northeast Document Conservation Center. https://www.nedcc.org/free-resources/preservation -leaflets/6.-reformatting/6.1-microfilm-and-microfiche.

Pedersen-Summey, Terri. 1990. "Theft and Mutilation of Library Materials." *College & Research Libraries* 51, no. 2: 120–28.

Prestamo, Anne M. 2018. "Libraries and Natural Disasters." *Journal of Library Administration* 58, no. 1: 101–109.

Rinehart, Amanda, Patrice-Andre Prud'homme, and Andrew Huot. 2014. "Overwhelmed to Action: Digital Preservation at the Under-Resourced Institution." *OCLC Systems and Services, Digital Preservation Special Edition* 30, no. 1: 28–42.

Rinio, Tyson. 2016. "Collection Condition Assessment in a Midsized Academic Library." *Collection Management* 41, no. 4: 193–208.

Sheffield, Rebecka T. 2016. "More Than Acid Free Folders: Extending the Concept of Preservation to Include the Stewardship of Unexplored Histories." *Library Trends*. 64, no. 3: 572–84.

Silverman, Randall H. 2016. "Surely, We'll Need Backups." *Preservation, Digital Technology & Culture* 43, no. 3: 102–21.

Teper, Thomas H., and Stephanie S. Atkins. 2003. "Building Preservation: The University of Illinois at Urbana–Champaign's Stacks Assessment." *College & Research Libraries* 64, no. 3: 211–27.

Tolppanen, Bradley P. 2000. "Electronic Detection Systems: Is Your Library Ready for One?" *Louisiana Libraries* 63, no. 2: 7–11.

Tripathi, Sneha. 2018. "Digital Preservation: Some Underlying Issues for Long-term Preservation." *Library Hi Tech News* 35, no. 2: 8–12.

Walker, Gay, Jane Greenfield, John Fox, and Jeffrey S. Simonoff. 1985. "Yale Survey: A Large-scale Study of Book Deterioration in the Yale University Library." *College & Research Libraries* 46, no. 2: 111–32.

White, Kaila. 2018. "Phoenix Fires, Punishes 5 More Workers over Burton Barr Library Flood." *The Republic*. January 31, 2018. https://www.azcentral.com /story/news/local/phoenix/2018/01/31/phoenix-fires-demotes-suspends-fire -department-employees-burton-barr-library-flooding-disaster/1079796001/.

Zerek, Bogdan Filip. 2014. *The Preservation and Protection of Library Collections: A Practical Guide to Microbiological Controls*. Chandos Information Professional Series. Oxford, UK: Chandos Publishing.

15
Legal Issues and Collection Management

When we consider how much of our web content comes from outside vendors, we may feel like we don't have much control over our users' experience. That is simply not true. My library has chosen not to subscribe to certain platforms because they were not ADA-accessible and the vendor had no plans to change that.
—Meredith Farkas, 2016

The most challenging part—but in many ways the most important—is to make sure you are in compliance with the law relating to public screenings of films.
—Kati Irons, 2015

New librarians benefit from seeing how seasoned colleagues have helped their institutions and patrons navigate copyright issues and how these issues are addressed on campus. They must learn how others have developed a solid, general understanding of copyright law and kept abreast of major issues that affect academic institutions.
—Bridget Carter Conlogue and
Leslie W. Christianson, 2016

You might have paused after reading this chapter's title and thought, "What possible legal concerns are associated with CM, other than perhaps copyright? This seems like a stretch." We touched on some of the concerns in earlier chapters and the above quotations from Farkas and Irons provide hints about the complex interactions between laws/regulations that can impact library services. Meredith Farkas' quotation is an example of the complexity between general laws and what we do in terms of CM. Even the issue of library privacy and the law may come into play when a library decides to use a Radio Frequency Identification (RFID) system, for example.

Ah, for the days when CM officers only needed to know the basics of one copyright law and stay up-to-date regarding the Internal Revenue Service's regulations regarding gifts in kind (generally books and magazines). Both of those issues are still with us; however, things have become ever more complicated. CM officers must become familiar with electronic resource contracts and licenses (they are legal documents—we covered this aspect of law and CM in chapter 13). Yes, the library's legal counsel, assuming there is one in place, can be consulted. However, doing so is expensive, especially if that is done each time the library thinks about adding a new electronic product or service. There are a number of technical issues that are also partially legal in nature, such as Digital Rights Management (DRM, discussed below) and how and to whom the library may provide access to e-resources (proxy servers, passwords, accounts, and the like). There is also the problem of how far the library staff may go in answering usage questions before the person asking for help might reasonably think it was legal advice. To that end, *keep in mind we can only highlight the issues and certainly none of the following should be construed as legal advice.*

We begin with two topics (copyright and gifts) that are probably somewhat familiar to you. Understanding copyright is important as librarians often serve as one of the major liaisons between users and copyright holders. Library staff members (especially the librarians) play an important role in how people gain access to and make use of copyrighted materials. They play such a role because they are often the point of contact between users and protected material. More often than not they have to explain to people just what a person may or may not do with covered materials. The reality is the vast majority of people have, at best, a nodding acquaintance with just what copyright means. When it comes to Web-based materials, some people do not realize that copyright might be an issue. Carol Henderson made our point most concisely when she wrote, "libraries are creatures of the historical and statutory balance in copyright law. . . . Libraries are places where the public and the proprietary meet. The multiple roles of libraries as social organizations address the balance in the law, and are shaped by it" (2017).

In many ways, public and school librarians are the individuals who can begin to instill in the public the notion that there are copyright laws that impact what a person may legally do with materials. And, yes, there are several laws that protect a creator's intellectual property—be it words, images, or actions in both the print and digital world.

Copyright Laws and Libraries

Copyright grants the creators of works certain exclusive rights that protect their interest in their creative work, such as realizing some income/benefit from the effort to create the item. The term copyright originated from the law's original purpose, which was to protect against unauthorized printing and selling of a work. It was a straightforward and seemingly reasonable method of encouraging individuals or businesses to take a financial risk to produce and distribute information. Over time, the concept has grown ever more complex. It is far beyond someone copying another person's creative work and selling it. Today, it is thought of in terms of protecting "intellectual property"—a concept that relates to almost all types of creative works of individuals or organizations. Most countries have such laws, with varying definitions of issues. In addition, there are international conventions that further complicate matters.

Today's laws confer six rights in a work that a person creates. (The following discussion is based on the 1978 law, which is still in place, if frequently amended. That law serves as the foundation for all that has followed in the U.S. context.)

1. To reproduce the copyrighted work in copies or phonorecords.

2. To prepare derivative works based on the copyrighted work.

3. To distribute copies or phonorecords of the copyrighted work to the public by sale or transfer of ownership, or rental, lease, or lending.

4. In the case of literary, musical, dramatic, choreographed works, pantomimes, and motion pictures and other audiovisual works to perform the copyrighted work publicly.

5. In the case of literary, musical, dramatic, choreographed works, pantomimes, and motion pictures and other audiovisual works to display the copyrighted work publicly.

6. In the case of sound recordings, to perform the copyrighted work publicly by means of a digital audio transmission. (§ 106, U.S. Copyright Law)

Such rights are limited by provisions in § 107-118. It is those sections that become significant for libraries and people who wish to use copyrighted material.

There are at least five significant areas where the law and library collections intersect—fair use (§ 107), photocopying/scanning (§ 107 and 108), interlibrary loan (§ 108(d)), performance (§ 107), and out-of-print status (§ 108). These provisions have implications for such areas as resource sharing, establishing the number of copies needed to legally meet demand, and maintaining collection integrity. As is true of most legal issues, copyright is not cut and dried. "It depends" is the all too common beginning to answers to the question, followed by "Is this legal?" especially when it relates to the library.

The following list of resources that libraries collect and are covered in the U.S. law provides a sense of how copyright may impact CM activities:

- Audiovisuals (such as news broadcasts) § 108 (f) (3)
- Other audiovisuals § 107, 108 (h)
- Books § 107, 108
- Graphic works § 107, 108 (h)
- Importing copies § 602 (a) (3)
- Instructional transmission § 107, 110
- Motion pictures § 107, 108 (h)
- Musical works § 107, 108 (h)
- Periodical article § 107, 108
- Pictorial work § 107, 108 (h)

- Public broadcasting programs § 107, 108 (d) (3)
- Sound recordings § 107, 108, 114

As you can see, the two major sections of the law are 107 and 108 in terms of library issues. However, other sections of the law may also come into play, especially for educational libraries supporting instructional activities.

Perhaps the two most vexing copyright issues for both the library and users are legal copying and what is fair use. The two concerns are interlinked both for individuals needing information and for teachers wishing to use copyrighted material(s) in their courses. There is no question that some people copy materials for commercial purposes, especially music and video products. However, much of the "improper" usage is a function of not understanding the nature of copyright and what fair usage may be in various circumstances. There are many misconceptions about copyright and we can only touch on a few of them.

One common misconception is that if you do not charge for, or gain financially, from the usage, there is no violation of copyright. We noted earlier that libraries should purchase performance rights for the videos they purchase if they are to be used in library programming. Even a free public performance during a children's program requires permission, if one did not pay for performance rights. Use in face-to-face instruction has been thought to be "fair use," but even that idea is questioned by many copyright holders.

Yet another common misunderstanding relates to the notice of copyright (the presence of either the word copyright or © on the item). "It did not indicate that it was copyrighted, so it must be public domain" is a common response to an alleged violation. One factor in such confusion is it *was* necessary until 1989. It changed when the United States joined most of the rest of the world as a signatory to the Berne copyright convention. That convention grants coverage with or without notice. Thus, the only safe assumption now is that everything is copyrighted after 1989.

There is a perception, especially among younger people who grew up with the Internet and its philosophy of openness, that anything accessible on the Internet is unconditionally available for their use. Further, the notion that the contents of a website may be copyrighted does not enter into their thinking until they face an allegation of violating someone's copyright.

Fair Use and Copying

Fair use is an area full of "yes, you can/no, you can't." Old guidelines seem to be under scrutiny and the goal appears to be a further lessening of fair use rights. The public still does have some rights to gain access to and use copyrighted material. Where to draw the line between creators' and users' rights is a complicated problem, and has become more so with digitization of material and scanning devices.

So what is fair use and does it have legal standing? Yes is the answer to the second question, and the answer to the first is "it depends." The devil is indeed in the details of what you do with the copyrighted material. Fair use doctrine was codified in general terms in § 107. That section refers to such purposes as criticism, commentary, news reporting, teaching, scholarship, or research, and it specifies four criteria to use in determining whether a particular instance of copying or other reproduction is fair. The statutory criteria in § 107 are:

Check These Out

The Library of Congress has produced a teaching site for schools on copyright called "Taking the Mystery Out of Copyright" (http://www.loc.gov/teachers/copyrightmystery/) with interactive modules that include the basics of copyright law and fair use, a timeline of copyright history, and steps to registering for a copyright.

ALA also has a site devoted to copyright and fair use (http://www.ala.org/advocacy/copyright-tools), including links to a "Public Domain Slider" and other resources.

The U.S. Copyright Office also maintains a "Fair Use Index" (https://www.copyright.gov/fair-use/) of decisions on copyright from district, circuit, and appeal courts as well as the U.S. Supreme Court.

---

1. The purpose and character of the use, including whether such use is of a commercial nature or is for nonprofit educational purposes.

2. The nature of the copyrighted work.

3. The amount and substantiality of the portion used in relation to the copyrighted work as a whole.

4. The effect of the use upon the potential market for or value of the copyrighted work.

The first point is rarely an issue from a library perspective. The second and third points are very much an "it depends" issue. Even a short poem cannot be copied without permission. Publishers have differing rules for authors quoting copyrighted material. The authors of this publication have experienced anywhere from 150 to under 100 permission-free words; beyond that limit publishers generally require a document indicating permission to use the material was granted by the copyright holder. A single graphic usually requires permission. Multiple copies can be legal in face to face instruction on a one-time-only basis.

There are some library safeguards ("safe harbors," in legalese) from being liable for someone misusing a library photocopy machine for illegal purposes. Clearly libraries should not be liable for what a user does with copyrighted material from their collections. It is also clear they must offer copying capability and, realistically, that must be a self-service activity. The law allows libraries to post signage that spells out copyright restrictions (you can find the exact wording required in the *Federal Register* for November 16, 1977).

Libraries are caught in the middle of these issues. Librarians may agree that prices are high, but they also know that if there was no income and profit for the producers there would be no information. They believe in free access to information, especially for educational purposes, once the library acquires the material or information. Finding the balance is the challenge. In many ways, the only organized voice for users is library and educational associations.

Digital Millennium Copyright Act (DMCA)

We first mentioned the Digital Millennium Copyright Act (DMCA) in chapter 12. The purpose of the DMCA was to update existing U.S. copyright law in terms of the digital world, as well as to conform to World Intellectual

Property Organization (WIPO, http://www.wipo.int/portal/en/index.html) treaties. The 1978 copyright law is still in force, but changed dramatically as a result of amendments and the DMCA. While DMCA amended U.S. law to comply with WIPO treaties, it did more. It also addressed a great many of the technology aspects of copyright, for example digital rights management software. (The Electronic Frontier Foundation provides an overview of the purpose of such software on its site: https://www.eff.org/issues/drm.) One of the education/library community's concerns about the decline of fair use rights relates to § 1201. This section prohibits gaining unauthorized access to material by circumventing any technological protection measures a copyright holder may have put in place. Section 1201 is not intended to limit fair use, but fair use is *not* a defense to circumventing technological protection measures. These other elements in the section have limited implication for collection development, at least at the time we wrote this chapter.

Section 1202 prohibits tampering with "Copyright Management Information" (CMI). The DMCA identified the following as constituting copyright management information:

- Information that identifies the copyrighted work, including title of the work, the author, and the copyright owner.

- Information that identifies a performer whose performance is fixed in a work, with certain exceptions.

- In the case of an audiovisual work, information that identifies the writer, performers, or director, with certain exceptions.

- Terms and conditions for use of the work.

- Identifying numbers or symbols that accompany the above information or links to such information; for example, embedded pointers and hypertext links.

- Such other information as the Register of Copyrights may prescribe by regulation, with an exception to protect the privacy of users.

One aspect of the DMCA that will probably be very important to libraries is "Title II: Online Service Provider Liability" (§ 512(c)). The reason for this is that the DMCA defines "online service provider" (OSP) very broadly, and libraries that offer electronic resources or Internet remote access could be considered OSPs. The law creates some "safe harbors" for certain specified OSP activities. When an activity is within the safe harbor, the OSP qualifies for an exemption from liability. One should read the most current material available about this title, as it is complex and legal interpretation of it is likely to evolve.

Title IV provides some clarification about library and archival digitization activity for preservation purposes. It allows the creation of up to three digital preservation copies of an eligible copyrighted work and the electronic

Check This Out

Bobby Glushko provides suggestions for libraries to consider when planning digitization projects in his 2011 article "Keeping Library Digitization Legal" (*American Libraries* 42, no. 5/6: 28–29).

loan of those copies to qualifying institutions. An additional feature is that it permits preservation, including in a digital form, of an item in a format that has become obsolete.

Distance education activities are also addressed in Title IV. The Register of Copyright provided Congress with a report on "how to promote distance education through digital technologies" (U.S. Copyright Office, 1999, p. 1). Part of the report was intended to address the value of having licenses available for use of copyrighted works in distance education programs.

Enforcement

Asking permission to use some copyrighted item is a straightforward compliance method and avoids trying to follow the various fair use guidelines. For some libraries, the guidelines are too narrow and the cost of acquiring, processing, and housing the needed copyrighted material is too high. Gaining individual permissions is rather akin to buying collection items from the publisher/producer rather than a wholesaler—there are large quantities of staff time required. Are such libraries and information centers cut off from needed information? No; there are some options for gaining access for users to materials not in the collection at a relatively modest cost in staff time.

The Copyright Clearance Center (CCC, http://www.copyright.com/) is a not-for-profit organization designed to serve rights holders, libraries, and other users of U.S. copyrighted material by providing a central source from which to secure necessary permissions and to pay any required fee. It is, in a sense, a licensing system; CCC does not copy documents, but functions as a clearinghouse for both print and online content. Several thousand organizations are members. There are millions of titles and individual images registered with the CCC. Although it handles mostly U.S. publications, some publications from other countries are included as well. Its website states that:

> At the heart of every company and academic institution, there's information. It's the content that fuels discovery, product and service innovations and learning. At Copyright Clearance Center (CCC), our mission is to make it easy for people to get, use and share content worldwide, while protecting the interests of creators, publishers and other copyright holders.
> Our vision is to create global licensing and content solutions that make copyright work (http://www.copyright.com/about/).

CCC's services include pay-per-item and an annual license for print and online materials, pay per image, and educational material related to copyright and IP (Intellectual Property) issues. An annual subscription covers both single copy and multiple copy needs for course packs and classroom handouts as well as for electronic courses and reserve purposes. The primary advantage of the subscription is that it provides access to the search interface to CCC's database. Such access greatly speeds up the permission process. Also, for academic institutions that hold an annual license, CCC offers the "Get It Now" service, designed to work with existing ILL services by "providing library patrons with the immediate fulfillment of full-text articles from unsubscribed journals—24 hours a day, 7 days a week—through a cost-effective, and easy-to-use application integrated into your ILL workflow and/or OpenURL Link Resolver" (http://www.copyright.com/academia/get-it-now/). Quite frequently, faculty requests for course packs, class use, and course reserves arrive at the last moment and faculty want the material made available immediately. This service can help expedite their request.

Although CCC does have material from other countries, it is a small fraction of what some users may want. Some countries have an organization similar to CCC, such as the Canadian Copyright Licensing Agency (http://www.accesscopyright.ca) and the UK's Copyright Licensing Agency (https://www.cla.co.uk/). Both of these agencies offer educational institution licensing programs.

As you might expect, you need permission of one type or another for other collection formats. Perhaps the most common are video formats, including theatrical motion pictures. We have mentioned a number of times the necessity of securing performance rights for video formats. Most of the educational video vendors include the cost of performance rights in their advertised prices; however, you should insist on getting a written conformation for each title acquired and keep the document as long as the item is in the collection. Vendors not specializing in the educational market rarely include performance rights in their basic pricing. You must ask about performance rights fees. Should you not get the rights at the time of purchase, you can contact the producer and pay for that right at a later date. The underlying message is that it is unwise for a library to use a video if it is not certain it has performance rights.

For theatrical motion pictures, there are several options. One such option is available from the Motion Picture Licensing Corporation (MPLC), which in recognizing the complexities of licensing films created the Umbrella License® (https://library.mplc.org/). This product allows subscribers to have unlimited exhibitions of a title for the cost of an annual license fee. For public and school libraries, there is also the option of using Swank's® K–12 movie licensing services (https://www.swank.com/k-12-schools), which has agreements with most of the major Hollywood movie studios, including Paramount, DreamWorks, and Sony. The fees for such services can be substantial; however, the cost of a lawsuit would be higher, and if the organization lost, it could be forced to pay at least $50,000 plus other costs and fees. When in doubt, ask for permission or pay the requisite fee upfront.

One other difference between print materials and media relates to archiving. Under Section 108 of existing law, a library does not have the right to make a backup/archival copy of media items, except under very specific circumstances.

Check This Out

Just because a library owns a particular VHS tape it wishes to digitize, that does not automatically give the library the right to do so. Section 108 of copyright law requires that, prior to duplication, a reasonable search be conducted to determine that an unused copy of the same video is available at a fair price. One resource for libraries considering digitizing video content is the Academic Libraries Video Trust (ALVT), launched in 2018 by National Media Market (http://www.videotrust.org/). The ALVT is an outgrowth of the Section 108 Due Diligence project, first created by Chris Lewis (American University) and Jane Hutchinson (formerly of William Paterson University Library), and its primary purpose is to serve as a clearinghouse of digitized selected AV works otherwise unavailable elsewhere. Under certain conditions, libraries can upload digitized copies of works from their collections to the clearinghouse and download replacement copies of needed works subject to Section 108 of the copyright law (http://videotrust.org/about/faq). The service is worth a look.

Digital Rights Management (DRM)

Digital Rights Management (DRM) is not itself based in law; rather, it is part of a business model that focuses on controlling the *rights* that are based on law. Piracy, misuse, and misunderstandings have been a part of the copyright scene since the 1710 Statute of Anne (UK) became law. In today's digital world, the possibilities for piracy and misuses abound and are very easy to accomplish, especially if the intellectual property is left unprotected. Many rights holders worry, with cause, that they may lose all control over their IP work(s). DMCA's passage with the anticircumvention clause links DRM and copyright.

U.S. Code 17 Sec. 1201(a)(1) (DMCA) indicates that "No person shall circumvent a technological measure that effectively controls access to a work protected under this title." Section 1201(a)(3) reads as follows:

(A) to circumvent a technological measure means to descramble a scrambled work, to decrypt an encrypted work, or otherwise to avoid, bypass, remove, deactivate, or impair a technological measure, without the authority of the copyright owner; and (B) a technological measure effectively controls access to a work if the measure, in the ordinary course of its operation, requires the application of information, or a process or a treatment, with the authority of the copyright owner, to gain access to the work.

Certainly in the past, the question of what constitutes reasonable/fair use has been contentious. DRM and the digital world have only magnified the division between producers, be they individual creators or companies, and end users. The opening sentences of Sarah Houghton-Jan's (2007) article on the topic convey the feelings of many who dislike DRM: "Digital Rights Management . . . Also known as 'Digital Restrictions Management,' 'Despicable Rights Meddling,' or even 'Delirious Righteous Morons' by some, the technology and its controversial application of controlling digital content has sparked an escalating battle over copyright protection and fair use. The stakes are huge for content producers and consumers and, yes, libraries too" (p. 53). A view in favor of DRM comes from Shri C. V. Bhatt (2008), who concluded his article on the topic by noting, "For creators and all sorts of content communities, DRM is likely to enable the growth and success of the e-market and finally will be the key point in the e-commerce system for marketing of the digital content, and will enable a smooth, safe, secure movement of the digital work from the creator and producer to retailers and consumers at a reasonable cost" (p. 42).

What are some of the typical "uses" a person, and a library, makes of digital content that may be controlled by DRM technology? The most obvious uses are to read, listen, and view such material. Others that may not come to mind are copying, pasting, printing, and emailing. All of these uses can be interfered with by DRM to a lesser or greater extent, even when that use would clearly be considered fair use in the analog/print world. These are especially significant factors in the educational library setting. Kristin Eschenfelder (2008) explored what she labeled soft and hard restrictions in the area of scholarly digital resources. Although her focus was on academic libraries, many of her points apply to almost any library environment where e-database access is available. To Eschenfelder, "soft restrictions" are impediments to easily using the material, while "hard restrictions" are forbidden uses (p. 208). Some of the soft restrictions are a function of DRM technology,

---

Check This Out

One recent work examining DRM from multiple angles is *Digital Rights Management: The Librarian's Guide*, edited by Catherine A. Lemmer and Carla P. Wale (Lanham, MD: Rowman & Littlefield, 2016). This edited work includes chapters on DRM and information privacy, as well as workflow issues and managing DRM with open access titles. It is well worth the look.

---

while others are license issues. An example of a license soft restriction she gave was that some vendors indicate they block suspicious or "excessive" use without clearly stating what constitutes either usage (p. 209). Statements such as "if a suspicious usage pattern indicates excessive copying, the activity is logged and you are sent a copyright warning message" (p. 209) leaves a person in the dark as to what specific actions would cause the generation of such a message.

Other library concerns regarding DRM include device compatibility and e-readers, archival/long-term preservation challenges, and access to digital material in compliance with the Americans with Disabilities Act (ADA). Many of the DRM-protected materials keep "assistive technologies" from working, essentially denying a visually impaired person from having access even when the material is legally acquired. A good article by Guy Whitehouse (2009) describes the challenges for the visually impaired and DRM, while Beth Caruso (2016) speaks to issues concerning accessibility of electronic collections in her article. Our quotation for this chapter from Farkas is a specific example of such challenges for CM.

There is some hope that over time the above issues will be resolved, at least for libraries and archives. The U.S. Copyright Office is mandated to review the impact of the noncircumvention clause of DMCA every three years. One interesting pattern in the exceptions allowed is that some exemptions do not get renewed in each review cycle. Thus, even if you are pleased that the review panel allows for an exception for something you wanted in one cycle, you can only count about three years to take advantage of the opportunity. It may or may not be allowed in the next review cycle.

Barry Sookman and Dan Glover (2010) summed up the nature of copyright, use, and licenses when they wrote, "In the digital space, however, rights that once seemed crisp and clear are blurred. Digital acquisition and lending invariably involves the act of making new copies. It also tends to involve agreements (licenses) between libraries and publishers that define the scope of the permitted copying" (p. 14). What is the relationship between copyright and licenses? Perhaps the best short description of the similarities and differences was written by Ann Okerson (1997), who noted:

- Copyright represents a set of general regulations negotiated through statutory enactment.

- Licenses or contracts . . . represent a market-driven approach to such regulation. Each license is arranged between a willing surveyor and willing licensee, resource by resource. The owner of a piece of property is free to ask whatever price and set whatever conditions the market will bear. (1997, p. 137)

Check These Out

The following are very useful guides to the complex issues of copyright and its compliance:

Butler, Rebecca P. 2011. *Copyright for Teachers and Librarians in the 21st Century.* New York: Neal-Schuman Publishers.

Butler, Rebecca. 2016. "Copyright and School Libraries in the Digital Age." *Knowledge Quest* 45, no. 2: 6–7. Introductory article to a series of four articles on the issue addressing various aspects of copyright in K–12 settings.

Dawson, Patricia H., and Sharon Q. Yang. 2016. "Institutional Repositories, Open Access and Copyright: What Are the Practices and Implications?" *Science & Technology Libraries* 35, no. 4: 279–94.

Copyright & New Media Law (formerly The Copyright & New Media Law Newsletter) 1997- . Handshake Productions: Toronto. http://copyrightandnewmedialaw.com/.

Crews, Kenneth D. 2012. *Copyright Law for Librarians and Educators: Creative Strategies and Practical Solutions.* 3rd ed. Chicago: ALA Editions.

IFLA. 2018. *Copyright Issues for Libraries.* World Library and Information Congress. April 23, 2018. https://www.ifla.org/copyright-issues-for-libraries.

Padfield, Tim. 2015. *Copyright for Archivists and Records Managers.* 5th ed. New York: Neal-Schuman.

Phelps, Marilyn, and Murray J. Jennex. 2015. "Ownership of Collaborative Works in the Cloud." *International Journal of Knowledge Management* 11, no. 4: 35–51.

Russell, Carrie. 2012. *Complete Copyright for K–12 Librarians and Educators.* Chicago: ALA Editions.

Gifts and the IRS

People, as we noted in chapter 8, often believe that any gift to a library is a valued contribution and worthy of a tax deduction. Reality is that these contributions are more mixed in terms of value. Even so, the library can and should acknowledge all gifts ("in-kind" or cash) with a letter/receipt that could be useful for tax purposes. Gifts "in-kind" (most commonly books, magazines, media, and the like) may or may not be highly valued by the library. Processing such items requires staff time to sort and make decisions similar to those involved in purchasing an item. Rejected items may be fodder for an existing book sale program, but even then a careful cost analysis may show the staff costs are higher than the income. What to do with the rejects adds additional staff time to the process. Regardless of the "value" of the gift for the library, most libraries accept the donation and say thank you. That thank you is where the legal implications arise. At a minimum, the description of in-kind gifts should state the number and kind of gift (for example, 100 mass-market paperbacks, 40 hardcover books, and 20 unbound volumes of *National Geographic*). Accepting gifts (with the understanding the library may use the material as it deems necessary) can generate goodwill, and they may generate some income for collection building through local and online book sales.

What follows reflects the 2018 summary of IRS donation rules for deductibility (http://www.njnonprofits.org/giftsubs.html). There are two categories of gifts that are typical for libraries, in-kind and cash. For a cash donation, in *any amount,* to be deductible the donor must have either a bank document or a document from the library (on official library paper) showing the date of the gift as well as the amount given. A person buying something at a book sale and wishing a receipt that the IRS would accept can be a problem unless the library has a receipt form that has the library's name and address printed on it. Another point about cash gifts is often the library has a foundation that handles cash gifts and bequests. The foundation's role is to manage investments and raise money for the library. Certainly that body's stationery also is acceptable to the IRS.

Any library, or its parent institution, that receives a gift in-kind (books, journals, manuscripts, and so forth) with an appraised value of $5,000 or more *must* report the gift to the IRS. A second regulation forbids the library to provide a valuation figure for a gift in-kind. A third disinterested party or organization must make such valuations. The latter requirement grew out of concern that recipients were placing unrealistically high values on the gifts in order to please a donor. Normally, an appraiser charges a fee for valuing gifts, and the donor is supposed to pay the fee. Most often, the appraisers are commercial dealers who charge a flat fee for the service unless the collection is large or complex. If the appraisal is complex, the appraiser often charges either a percentage of the appraised value or an hourly fee.

Typically, with gifts thought to be less than $250 in value, the library may write a letter of acknowledgment indicating the number and type of items received. (The IRS requires its form 8283—Noncash Charitable Contributions—for all gifts of $500 or more.) For gifts of less than $250, the IRS does not require a letter; however, a letter from the library thanking the donor for a gift is also a good idea regardless of the assumed value. The donor can set a value on the gift for tax purposes.

If asked, the library can provide some websites such as Abebooks (http://www.abebooks.com/) and BookFinder (http://www.bookfinder.com/) so a donor may review retail prices for items similar to their donation. However, the final value of the gift is established by the donor, her or his tax accountant, or a certified appraiser. *Note:* CM staff have a major role to play in the acceptance of gifts and must have a sound knowledge of material prices. Just because the gift is small in terms of number of items does not mean that the fair market value is below $5,000.

From the Authors' Experience

While at Loyola Marymount University Library, Evans received a gift of 483 books about Japanese art, architecture, and landscape design. The donor merely wanted a letter listing the items. A check of what appeared to be special or unique books using Abebooks' website indicated that the collection was probably worth a substantial amount of money. After some negotiation with the university's development staff, the collection's appraised value was $39,743. The donor might well have accepted a letter simply stating the number of books given and would have lost a substantial tax deduction.

As a result of that positive experience, the donor became a major supporter of library projects that would not have been possible without the donor's financial commitments to the projects.

Americans with Disabilities Act and Collection Management

The Americans with Disabilities Act (1990, ADA) is fairly well known, in broad terms, due to the many physical changes in our environment that occurred as a result of the act. Wheelchair ramps at buildings and the small "ramps" cut into the curbing at most street corners are two of the most commonly seen changes that arose from ADA's passage. What, if anything, does ADA have to do with CM? Actually, rather a lot. Title III of the act states that it is a violation to discriminate "on the basis of disability in the full and equal enjoyment of the goods, services, facilities, privileges, advantages, or accommodations of any place of public accommodation" (42 U.S.C. § 12182(a) 2000).

A question to ponder from time to time is, what percentage of your library's collections is accessible to visually impaired users? Does collection access meet the "full and equal" provision of ADA? Large-print books are one way to meet this need; however, only a small fraction of the total publishing output is available in that format. Also, there is a question of how far you should go in creating such a collection—what fulfills the "equitable" aspect you see in ALA documents regarding services? What accommodation has the library made for access to the balance of its resources? Have the visual challenges of the available e-resources and the library's website been addressed? These are some of the questions to think about and legal issues to consider with regard to collections. There are solutions available, but you must think about the issues on an ongoing basis. Two tools designed to assist with accessing accessible electronic technologies are the Voluntary Product Accessibility Template (VPAT, https://www.section508.gov/sell/vpat), developed for federal contractors, and the Web Content Accessibility Guidelines (WCAG, https://www.w3.org/WAI/standards-guidelines/wcag/) established by the World Wide Web Consortium (W3C). As noted by Ostergaard, WCAG "is a technical standard that can be applied to academic institutions. It consists of 12 guidelines organized into four principles: perceivable, operable, understandable, and robust" (2015, p. 161). The updated version of the standard (WCAG 2.1), now incorporating 13 standards, was issued in June 2018 (https://www.w3.org/TR/WCAG21/). These tools can be useful when negotiating with vendors. The authors know from first-hand experience that failure to address these issues for just one user can lead to at least a visit from the user's lawyer and perhaps even a lawsuit.

Check These Out

Diane Murley provides some sound advice regarding improving accessibility for websites in her 2008 article "Web Site Accessibility" (*Law Library Journal* 100, no. 2: 401–406). Additionally, Kyunghye Yoon, Laura Hulscher, and Rachel Dols provide background on applying principles of inclusivity and diversity in library website design in their April 2016 article "Accessibility and Diversity in Library and Information Science: Inclusive Information Architecture for Library Websites" (*The Library Quarterly* 86, no. 2: 213–29). Additionally, consortia such as the BTAA coordinate accessibility testing of licensed resources. Results of BTAA reviews are available at https://www.btaa.org/library/accessibility/library-e-resource-accessibility--testing.

Privacy

Why include a discussion of privacy in a textbook about collection management? The answer is because it is part of the complex issue of intellectual freedom and libraries may, unknowingly, be allowing outsiders to collect personal information from those using our services. Many libraries have a confidentiality policy, and ALA's *Policy on Confidentiality of Library Records* (http://www.ala.org/advocacy/intfreedom/statementspols/otherpolicies/policyconfidentiality) offers guidance here. The policy in most libraries requires that staff eradicate past circulation data from the system in order to preserve user confidentiality. Libraries with automated circulation systems are in a good position to ensure confidentiality as today's systems are designed to break the link between the borrower and the items upon the material's return and when any associated fees are paid.

Angela Maycock (2010) noted, "Privacy, one of the foundations of intellectual freedom, is a compelling concern for school librarians. We live in an era when more and more personal information is available online" (p. 68). She was discussing the fact that many library database vendors, like almost all commercial Web organizations, collect data about people using their services. Certainly the concerns libraries have regarding user confidentiality go beyond online database usage. There are three major user privacy issues for libraries. One relates to personal information the library collects about a person as part of its normal business practices (such as basic contact information for borrowers and what they borrow). The second issue is what vendors may collect from library users. The third issue is most important, that being who may access that information and under what conditions.

At a minimum, libraries have the name, address, and telephone numbers for all of their registered borrowers. Many also ask for, but usually do not require, an email address. Not too long ago, when ILS circulation systems first became available, Social Security numbers were employed as the borrower's identification number in the system. That is no longer the case; however, the information may still be in the system unless there was a proactive effort to delete the data. Although today's circulation modules break the link between borrower and item upon return, the data may be on one or more system backup tapes. This information is something a library can control; further, it has a legal obligation to do so—all the states and the District of Columbia have regulations or laws relating to library patron confidentiality. Libraries are also ethically bound not to reveal the reading habits of borrowers. This is consistent with ALA's *Library Bill of Rights* principles, intellectual freedom (the right to read and think whatever one wishes), as well as ALA's *Code of Ethics*, which states: "we protect each library user's right to privacy and confidentiality with respect to information sought or received, and resources consulted, borrowed, acquired or transmitted" (http://www.ala.org/advocacy/proethics/codeofethics/codeethics). Only the reader and library staff, in the legitimate performance of their duties, have a right to know what resources a user consulted or checked out.

One area that the library does not have much control over is what vendors may be collecting about our users' interests as reflected in their interactions with the vendors' online databases. Trina Magi (2010) noted that the current Web 2.0 environment "poses new challenges for librarians in their commitment to protect user privacy as vendors of online databases incorporate personalization features into their search-retrieval interfaces, thereby collecting personally identifiable user information not subject to library

> ## Something to Watch
>
> One privacy issue that is not directly related to CM activities, but still bears watching, is the use of Radio Frequency Identification (RFID) in libraries. With RFID, transponders located in library materials are "read" wirelessly by a remote antenna, and data is collected on the item(s). As noted by Deborah Caldwell-Stone (2010), "Because RFID tags do not require a clear line of sight and allow multiple items to be read in a stack, far less time and human effort are spent on processing materials. Patrons using RFID-enabled self-check stations and automated sorting equipment further free up library staff for essential work. Handheld RFID readers can be moved along the shelving units to read the tags attached to books on the shelves, allowing for more efficient and frequent inventory of the library's collection" (pp. 38–39). However, privacy concerns and security flaws in RFID led ALA to create a resolution and series of "privacy principles" related to RFID in 2006 (http://www.ala.org/advocacy/intfreedom /statementspols/otherpolicies/rfidguidelines).
>
> Caldwell-Stone's review of RFID technology ("Chapter 6: RFID in Libraries," *Library Technology Reports* 46, no. 8: 38–44) is well worth reviewing.

oversight" (p. 254). Most of the major online library product vendors have a sign-in option on their opening search page that allows users to personalize their search—some examples are Emerald's "Your Profile" and EBSCO's "My EBSCOhost" features.

All library staff must be familiar with the concept of confidentiality because it is also certain that someday a parent, citizen, or government official will approach the staff with a request for information regarding someone's reading habits or use of other services. A staff member receiving such a request should politely, but firmly, refuse to comply and immediately report the request to their supervisor and otherwise follow the library's confidentiality policy. A good resource for handling requests about children's library usage is ALA's 2016 *Library Privacy Guidelines for Students in K–12 Schools* (http://www.ala.org/advocacy/library-privacy-guidelines-students-k-12 -schools).

What might vendors collect and do with such data? Even without personalization, many vendors have the option of emailing the requested file(s) to the person. That alone provides a vendor with two pieces of marketable information: what the person may be interested in and a means

> ## Something to Watch
>
> In spring 2011, the Reader Privacy Act of 2011 (SB 602) was introduced in the California State Legislature. The bill was sponsored by the Electronic Frontier Foundation (EFF) and the California affiliates of the American Civil Liberties Union (ACLU), in recognition of the amount of patron use data that electronic book vendors, such as Amazon, have at their disposal. The bill was successful and was enacted January 1, 2012 (California Reader Privacy Act [1798.90-1798.90.05]. Title 1.81.15. Stats. 2011, Ch. 424, Sec. 1). Background information on the bill is available from EFF (https:// www.eff.org/nl/cases/sb-602-californias-reader-privacy-act-2011). To date, New Jersey is the only other state to enact a similar law. Their law was enacted in 2014 (http:// www.njleg.state.nj.us/2014/Bills/S1000/967_R1.HTM). It remains to be seen if other states follow suit.

From the Authors' Experience

A longtime colleague of the authors commented on privacy and access to library materials:

Access issues are problematic for many children's librarians who consider themselves to be advocates for children. Yes, the ALA "Bill of Rights" affirms that access should not be denied because of age. Yet they acknowledge that parents have the right to control their child's access to library materials, or even to the library itself. Children are both legally and in practice dependent on their parents. They are often dependent on their parents to bring them to the library in the first place. Their parents must sign before a child can get a library card (although more than one street-savvy kid has forged his parent's signature). They can determine what a child may or may not read. Many fundamentalist religious parents refuse to let their children check out books about the occult, including folk tales about witches or those popular books about the boy wizard, Harry Potter. Sex education books can be another delicate area. Children's librarians know that it is usually NOT in the child's best interest to exacerbate the conflict between a parent and child who wants the latest popular vampire book, but they usually wish there were some way to empower these children to read what they want.

Privacy is another interesting issue. Almost every public library I know allows parents to routinely check their children's library records, usually because they want to know if everything has been returned. However, a few libraries—Santa Clara City, for one—require that the child approve a parent's access to the child's records. One rationale for this, aside from the legal opinion of some city attorneys that the right to privacy is not abrogated by age, is that the information on a child's library record has been used to determine a child's address and acquire access to a child that had been blocked legally, usually in a court case involving custody.

---

of contacting the person. The personalized profile can generate more marketable data. Magi reported that LexisNexis sells marketing lists such as "Homeowner" and "Relatives and Room Mates" (2010, p. 268). Even without selling the information to third parties, a vendor may have potential income-generating data. Did you know that EBSCO is part of EBSCO Industries, which includes, among other operations, a fishing tackle manufacturer, a real estate firm, an office and technology furniture retailer, and a rifle manufacturing company?

Magi's analysis covered 27 library vendor privacy policies—they all had such a policy. However, most were vague about what data they gather as the result of using their services and how they, or third parties, might use that information. Only a few had "opt out" features when it came to personalization. Overall, her assessment of vendor policies suggested that none would fully meet ALA's view of user confidentiality. She suggests that it is more a matter of vendors' lack of knowledge of the field's position on privacy and IF rather than some sinister profit-making effort. Essentially, the vendors are merely following the practices of most commercial Web companies (p. 267). She, and we, strongly suggest CM personnel, at the time of assessing the possible purchase of an online product, ask for and evaluate the vendor's privacy policy and, if necessary, negotiate changes that more closely reflect the profession's IF concerns.

Check These Out

The following items explore the issues of privacy, libraries, and digital environment in more detail:

Adams, Helen R. 2013. *Protecting Intellectual Freedom and Privacy in Your School Library*. Santa Barbara, CA: Libraries Unlimited.

Beckstrom, Matthew. 2015. *Protecting Patron Privacy: Safe Practices for Public Computers*. Santa Barbara, CA: Libraries Unlimited.

Givens, Cherie L. 2015. *Information Privacy Fundamentals for Librarians and Information Professionals*. Lanham, MD: Scarecrow Press.

Magi, Trina J. 2011. "Fourteen Reasons Privacy Matters: A Multidisciplinary Review of Scholarly Literature." *Library Quarterly* 81, no. 2: 187–209.

Newman, Bobbi, and Bonnie Tijerina, eds. 2017. *Protecting Patron Privacy: A LITA Guide*. Lanham, MD: Rowman & Littlefield.

Woodward, Jeannette. 2007. *What Every Librarian Should Know About Electronic Privacy*. Westport, CT: Libraries Unlimited.

Points to Keep in Mind

- There are several legal issues that impact CM activities.

- Copyright laws are complex and impact CM work in various ways— fair use, copying activities, and "performance" activities in particular.

- DRM, although not a law, does have its basis in law and presents challenges to some CM efforts, especially fair use and copying that would not be questioned in an analog situation.

- Accepting donations of material for the collection may have legal consequences for both the donor and the library.

- Providing equal access to library resources for all people, even the visually impaired, is both a legal and ethical issue.

- Privacy issues in libraries are related to intellectual freedom and are complex.

References

Bhatt, Shri C. V. 2008. "Is Digital Rights Management an IPR?" *Journal of Library and Information Technology* 28, no. 5: 39–42.

Caruso, Beth. 2016. "Post-Acquisition Management and the Issue of Inaccessibility." *Proceedings of the Charleston Library Conference*. http://dx.doi.org/10.5703 /1288284316460.

Conlogue, Bridget Carter, and Leslie W. Christianson. 2016. "Navigating the Copyright Landscape: Practical Considerations for Librarians." *PaLA* 4, no. 1: 35–47.

Eschenfelder, Kristin R. 2008. "Every Library's Nightmare? Digital Rights Management, Use Restrictions, and Licensed Scholarly Digital Resources." *College & Research Libraries* 69, no. 3: 205–26.

Farkas, Meredith. 2016. "Accessibility Matters: Ensuring a Good Online Library Experience for All Our Patrons." *American Libraries* 47, no. 9/10: 54.

Henderson, Carol C. 2017. *Libraries as Creatures of Copyright: Why Librarians Care About Intellectual Property Law and Policy.* Chicago: American Library Association. http://www.ala.org/advocacy/copyright/copyrightarticle /librariescreatures.

Houghton-Jan, Sarah. 2007. "Imagine No Restrictions." *School Library Journal* 53, no. 6: 52–54.

Irons, Kati. 2015. "Screening Legally: Film Programming for Public Libraries." *American Libraries* 46, no. 1/2: 38–41.

Magi, Trina J. 2010. "A Content Analysis of Library Vendor Privacy Policies: Do They Meet Our Standards?" *College & Research Libraries* 71, no. 3: 254–72.

Maycock, Angela. 2010. "Choose Privacy Week and School Libraries." *Knowledge Quest* 39, no. 1: 68–72.

Okerson, Ann. 1997. "Copyright or Contract?" *Library Journal* 122, no. 14: 136–39.

Ostergaard, Kirsten. 2015. "Accessibility from Scratch: One Library's Journey to Prioritize the Accessibility of Electronic Information Resources." *Serials Librarian* 69, no. 2: 155–68.

Sookman, Barry, and Dan Glover. 2010. "Digital Copying and Libraries: Copyright and Licensing Considerations." *Feliciter* 56, no. 1: 14–16.

U.S. Copyright Office. 1999. *Report on Copyright and Digital Distance Education.* Washington, DC: United States Copyright Office. https://www.copyright.gov /reports/de_rprt.pdf.

Whitehouse, Guy. 2009. "A New Clash Between Human Rights and Copyright: The Push for Enhanced Exceptions for the Print-Disabled." *Publishing Research Quarterly* 25, no. 4: 219–31.

Index

Abram, Stephen, 9

access. *See* information, access to

acquisitions, 37, 130, 141–44, 175; basic steps in the acquisitions process, 144–46; demand-driven acquisition (DDA), 45, 146, 149–50; evidence-based acquisition (EBA), 149–50; financial and budget considerations of, 144, 149–50; goals of an acquisitions department, 142; importance of public services staff to an acquisitions department, 143; key to successful acquisitions programs, 143; and the outsourcing of technical service processes, 144; patron-driven acquisition (PDA), 45, 149; Print-On-Demand (POD) acquisition, 46; requests for particular acquisitions, 145; speed of in meeting user demands, 143. *See also* acquisitions, fiscal management of; acquisitions, methods of; acquisitions, and the vendor selection process; integrated library system (ILS), acquisitions module of

acquisitions, fiscal management of, 166–67; allocating the budget, 168–70; and encumbering, 171–73; estimating costs, 167–68; financial, compliance, and operational audits, 174–75; keeping financial records, 170–71; and stewardship, 173–74;

acquisitions, methods of, 146; approval plans, 147–49; blanket orders, 150–51; exchanges, 155; firm orders, 146; gifts, 153–55; leases, 152–53; standing orders, 146–47; subscriptions, 151

acquisitions, and the vendor selection process, 156; customer service considerations, 159–61; evaluating vendors, 161–62; financial considerations, 157–58; importance of knowing what a vendor stocks, 156; out-of-print and antiquarian dealers as vendor sources, 164–66; retail outlets as vendor sources, 163–64; speed of vendor delivery, 157; technological capabilities of vendors, 156–57; variety of services offered by vendors, 158–59

Advanced Computer Innovation, Inc., 329

Albee, Barbara, 167

Alexander Street Press, 45, 293–94, 296

Algenio, Emilie, 288–89

Allen, Melissa, 200

Amazon.com, 163–64, 234, 289

American Association of School Libraries, 188

American Library Association (ALA), 25, 109, 167, 214, 240; guidelines of for handling complaints concerning library procedures, 65; primary position statements of, 7–8. *See also* Association of College & Research Libraries (ACRL); Association for Library Collections and Technical Services (ALCTS); Association for Library Service to Children; *Code of Ethics of the American Library Association*; Office for Intellectual Freedom (OIF)

About the Authors

MARGARET (MAGGIE) Z. SAPONARO is currently Director of Collection Development Strategies at the University Libraries, University of Maryland (UMD), where she is responsible for leadership and vision for the content of purchased and licensed collections across all disciplinary areas and formats. She also directs the collection development work of the Libraries' subject specialist liaison librarians, with primary responsibility for content and budgeting of the UMD Libraries' general collections. Her prior work experience includes serving as Manager, Staff Learning and Development at the University of Maryland, as Associate Director of Learning Resources at the Alexandria Campus of Northern Virginia Community College, and as Librarian for the College of Human Resources at Virginia Polytechnic Institute and State University. She has also served as an adjunct faculty member for the University of Virginia. Ms. Saponaro is a member of the American Library Association and ACRL. She holds an MLS from UCLA, with postgraduate work in the areas of personnel programs and public administration. Her research interests are in the areas of collection management, instruction, and emerging technologies in libraries.

G. EDWARD EVANS is an administrator, researcher, teacher, and writer. He holds several graduate degrees in anthropology and library and information science. As a researcher he has published in both fields and held a Fulbright (librarianship) and National Science Foundation (anthropology) Fellowship. His teaching experience has also been in both fields in the U.S. and the Nordic countries—in particular UCLA's Graduate School of Librarianship and Information Science. Most of his administrative experience has been in private academic libraries—Harvard and Loyola Marymount Universities. He retired from full-time work as Associate Academic Vice President for Libraries and Information Resources at Loyola Marymount University. In terms of his writing, he currently has eight titles in print, several of which have been translated into one or more of eight languages. Semi-retired, he consults for and volunteers at the Museum of Northern Arizona library and archives and is a member of the Flagstaff City–Coconino County Library System Foundation Board.